Body Renewal:
The Lost Art of Self-Repair

By

Jay Glaser, MD

LOTUS
PRESS

P.O. Box 325
Twin Lakes, WI 53181 USA

Edited by David Freedman

Copyright © 2010   Jay Glaser, MD

First Edition 2010

Printed in the United States of America

ISBN   978-0-9102-6196-8

Library of Congress Catalog Number   2010921539

Published by:
Lotus Press, P.O. Box 325, Twin Lakes, WI 53181 USA
web: www.lotuspress.com
Email: lotuspress@lotuspress.com
800.824.6396

To Danielle

Whose constant presence has brought
the healing silence of Mother Divine onto every page

ACKNOWLEDGMENTS

Above all, I owe my gratitude to His Holiness Maharishi Mahesh Yogi. His refined awareness enabled him to revive on a practical level all the Vedic sciences, from Ayurveda to yoga, so that future generations in East and West might benefit from their full value. I feel fortunate to have been able to participate, in whatever small way, in his lifetime endeavor.

The ancient Vedic rishis are the fountainheads of this knowledge. I am grateful to those following in their footsteps, the dozens of Ayurvedic physicians who have presented to me their insights into this science in the context where it becomes indelible, in the examination room. My late father and surgeon Joseph Glaser, MD, inspired me by his example to study medicine and PJ Deshpande inspired me in 1972 to study Ayurveda as I assisted him in Ayurvedic surgery. Drs. Brihaspati Dev Triguna, the late VN Dwivedi, the late Balraj Maharshi, J.R. Raju, P. Subhedar, Harish Garge, N. Mhaiskar and Manohar Palakurthi have been generous clinical mentors. Prof. Michel Angot, PhD, translations and commentaries, has clarified the Sanskrit texts with his broad perspective.

I thank Maharaj Adhiraj Rajarām for his supportive silence and for illuminating the human physiology in its cosmic dignity. John Hagelin, PhD has delineated the quantum physics of consciousness. R. Keith Wallace pioneered research into the neurophysiology of enlightenment. These three scientists have made important contributions to the growing understanding of the fictitious distinction between mind and body. Santosh and Shanta Krinsky, my publishers, have had the vision to recognize the importance of bringing Vedic knowledge to the public. Michael Dick has generously offered grammatical and content editing. Finally, my wife, Danielle, has patiently sustained me with her wisdom, perspective, silence and song.

About the Transliteration of Sanskrit Terms

The transliteration of the 64 Sanskrit characters is generally best accomplished using an established convention in order for a Sanskrit expression in the text to be clearly identified and pronounced. For the purpose of this book, however, I have opted to make the Sanskrit more approachable, using a spelling that is commonly recognized among students of yoga, meditation, Ayurveda or speakers of South Asian languages. Diacritical marks, except for some long vowels, have been omitted.

CONTENTS

INTRODUCTION

DEEPAK CHOPRA, MD

Your body has an ancient song. Its score flows through the rivers of time as it runs through the rivers of your vessels, carrying the miracle of life to every cell. Its rhythms beat to the pulsation of your heart and with the surge of hormones and neuromessengers whose fanfare heralds your waking day. Its melodies sing out a sequence of information that encodes your body's functions with your unique countenance, talents and foibles. Its harmonies blend into a perfect mixture of acids, bases and buffers, neurotransmitters, antibodies and killer cells, making you nearly invincible. Its counterpoints allow you to put your attention on your task at hand, blissfully unaware of the symphony of intertwining intelligence that keeps you vibrant and constantly repairing imbalances as they arise. And it reveals itself in your pulse.

This song is available to anyone, from any culture, at every moment. A riff of its melody is available as you feel yourself salivate while your meal is prepared, as you feel the stimulation and stretch in your body while jogging or during your morning yoga, in the excitement as your lover touches your lips, and even in the distress from your gut when you get bad news, because the song's refrain is available in every sensation and perception, the interface between your body and your mind.

Our culture presents this song to us in many ways – through arts, but in the west also through science – as we gain a collective awareness of the evolution of DNA and of the evolution of our cosmos. We watch films about genetically reconstructing dinosaurs and view in exquisite detail pictures from the Hubble telescope of distant nebulae exploding and galaxies colliding. Growing up in India I heard this ancient song in the refrains of my parents and grandparents which recounted the expression of the intelligence of life. India's rich cyclical interplay of festivals, fasts, feasts and pilgrimages revealed this song to me through tales, music, theater and dance. My Vedic heritage, focused on the song of the Veda, seeded the awareness of the interplay of gods, demons and sages within my own developing body, which was poised to experience the entire range of life. Today, my modern medical journals simply recount these same tales through a different language.

Once I fully appreciated the role of the harmonizing value of nature's intelligence in the maintenance and restoration of health, my life as a physician would never be the same. My life became devoted to making knowledge of the body's natural healing capacity available everywhere, not only to benefit health and prolong life, but also to make life more rich and creative.

Without a sense of the rhythms and intelligence inherent in our physiology and our consciousness, we ignore the critical signals that our body has been cultured over eons to express in order to maintain balance. We neglect to sleep and exercise, indulge beyond our capacities, retire too late and then arise when the sun is well aloft, wondering why we feel out of synch. We sabotage the delicate harmony and order encoded in our chromosomes, our genetic gift of longevity that comes from keeping our tissues free from plaque and debris. A little imbalance in time becomes a disorder and then a disease, bringing on more stress and neglect. Our body's ancient song is sung off key.

When, on the other hand, we imbibe the flow of the universe into our rhythms and habits, culture tastes and pleasures that nourish us, drink in experiences that uplift us while preserving inner repose, we evolve with an evolving universe. Such a life promotes an integrated interaction of our brain's one trillion neurons, allowing us to be present to the multitude of perceptions we are incessantly bombarded with, to enjoy them for their beauty, to process them into creative action and to intuit the future and our role within it. For those so inclined, in nearly every tradition, such a life is held to be conducive to the contemplation of the cosmos and its Creator.

Modern physicists, ancient physicians as well as artists and poets have described this intelligence in terms of sound and light, because of its vibrational and harmonic values. Its expression at each level of your physiology, from the subatomic level of quarks and leptons through the macromolecular level of DNA and proteins, to its ultimate functioning in tissues and organs, means that it can be accessed for its practical benefit: a long, productive life free from disease. Growing up in India, I found this refrain available on the surface of life in my Vedic tradition: in the kitchen where my mother and grandmother used herbs and spices for their healing values on our bodies and minds; in the stories and songs of my elders who breathed to me and my brother the dynamics of the unmanifest values of life underlying the concrete world of health and disease, joy and suffering; and in the chants and rhythms of the Brahmins in the temples. I have since discovered that it is available everywhere if you are ready to look.

Adopting or learning the Vedic traditions is not necessary to gain the practical benefits of Vedic medicine. Jay Glaser has made the essence of Vedic medicine available to anyone in this immensely practical book. He has presented the true roots of Ayurveda and the other Vedic healing arts in a context that does not require any previous knowledge of these sciences or a trip to India. Here in one volume is an approach to preventing and treating the most common chronic diseases that almost everyone gets. This work should be an owner's guide to anyone planning on someday finding herself in possession of an aging body, or already the owner of one. Since over forty percent of us will die of heart disease, thirty-five percent experience sleep difficulties in a given year, 23 percent will develop high blood pressure, and 46 percent of men 40-69 years old will experience sexual difficulties, you are almost guaranteed to develop a handful of conditions whose prevention and treatment are discussed in this book.

Dr. Glaser had already been studying Vedic medicine for over fifteen years when he joined me at a newly opened Ayurvedic clinic in the late 1980's. In this setting we were able to witness together the effect of Ayurvedic treatments applied to western patients and to understand how the classical description in the ancient texts may need to be adapted to modern health consumers who are inquisitive yet skeptical, and who are willing learners if motivated and informed in a logical, scientific dialect. The result of his experience, including the years we spent practicing medicine under the same roof is this book of Vedic wisdom in a language of the twenty-first century.

My late father, Krishnan Chopra, MD, was a cardiologist and medical director of a hospital in New Delhi, which offered separate wings for both Ayurvedic and western medical approaches. Interestingly, Jay Glaser met my father in India years before he met me and was asked by him to teach meditation to the medical staff. Jay told me it was at my father's hospital, where Vedic and conventional medicine had been seamlessly integrated, that he realized that complete medicine requires both the subtlety of the East and the rationalism of the West. Before Jay returned from Delhi my father told him, "Be sure to look up my sons in Boston." Since then, our mutual medical research, clinical practice and other collaborations have been based on the shared recognition that medicine is foremost a spiritual path for personal evolution. This book has been written from that same spirit, one that encourages adoption of daily habits of prevention and healing as a part of your spiritual evolution. It is a path of healing where the joy and well-being gained from the practices create the motivation to continue.

Whatever your interest in Vedic medicine, as an option for dealing with a chronic condition, a means to feel younger and live longer, or as a science to refine your nervous system to complement your practice of yoga or spiritual practices, you will find it available in Vedic medicine, which is simply and colorfully laid out here. May your journey to perfect health be effortless and fruitful.

Deepak Chopra, MD

PROLOGUE

Reviving the Lost Art of Self-Repair

If your palms get wet when you are reminded of Bette Davis' famous line, "Growing old is no place for sissies," then this book is for you. Its purpose is not to give you more years of misery, but more fun in some extra years, and to make you look forward to it, even if you already have a few infirmities.

There is nothing new under the sun, so this book is loaded with something that is nothing new. Its subject, the continuous renewal and repair of your body, has simply been lost, forgotten or neglected. This book may unsettle both medical providers and consumers alike, because modern medicine has made us drift away from health wisdom that has been time-tested. Doctors like to think their advice is based on scientific evidence, but much of what we do still lacks scientific documentation. Evidence-based medical recommendations may give a better outcome for populations as a whole, but may not necessarily be better for you as an individual, whose unique situation may instead require common sense, clinical judgment, restraint, procrastination or even, God forbid, something ancient and tested by time rather than randomized clinical trials.

Unfortunately, the people least benefited by the gains of modern medicine are those suffering from age-related chronic disorders addressed by this book. Moreover, most people open to natural options simply run out for the latest supplement heralded in the evening news, rather than address their problems with a systematic science.

We will be exploring a lost art of self-repair that despite its antiquity offers a revolutionary approach to stubborn conditions that have developed over time and which yield with extreme reluctance to modern interventions.

It is interesting that Vedic medicine has made a comeback in India recently due to an unlikely influence: the West. Just as South Asians have adopted high technology and some of the West's worst habits, they have also witnessed the popularity of western Ayurvedic clinics, and installed Ayurvedic spas in many of the finest hotels to cater to the western tourist. After sixty years of relegating its own traditional practitioners to the villages where few trained physicians choose to live and where the villagers cannot afford western medicine, the growing middle and upper classes of India and Pakistan are rediscovering, through books and programs developed outside of India, the genius of the Vedic sciences that were always under their noses.

A Chance Encounter with the Field of Self-Repair

My journey to the realm of self-repair began in 1971, in Kampala in the heart of Africa, where I arrived tired and hungry, having not eaten a decent meal for a fortnight. Three weeks previously, I had dispatched my research samples of tuberculosis bacteria from rural Zulus to my medical school in Colorado and had embarked on a trek by motorcycle, thumb and boat northward through the Rift Valley. I was eager to see Africa in its pristine state. The local fare of mashed tapioca root, grasscutter (rodent) stew and home brew left my taste buds begging for something savory. I asked the first Westerner I had seen in weeks where I could find the best meal in town. The tyranny of Idi Amin had left Kampala plundered, she replied, and the good restaurants had all closed. I could buy the inventory of a whole hardware store for a few hundred dollars cash because the Asian merchants were abandoning Uganda. The only good meal was at the Hindu temple. My first Indian feast has still been the best. As the servers brought dish after spicy dish of South Indian cuisine, I knew that the following year I would pursue my tuberculosis (TB) research in India.

Nine months later, I was staring at the dried herbs for a patient with tuberculosis at the All-India Institute of Medical Sciences in New Delhi, asking him how he could have been prescribed something so unquantifiable at such a prestigious research center. "If you will not tell my doctors that I am seeing an Ayurvedic doctor, I will tell you how to find the vaidya who prescribed them." he bargained. This patient opened my eyes to the science of life and led me to hear the body's ancient song.

For the next five months, as my research permitted, I apprenticed myself out to the most renowned vaidyas who would accept a foreigner under their tutelage, journeying from the Himalayas to the tip of the subcontinent in the south. In Benares, I met PJ Deshpande, who initiated me in the secrets of Ayurvedic surgery because he professed that if a western doctor was interested, his lost art had a living future; in Thanjavur, I coddled in my hands an ancient crumbling Ayurvedic text that scholars were translating. I visited the forests where the herbs grew and followed the crafters who collected, crushed and fermented them. Under trees in the villages and in clinics in the cities, Vedic physicians tried to explain to me Ayurvedic theory, coaxed me to sing the Sanskrit verses which comprise the medical texts, and placed my fingers in the proper position on the pulse. It was during this journey that I first heard the body's ancient song – transcendental Veda taking expression in a Brahmin's chant – droning a thrill up my spine to awaken me to the vibrancy of life.

Since Ayurveda was unknown in the West in 1972, I wrote a journal chronicling my adventures and upon my return to Denver was asked to present the paper before the University of Colorado Medical School faculty and students. The Waring Society received my paper with polite interest, appreciating it mainly as a firsthand, historical analysis of a quaint relic of medical science. I protested that they had missed the point and that contemporary medicine had much to learn from Ayurveda, which offered therapeutic possibilities in areas where medicine failed. In 1972, an era when breastfeeding was discouraged, the medical profession and lay public regarded these arguments as nonsensical. So I quietly continued reading the ancient texts and put up with the admonitions of my superiors who pointed out that I was wasting my time feeling the pulse when I could plainly see the tracing on the monitor. Four years later upon completing my internal medicine board examinations, I realized I still needed to learn real medicine. Having learned the Transcendental Meditation technique while in medical school, I approached the program's founder, Maharishi Mahesh Yogi, to learn the science of life.

Completing a Proper Medical Education

Ten years passed in the role of a brahmacharin, a reclusive Vedic apprentice. I had no idea this real medicine would be more demanding than medical school and hospitals: the routines, the lessons learned, the changing winds the teacher conjured to break my boundaries and structure flexibility. Sometimes I found myself washing pots (open ego surgery for a doctor used to giving orders), sometimes doing research or teaching.

In his study in the Swiss Alps in 1979, I asked Maharishi when we could take up the discipline of Ayurveda, which I had been studying on my own for seven years but which was still unknown in the West. He replied that Ayurveda was a beautiful flower that would soon be ready for picking. Three months later, he returned to Switzerland from India with Dr. VN Dwivedi, a learned Ayurvedic physician and authority in rejuvenative tonics called rasāyanas. Other renowned vaidyas began to arrive from the various regions of India, each with their expertise in a specific area of Vedic medicine.

The following years were witness to a gathering of Vedic luminaries to rival the assemblages described in the ancient books. The western doctors felt humbled in their presence. Each expert described a different part of the flower of Vedic medicine that we were now picking: some its roots in the Vedas, some its stem in the three great encyclopedic medical texts, some its petals and leaves in the ancient Upanishads and systems of Vedic philosophy like the Yoga Sūtras and Vedanta, and some the flower's reproductive organs, the texts that assure the perpetual transmission of Vedic sciences to other generations in their purity. From a discussion of *agni*, the digestive and metabolic fires, we would find ourselves considering *Agni*, the purifying source of intelligence, and then a poetic description of Agni in the experience of an ancient seer, and then back to the treatment of irritable bowel syndrome. The days dissolved into late nights and then into weeks and years as we buzzed around the flowers of Ayurveda and retreated to the hive, our own silent experience of the abstract field of Veda, the domain of self-repair.

On occasion, a Sanskrit verse describing a property of an herb, the treatment of a disease with an ancient physiotherapy technique or a benefit of meditation would set us wondering whether a remedy was really as good as the text implied and some of us undertook laboratory experiments to test the ancient record. The Ayurvedic doctors approvingly laughed, implying that being time-tested through the millennia was proof enough.

One day Maharishi surprised several physicians and me as we sat with him in his cottage, working on herbal preparations for treating chronic diseases. With a sweep of his hand he pushed the papers across the table and proclaimed, "This is fourth class Ayurveda!" We were startled and speechless, wondering why he would debase knowledge he seemed to value. He continued, "If a medicine is truly first-class, it should work on the deepest, most subtle level, on the level of consciousness. These herbs, diets, massage and tonics function mainly on the physical body. How good can this medicine be? After all, I was aware of the possibilities of Ayurveda in 1955, when I came out of the Himalayas, but how could I talk about herbs and diets when people were not even meditating?"

Validating Vedic Medicine in the Clinic

After several years, my medical colleagues and I realized that we had begun to reconstruct Ayurveda in its ancient dignity and integrity. It was a different Ayurveda than the Ayurveda practiced in India, where physicians with many years of training and recitation of Sanskrit medical texts find themselves practicing as herbal pill pushers or abandon Ayurveda to prescribe western drugs. Maharishi had restored the Veda to Ayurveda.

Meanwhile my former medical colleagues, family and friends wondered why a board-certified internist, who by then was over forty, had forsaken the standard medical model and could barely pay his debts. They were delighted when at last I announced my intentions to test these new clinical tools, joining Tony Nader, MD, PhD and Deepak Chopra, MD at an Ayurvedic medical center that Maharishi was establishing in Lancaster, Massachusetts.

I put Vedic medicine to the test in every soul who sought my help, referring to ancient texts when in doubt; keeping an experienced vaidya from India by my side during consultations; phoning to the land of the Veda for another option when the predicted response was not forthcoming; summoning my clinical judgment to conjure a new plan based on Vedic principles when neither the ancient or modern approaches kindled a cure; or simply singing a poetic Sanskrit verse from the medical texts predicting hopefulness to a disconsolate heart. I came to realize that the lost art of self-repair is still available to anyone.

Applying Vedic Wisdom to Self-Repair

My experience has shown me, however, that what the public has come to understand as Ayurveda, picking your body type and then avoiding foods and activities accordingly, had nothing to do with the principles used by experienced practitioners, who attempt to intervene at the source of a disorder's cause. Most patients have several interacting disorders that cannot be resolved by simplistic prescriptions. These physical disorders are further aggravated by marital problems, depression, anxiety, job dissatisfaction, destructive habits and lifestyles, all of which may contribute to or even cause the problems.

This book attempts to help you identify the critical parts of your own life that may be involved in the age-related and chronic disorders that almost everyone eventually experiences and offers effective, drug-free treatments. Since *ayu* means lifespan and Veda means knowledge, it is only fitting that Ayurveda and its associated sciences should be the key components in your program of body renewal.

Because you may sometimes be a less-than-perfect patient, I have given you a break by selecting my Ayurvedic prescriptions carefully. If, in my own life, I adhered to one-tenth of the lifestyle interventions my Ayurvedic teachers have prescribed to me over the years, I would have no time for living. If an intervention is included in this text, it is considered important.

An Ayurvedic consultation is about imparting the essence of Vedic wisdom that bears on a patient's problem, and it seems there never is enough time to convey what Maharishi called "first class medicine." This book has been conceived for those who cannot otherwise gain this knowledge. Except for a few instances, I have avoided introducing the concept of three doshas and the idea of body types, but have made these aspects of Ayurveda available as appendices for reference purposes. A book presenting the Vedic roots of healing may sound unfamiliar to people who have understood Ayurveda to be about the three doshas and yoga to be about postures. They should not be skeptical; these fundamentals are authentic, simple, intuitive and practical. The knowledge herein represents a distillation of the wisdom of the ancient texts, the insights of Maharishi and the dozens of vaidyas from India with whom I have worked over the past thirty-seven years, and the corroborating confirmation of this ancient wisdom from modern science.

This book is for those patients who have trepidation over future infirmities and who want to renew their bodies, those who could not come, and those who are still seeking to learn the art of self-repair.

BODY RENEWAL

CHAPTER 1

THE ROOTS OF HEALING IN A SONG

Every morning at four o'clock from the comfort of my cot, I can pick out the voice of Jagu from among the other young boys. His song is deep, rich, even hoarse, and has soul. Jagu is only eight and entered the academy for Vedic pandits in southern India the same week I moved in. Some mornings I force myself up and sit in a corner of the courtyard listening to the syncopated rhythms of the boys' daily morning practice of their Vedic recitation. I spot Jagu, his big brown eyes near shut, standing propped between the two biggest boys in his group, who keep him from falling over when he falls asleep, which is every two or three minutes. His eyes close and his voice fades for a spell. The morning recitation is performed standing so there will be less chance of falling asleep. The ten boys are so tightly packed together they could fit in a shower stall. They even sleep packed together under a fan that keeps off the mosquitoes, and they study together in the afternoon with their knees touching. There is no place in this academy for a loner.

Despite being the youngest, in his short time at the Vedic academy, everyone, including a Westerner like me, recognizes Jagu's special gift. His vibrant voice is like a prod in the back that makes the spine tingle. It also helps that his Sanskrit pronunciation is natural even if it is not his mother tongue, and that he effortlessly recites the Veda without hesitation. His mentor tells me he will enter Jagu into a competition for young pandits to display their voice and pronunciation.

Jagu represents a unique phenomenon of nature: his DNA has been cultured for thousands of years to code for a reciting machine. He and his brothers are able to track their family lineage not just for a few hundred, but for three to four thousand years. Jagu knows the name of the grandsire of his family, Bharadvaja, a man who lived at the dawn of modern history, perhaps 3800-4000 years ago, as well as details about his life. In India, what is old is termed ancient, and what is ancient is deemed eternal, so putting even a vague date on these events is considered heretical.[1] Jagu has the same Y chromosome as his ancient grandsire Bharadvaja, and the rest of his DNA is from purebred Brahmins. The need for this restriction of genetic material from his pedigree has a biological reason: to propagate the sound of the Veda. Jagu loves to recite as a thoroughbred loves to run, even at 4 a.m., eyes half shut in a semi-stupor.

After recitation, Jagu collapses in a heap for a few minutes before his friends wake him to perform personal morning rites. Facing the rising sun, he recites a verse as he glances at its red reflection in water drops he throws backward over his head, and then goes to meditate before breakfast, usually falling asleep again.

Unlike other boys their age, Jagu and his friends have no toys. Jagu opens a metal cookie box for me, proud that I am interested, and shows me his entire worldly possessions, beside the white lungi around his waist and the string over his shoulder. A spare lungi to wear while the other is being washed, a cotton shirt he wears only when he goes home, a picture of his family, a pen, a pencil, a paring knife, a set of tulsi beads, a few pieces of paper written in Tamil in a child's hand and a small picture of Maharishi.

In the streets nearby, boys Jagu's age play games, variations on cricket, soccer and kick-the-can, and create tomfoolery like eight-year-olds anywhere. The boys at the academy could care less; they just want to recite. They amuse themselves by climbing on the shoulders of the older boys to collect hibiscus blossoms to offer in their morning yajñas.

Compared to the boys in the nearby streets and even to the Brahmin boys I have observed in academies in north India, Jagu and his friends are models of decorum. A traditional Brahmin's life revolves around sound and speech, so Jagu's main vices involve singing, speaking, reciting, cajoling, laughing or doing something mischievous with his larynx. Discipline is delivered by making the boys do one-legged deep knee bends until they begin to wince, and from what I've witnessed, traditional Brahmins don't suffer physical stresses well, including exercise and sports. Jagu is saved from the knee bends, despite his natural penchant for mischief, because he is the youngest and too endearing to punish.

Twice Born

Jagu was born as a Brahmin a few weeks before he came to the academy, when he ceremoniously received a woven string that he will now wear for life across his shoulder and down to the opposite hip. He is now *dwija*, twice-born. From the moment of that ceremony onward, he would be married to the Veda, obligated to protect and preserve it. This means he needs to accomplish two things in his life: learn the Veda and pass it on to his sons. Jagu proudly tells me he is from the Bharadvaja clan,[2] meaning he is responsible for the part of the Rg Veda that was cognized by his grandsire, Bharadvaja. Jagu cannot marry a girl from the Bharadvaja clan, because, after all, she is considered family. In this profession, the younger Jagu is when he marries, the sooner he will be able to teach his own son Bharadvaja's cognitions of Rg Veda. So it may well be that, barely a man, he will marry a Brahmin girl who is barely a woman.

Jagu is at Maharishi's academy because Jagu's father and grandfather have taken government jobs and no longer are involved in the traditional practices. At the very minimum, Jagu is obligated to learn the cognitions of his grandsire, Bharadvaja, an especially gifted seer, who cognized the 765 suktas (collections of verses) that comprise the entire sixth Mandala of the Rg Veda. Fulfilling one's obligation ordained by the Vedic tradition is nearly incompatible with having another job, since it means sitting with your son for hours every day for fifteen to twenty years. Some preceptors hold their charges' head in one palm as they sit knee-to-knee, lowering or raising the head as the tones rise and fall, thus instilling a kinesthetic memory. It is an ancient professional tradition, needing no books, pencils or pens, nor even the ability to read or write.

Sanskrit: The Language of Name and Form

The sound of any Sanskrit word is held to be sufficient to evoke in a listener the understanding of its meaning, even if the listener has no knowledge of Sanskrit. This applies, of course, only to a listener like Jagu's ancient great-grandsire Bharadvaja, whose nervous system was free of noise, allowing his brain to fully register the sound with all its implications. This phenomenon is due to the *principle of name and* form (nāmarūpa), a quality of Sanskrit whereby the sound of any word contains its meaning.

An English word like *hiss* has a sound expressing its meaning, and someone learning English may understand its meaning in a conversation without an explanation. In Sanskrit, every word is onomatopoeic, because every prefix, root and suffix has its basis in a sound of nature. The Sanskrit prefix *pra*, meaning beginning or opening (and the ancient precursor for our Latin prefix, *pre-*), is the sound made by a nut cracking open. For people whose nervous systems crackle with static, thus rendering the meaning opaque, an ancient encyclopedic code of aphorisms[3] illuminates the surface and hidden values of any Sanskrit sound.

A *rishi* is a person whose nervous system is so pure that she or he can infer the deepest meaning of a Sanskrit expression and also receive or cognize unmanifest expressions of Veda to transmit them to posterity. The expressions of Veda that are available today, perhaps only a fraction of the total Veda, are all cognitions of such rishis. Even if your noisy mind cannot register a meaning when exposed to a Sanskrit expression, your physiology is affected. I lie half awake before dawn bathing in Jagu's alto libretto, even if it is unintelligible to my unrefined nervous system.

DNA, the Parchment of the Vedas

Had the Vedas been trusted to a written record, there would be none available today, because nothing survives long in the heat and humidity of the Indian sub-continent. To preserve truly old documents you need to hide them in places like the Gobi desert, Egypt or the Dead Sea.

Instead, the Veda was inscribed on the most fragile, yet permanent, of all possible materials: human DNA. These boys have an uncanny ability to memorize anything and everything in a language that means absolutely nothing to them. It is as if the sound is already in their physiology; they open their mouths and it flows out. Jagu is a scampering tape recorder; if he hears something two to three times he can recite it and, once chanted, it is indelibly inscribed. With over 600,000 syllables to memorize, comprising tens of thousands of verses, he has to be good. Some Brahmins learn all four Vedas, Upanishads, and more.

In addition to learning the cognitions of his grandsire, Bharadvaja, that are important in the Vedic rite, Jagu and his friends learn to recite some verses whose meaning is transparent and that Maharishi has deemed important for all the clans to chant. Now and then, I can pick out the word Purusha and know they are singing the verses describing the nature of the unmanifest. With beautiful poetic imagery that describes the indescribable by anthropomorphizing it into a living being, the verses describe a Purusha who has a thousand heads, a thousand eyes.

Purusha is verily all this visible world, all that is and all that is to be; all existence is one-fourth of him; his other three-fourths, being immortal, abide in heaven. Three-fourths of Purusha ascended; the other fourth that remained in this world proceeds repeatedly, and, diversified in various forms, went to all animate and inanimate creation.

Rg Veda X.7.6.2-4

Four Levels of Expression of Intelligence

As a field of virtual fluctuations, pure intelligence has many manifestations, from expressed to transcendental. On its most expressed level, Veda is the song, with its gaps of silence between syllables, coming out of the mouth of a deer-eyed boy. On this gross material level (called *vaikharī* in Sanskrit), Veda, the sound, cannot be divorced from the traditional lineage and the DNA that has conveyed it intact through time and space. The boy and the sound are the same. While the expressed sound of the Veda is its least subtle form, it is still important. The boys' recitation is outward and appears to create a physical stir throughout the community that is appreciated by the neighbors. Jagu circles his finger in all directions to tell me he is enlivening the universe.

What Jagu sings also has a meaning of sorts, invariably bickered about by Sanskrit scholars as well as greater and lesser masters. This meaning of the verses, although subtler than the manifest sound, ultimately does not mean much to a Brahmin, but is somehow important to western scholars, perhaps because we attach importance to the meaning of our own sacred texts. This literal level of Veda's song of life is called *madhyamā*.[4] Translations of the Veda are banal for a reader of modern literature. The pastoral verses describe cows and horses; pressing out and filtering the juice of the Soma plant; venerations of the impulses of intelligence as celestial beings; and formulas, rites and incantations. The meaning rarely appears to have a plot or an obvious direction. Moreover, the boys have little clue what they are singing and, like generations of mentors before them, they don't care. In this environment even a visitor understands that Veda's essence is not to be found in its meaning, but in its sound. The boys' resonant singing has a different purpose than their meditation, which is inward and silent, punctuated by the playfulness of normal boys.

Subtler than meaning is a third level, the notion of the verse, called *pashyantī*, the essence of the verse on the level of one's feeling. For a person with a nervous system unencumbered with noise and static, the sound of the verse should provide a clear notion of the quality of pure intelligence that the boys are singing about. For an individual with clatter in the nervous system, the impression would be vague. This is what Henry David Thoreau meant when he said, "Speech is for the hard of hearing."

Transcendent to the notion of a verse is the subtlest level of all. Called *parā*, it is uninvolved in the material level, yet is its basis and prime mover. The transcendental level is the level you feel in the moments of silent clarity of the mind as you fall asleep or awaken, in the space between breaths in meditation or in the transfixing of the mind by a sunrise. On the parā level, the Veda is as irrelevant as drinking water to a fish. While you may have some interest in Veda on its three grosser levels, this book is about learning to make pure intelligence – the transcendental value of all holy scriptures – practical in daily life.

Self-Interaction, the Essence of Self-Repair

In Jagu's world of abstraction, if you wanted to describe a relationship within the field of pure intelligence, perhaps in an age when writing was not available, you might give the relationship a personality, portraying that impulse or quality of intelligence holding the tools of her profession – a mace, a musical instrument, a begging bowl. If the personality is complicated, you may run out of hands to put the tools in. So, you add more arms and hands. Modern mathematicians use creation and annihilation operators to describe the change in numbers of particles in quantum mechanics. Similarly, Jagu and his friends sing of Brahma, Vishnu and Shiva to describe their physical world arising from or dissolving into the absolute. Every song they sing describes a relationship, and the Veda, or at least what is available of it, describes all possible relationships. For these little budding Brahmins, pure intelligence is a superposition of all truth and all falsehood. You are also a superposition of relationships, wearing simultaneously the hats of mother, daughter, wife, sister, friend, enemy, subordinate and boss. The reverberation flowing from the group of huddling boys with their dark brown eyes and young voices vibrating with the power of infinity is an echo of a field of all possibilities in a point.

A story goes that somehow a rope had been wrapped around a mountain in the middle of an ocean of milk and the forces of darkness and light were fighting for control of the mountain in a tug of war, making the mountain churn within the ocean. What churned out was a being, the primordial physician, Dhanvantari. Like butter out of milk, Dhanvantari is the precipitation of a specific value of wholeness, the aspect of the pure intelligence that is self-interacting and self-perpetuating. For a Vedic physician, if all possibilities arise from an unmanifest field that is everywhere yet nowhere to be found, that field must be perfectly orderly, perfectly integrated and perfectly balanced. When you churn the pot, breaking its symmetry, the qualities of the field emerge. Dhanvantari represents self-interaction, whereby the field of pure intelligence reflects back on itself to recreate itself. The maintenance of your health, and its restoration when it is lost, are functions of self-interaction. Most importantly, you can access this field to change your health.

A modern physician counts on self-interaction to heal her patient. While she might order fluid, potassium, glucose, magnesium and other solutes for a patient in shock from pneumonia, the physician must count on the patient's self-interacting feedback mechanisms to keep the countless other biochemical values in balance. She also counts on the wily infecting bacterium to try to use self-interaction to outwit her prescribed antibiotic. Self-interaction is the basis of self-repair.

Dhanvantari has but four arms. He holds an urn of healing herbs, a conch symbolizing purity, a leech used in surgery,[5] and a medical text inscribed on palm leaves.

He is fully expressed in you because your human body contains the rules of self-repair in every cell.

1 This date is preferred by most Vedic scholars based on the antiquity of the civilization in the Indus River valley where the Veda was thought to have been first cognized.

2 Shakha, a lineage or familial clan

3 The aphorisms of Panini

4 Searching for meaning in the verses of the Veda itself is frustrating, elaborate, and rife with pitfalls. The easiest means to grasp the essence of Veda is from a learned teacher or by feeling it on its parā or transcendental level. Veda's elaboration as the rest of the Vedic literature is considered its means of revealing its essence to people with coarser nervous systems.

5 Leeches were used by Ayurvedic surgeons to evacuate hematomas and are still employed by modern plastic surgeons for the same purpose.

CHAPTER 2

SELF-INTERACTION AND THE
PHYSICS OF SELF-REPAIR

"Is there a pattern in the apparent chaos of the cosmos? Who is the artist who laid out Orion and the big dipper? How many stars are in heaven? Can I possibly fathom it all before I fall asleep?" Perhaps you have gazed in wonderment at its vastness, as my fellow ten-year-old Boy Scouts and I, our heads sticking out the doors of our army surplus pup tents under a cloudless, starry firmament far from the city lights in an arid Colorado canyon. Perhaps for you this moment of mystery came in the mountains where the thin atmosphere and cold air brought the heavens to life with stars you never imagined existed, but reduced their twinkle, impressing on you its vast, cold, aloofness and the transient nature of your existence. Perhaps this is where you first asked yourself the same primordial awestruck questions about the Creator of all this, and your own pitiful role in it all.

Einstein posed these questions in a novel way: innocent of all assumptions about the laws of nature accepted by other scientists. He rethought the issues of motion, mass, light and energy, concluding that even the emptiest space should behave as if it had a mass and energy, and gave it the term "cosmological constant."

We need to address these questions in a book about body renewal because your body is made of exploded stars and because self-repair is propelled by the same prime mover that propels our expanding universe. Self-repair is dependent on a reality of the unmanifest, so we will start by appreciating, in the most macroscopic way, its expression in the cosmic bodies. When you know about the idea of pure intelligence and the life of the brown-eyed boy who will keep it lively in the awareness of humankind, it may help you to understand how to repair your human body, because self-repair locates its source in a field of consciousness in motion.

The Paradox of the Accelerating Universe

One of the most important cosmological discoveries of the late 1990's was that the expansion of the universe is accelerating – and this contradicted existing understandings of the universe. It had always been taken for granted that the rate of acceleration of galaxies receding away from our own Milky Way was constant[6] and had been calculated with reasonable precision since Edwin Hubble's postulation of the big bang.

Hubble used stars that have a regular size and luminosity[7] to determine their distance and speed, like identical streetlights that dim as they recede. He found that the galaxies in the universe, like the raisins in a rising loaf of bread, are moving away from each other as the loaf expands. For our universe, the expansion of the loaf was extraordinarily rapid right after the big bang, not only during the first few seconds but also for about 300,000 years. The expansion then apparently slowed under the gravitational attraction of its matter and was assumed to be steady.

In 1998, cosmologists analyzed light from type 1a supernovas, exploding stars that briefly shine like a billion suns and can be seen across the universe. Supernovas give a more exact standard of luminosity for distant bodies, providing surprising new data for calculating the rate of expansion. For the last seven billion years, the universe seems to be expanding again. As the galaxies sprawl across the firmament, something unseen, which is not matter and not energy, as we know it, continues to drive them apart despite the expected slowing due to gravity.

All matter and energy is self-attracting. This contribution of Einstein's general theory of relativity states that energy, like matter, has a gravitational influence on everything else. The universe should therefore be self-attracting and decelerating in its expansion outward. For the galaxies close to our own, the rate of expansion fits the calculations made from the mass of the measurable universe. But for the farthest galaxies, it is much faster.[8] This can mean only one thing: something is creating a force opposing gravity that dwarfs the effect of the universe's visible (or otherwise measurable) matter, i.e. the gazillions of galaxies with their stars, planets, asteroids, interstellar dust and plasmas.

Dark Energy – the Discovery of the Unmanifest

This invisible "non-matter" is not made of leptons, quarks, photons or other subatomic particles. It is also not energy, as physicists classically understand it. Nor is it anti-matter. This non-matter, non-energy is nearly non-manifest in every sense. It barely has density, yet uniformly fills empty space, creating a dramatic and measurable anti-gravitational influence. Our universe is self-attracting at a scale that is too weak, and is therefore inconsistent with its apparent content of luminous matter. There is a negative gravitational pressure driving it apart. Physicists call this new entity accounting for the bulk of our universe *dark energy* because, similar to dark matter, it cannot be observed using light. Our universe's prime mover has somehow been saddled with a disparaging misnomer right out of a space war series.

Physicists have been able to calculate the effective gravitational mass of the universe and the undetectable part is 73%,[9] just the proportion of the Totality that Jagu sings about every morning.

When he first learned of Hubble's discovery that the universe was expanding, Einstein, with his typical humility, rejected his own previous idea of a cosmological constant, calling it his greatest blunder. Einstein's "blunder" appears to not only exist as dark energy, but is likely the unified field he spent the latter part of his life hopelessly trying to define. Its effect dominates the total mass-energy content of the universe, pulling it apart. With the recent discoveries of the magnitude of the universe's acceleration and the mathematics of string theory, the shape of this dark energy field is calculable, and many physicists say there is only one viable alternative: it is a precisely balanced superposition of all possible shapes.

Pure Wakefulness – Vigilance at work in Self-Repair

Jagu tells me his full name is Jagannath, the name his mother uses when she is serious. *Jagan* is universe and *nath* is lord, a lord of the universe. We get our word *juggernaut* from the same name, the American usage being a relentlessly powerful force, a universe of dark energy. Unlike other personifications of pure intelligence, Jagannath has no hands; in fact, he barely has a body. He looks, and literally is, an unfinished mound with miniature feet and huge open eyes without lids to close them. Jagannath personifies pure wakefulness, the eternally self-interactive nature of the virtual fluctuations underlying the visible universe.

In Puri, a quiet Bay of Bengal town on the perfect beach, every June or July the Brahmins place the images of Jagannath and his two wide-eyed sisters on enormous chariots and parade them from the temple in which they are enshrined to another temple a mile and a half away down a dusty street wider than a twelve-lane turnpike. The chariots are so massive it takes tens of thousands of people to pull them – to the cheers of another million. To the British, a juggernaut is a heavy truck, probably because the procession was so impressive.

Pure wakefulness describes a state of restful alertness, an intergalactic vacuum of nothingness, but pregnant with dynamic potentiality, silent though never sleeping or inert. Over hundreds of millions of years, the pure wakefulness value of the virtual fluctuations have been silent participants as time coerced your human body out of a primordial methane soup.

Biological self-interaction has a pure wakefulness value. It is constantly at work to keep you comfortable in your skin, to heal a laceration and to dissolve deposited plaque in the vessels of the heart. Before you can even think, "I'm cold!" thermoregulatory feedback loops based in the hypothalamus have compared the temperature of your blood to an internal thermostat and, finding it too low, initiated the constriction of your peripheral blood vessels that could lose heat, increased your burning of carbohydrates and fats, shunted blood to the core of your body and made your hairs stand on end to provide insulation. The intelligence behind this is an expression of the evolutionary effect of the presence of all possible shapes in every point.

If sedentary habits, overindulgences in rich foods, lousy genetics, a fondness for tobacco, the ravages of time, and plain bad luck conspire to plug your vessels with cholesterol-laden plaque, Dhanvantari, the principle of self-interaction, has blessed your boat with life preservers: good high-density cholesterol to scavenge your nasty, foamy, low-density cholesterol; blood factors that reduce the formation of fibrin clots that could attach to the plaque; factors to reduce inflammation that could accelerate the accumulation of plaque as your vessel perceives it is being injured; and natural factors to inhibit platelets from attaching to the plaque in the mistaken impression that it were a hemorrhaging leak requiring a plug. Hundreds of millions of years of self-interaction, condensed to fit into every cell's nucleus, has made your human body a genius of self-repair. Call yourself Dhanvantari.

Today at the entrance to many medical colleges, both western and Ayurvedic, from the Himalayas to Sri Lanka, you may see a statue of Dhanvantari, with his leech, herbs, conch and palm leaf texts, rising out of the foam of the churning ocean of consciousness in motion. Students and professors may adorn him with garlands as their patron saint, just as every western student swears allegiance to Hermes, Apollo and the other gods of healing when they become physicians – although for the latter the oath is often regarded as required and quaint rather than sacred.

Dhanvantari represents self-interaction, so the purpose of this book is to make it practical as body renewal and self-repair in the most common chronic disorders or health issues.

6 This rate is called the Hubble constant, red shift or Doppler shift.

7 Called Cepheid variables

8 With new tools such as radio telescopes, the Hubble telescope and other instruments, cosmologists have been able to gaze much farther away, 13 billion light years across the universe to its very frontier. The photons of light arriving at these telescopes left their galaxies 13 billion years ago, just several hundred years after the big bang.

9 The visible universe's matter and energy is 4% of the total, dark matter is 23%

CHAPTER 3

THE STRUCTURE OF PURE INTELLIGENCE

Jagu and his fellow students are grouped for their classes and sleeping space not by age, but according to the Veda of their clan. The biggest group represents families responsible for the Yajus, the Veda that is used directly in *yajñas*, sacrificial rites where a material essence of the world of humans is transferred to the world of the devas – the impulses of intelligence – with the purpose of nourishing and enlivening these impulses in a human's daily life. These boys may find it easier to find employment in temples because their services are the most practical. The boys reciting the Yajus sound very different from Jagu's Rg Veda group. Their recitation is highly rhythmic and syncopated, but seems monotone because they only use three or four notes. The boys are adept at making it vibrate in their noses, like a drone.

Before reciting a sukta, the boys first invoke the name of the rishi or seer, who cognized that verse, followed by the devatā – the impulse of intelligence that the verse describes – and then the chhandas (meter) in which the verse has been composed. Before the first verse of *Rg Veda*, for example, they sing, "The rishi is Madhuchhandas, the devatā is Agni, the *chhandas* is gāyatri!"[10]

Jagu will be a Rg Veda pandit, and his voice is perfectly suited to the loud resonance that the recitation of these verses requires. With his playful nature, if he grew up in a schoolyard in Chicago he would likely attract a crowd by imitating a jazzman on an alto sax.

One evening before lights out in the boys' quarters (which also serves as their dining hall and classroom simply by rolling up their straw sleeping mats), Jagu approaches me on my porch. Jagu knows 20 words of English, and I know about as much Tamil, but somehow, using fingers and Sanskrit, we communicate frictionlessly. "Three Jagu today." I try to look surprised. "Jagu is rishi, Jagu is devatā, Jagu is chhandas." He leaves me to contemplate the cosmic mystery in his words, learnt with his preceptor today, their two knees touching.

This afternoon Jagu's preceptor had told him and his group why they recite the name of the verse's seer (rishi), its rhythm (chhandas) and the name of the impulse of intelligence (devatā) to whom the verse is dedicated. The seer is the verse's knower, the rhythm is its known, and the impulse of intelligence is the relationship that connects the two, (the process of knowing), the tutor had explained. Embedded in the heart of every interaction, whether it is a quantum interaction such as the collision of an electron with a proton, or the witnessing of a sunset, is a relationship between the interaction's elements – the particle and its field, the witness and the sunset.

From the perspective of someone interested in learning the rules of self-repair, the most important interaction is the witness becoming one and the same with the object witnessed: the knower knowing the Self. It is the essential experience not only of healing and self-repair, but also of the most fulfilling and profound spiritual moments. The interaction of the Self with the Self is the dynamics of wakefulness and is a relationship we need to explore in detail in order to fully enliven the rules of self-repair within your human body.

A Constitution of the Universe

Quantum physicists attempt to describe the complex self-interactions of the vacuum fluctuations with composite equations called Lagrangians. The Lagrangian for the superstring field is the physicist's attempt to capture the idea of pure intelligence in symbolic language as opposed to in syllables, melody and rhythm. If a physicist were asked to write a constitution of the universe to express the laws of nature, it would be a Lagrangian equation. For those like me, whose intellects will never access this abstract realm of mathematics, Veda is there with its four different levels of expression – including the sound I hear when Jagu and his friends wake me with their recitation two hours before dawn, the imagery I see when I read of a thousand headed Purusha, the notion I feel when I experience the boys' refrain coming from an inner voice, and its transcendental value that sneaks in and out of my awareness during the gaps between thoughts while I sit in meditation or drift into sleep.

The best healers from both West and East know this field of intelligence as the source of self-repair and give their patients the means to cultivate it in their lives. We will be exploring its healing nature and analyzing its "Lagrangian" in practical terms in later chapters.

Jagu's preceptor had surprised his group by telling them that they as individuals were composed of the same three-in-one structure of pure intelligence that they spend all day ingesting as song. The boy was impressed that he, like the Veda, is cosmic and has the ability to reflect the intelligence of the underlying creation. At the age of eight, Jagu was grasping the abstract principle that he is at the same time knower, known and process of knowing, and that every point of creation can be said to have that same underlying dynamic, but non-manifest, structure.

The next evening, Jagu steals a moment to see me again. "Jagu is three, Jagu is one," he informs me, eyeing me intently to see whether I have understood. Satisfied, he heads for his grass sleeping mat. Jagu seemed to grasp that whenever the knower and known are the same, the awareness is self-interactive, independent of any other outside point of reference. The knower's awareness turns back on itself to know itself. This abstract paradox, how something could be unity within diversity, simultaneously dynamic and silent, did not trouble Jagu and his eight-year old twice-born companions as it did the early pioneers of particle theory; they naturally think in abstractions. Jagu leaves me alone on the porch; he is done in, and wise enough to realize he will be standing to recite before the birds sing.

The Mistake of Judgment – Root of all Disorder

The Rg and Yajus boys are quite happy forming recitation groups next to each other, but the Sāman boys are happier by themselves. The Sāma is the only Veda that is sung as opposed to chanted. Although it is nasal and loud, its long, sustained tones are more restful and soothing. My drowsy brain naturally selects the Sāma melody out of the cacophony when the young voices inevitably rouse me. I distinguish the words of the Sāma with great difficulty. The boys learn to purposely obscure the syllables by drawing them out for up to a minute at a time, cutting off and repeating words, or inserting and drawing out exclamatory syllables such as "ha," or "u." The Sāman boys can spend ten minutes singing half a dozen words. Although it is not the Veda of his clan, Jagu can recite it on cue, mischievously trying to look bored. Its effect is potent – the best remedy for my sleep deprivation.

Jagu's pronouncements have made me think deeply about the health implications of Jagu's understanding of his three-in-one nature. I consult a dusty copy of *Charaka Samhitā*, the oldest Ayurvedic text, at a local dealer in Sanskrit texts. Charaka writes, "Unhealthy practices performed when the intellect, resolve and memory are imbalanced are known to arise from *prajña-aparādham*, 'a mistake of judgment;' this mistake of judgment provokes all the agents of disease."[11]

From the perspective of Charaka's teacher, the ancient physician Ātreya, a mistake of judgment occurs when you erroneously understand life to be diverse and finite, and behave accordingly. Under this illusion, common to nearly everyone, the unified, infinite value of life is ignored or forgotten. Your connection with your source is lost. You start to work too hard, eat or drink too much or partake of the wrong things, and then violate other laws of nature because you are not grounded in your source, the prime mover on which the laws of nature are based. Charaka calls this prajña-aparādham – the mistake of judgment.

Overshadowed by the mistake of judgment, when your awareness does not have intuitive access to the full value of the laws of nature, your intellect, resolve and memory conspire to forget or ignore what your body and your common sense are screaming at you. The Ayurvedic texts characterize the various types of violations (suppressing natural urges, getting out of healthy routines, abusing food, drugs, etc.). When you are sick or injured, you can often identify some behavior that leads to suffering. The pain, in turn, is a mechanism to motivate you to restore your connectedness with the source and enliven the rules of self-repair.

Jagu does not think too deeply regarding his new discovery that he is three Jagu's in one, although there are profound implications for his own health and the health of society. He is too busy singing creation's ancient song and seeing it unfold in his life with his fellow students.

The Practicality of Pure Intelligence: Access to the Laws of Nature

This academy does not offer instruction to boys from Atharvaveda families because this fourth Veda is used for specific purposes – such as attaining a goal or healing. Atharvaveda has no role in the rites that are performed for no good reason, which, paradoxically, is deemed the best reason to perform them. The academy boys seem to look down on Atharvavedins. The fourth Veda is too practical. It can be used to accomplish seemingly anything, including not only healing disease but also even malevolent undertakings like poisoning a neighbor or seducing his wife. If Veda is an expression of totality – truth and falsehood, good and evil – then, the reasoning goes, nothing falls outside its scope. For a physician, the Atharvaveda is the most interesting read.

Vedic verses are also divided into those that are useful and those that give knowledge. The biggest share is the verses used in the Vedic rites. Every group of boys sings several Rg Veda verses that impart knowledge at the end of their dawn recitation. I know I can soon sleep again when they intone:

richo akshare parame vyoman yasmin deva adhivishve nishedu

The richas, the verses of the Veda lie in the transcendental field
(parā) in which reside all the impulses of intelligence (deva).

The boys sing of the compactification of a fullness of forces and energy within
an unmanifest field beyond the senses, beyond time and space and yet which is the
basis of time and space.

How so much matter and energy can be superposed in a virtual transcendental
field is something I have not yet begun to grasp, but a lot of very bright physicists tell
us it involves superstrings and their reverberant frequencies. The virtual fluctuations
impelling our universe have a distinct, calculable structure. These fluctuations
within the unmanifest are the template from which the structure of the universe
is expressed. Moreover, some of these bright physicists have shown good logic to
equate pure intelligence with the unified field.[12]

"Jagu is three, Jagu is one." The eternal enigma of how unity transforms itself into
multiplicity, yet remains unity. The vision of Jagu, waving his fingers in all directions
showing me how he brings Veda to permeate creation, has haunted me all these
intervening years. It is that same song that permeates every cell in our physiology
with intelligence, giving us the power of self-repair.

Insight into the connection between physical theories of the cosmos and the
world's oldest and newest medical textbooks is needed to bring the latent potentiality
of pure intelligence into action to improve our health. We need to hear this song
of intelligence from many perspectives because nothing falls outside its purview.
The song's traditional custodian, a Brahmin like Jagu, calls it Veda; a quantum
physicist calls it the vacuum state; a cosmologist, dark energy with its virtual
fluctuations; an Ayurvedic physician calls it Ātma or, as applied to the task of self-
repair, Dhanvantari; a neurophysiologist calls it pure consciousness; a Buddhist,
nirvana; a Jew, shekhinah, the divine presence; and a Christian might call it the will
of God. Each perspective has its own language and metaphor and each has a value
in permitting us to embrace the power of self-repair at our finest level of feeling.

We need all these perspectives because pure intelligence is not something you
can simply confront intellectually to gain its healing power. Self-interaction must be
lived to make self-repair work for you. As you learn to kindle the healing response,
naturally you will be making a radical change in the way your nervous system
interfaces with your immune and endocrine systems.

Jagu is now grown, undoubtedly married and perhaps preparing a ceremony to
give his own son his string, rebirthing him as a Brahmin to begin teaching him the
Veda, thus playing out his role in perpetuating Veda's transmission through human
generations. You do not need to learn to recite Veda to gain its power. You are
already Veda, cosmic, multiplicity in unity. Veda is hardwired in your cells and only
remains to be discovered in your consciousness. It is a fire that only needs lighting.

10 *Gāyatri meter (chhandas)* has 3 lines of 8 syllables each

11 *La Charaka Samhitā*, Sa 1.99. p. 81. Translated by Michel Angot. 1996 Paris. This verse translated
from French by Jay Glaser, MD.

12 *Is consciousness the unified field? A field theorist's perspective.* Modern Science and Vedic Science. John
S. Hagelin, Ph.D. Vol. 1, no. 1, 1987, pp. 29-87.

CHAPTER 4

THE ILLUSION AND REALITY OF SELF-REPAIR

Repairing a human body is usually not very difficult as long as the repairman and the human body in question are the same. This is self-repair, the subject of this book, and we do it all the time. When another technician – such as a doctor – needs to be called in, things rapidly become problematic. Self-repair is simple because the human genome within nearly every one of the body's trillions of cells contains not only a complete blueprint, but a full set of repair manuals.

In nature, self-repair is taken for granted. The halobacterium living in the extreme salinity of the Dead Sea, six times saltier than the ocean, because of the extreme hostility of its environment, has evolved highly elaborate repair enzymes. You can mince its DNA with radiation or intense UV light and within a few hours the bacterium has made itself whole and is ready to reproduce.[13, 14]

Salamanders sacrifice a leg and grow another at will. And you can lose a good part of your liver and regenerate it without visualization, affirmations, organic groceries, healthy lifestyles or stopping smoking.

Repairing a human body is especially easy if that body is youthful and the breakdown acute. An inventory of the various repair contracts my not so youthful body has taken on any given summer day shows just how easy it really is. A splinter from working the garden and calluses from the shovel are no problem. An abrasion from surfing a rocky reef plus the sore shoulder muscles from all the paddling are brief annoyances. A hint of athlete's foot from not drying my feet. Sore, red gums from eating steaming corn on the cob. Even more miraculous is the ease with which my body deals with imbalances of which I remain blissfully oblivious: eliminating an overdose of chai, neutralizing the free radicals in my retina from staring too long at my monitor. My body intuitively knows how to scavenge the foamy, oxidized cholesterol deposited by a second helping of chocolate cheesecake that I impulsively decided not to forego. My body is fortunately much more brilliant a physician than I could ever hope to be, and a better parent, caring for and nursing itself after I repeatedly subject it to both physical and emotional abuse.

Repairing a human body generally begins to get problematic when the instructions in the genetic repair manual are insufficient to compensate for the degree and duration of the overdose, underdose, misuse or injury. At some point, the body goes beyond simple imbalance and enters into the ill-omened territory of chronic disease, which is the subject of this book.

The Doctor Within

I remember the moment I entered that inauspicious domain of chronic disease, still in my twenties. I had enjoyed a sunny March morning pummeling my quads while skiing on a steep, bumpy run. Getting off the lift with joy in my heart for a last run before lunch, I became aware of a vague ache in a knee that seven years previously had lain wide open on an operating table prior to the era of arthroscopy.

Having personally experienced how remarkably efficient a youthful body can be at the difficult task of self-repair, I had always assumed, or perhaps hoped against my better judgment as a first year medical student, that acute trauma was simply something I naturally recover from, given a day or two off and a few tablets of ibuprofen. Looking down the hill and feeling a faint fullness and twinge in my knee, I knew my life had changed forever. What once was a trick knee would now always be my bum knee. I thought, "I'm not yet thirty and I have arthritis!" I sensed the rest of my days would be encumbered with its repair, in contrast to the much simpler job of prevention. Deciding that I'd better start to acquire some common sense, and realizing that pain had a purpose, I chose the less traumatic way down the mountain.

Learning the lost art of self-repair implies a process of giving your body's intelligence an opportunity to function in a different mode than the one that brought it to its current state.

In states of extreme disease, however, sometimes the body is too smart for its own good. For example, an unstable, arthritic knee initiates a process of building osteophytes, calcifications that help to stabilize the joint. Unfortunately, they eventually also decrease its range of motion, impose sharp spines into the joint space and promote more irritation.

In response to a weakening heart, the body activates many hormonal and muscle responses that stretch, dilate and thicken the heart's walls to compensate. This strategy works up to a point. After that, the same compensatory responses, which initially helped the heart cope, begin to sabotage its wall's motion. Too much stretch makes it weaker, as in blowing up a balloon the thinning walls become easier to fill.

The ideal response to a chronic process is not always intuitive to a diseased body. The goal of Vedic medicine is to enliven the best of the possible responses inherent in the genome in reaction to a stress, an imbalance or disease.

Each patient carries his own doctor within. They come to us not knowing that truth. We are at our best when we allow the doctor who resides within each patient a chance to go to work.

Albert Schweitzer

The Illusion of the Physical Body

The ancient art of self-repair, the secrets shared by the ancient Vedic physicians and their disciples, eerily envisages the nonlinear perspective about biology discovered by modern science over the past fifty years. This non-linear paradigm from quantum mechanics, molecular biology and psychoneuroimmunology has been largely ignored, neglected and dismissed in clinical medicine.

Quantum mechanics understands matter not as a solid substance, but as a wave function or probability on one hand, or as a kink in space-time on the other. In essence, your body is nothing material. It is a song. Depending on your perspective your body is a quantum mechanical wave function, recurrent waves of a repetitive sequence of genetic information, or the cosmic embodiment of Veda. "Reality is an illusion," said Albert Einstein, "albeit a persistent one."

Whatever this nothingness is, cell turnover studies have shown it is in constant flux. Your tissues renew themselves on a regular basis. You shed your skin every 28 days – unless you have psoriasis and turn your skin over in 7 days. You make new red cells every six months, breaking down the old weak ones in your soles as you walk and excreting them in your stool. Your white cells have an even shorter life, from a few days to a few weeks. The cells that line your stomach are replaced in a matter of hours. In short, you are a nothingness in progress. Carbon-14 dating of genomic DNA, which has the lowest turnover rate of all the molecules in a cell, has shown that most tissues are much younger than your body.[15] Your intestinal tissue (except the lining which you shed every few days) is 11 years old. Skeletal muscle is 15 years old. Your brain's neurons are the most stable. This study suggested that the average age of your tissues is seven to ten years. You literally urinate out your bones as soluble calcium as you replace them with this morning's yogurt, and exhale the lymphocytes of your spleen as carbon dioxide and water as you build new ones from the burrito at lunch.

Molecular biology has demonstrated that your physical essence is not its material components, but the software, the biological intelligence flowing from the gene sequences of DNA that program you. If you are indeed a nothingness in progress, you are not even a material nothingness, but a nothingness of information, consciousness in motion, a wave function.

These modern insights have profound implications for chronic disease because most people, including physicians, feel that most disorders have rigid anatomical consequences that cannot be modified: torn cartilage, growth of osteophytes, thinning of intestinal walls, brittle bones. If a good part of your calcium will be exchanged over the two years before your next bone density measurement, why should it not happen in a more positive way than heretofore? In two years, you will examine your most recent scan showing that you have the bone density of a seventy-year old while your driver's license reads only fifty. You may think, "Same lousy, brittle, old hip!" The reality is that you do not have the same old hip at all. In those intervening two years, you have literally exchanged a new hip for the old one. The only factors that remained the same were the software (your DNA) and your lousy old habits, which are mere memories ("I hate walks, veggies and dairy, but I love coffee.") Much of chronic disease is but memories and information, mostly smoke and mirrors.

Your Brain and the Repair Response

A merry heart doeth good like a medicine: but a broken spirit drieth the bones.

Proverbs 17:22

Psychoneuroimmunology, a new discipline studying the interface between our nervous and immune systems, has added other insights to dispel the idea that the body is but flesh with feelings. In 1982, Robert Ader performed a remarkable experiment, feeding saccharine to one set of lab mice while injecting them with the immune boosting drug interferon.

He gave the other set saccharine while it was injected with the potent immune suppressant cyclophosphamide. When he gave the saccharine alone, the immune system was either stimulated or suppressed depending on the animal's previous experience.[16] Humans respond in similar ways. Depending on our past experience a stimulus like the smell of a box of chocolates or the lilacs blooming can make us remember happy times or sad.

This also implies that every thought and emotion is accompanied by its own neurochemical mix – the neurotransmitters and neuropeptides such as serotonin, endorphin, GABA, vasopressin, epinephrine, and acetylcholine. These neurotransmitters are involved not only with signaling and synapses in the brain, but with the regulation of the immune system, gut, circulation and other vital functions. The body's glands, intestines and bone marrow appear to be a part of our memory bank, storing and exchanging information with the brain mediated by these neuromessengers. Depending on what we think and feel, we can have heartfelt feelings or heart attacks, strong immune defenses or a series of colds.[17] Dhanvantari is self-interaction. Your every thought, emotion and perception, including what TV shows you watch and the company you keep, affect your health.

The soul is dyed the color of its thoughts. Day by day, what you choose, what you think, and what you do is who you become.

Heraclitus

The connection between the nervous and immune systems can also be extended to a culture. Sociological studies have shown that poor people have worse health than the rich. Only a small fraction of that difference can be explained by access to doctors, hospitals, medicines, good food, better hygiene, more leisure time and exercise. Good research suggests that one of the main determinants in this disparity is the shame, anger and frustration that come with the perception of being comparatively poor.[18] In the US where even the poor have mobile phones, televisions, cars, microwaves and reasonable access to hospitals, we rank 25th in the most important measures of health. This is well below many countries that are much poorer than ours, including some countries where the necessities in life are truly marginal and where there is little disparity between rich and poor. Could it be that a person creates within herself a culture of wealth or poverty, regardless of her actual financial status, together with the emotions and corresponding neurochemistry of health or disease? Perhaps the quantum physicists are right and the body is but a song, a tapestry of harmonics and rhythms, a field of all possibilities with a flavor of its own. Can you turn your family's culture into one that promotes self-repair?

13 Grant W.D., Gemmell R.T., McGenity T.J. (1998) *Halobacteria: the evidence for longevity.* Extremophiles 2:279-287

14 McGenity T.J. et al. (2000) *Origins of halophilic microorganisms in ancient salt deposits.* Environmental Microbiology 2(3), 243-250

15 Spalding KL, Bhardwaj RD, Buchholz BA, Druid H, Frisen J. 2005) *Retrospective birth dating of cells in humans.* Cell. 122:166-43. The authors correlated the carbon-14 content of the atmosphere, which is declining since above ground atomic tests of the 1950's, with the content in human cells, beacuse humans incorporate plants and plant-eating animals which fix atmospheric $CO2$.

16 Ader R, Cohen N. *Behaviorally conditioned immunosuppression and murine systemic lupus erythemotosis.* Science 1982; 215:1534-6.

17 For a more detailed discussion of this topic, see *Quantum Healing*, by Deepak Chopra, MD; Random House, 1989

18 *Health and Wealth.* Transcript of a talk on Alternative Radio. Stephen Bezruchka. Seattle, WA, 9 Dec. 2003.

INVOKING YOUR
BODY'S REPAIR RESPONSE

CHAPTER 5

THE SECRETS OF EXTREME LONGEVITY

Life insurance actuaries earn a good living by staking wagers on how long you are likely to live. They tell us that when you are turning eleven years old, you have the best chance of living to see your next birthday. By eleven, you have survived your toughest year, the first, as well as the next ten years beset with infections, household poisons, accidents, congenital deformities and childhood tumors. At eleven, you generally have not yet started hanging out with people who carry weapons and drive recklessly nor have you seriously contemplated suicide. By twelve, your risks of dying are heading the wrong way.

The science of gerontology, the study of aging, begins in utero, the period of life when the rate of cell death is the highest. The science of geriatrics, the management of age-related disorders, apparently begins at eleven, the onset of age-related disease.

If we assume geriatricians could treat any chronic disorder with complete success, barring an accident, you would have a high probability of living out your full life expectancy. But most of us would still die somewhere between 85 and 95, not from any disease but from old age, like Oliver Wendell Holmes' "Wonderful one hoss shay that ran a hundred years to the day."[19] His carriage-maker argued that in any vehicle,

"there is always somewhere a weakest spot
Find it somewhere you must and will, – Above or below, or within or without,
– And that's the reason, beyond a doubt, A chaise breaks down, but doesn't wear out."

This good New England Yankee proposes a remedy:

"t's mighty plain That the weakes' place mus' stan' the strain; 'n' the way t' fix it, uz I maintain, Is only jest T' make that place uz strong uz the rest."

Unlike your car, Holmes' wonderful shay never did break down, but died of old age. After one hundred years "it fell to pieces all at once."

Some physicians are dissatisfied with the claim, "She died in her sleep of old age," preferring to write on the death certificate a more definitive sudden event such as heart attack or stroke. Your body, however, truly decays like the one hoss shay. The most important determinant of the rate of decay is not whether you buy organic produce or are vegetarian. It is your genes. As in all species, humans are genetically endowed with a maximum lifespan.

Gerontology attempts to extend the maximum human lifespan. In the twentieth century, civil engineering collaborated with medical science to extend our life expectancy from 45 at the century's start to over 77 at its end. Despite this dramatic progress, and the advances in intensive care and cardiology including pacemakers, bypasses, stents and implantable defibrillators, there has been no change in the maximum human lifespan. Once you get to 85 or 90, your chances of living considerably longer are not much better today than they were when Holmes penned his poem in 1858. It is up to your genes, the hand of DNA you were dealt.

Change, Entropy and Growing Older

Change by itself appears to be no barrier to immortality because from birth until around 25 we are changing for the better. After that, as almost any elite athlete will tell you, change is usually for the worse.

Physicists call this kind of change *entropy*, the tendency of a system left to itself to evolve in the direction of greater disorder – like a heap of red and a heap of white sand side by side turning into a heap of pink sand and never vice versa. Entropy, says the second law of thermodynamics, is a one-way street. It's a statistical issue: there are a million ways to throw bricks off a truck in a heap, but only a few ways to throw them off into a perfect pile. Similarly, rusting cars in a scrap yard, like residents rusting in nursing homes, inexorably deteriorate and never spontaneously reorganize themselves into orderly new cars.

Fortunately, hope for this bleak picture for a changing human body is available in the third law of thermodynamics, which states that cooling any system reduces its entropy. Superconductors near absolute zero exhibit the frictionless flow of electrons within their circuitry. Superfluids at 4 degrees above absolute zero can swirl without turbulence around a beaker forever because their atoms display a perfectly coherent, orderly interaction.

Reducing Biological Entropy

The physiological equivalent of a superfluid would be a physiology that maintained a low metabolic rate. Indeed, it has long been noted that the longest lived species such as elephants and hippopotami have the lowest metabolic rates compared with the short-lived high metabolizing mouse. These observations led Clive McCay in the 1930's followed by George Sacher in the 1960's to report that you could get caged lab rats to live up to 75% longer without the aid of nutritional supplements or body wraps.[20] You simply had to restrict their caloric intake 30-40% from what they normally ate. Animals in captivity are known to live much longer than wild animals that suffer from the chronic stresses in their dog-eat-dog world. McCay and Sacher showed that caged animals on a low-calorie diet live longer than even pampered captive ones.

These observations have been verified and extended to other species, including a report in July 2009 showing that monkeys, our closest cousins, look younger and live longer when kept on a lifetime calorie-restricted diet. To this day, caloric restriction is one of the only reproducible ways to make an animal live longer than its littermates. The rate-of-living theory was born. This theory essentially states that if all the food you will require during your lifetime is put into an enormous pile, your lifespan will be the time it takes you to eat the pile. You can stretch your life out by applying great self-discipline or flame out young in hedonistic overindulgence. Rate of living proponents may also point to recent research showing that women who keep within ten pounds of their college weight lived longer.

There are a few problems with this theory. First, leg banding has shown that bats smaller than a mouse have been noted to live for thirty years and more. Theory proponents argue these bats have long lives because they spend most of their time hibernating in literal suspended animation, hardly metabolizing at all. On the other hand, some bigger animals, especially marsupials like kangaroos and opossums, may live only as long as a mouse. Another problem with this theory, say its detractors, is that the control lab animals in the cages eating as much as they desire are simply overfed couch potatoes, not unlike the rest of us, and are not subject to the exercise requirements of an animal in the wild.

Error Theories of Aging

There are other theories explaining why we age, together with possible cures for this universal disorder, One good theory sees aging as caused by the inability of the aging body to repair damage, especially in its DNA, creating metabolic errors that result in the accumulation of debris in the cells. The finding that fetal cells can only divide about 55 times, called the Hayflick limit, before they fill with debris and stop proliferating, supports this theory. All organisms have proteins to make these repairs. So why do the repair mechanisms get overwhelmed?

Biological Rust

Perhaps aging is just so much oxidation or weathering, turning our supple cell membranes into leather, an extension of the rate-of-living theory. More practically, perhaps this oxidation could be countered by taking huge doses of antioxidants. Ironically, there was a time when health food zealots who fought to banish BHA and BHT as additives to retard spoilage from oxidation found themselves popping it in enormous doses when it was marketed as an anti-aging cure.

Or perhaps aging is a hormonal issue. After all, growth hormone and DHEA (dehydroepiandrosterone) decline with age and when replaced in large doses produce rejuvenating changes in humans and lab animals that had some researchers calling them the fountain of youth. Unfortunately, growth hormone supplementation also has serious side effects and although you may gain lean muscle mass, energy and endurance, similar benefits of youthfulness can be had, but with more work, through improvements in diet and exercise. These impositions on your life of pleasure, however, still do not extend the maximum lifespan.

Your Selfish, Immortal DNA

Perhaps the price we pay for the immortality of our genes is aging and death. In River Out of Eden, Richard Dawkins writes,

"A river of DNA flows through time, not space. It is a river of information, not a river of bones and tissues: a river of abstract instructions for building bodies, not a river of solid bodies themselves. The information passes through bodies and affects them, but it is not affected by them on its way through."

The evolutionary change on our human species through 100,000 generations appears to not be concerned with making our lives prolonged beyond the time it takes to conceive and raise a child to carry on the task. This makes DNA selfish: DNA's only concern is its own propagation – beyond that your body is dispensable.

Another good theory sees your DNA as programmed with a death hormone or messenger molecule that kicks in after seven to nine decades to bring your days to an end so your more viable progeny will be less encumbered as custodians of your DNA. Intriguingly, such a genetic booby-trap might be defused.

Examples of Extreme Longevity

Is there any proof that extreme longevity is possible? Although some areas of the world have been claimed to be home to people living to 130 or 140, such as the Hunzas of Kashmir, the people of the Caucasus Mountains of Georgia and the Incan descendants in the Andean valley of Vilcabamba of Ecuador, the authenticity of these claims is not supported by any documentation. One thing all these places have in common, besides their being remote and mountainous, is the reverence the culture has for the elderly. Unlike in our culture, in these societies there is a strong incentive to exaggerate one's age.

Jeanne Calment was a centenarian who gives hope to the person turning fifty and who laments finding himself on the back nine.[21] Descended from generations of extremely long-lived ancestors, she passed away in 1997 in Southern France where she had lived for her entire 122 years. She was riding a bicycle until 110 and for most of her life was a smoker. Most importantly, a demographer, a gerontologist and her physician were able to document every event in her extraordinarily long life with existing historical records. Most remarkably, despite her frailty and deprivation of hearing and sight, she maintained a sharp, alert mind.

If this woman could live so long and well, why can't you? This brings us to the critical issue for anyone serious about longevity: even if you are a toddler, it is unlikely you will ever be able to swallow in confidence a harmless magic bullet to reverse aging due to the sheer length of a human lifespan and the time it takes to test such a remedy.

There are a few good studies like the ones supported by the MacArthur Foundation Consortium on Successful Aging. It found that people entering their eighth decade healthy and independent have several qualities in common that might explain their successful aging: participating in regular exercise, continued social connections, a sense of self worth, and resiliency in the face of a major loss. These are attitudes and lifestyle patterns you culture over seventy years to keep you young and not something you can swallow today to live longer.

Structuring a Personal Anti-Aging Program

Assume a new hormone were discovered tomorrow that has promising potential at arresting the aging process. You would be reluctant to take it yourself without knowing if the benefits outweighed the long-term side effects. Before swallowing your first dose you would want to see the results of a randomized controlled trial, whereby scientists draw straws to assign a few hundred newborns to receive the hormone or a placebo, then follow them for the next 100 years or so, keeping all the other conditions the same, to see which group lived the longest.

Since you will never have gold standard evidence upon which to base your choice of an anti-aging regimen, you are left with a few other options:

1) Forget trying to alter the rate at which you are aging and instead simply opt to avoid all the possible diseases that could shorten your life, even if most of them are the degenerative ones caused by aging.

2) Follow your own common sense and live every day as if it were your last – one day it will be.

3) Adopt time-tested medical traditions purported to promote longevity, not feeling per-

fectly convinced they will give you the 122 years you deserve, but at least comfortable in the knowledge that if the interventions have stood the test of time, they can't be harmful and at worst might even help dodge a few of the biggest bullets.

If you opt for number one, this book has what you are looking for in the subsequent chapters.

If you opt only for number two, you don't need any help; put down this book and light the barbecue.

If you opt for number three, here are a few practical points you can follow without much trouble, and which have the side benefit of making you feel and look better even if they haven't been definitively proved to make you live longer. Some of these tips are derived from observational studies of commonalities found in aging populations or in the oldest of the old. Some are extrapolations of observations made in younger humans, animals or test-tube experiments that appear to improve general health in human populations.[22] Some are derived from ancient medical texts, including those of Ayurveda.

- **Transcend time and space on a regular basis.**[23][24] Visit the field of pure consciousness that is described as infinite, eternal and unbounded for a few minutes each day in order to bring infinity back into your life of boundaries. See these footnotes below or begin with the techniques in Chapter 8.

- **Culture an attitude of childlike innocence.** This does not mean being naïve. See every circumstance as fresh and new.

- **Practice hatha yoga āsanas**, even ten minutes a day.

- **Practice prānayāma** (yoga breath refinement techniques) designed to slow your metabolism by slowing the breath – inducing mini-hibernation throughout your day. Prānayāma, like meditation, which has been shown to reduce oxygen consumption and CO_2 elimination,[25] empirically counteracts the rate of living theory described above. Don't worry; it will not slow the rate at which you burn fat. See Chapter 15 for a description of how it is performed.

- **Purify your body with regular eliminative physiotherapy programs.** Plan on one week in residence twice yearly for optimal results, or see Appendix 6.

- **Get regular physical activity.** Whatever you do, however, avoid arthritis and injury! If you need a rolling walker in your 80's, your chances are slimmer for making it to 100. Chapters 13 and 29.

- **Establish structured daily routines.** Opt for a schedule that is royal, unhurried and free of hassle, including time for meditation, exercise and the other strategies below that you find important. Chapter 10.

- **Adjust your routines with the season and, for women, the time of month.** Chapter 32 and Appendix 7.

- **Practice devotion:** to your partner, your family and your higher power. Chapter 9.

- **Stay slim and eat frugally.** This is one of the most important things you can do to reach your maximum lifespan, and the research above suggests perhaps even beyond it. People enjoying life vibrantly in their nineties and beyond are almost invariably slim. (Chapter 20.)

- **Avoid toxins in your food and environment.** This includes tobacco. Forget Jeanne Calment's cigars. The chances are one in a billion that you have similarly lucky genes.

- **Take alcohol only in extreme moderation.** Some evidence suggests a drink here or there may help prevent heart disease, but not if it is a habit.

- **Culture the ability to be flexible.** And find creative ways to make the best of adversity. This was one of the most important qualities in a Harvard study of the oldest of the old. For hints where to start, see #1 and #2 above.

- **Avoid being critical or judgmental of yourself and others.** The alternative saps life and energy.

- **Moderation in meat, fowl and eggs.** In those remote mountainous cultures reputed for their longevity, animal products are taken sparingly. North American Seventh Day Adventists and other vegetarians appear to have less heart disease and cancer.

- **Get adequate rest.** Schedule it in. (Chapter 10, 11.)

- **Find a job you enjoy doing and that brings you a sense of satisfaction.** A common finding in the oldest old.

- **Avoid "going to pasture."**[26] (See Chapter 27.)

- **Culture a happy marriage/relationship.** Fights and discontent create the worst kinds of wear and tear.

- **Properly metabolize the notion of time.** Einstein said, "When a man sits with a pretty girl for an hour, it seems like a minute. But let him sit on a hot stove for a minute and it's longer than any hour. That's relativity." If time seems to fly because you are absorbed in the present, you may be aging much more gracefully.

- **Take a diet rich in natural antioxidants,** i.e. fresh food of all different colors. It is fine to add vitamins and supplements, but no proof of their benefits has yet been shown. Start with celery, broccoli, carrots, seeds and nuts. Brazil nuts in moderation[27] are rich in the antioxidant selenium. (Chapter 18.)

- **Olive oil.** A component of the Mediterranean diet which seems to be associated with less heart disease and hypertension. Side-benefit: tastes great.

- **Avoid excessive sun exposure.** Use sunscreen and wear a hat. At the very least, you will look younger.

19 *The Deacon's Masterpiece* or *The Wonderful One Hoss Shay.* Oliver Wendell Holmes. Houghton, Mifflin and Company. Boston and New York, 1891.

20 GA Sacher, *Life Table Modification and Life Prolongation, Handbook of the Biology of Aging,* 1st edition, ed. CE Finch and L. Hayflick. New York: van Nostrand, 1977

21 Allard M, Lebre V, Robine JM., Calment J. Jeanne Calment: *From Van Gogh's Time to Ours: 122 extraordinary years.* WH Freeman & Co.: New York; 1998.

22 Such evidence is highly subject to change from year to year, creating cynicism and frustration among health consumers. You should make diet and lifestyle choices based on common sense, how it feels to you and how it makes you feel, realizing that the issues related to your state of mind appear to be the most important with respect to modifiable factors in longevity. Fretting over what scientists still call controversial may itself be a good accelerator of aging.

23 Schneider, Robert, *American Journal of Cardiology,* Dec. 17, 2005

24 For starters, look into meditation: the research on TM shows that it cultivates a hypometabolic state opposite to the life-shortening stress response, increases DHEA sulfate, and improves scores on standardized tests of biological age. A NIH funded study of the effects of TM on blood pressure on inner city blacks followed from 7 to 18 years showed that those that learned TM compared to those in the mindfulness training and progressive relaxation groups had a 23% lower overall death rate and 30% lower reduction in death from cardiovascular disease. These reductions are equivalent to those seen in people who take cholesterol and blood pressure medications. See Footnote immediately above.

25 Wallace RK *Physiological Effects of Transcendental Meditation,* Science, 167:1751-1754.

26 Silver, M.H., Jilinskaia, E., Perls, T.T. *Cognitive functional status of age-confirmed centenarians in a population based study.* Journal of Gerontology, Psychol Sci 2001,56B:P134-P140.

27 Brazil nuts are also rich in isotopes.

CHAPTER 6

MASTERING THE MIND-BODY CONNECTION

During the interval between the discovery of an antibody test to diagnose HIV infection and the discovery of antiviral drugs active against the virus, there was desperation among people diagnosed with HIV. AIDS was a mortal disease with no effective therapy. I was asked to create mind-body programs to be used at clinics in San Francisco and New York. To my amazement, the patients who showed up had never been tested for the HIV antibody. Instead, they had guessed, intuited, deduced, assumed or supposed but never definitively confirmed that they were infected. In those communities, avoiding diagnosis was seen as critical to maintaining a foot in the world of hope because a positive test at the time was a sentence to a certain, cruel death.

"Even the dream that I am HIV negative is a therapy for me," one man told me, "because I have seen that as soon as my friends were confirmed to be infected, their disease accelerated. I don't want to know." At the time, such a person was considered to be in denial and worse, a walking public health hazard. Infectious disease specialists said there was no basis for this concern, that you cannot worry yourself from HIV positivity to full-blown AIDS. I soon began to realize that there was plenty of truth in their folly. As soon as zidovudine became available as the first antiviral agent against HIV, even though by itself it was nearly useless as well as toxic, all my putative AIDS patients rushed out to get the confirmatory tests so they could start the drug. Within weeks the T cell counts of some of them dropped precipitously, sometimes even before they got their hands on the first dose.

Recently researchers at UCLA confirmed the link between one's state of mind and the course of HIV infection. Men infected with the virus who were introverted, reserved and loners had eight times as many viral particles in their blood as outgoing men. The extroverted men also had a better response to therapy. After 18 months taking anti-retroviral drugs, their viral load fell 162 fold, while the withdrawn men had a drop of only 20 fold. [28]

This study suggests that your constitution or makeup, a trait that changes at best extremely slowly, can influence your immune system. It has been well documented that chronic mental disorders like depression are also linked not only with AIDS, but also with cancer and osteoporosis. Researchers following 5,000 people with depression found they had twice the risk of developing cancer as people without the blues. Research going back 40 years has shown that people with high scores on indices of stressors – life-shaking events such as divorce, death of a spouse, loss of a job or even marriage – have not only more high blood pressure and heart disease, but also more cancer than those with lower scores.

The interface between body and mind is a determinant not only of health but also of longevity. As discussed in Chapter 5, one of the characteristics of the eldest of the old, people over 95, is an uncanny ability to shrug off adversity such as the loss of a loved one and get on with their lives.

Accessing the Mind-Body Interface

It is important to explore this interface. It affects every waking and perhaps sleeping moment, and it is a portal we can access to bring about positive changes in our health, physical performance and mental well-being. We also need to master this interface to prevent the opposite: the body holding the mind hostage, as in a panic attack. A simple sensation, "Oh, I can feel my heart beating," sets off a chain reaction where the body now dictates the state of the mind. The next thought, "Oh, no, now I can't breathe!" The stricken person tries to increase airflow and feels the symptoms of lowered CO_2 from hyperventilation, "My face is going numb. I must be having a stroke!" This increases the anxiety, a vicious cycle of the mind-body interface run amok.

The expression mind-body interface is both a misnomer and a fallacy because in reality, there is no identifiable boundary between them. I have an electron microscope image of a neuron synapsing on an immune cell, a monocyte. You could argue that this is an example of the mind-body interface – the nervous system, the seat of the mind, directly connecting with our immune system. Both cells are nevertheless still the physical body. The nervous system connects with nearly every other system in innumerable ways – not only through synapses, but also through chemical messengers like neurotransmitters and hormones – and it may be through these countless interactions that our mind and body become one. It is better to use the terms consciousness and physiology, because they describe the relationship better between the non-manifest world of our inner experience and the physically expressed nature of your body's underlying intelligence.

Consciousness can be conceived as a field, not unlike a magnetic, gravitational or quantum field. We can experience consciousness but its non-physical nature makes it available only to indirect measurement. Mind on the other hand, we will define as the expression of consciousness that thinks. Similarly, the intellect is the expression that discriminates; emotion is the expression that feels; the senses are the expression that perceives; ego is the expression of consciousness that provides awareness of self. Mind, intellect, emotion, ego and senses are all tangible expressions of consciousness that we regularly probe and quantify.

The Anatomy of the Mind-Body Interface

Our purpose is to master the laws of nature governing self-repair, to gain the ability to choose our state of mind and thus to permit our body to do what the mind dictates. This means peeking into the chapters of the owner's manual for the human body not found in a medical library.

An anatomy lesson of the mind-body interface would show a diagram depicting the hierarchy of expression of the parts of our experience arising from the field of pure consciousness. Ascending sequentially from most subtle to most manifest, the mental organs that permit us to experience and cognize appear like this:

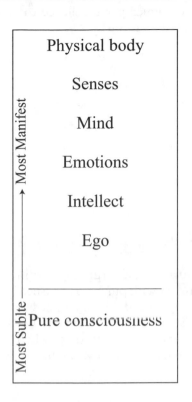

Like waves on an ocean, all the mental and physical processes above the line are expressions of the unmanifest field of pure consciousness, consciousness without its content – the ocean's silent depth. The workings of the mind, intellect, emotions, ego and senses are the superficial turbulence, while pure consciousness always remains the unmoving basis for mental activity.

One could similarly compare your cognitive organs in this diagram to a tree finding its roots in the earth, an apt analogy because the best way to nourish the mind, intellect and emotions is through practices that put us in touch with pure consciousness.

The Simplest State of Awareness

There are two approaches to the study of consciousness. Modern psychology studies the diverse expressions of consciousness above the line. Unfortunately, this is a cumbersome way to gain insight into the core of a person's quirks and foibles. Before attempting to fathom a complex system, scientists study its simplest model, a hydrogen atom with one proton and one electron, the metabolic pathways of a one-celled bacterium or the simple neuron of a squid. Similarly, to understand complex human behavior such as the T cell counts of a patient with HIV that rise and fall with his state of mind, we need to analyze those moments of pure consciousness. Can we analyze the moments where time stops still upon seeing a sunrise or the beauty of an innocent child? Or the gaps between waking and dreaming or sleeping, when we are awake inside yet the mind is still? Or a moment of sudden insight, a Eureka moment where the brain reboots, discharges old ideas and resets itself using new paradigms? Or a moment in meditation when the mind is found to be awake and alert but its content is suspended? A moment of pure wakefulness without thought, emotion or perception? Or a moment at a Beethoven symphony where the musicians in black lead you on an exploration of the field of possibilities of four notes, incessantly repeated in startling ways, each iteration different from the other, as you let yourself be charmed by their variation and familiarity, until your breath and your brain are simultaneously suspended?

We can indeed analyze these experiences and the tools of research are the fabrics of your nervous system. This is transcendence. You have gone beyond the mind, intellect and senses into another realm which is wakeful but still. It is not a trance. It is not flashy. No fireworks, no angels. The experience is natural, simple and uncomplicated. Your problems and cares don't exist in this field. Here is where they can be dissolved.

Visiting this field of pure consciousness on a regular basis is the first exercise in gaining mastery over the mind-body interface. Spiritual practices including yoga, prāṇāyāma and especially meditation are techniques par excellence to gain familiarity with this state. William Wordsworth described it thus:

"that serene and blessed mood,

In which the affections gently lead us on, –

Until, the breath of this corporeal frame

And even the motion of our human blood

Almost suspended, we are laid asleep

In body, and become a living soul:

While with an eye made quiet by the power

Of harmony and the deep power of joy,

We see into the life of things."

William Wordsworth. Tintern Abbey.

Some people say pure consciousness happens during tai chi, running, writing or even drinking a beer. This may be, but these encounters with pure consciousness are less practical because the next step after having experienced pure consciousness is mastering how to think and act established in this state. This requires us to be able to invoke pure consciousness at will, systematically, and in a circumstance where we can begin to cultivate it. If we want to teach our pet some new tricks we had better pick an environment without distractions.

Fluctuations in Consciousness

Let us return to our example of waves on the ocean: the thoughts, feelings, judgments, insights, desires, memories and other experiences that superimpose themselves on the silence of pure consciousness. Suppose you entertain the thought, "I need to cure my asthma." Due to the brain's many simultaneous activities, it is unlikely that the thought would be experienced throughout the brain because of its surface turbulence.

If you throw a boulder in a choppy sea, all you see is still just foam. This is like trying to attempt visualization, affirmations or even prayers to improve your asthma while in an "agitated" state of mind without pure consciousness. The results are usually less than dramatic. However, if you drop even a grain of sand into a still pond, the ripples emanate perceptibly in all directions. *Perceptibly* means the import of the desire touches the whole brain. Since your brain is the master organ, like the maestro of the orchestra, connected to and directing every other member, it has a bully pulpit to spread your desire throughout your physiology, alerting not only your lungs but also your adrenals, gut, heart, and immune system that the wheezing has to stop. Your body's song, the silent score underlying its mental and physical functioning, contains the program to synchronize and harmonize its parts.

In the state of pure consciousness, a brain impulse affects the brain in a more global manner. Prof. Nicolai Lyubimov of the Moscow Brain Research Institute found that sensory evoked potentials (faint repetitive stimulations of a finger to evoke a brain wave response) during the practice of Transcendental Meditation spread throughout both brain hemispheres, but during normal waking in the same subjects, the brain responses were confined to the sensory cortex.

To gain mastery of the mind-body interface to heal your chronic disorder, you need to begin to speak to the body from the state of pure consciousness, where a whisper is appreciated more than a shout. This does not mean having a less intense desire. Rather you need to learn to hold your desires ever so subtly on the finest level of feeling within a settled nervous system. Such a skill can hold sway over the physiology so the body collaborates with your desire for radiant health.

Locating the Mind-Body Interface

The most effective practices for enlivening this interface, by tradition and for a good reason, are taught one-on-one by a person authorized by her teacher to teach others.[29] Here is an exercise that anyone can practice to begin to appreciate the different expressions of pure consciousness and to recognize pure consciousness itself. Since the exercise is performed with the eyes closed, you can read the exercise through several times until you understand it well, then put the book down and begin. This is the preferable way to proceed because the exercise is simple and it is better to do the exercise at your own pace and in silence. You could also ask someone to read it to you slowly, giving you plenty of pause time. You can read it into a tape recorder if you prefer.

Lie down with your eyes closed, the arms by the sides, palms up. Notice how thoughts move in and out of your awareness. Allow your awareness to locate the silent basis of thought but which is not the thinking mind. Savor this silence a few moments.

Next, notice how you also have a tendency to analyze the thoughts. This is the discriminating intellect. Allow your mind to locate the silent basis of the discriminating intellect, yet which is not the intellect. Savor this silence for a few moments.

Now notice your emotions: your joy, guilt, relief or blues. Allow your awareness to experience the silent basis of your feeling "heart," yet which is not the heart. Enjoy this silence for a few moments.

Now notice the perceptions, the constant flow of input from the five senses. Allow your awareness to fall on the silent basis of your perceptions, yet which is not perception. Be with this silence a few moments.

Finally, notice the ego, the sense of self, the awareness that "I am." Allow your awareness to fall on the silent basis of "I am," yet which is not "I am."

That which is the basis of all your faculties, yet which is not the mind, intellect, emotions, senses or sense of self is pure consciousness, pure wakefulness. Allow your awareness to enjoy the experience of approaching in the vicinity of pure conscious for a moment. Listen to your body's ancient song.

After performing this exercise, you should begin to locate pure consciousness in your awareness. Many people are able to identify the experience readily as they have already had the simple experience described by Wordsworth above. The experience does not involve the senses with music, golden lights or physical sensations. It is simple and natural.[30] The purpose of this exercise is simply to recognize and habituate yourself to the presence of pure consciousness, the ground state upon which all other experiences are but excitations. Later we will be learning other ways to put pure consciousness to work to bring about self-repair.

28 Cole S, et al. *Biological Psychiatry*, Dec. 15, 2003.
29 See Chapter 8 for instruction in mind-body techniques. In my medical practice, I recommend the Transcendental Meditation technique because it comes from an ancient tradition and is taught by carefully trained instructors in a standardized way that can be learned by anyone. It is also the technique that has been researched with respect to its effects on the mind, health, and behavior. Unlike most other techniques, a practitioner thereby has a good idea what influence this technique will have on her life after many years and many thousands of hours of practice.
30 The role of meditation is to make this experience more systematic, regular, longer and more profound, to the point that the experience becomes present also outside your sittings of meditation. The author hopes that this exercise will not substitute for learning to meditate properly, but will inspire the reader to do so.

CHAPTER 7

HOMELAND SECURITY AND YOUR IMMUNE SYSTEM

Agnivesha, a medical student who lived thousands of years ago, poses in the Ayurvedic medical text, Charaka Samhitā, a question about immunity that is still pertinent today. "Why is it that some people eat all the right things and they still get disease and infections, while some people never eat well and they seem to never fall sick?" His professor, Atreya, tells him, "Predisposition to disease also depends on how and when the food is eaten, the environment of the individual, as well as on genetics. "Life, he implies, is not necessarily fair, but we can do something with the hand we are dealt.

Administrators in politics, social policy, security, intelligence and defense have been grappling in the wake of turbulent world events with how to re-engineer a free society that is immune to disruption from within or without. They should consider a lesson in immunology from both a western and eastern perspective.

A Sanskrit expression from Yajurveda states, *yatha pinde tatha brahmande*, i.e. "as is the individual physiology, so is the universe." This means that the body is an expression of an underlying field of intelligence, the same intelligence that also governs the functioning of larger structures such as galaxies, ecosystems and societies. You may have often wondered if any intelligence whatsoever can be located in the functioning of a human society. Chaos theory mathematicians insist, "Yes, but as in biology, a society obeys laws that operate with probabilities and uncertainty." This means that social systems also have a physiology, one that must be structured from the same underlying intelligence as your body's ancient song. Perhaps we can find some similarities with regard to their self-repair.

Immune disorders, like problems with security systems or militias, can be politically categorized as either 1) too weak or 2) too strong and lacking organization and leadership. AIDS and chemotherapy induce the former because the immune cells are both scarce and weak. Allergies and autoimmune disorders are examples of the latter. In allergic conditions, a strong immune system aims its formidable weapons at a non-threatening foreign irritant, the proverbial cannon against the mosquito.

Discrimination – the Key to Healthy Immune Functioning

Autoimmune disorders are the most interesting to a student of social policy and domestic security, because they represent an imbalance between adequate internal vigilance and tolerance of individuality. Autoimmune diseases are disorders caused by activation of immune cells without an appropriate purpose, such as against an infection. The immune response is directed against one's own tissues, perhaps tissues that, to a T cell, look a lot like an invader. This includes common disorders such as hypothyroidism, rheumatoid arthritis, psoriasis, juvenile diabetes, inflammatory bowel disease, multiple sclerosis, as well as uncommon problems such as lupus, pemphigus and spondylitis.

Healthy immune cells are able to discriminate self from foreign as well as to attack in an environment of inflammation triggered by chemical signals. Autoimmune disease often involves both a genetic predisposition and the presence of triggers such as viruses or bacteria, drugs, a woman's natural estrogen, or even stress.

The standard medical approach to autoimmune disease is to subdue the immune system with steroids and other immune suppressants commonly used for preventing transplant rejection and cancer chemotherapy. Continuing our analogy, this is comparable to weakening the FBI and other domestic security agencies simply because they lacked perfect discrimination between the innocent citizenry and subversives, thus endangering the whole society.

The Role of Stress in Autoimmunity

It has long been known that stress aggravates allergic disorders like asthma, eczema and hives. Every experienced ER doctor has known kids with severe wheezing at home who are fine as soon as they arrive in the waiting room. Now several studies have shown that stress can also be a trigger for autoimmune disorders, including Grave's disease, lupus, colitis and rheumatoid arthritis. Our forebears fleeing a predator had a good chance of being wounded and needed an immune system that would be mobilized and stimulated from the chase alone. Today our environment is benign, but we go about our business with our nervous systems in high gear as if these dangers were present, creating neuropeptides and stress hormones in the brain that circulate through our bodies to turn our immune systems on inappropriately. Serenity, on the other hand, allows proliferating cells to be quiescent.

The discipline of psychoneuroimmunology has revealed the intimate connection between our nervous and immune systems. Brains and immune cells both have memories and intellects, and some cells have roles in both systems. Most importantly, a nervous system free from anxiety and depression creates a neurochemistry that signals the immune system to deactivate. Similarly, countries at peace, like Switzerland and Costa Rica, marshal small, inconspicuous armies.

When I was in medical school, we thought that the body naturally eliminates clones of cells that attack one's self, leaving intact only the T and B cells directed against foreign antigens such as bacteria. Now we understand that a low level of autoreactivity is natural and even critical to normal immune function. Apparently, tissues that harbor a mild immune response help naïve immune cells to differentiate and survive. In addition, since our bodies create cancer cells every day, a hint of autoreactivity may be one of the ways the immune system is recruited to eliminate these abnormal cells which don't look quite like "self." In addition, a recent study has shown that inhaling or ingesting certain strains of soil-borne mycobacteria through gardening stimulated the human immune system. These mycobacteria can trigger a cascade of neurosignaling that both stimulate immune cells and raise their threshold for causing inflammation.[31] Playing in the dirt, and not avoiding a little schmutz on your veggies may actually be good for you.

Vedic medicine similarly conveys the idea of immunity with two Sanskrit words. The first, *bala*, means strength or vigor, and implies the ability of extreme resistance of disease. The second, *vyādhikshāmta*, literally means "forgiveness of disease." This implies that a healthy immune system is not only strong, but also accommodating to harmless differences from the "self," forgiving them for their presence without attacking inappropriately.

These findings imply that the healthiest relationship between the immune system and the body is akin to a society that generates a low but persistent number of dangerous elements in order to train and challenge the critical elements of homeland security for bigger potential threats, while the security forces are forgiving of the society's minor infractions.

We will be exploring the practical implications of immune functioning in chapters on specific disorders. Good research has confirmed what your grandmother, your common sense and Vedic medicine tells you: the best way to boost your general immunity is to keep your physiology and consciousness balanced by following the guidelines in this book with respect to diet, exercise, daily rhythms and reducing stress. For example, in 2009 researchers reported studying the sleep patterns of 153 healthy young subjects and then isolating them and infecting them with a rhinovirus that causes the common cold. Subjects getting less than seven hours sleep and waking frequently were nearly six times more likely to come down with cold symptoms than the group with good sleep.[32] Practicing Transcendental Meditation has been shown to reduce inflammation[33] and improve the lymphocyte response to stressful situations.[34] Even singing improves immunoglobulin secretion.[35] Immunity, like energy, creativity and a clear mind, comes not from supplements, but is the result of maintaining equilibrium on many levels of your life.

One of the most important herbs for boosting general immune function for prevention of colds and other infections, as well as for reducing inappropriate inflammation and allergic responses is the ubiquitous and delicious spice, turmeric. It can be taken by anyone, at any age. Turmeric can be purchased inexpensively as bulk powder at Asian markets and added liberally to your cooking, or it can be swallowed as tablets. For general immune protection during cold and flu season, one tablet twice daily for children or two tablets twice daily for adults is the proper dose. Significant research has documented its anti-inflammatory and anti-allergic effects. See Chapter 29 Degenerative Arthritis for a more extensive discussion of turmeric.

31 Lowry C, et al. University Bristol. J Neuroscience, 2007
32 Cohen S, et al. Arch Intern Med. 2009; 169: 62-67.
33 Klemons, Ira. 1972. In Collected Papers. *Scientific Research on the Transcendental Meditation* program. Vol 1. ed Orme-Johnson D and Farrow, J. Meru Press, New York, 1977.
34 Blasdell, Karen Sue. *Acute immunoreactivity modified by psychosocial factors: type A/B behavior, Transcendental Meditation and lymphocyte transformation.* Ann Arbor, Mich.: Dissertation Information Service, 1991.
35 For more details, see the opening paragraph of Chapter 9, Behavioral Tonics.

CHAPTER 8

LISTENING TO YOUR BODY'S SONG

Our research team once hired a data input operator who, to our dismay, had the aggravating tendency of mistyping numbers using the proper finger of the wrong hand, substituting 3's for 8's and 8's for 3's. Her habit rendered useless the other 99% of her rapid keystrokes and we were forced to duplicate everything she had entered.

Like the distortion in this operator's string of data, age-related and chronic disorders are generally an issue of cellular intelligence: the body persistently repeats the same error. Usually the intelligence is completely intact and not distorted as in this example, but it is not utilized because the cell does not express or actively suppresses the appropriate genetic information. Unlike a limited event such as the trauma of a broken leg, age-related disorders are chronic because of the tradition of error. Fortunately, self-repair is often only a matter of restoring the cell's access to its intelligence.

The Milligram Solution

The biological error can manifest in many ways: an immune cell mistakes healthy tissue (self) for a foreign invader (non-self) such as a bacterium, virus or parasite, thus creating autoimmune disorders. Or an inflammatory process runs amok, whereby the body's intelligent mechanism for repairing an injury gets out of hand, sending inappropriate amounts of signaling molecules (cytokines) to a joint's membranes, thus triggering a massive inflammatory response, as seen in osteoarthritis, the common overreaction to the wear on a joint. Or the inability of a tissue to respond to a hormone, as in adult-onset diabetes. Or the manufacturing of too much of a good thing, such as when the kidneys make excessive angiotensin and renin in response to stress: appropriate for the low blood pressure of a person who is losing blood and in shock, but a recipe for high blood pressure for a person whose only threat is a cranky boss. Or the inappropriate jazzing of the brain's reticular activating system by a minute amount of a stimulating molecule like adrenaline, cocaine or caffeine, which creates wakefulness when you are trying to fall asleep.

In these chronic conditions, the physiological imbalance can be rectified by a few milligrams of the right molecule. The proof: take five milligrams of a sleeping pill and you're gone. Have 30 mg of a steroid injected into your bum knee and you're fine for a week. Take 5 mg of a drug that blocks the formation of angiotensin[36] and your blood pressure is lowered for the next 24 hours. A small dose of insulin and your diabetes is as good as gone until your next meal. A few milligrams of a biphosphonate once a year and your brittle bones become denser.

Treating chronic disease is only a question of milligrams – but it is also a function of faulty intelligence that uncorrected can last forever. Why can't the body be trained to deliver the appropriate dose on an ongoing basis? Is there a concert master for the orchestra of your body's ancient song whose violin gives a perfect A note to bring your flat notes back into harmony? There is, and it happens all the time. Every physician has personally seen many overweight, sedentary diabetics lose weight, get in shape and have all traces of their diabetes completely disappear. Ditto with high blood pressure, sleep apnea, chronic insomnia, and other stubborn disorders.

Spontaneous Remission

The term we use for a disease that goes away "unexpectedly" without medical intervention is *spontaneous remission*, and we usually apply it to a seemingly miraculous cure. However, even the people who have had the most miraculous of unexpected remissions always seem to offer a reason: a supplement, an attitude, an exercise, dietary program or yoga posture. Only rarely will someone say, "I can't explain it. I guess God just answered my prayers." In this sense, if God helps those who help themselves, the spontaneous remissions I have observed in my patients who elect to forego standard medical therapy have been in people who were making major changes in their lives.

In 1989, Brendan O'Regan, a young publisher and himself a terminally ill patient, approached me about his research. He had heard about our clinic and invited me to contribute our case studies of unexplained spontaneous remissions to his compilation of similar cases. He had a grant to gather the published medical documentation of unexplained remissions over the past 100 years. The resulting volume is nothing less than astounding.[37]

In this thick tome, generations of physicians recount, in their own scientific language, thousands of stories of patients who defied all odds. These are people with metastases or otherwise incurable tumors to their bones, liver, lungs and brains, who had exhausted their medical options, and who incomprehensibly began to recover. In a typical case study, the author describes a patient with an untreatable tumor documented by biopsy which began to decrease in size over a period of six monthly office visits until it could no longer be detected. The patient became asymptomatic and, at autopsy following an unrelated illness dozens of years later, no traces of tumor were identified.

In many of these cases the physician offers a hypothesis for the mystery such as, "the patient developed an overwhelming infection that may have triggered an immune response against the tumor." There is even an entry from an Australian physician entitled, "Remission of metastatic breast carcinoma following intensive meditation."[38]

Affirmation, Visualization, Suggestion and Prayer

When I recommend to patients that they should strongly consider learning techniques to master the mind-body interface (rather than let that interface master them), they often reply in frustration that they have tried everything, including affirmations, visualization, subliminal suggestion, and self-hypnosis. The result of this for them was only boredom. If this is your experience, your boredom and lack of good results have several causes.

- First, affirmations and visualization force your mind to think thoughts that contradict your own experience. It is conflicting to think sincerely, "My MRI shows a herniated disc pressing against my sciatic nerve roots, but thinking positively will relieve the pressure." Similarly, can you really make yourself believe, "I see a natural killer cell, gobbling up my tumor cells," when your oncologist has told you the cancer has metastasized?

- Second, you are always focusing or concentrating on the same thought. This is a recipe for boredom because the nature of the mind is to migrate to a thought that is more attractive than the present one, including sometimes your troubles. Trying to hold onto an electron microscopic image of a healthy T cell unaffected by the HIV virus will soon lose its charm.

- Third, enjoyable practice requires an attitude of innocence. Embarking on a mental practice with a specific intention is often inherently boring and doomed to failure because you have taken away any possibility of experiencing a delightful or unexpected surprise. This lack of innocence goes against the mind's nature and produces tedium because you may be affirming, "My back pain will go away," or praying, "May my back pain go away!" You are looking during your practice for a specific experience to take place in your back and it may or may not happen. However, something else unexpected and subtle may transpire that you are missing because you are only open to your intended result.

Cultivating Innocence

The key to the practice of any mental technique is an attitude that is non-judgmental or innocent. If you anticipate or desire a certain outcome, you are not approaching your practice or technique with innocence. You will end up disappointed because you are rarely going to get what you predict. The possibilities are simply too endless. One of the primary purposes of any proper mental technique or spiritual practice, therefore, is to cultivate the habit of maintaining an attitude of innocence. This is a better way to think of the popular spiritual goal of "living in the present." After all, if you want success in the present, you have to plan for tomorrow and recollect the events of the past while "being in the moment." Trying not to think about the past and future when they influence your next action can be conflicting. Innocence is the attitude that allows you to live "in the moment" without really thinking about it. It is the mechanism underlying self-repair because you can detect and address the most profound imbalances in your physiology.

Listening as You Sing

Every cell is engaged in self-repair at every moment. Verily, self-repair is the cellular expression of your body's ancient song. The cells of your pituitary and hypothalamus are continually identifying the level of circulating thyroid hormone, cortisol, testosterone, estrogen, and other hormones and comparing the results with a set point located on your genes. When levels are low, those cells secrete stimulating hormones that signal the gland to make more. Your body's cells relentlessly control the health of their own internal milieu and watch out for the health of the whole. They manufacture the right amount of proteins, fats and sugars, and avoid creating residues. Cells even sacrifice themselves for the greater good, self-destructing on command (apoptosis) from their inner intelligence to protect the whole. Biologists call these processes feedback. Vedic science calls it self-interaction. Musicians call it listening as you sing. We adjust the tension in our vocal cords to bring the pitch of our new notes into accord with the notes we have just sung or with the notes of our accompanists or piano.

Self-repair is one of many side-benefits of self-interaction, together with mental clarity, creativity, a good disposition, compassion and good luck. Naturally, it is better to go for the highest goal first and gain the ability of self-repair in the bargain. When you cultivate the ability to remain firmly established in the Self, your medical, financial and social problems are more likely to dissolve due to your increased power of thought and influence over your environment. In theory, it sounds good, maybe too good, but you may have no interest in waiting months or years to gain the rewards. If you have a chronic disorder, if your spouse is leaving because you have become a burden, or if you do not know how you will make the next mortgage payment, then you may not necessarily see the immediate value in starting to culture self-interaction. In fact, this is when most people begin to think more about intercessory prayer than meditation.

Meditation

You might think that Jagu would be the last person who needed to meditate. He spends most of his day absorbed in the Veda and the most stressful decision he makes is whether to pick hibiscus or bougainvillea blossoms for his morning offerings. But Jagu and his fellow students spend time morning and evening practicing Transcendental Meditation, which allows them to bring the transcendental level of pure intelligence into their outward song. For Jagu, his meditation has a purely spiritual purpose. You likely have important spiritual goals in addition to your desire to renew and repair your body, and both of them are valid reasons to meditate.

Meditation should bring the conscious awareness to the experience of pure consciousness in a systematic way. It should culture the mind to function in a mode of innocence, the prerequisite for spiritual discovery and daily creativity. Even a moment of awareness without thoughts, emotions, and perceptions imbues the mind with the qualities of the field of pure intelligence: silence, orderliness, balance, integration and dynamism. For someone with a body to renew or disorders to repair, this experience of the nervous system is translated into corresponding benefits in the function of your immune, endocrine, cardiovascular and other organ systems.

To derive both spiritual and physical benefits, your practice must be regular. Your motivation to take the time to meditate every day can never be the promise of future benefits – it has to be personal experience. Unless you enjoy your practice while your eyes are closed and unless you feel calmer and more energetic when you re-open them at the end, your chances of long-term success are slim. You will likely spend several hundred hours practicing yearly, and many thousands of hours practicing over your lifetime. You should therefore carefully consider the technique to which you will expose your nervous system. While there are many meditation techniques available today, few are taught by professionals with extensive training and experience, and even fewer have been scientifically documented to give any of the benefits their proponents might claim.

For this reason, I recommend that if you are interested in meditation as an important part of your program to renew and repair your mind and body, that you strongly consider learning the Transcendental Meditation technique®. It is simple and effortless, available from trained experts throughout the world, and backed up by 1500 scientific studies showing that the time you spend will be fruitful in many aspects of your life. It involves a systematic sequence of learning both the proper mantra for your nervous system and the technique how to use it properly.

Self Pulse Reading

Self pulse reading, a simplified version of the diagnostic technique used effectively by skilled Ayurvedic physicians, is an important tool for self-repair. The goal of this preliminary exercise in self-pulse reading is not to diagnosis yourself, but rather to develop an intimate connection between your mind and body. The sites in your body where the pulse is available to your fingertips function as interfaces for your awareness to be projected into your physiology and to locate imbalances – advanced imbalances associated with disease and incipient ones that are still asymptomatic. We will use your radial pulse at your wrist.[39]

How to Practice Self Pulse Reading

Males take the pulse at their right wrist and females at their left. With the palm and wrist facing upward, pass the fingers of your sensing hand under the wrist of the pulse you are assessing so that your fingertips come up on the outside of the wrist. Place the index finger about an inch below the base of the thumb. Place the middle finger next to it along the line of the pulse, closer to the elbow. Lastly, place the ring finger next to the middle finger. Curl the fingers so you feel the pulse with the tips of the fingers, which are more sensitive than the pads. See the diagram above of a woman taking her own pulse for proper positioning. Fold your arms closer to your body until you find a comfortable position. Close your eyes and bring your attention to your fingertips.

Examine the pulse for three qualities:

- **rate**

- **contour**

- **location of maximum impulse**

Rate. Is your pulse relatively fast or slow? Can you notice a change in its rate with meals, exertion, a good or bad night's sleep, stress, a change in mood, or during your period? Don't count your pulse rate. Whenever you assess your pulse, use your intuition, judgment and subjectivity.

Contour. Notice the form of the pulse wave. Does it slither away from your finger like a leech or a snake? Does it hop like a frog or crow? Does it move slowly, like a swan? These are the ancient descriptions from an Ayurvedic text, corresponding to the three doshas, vāta, pitta, and kapha respectively.[40] See Appendices 1-3 for more on three dosha theory. Can you associate the rate and contour with the movement of another animal? Does this animal's movement correlate with the way your body feels?

Location of maximum impulse. In which fingertip do you feel the pulse most clearly? Where does it strike most firmly? The index finger is located over the vāta impulse, the middle finger over the pitta impulse and the ring finger over the kapha impulse. The finger with the maximum impulse suggests which is the principle dosha imbalance. You do not need to concern yourself with three dosha assessment at this point. Your goal is to acquire the ability to detect subtle changes in your body's functioning.

Feel your pulse for a half minute twice daily. Read the pulse after yoga, before and after meals, when you are rested and fatigued, etc. Note the changes in the pulse with different states of your body. Allow your awareness to enter into the body at the site of your radial pulse and feel where in your body you might harbor discomforts or imbalances. Like the attention a mother gives a child, allow your awareness to spend a few moments attending to any sensation or need. The following exercise will be useful in developing an awareness of subtle changes in your body and attending to them.

Awareness in the Body

A simple exercise that recapitulates your cells' biological feedback mechanisms for self-repair uses its three elements: identification of the body's requirement, continuous flow of attention to the requirement and a ground state of reference. Although this exercise is so natural that many people do it spontaneously, it is also a medical therapy. It should not replace the proper learning of Transcendental Meditation. Practiced correctly i.e. without trying, like all things Vedic, it should nevertheless provide an experience of naturalness and well-being – as one would expect from effortless meditation. It involves awareness of the body and its responses using your finest sense of feeling. With this exercise, you can begin to heal your body and from there, other aspects of your life.

Practice this exercise regularly. This should be easy, because it requires only a few minutes. If you learn the Transcendental Meditation technique or another well-researched meditation that you integrate into your life as a regular routine, practice this exercise at the end of your sitting of meditation. Transcendental Meditation is usually practiced before breakfast and supper. Otherwise, find a time that is convenient during your day when you are fresh and rested. Decide how much time you have to give to this practice and stick with it. There should be little in your life more important than repairing your body. Practice the same number of minutes at about the same time every day. If you have a conflict with another appointment, don't skip your exercise, but do it at another time. Even bedtime, when you risk falling asleep, is acceptable and better than no practice at all.[27]

You can practice this exercise either sitting or lying on your back with your arms by your sides, or in any comfortable position. Follow these instructions:

> "Innocently allow the awareness to dwell in the body. Easily allow the awareness, imbued with balance, harmony, orderliness and bliss to flow where it will in the body."

During your practice you do not need to remember these words or think these thoughts. Just have the intention of projecting your awareness in the body. Simply remember that your awareness, in its quiet state, is the vehicle of pure intelligence and carries with it the qualities necessary for self-repair: perfect balance, harmony, orderliness, integration and bliss. As you project the awareness in your body, your body may naturally feel a pleasurable thrill of the flow of self-repair. This is your body's song.

When you realize that you are thinking other thoughts, allow your awareness to come back to the body. You need not force the awareness back to the body if it is engaged with an intense thought. Be easy. When you sense the thought letting go, return to the exercise easily and without forcing.

Lack of expectation or innocence in this exercise is essential and means you should not approach it with a specific healing intention. You may have diabetes and think the problem is in your pancreas, but you find that your awareness persistently is drawn to your head or chest. Perhaps the underlying cause of your diabetes is overeating and obesity, an emotional problem, and not in your pancreas. Being innocent means you accept the experience that spontaneously comes, not trying to override your mind's natural tendency to flow where it will by thinking, "My problem is in my pancreas, so I should focus on my upper abdomen." Manipulating your attention is doomed to cause an experience of conflict, effort, and boredom. If the exercise seems difficult, it means you are trying and not being effortless in your practice. If you find this exercise difficult, do not continue to try to practice.

Recommended time of practice: start with three minutes and increase gradually to ten minutes.

The nervous system, being connected to every other part, is designed to function as the boss and the rest of the body as the subordinate. When the awareness flows to the body, the boss is watching, and the employee is naturally inspired to work more effectively and with more delight in his task, in this case, self-repair.

The biological mechanisms of feedback (the integration of fixity, continuous flow of attention and reference to the ground state) form the basis of this exercise for initiating self-repair. Like self-pulse reading, it is both a diagnostic and therapeutic tool. When you begin to conceive of your chronic disorder as an issue requiring only a few milligrams of change in your body's chemistry, your goal may feel within your reach.

36 An angiotensin converting enzyme (ACE) inhibitor, initially isolated from snake venom, prevents the contraction of the smooth muscles in the arterial walls.

37 *Spontaneous Remission.* ed. Brendan O'Regan and Caryle Hirschberg. 1993. Institute of Noetic Sciences.

38 In addition to shedding light on the mechanisms involved in self-repair, one of the most important uses of this book, Spontaneous Remission, is simply inspiration. I pull it off the shelf for patients who are out of options and out of hope, open it to the chapter for their tumor, where there are invariably at least a few cases, and say, "If these people had a spontaneous remission, why not you?" People who feel it is inappropriate to give false hope may criticize this approach. But for a patient who is realistic and takes practical measures about her life constrained by a chronic or even terminal illness, there is a difference between a positive attitude and false hope.

39 Start your search at www.tm.org to learn more about TM, a technique that is effortless, comes from an ancient tradition, and has been documented to give health benefits to novice practitioners regardless of their culture, age group or intentions to start the practice.

40 Dash, B. and Kshyap, L. *Diagnosis and treatment of diseases in Ayurveda- based on Ayurveda Saukhyam of Todarananda.* Vols 1-5. 1984-1994, Concept Publishing Company, New Delhi.

THE PILLARS OF SELF-REPAIR

CHAPTER 9

TONICS YOU PERFORM INSTEAD OF SWALLOW

Scientists have reported that singing in a choir is good for your health. Saliva samples from choir members were richer in secretory IgA antibodies – that boost the mucous membrane's immune response – following a performance of Bach's Missa Solemnis than samples taken before the performance. The singers revealed that they felt invigorated and inspired despite the stresses of the two-hour performance.[41]

Singing, especially songs of a spiritual nature, is an example of a "behavioral tonic," (achāra rasayana), a tonic that is not swallowed but rather performed. A behavioral tonic is technically ingested because our thoughts, emotions and perceptions have as great an influence on our biochemistry as what we eat. The Ayurvedic medical scriptures say that you need to digest and metabolize your experiences, and they describe a digestive fire for that purpose, located in the region of the heart, as well techniques to strengthen it.[42]

Everything you imbibe through your senses including music, television and film; memories you conjure up; the hours feeding your intellect in front of a computer; aromas; and even the company you keep; all these experiences need to be digested and metabolized, as surely as this morning's bagel and latte. The heaviest mental load that you need to metabolize, besides your perceptions, are your thoughts, so you need to be careful what you think. Otherwise, you may find yourself awake at night still chewing on anxieties and doubts.

For a Vedic physician, singing is an important treatment strategy. A young man with inordinate intensity and drive was organizing a North American speaking tour for one my teachers, a respected Ayurvedic vaidya. Observing his assistant singing while preparing a lecture hall, the physician remarked, "Singing has saved you."

Sitting in consultations with him, I take note of the behavioral tonics he prescribes. To an older gentlemen he said, "Play with children." The man protested, "My children are gone." "Then play with any children." He would tell people who looked depressed to "Read funny books and laugh." That was years before research showed that laughter could shorten your hospital stay.

Once he told a couple having marriage problems to put a picture of Shiva with two heads (one female, one male) on their wall and look at it daily. He said it would remind them that marriage creates a state of unity wherein both partners function as one, focused on creating a whole that is more than the sum of the parts.

After prescribing herbal remedies to a man with chronic digestive problems, he took the pulse of his pestering wife and declared, "You are perfectly healthy, no herbs are needed. Just wear an amethyst of at least eight carats." A minute later, she stuck her head back in the consultation room. "Why must I wear a medicinal gem, if I'm so healthy?" she inquired. He replied, "For your husband's stomach."

Giving is Healthier than Receiving

While virtue is supposed to be its own reward, a growing body of research suggests that there is more in it for the virtuous than just feeling good about oneself.

By helping others, you may be improving your mental health and even longevity. Among a group of 423 older couples followed for five years, the ones who reported helping other people had a probability of dying that was half of those who did not, even if it was only giving emotional support to a partner.[43]

It seems that the old adage, "It is better to give than receive" can be scientifically documented. In a group of over 2,000 Presbyterians, those who gave help had improved mental health over the studied interval compared to those who were more likely to receive help.[44] It may be that the altruistic act involved in a behavioral tonic decreases cortisol or increases endorphins, creating a sort of "helper's high." And researchers tracking the activities of 2,713 people over many years reported in the British Medical Journal that those who engaged in social activities, either volunteering or being with friends, were as likely to be physically conditioned as those who engaged in exercise and no socializing. Swedish researchers studying over 12,000 people of all ages found that those who attended only 20-40 cultural events a year such as theater, cinema, concerts, art exhibits and sports competitions were 60% more likely to have died by the end of the study period than people who attend more than 80 events a year.[45] The researchers suspected that pastimes help people get their minds off their problems, a phenomenon that is well known to improve immune function.

> *Adopting wholesome practices is like perpetually ingesting a rejuvenating tonic.*
> Charaka Samhitā, Chikitsasthāna 1, 30-35

You can feel free to interpret the tonics that I have assembled from Charaka's text and apply them to your own life in the light of their antiquity. They are not only less expensive than any tonic you have to ingest, but easier to swallow. They are translated loosely from the Sanskrit, which I have preserved in some cases to give a flavor of the verse.

- *Sadyavachanam ayushyanām.* Speaking the truth, but only the sweet truth, is the best tonic for prolonging ayu, the span of life.

- Show respect to your elders (even if you are yourself an elder). Practice greeting persons older than yourself before they greet you.

- Be a knower of the proper time, place and measure of activities. (Hint: Use each room in the home for its proper function, such as not eating or watching TV in bed. Avoid working during mealtimes, exercising just before bed and listening to hard rock before retiring or on arising).

- Serve ministers, sages, renunciants and the devout, who have offered their lives for spiritual purposes.

- Respect teachers, mentors and animals.

- Be merciful and forgiving. Avoid cruelty.

- Engage in cultivating the state of pure consciousness (awareness devoid of its content: thoughts, emotions and perceptions).

- Donate generously and regularly.

- Always have a purpose if not a plan and persevere in its fulfillment.

- Keep your body, your apparel and your environment clean and orderly. Wear garments that are simple, elegant and graceful.

- Keep flowers in and around your home and workplace. Spend time in nature listening to birds, brooks and the wind in the trees.

- Follow a structured daily routine. Avoid sleeping in the day and staying awake into the night.

- Take cooling walks by lakes and rivers or in the moonlight.

- *Brahmacharyam anushteyānām.* Practices that cultivate the nervous system to support the experience of the underlying Totality of the cosmos (Brahman) are the best tonics for health. (This includes balanced indulgence in sex, food and spirits.)

- *Indriyajayor nandananām.* Conquering the need for gratification of the senses is the best tonic for experience of Bliss.

- *Vidya bhrmananām.* Knowledge of the Self is the most nourishing of all tonics. Practice yoga and meditation daily. Read spiritual texts.

- Practice effortlessness, serenity and compassion. Cultivate your heart's ability to love, even in the most senseless of circumstances. (After all, if it were easy, it wouldn't be called "practice.")

- Avoid holding onto anger and negative thoughts.

- Practice non-violence.

- Be courageous by not losing patience in any situation.

- Keep the company of the wise.

- And don't forget to sing.

41 Journal of Behavioral Medicine 27;6:623-635, Dec 2004.
42 See a discussion of sādhaka pitta in Chapter 20.
43 Stephanie L. Brown, Institute for Social Research, University MI.
44 Carolyn E. Schwarz, J Psych Som Med, Fall 2003.
45 Bygren LO et al, British Medical Journal 313:5-8, 1996.

CHAPTER 10

THE RHYTHMS OF LIFE

A thousand years ago, the forebears of the Nipmucs and Narragansett peoples who inhabited the shores of our central Massachusetts lakes had it tough compared with today's Yankees. I think of them as I chip freezing rain from my windshield. Their life was a cakewalk, however, compared to the Thule and Inuit peoples north of the Arctic Circle. Like us, these native peoples had their winter traditions, but for them it was a matter of necessity.

Anthropologists say that one key to their success was their mastery of chronobiology, the knowledge of biological rhythms and its applied science that outlines how you can coordinate your behavior to the cycles of the day, month and season in order to maximize performance and health. Of course, these native people did not see their behavior as scientific; they were simply following the dictates of their traditions, their ancestral elders, their grandparents, their community values and the desires of the Great Father. Their scientific behavior was actually very simple: they went to bed when the sun went down and got up before the dawn. Their bodies, like ours, were hardwired to maximize every precious second of daylight. They followed traditions that maximized their ability to digest a heavy diet consisting mainly of animal proteins, fats and roughage – personally hunted or scavenged. They had traditions prescribing seasonal routines that enabled them to survive a winter's famine.

Modern chronobiology has shown why our physiological cycles are conducive to certain activities at different times of the day. Hormones promoting sleep, such as melatonin, kick in around 10PM if the lights go out and kick out when the sun comes up, just when hormones such as cortisol, which promotes arousal and stress responses, begin to be secreted. This means that six hours of sleep from 10PM to 4AM, chronobiologically speaking, may be worth eight or nine from 3AM on.

It was recently shown that studying in the morning provides greater retention of the material than cramming in the wee hours. Yet, a survey showed the average bedtime for Harvard and MIT students is 3AM.

Ancient medical texts intuited what the modern science of chronobiology has only begun to discover: humans are diurnal beings with clear biological rhythms, which when obeyed, promote optimal performance, and when violated, promote depression, insomnia, chronic fatigue, chronic constipation, PMS and a host of other modern maladies that were rare before the advent of the electric light. Studies in night shift workers have shown increased rates of medical disorders-especially gastro-intestinal – as well as social problems. These disorders improve when the worker returns to the day shift.

Chronobiology influences every aspect of medicine but doctors ignore this fledgling science. Seventy-six percent of 1200 pre-menopausal women having breast cancer surgery during the week following ovulation were still tumor-free after five years, compared to 63% who had the surgery earlier in her cycle.[46] Despite this evidence, it is rare to find a surgeon who schedules their patients based on this study. A friend of mine did pioneering research demonstrating that a safe dose of radiation given to an animal at one time of day could be lethal at another. Yet his daughter, a radiation oncologist, admitted that patients were simply scheduled in her department out of convenience.

Amazingly, chronobiology is not generally taught as a specific discipline at most medical schools. I got my only lesson in chronobiology as a medical student when I was working at a hospital in the remote regions of Zululand. Walking at dusk down the single lane in a hut village, I noticed bustling in every home. On my way back as darkness descended, every hut was silent except for a few tuberculous coughs. I was astonished to realize that the villagers were going to bed when my evening was just beginning. At the hospital, we had electricity, a commodity unavailable in the village, to stay up until all hours of the night. By the following noon, the Zulus had already been working eight hours in the hot field and were ready to call it a day.

Using Your Body's Pacemakers

The ancient Ayurvedic texts were prophetic in predicting the behaviors that in the 20th century would prove to be associated with disorders caused by shift work. Scientists have identified the existence of "synchronizers," biological influences that have the most profound effect on creation of rhythms, such as light hitting the retina, food hitting the stomach, rest, and exercise. Ayurveda used these same synchronizers to make simple recommendations for good chronobiological hygiene:

Early to bed and early to rise. Lights out by 10PM to prevent having to deal later in life with insomnia and fatigue. Henry David Thoreau once wrote, "Measure your health by your sympathy with morning and spring."

Start the day with a glass of warm water to stimulate elimination. After evacuating, brush the teeth, scrape the tongue and then rinse the mouth and gargle with 2-3 teaspoons of cold pressed sesame oil. (Sesame oil is a good antimicrobial and has been shown to reduce the plaque between the tooth and the gum in dental hygienists who followed this Ayurvedic mouth care program.[47]

Before your shower, spend a few minutes massaging yourself with sesame or coconut oil. At least try to do this twice a week for healthy skin. Most of the oil comes off leaving you with a thin film to moisturize the skin all day.

Spend 10-15 minutes practicing gentle hatha yoga followed by prānayāma (yogic rhythmic breathing exercises – See Chapter 15) and meditation or prayer before breakfast.

Plan your day to do the work requiring greatest creativity and clarity of mind in the morning. Reserve the routine tasks for the afternoon.

Eat a good lunch and take a light supper before 7PM. The digestive fire follows the sun, so your meal with heavier foods such as meat and cheese are more easily digested at noon. A heavy evening meal has a better chance of sticking around as unwanted weight and promotes reflux and indigestion when you lie down.

Get a good half hour of exercise daily to promote metabolism, fitness and bone density. Simple walking is enough. If you are over sixty, stroll before work in the morning and get a good workout before supper in the evening. This saves your energy for a good day's work. If you are younger, you can exercise vigorously anytime up to supper. Our athletic club is busy from 8-10PM. It is probably better to exercise late than not at all. If it becomes a routine, avoid an intense attitude and keep it enjoyable. You may be fighting your body's natural tendencies by stimulating it to secrete adrenaline and steroid hormones that have already been shut down for the night.

Make the evening a time for relaxing, being with family or friends and light activities. Insomnia often finds its root in a lifetime of intense work or over-utilization of the mind and senses (e.g. computers, intense entertainment) before retiring.

Keeping your Body in Balance

According to Vedic medicine, the qualities of all objects and tendencies can be known and utilized to create balance – in an individual, the society and the environment. The corollary of this precept is the *Principle of Similars and Opposites* (Samanya-vishesha siddhanta), which states that in order to create a balancing influence in your physiology and mind you need to adopt influences that have an effect opposite to the imbalance. Stated simply, if you are too warm, stay cool; if you are too dry, hydrate. You would be surprised how many people routinely violate this common sense. This principle should be applied to nearly every aspect of your life including diet, exercise and routines. It reflects the body's own mechanisms to maintain homeostasis, a balanced internal environment. Deciding what to do at different times of the day and year is generally intuitive. People who live above the Arctic Circle or in the tropics are much more sophisticated about living in accord with seasonal routines. Because we often stray from or neglect good seasonal routines, detailed guidelines for maintaining balance during the six seasonal changes are included in Appendix 9. For women, guidelines for monthly routines are provided in Chapter 32.

Gaining Freedom though Structure

Start to experience the benefits to your health of establishing regular rhythms. Write out your ideal schedule for every day of the week, making time for everything important in your life. Post it in several places to keep yourself on schedule. Engineer the best time to meditate, walk, cook, play and even to eliminate using the guidelines above and your own schedule's constraints. Soon your whole body and life will begin to function like the Swiss train system. Your ancestors would be proud that chronobiology is finally coming back into vogue.

Most importantly, remember that routines are liberating. Great musicians don't need sheet music; they have so thoroughly imbibed the scales, rhythms and melodic patterns into their nervous systems, that they can allow their creativity to soar to the heavens, forgetting their limitations, and knowing that their playing will always sound good as long as certain notes fall on the right beat. Similarly, we can set ourselves free to be more creative and productive in our lives by imposing a structure. This is a paradox inferred through the study of chronobiology: we gain freedom through routines.

46 Veronesi, Umberto. Int'l Conference on Breast Diseases. Houston, TX. May 1996.
47 Steven MM et al. Cleveland Int'l Symporium on Dental Hygiene. June 1989

CHAPTER 11

A GOOD NIGHT'S SLEEP: NATURE'S SOFT NURSE

When I was growing up in Colorado, a local disc jockey dreamed up a PR stunt to see who could guess how long he could broadcast music without falling asleep. I must have been fascinated by his masochism, because it impressed me as one of the worst possible violations of the laws of nature. He lasted eight days.[48]

When Shakespeare wrote, "Gentle sleep is nature's soft nurse," he invoked the idea that there are few panaceas like a good rest, and restful sleep is the norm of all animals except humans. Even animals that are prey manage to sleep. It is amazing how humankind has manipulated something so natural into something so complicated. Chronic sleep disorders have their roots in poor lifetime sleep habits. The epidemic likely began with the invention of the electric light, which permits us to rearrange our circadian rhythms on a whim. Sleep problems happen to one half of us according to a National Sleep Foundation survey, with a quarter of Americans using sleeping pills at some time during a year. One of the worst forms, chronic sleep maintenance insomnia – regularly spending long periods awake after initially falling asleep – is the commonest and hardest to treat of sleep disorders, affecting 10-35% of the population in a given year.[49] The situation is getting worse, probably fueled by late night talk shows, cable television, irregular and long work schedules and the Internet. Worse, Americans have simply never been taught how to sleep properly. One-third of us have no set sleep schedule, the toxic ingredient for chronic insomnia.

In a good proportion of people with insomnia, especially if it is of recent onset, an underlying cause can be found. Before undertaking this Vedic approach, you have to rule out a treatable cause for your wakefulness, including other diseases and medications. Consider nervous disorders like anxiety, depression, grief, stress, bipolar disorder and restless legs; GI problems like overeating, reflux or constipation; endocrine problems such as obesity, menopause and an overactive thyroid; frequent urination including the type caused by diuretics; chronic pain such as arthritis, headache and back pain; respiratory problems like sinusitis, allergies, asthma, and obstructive sleep apnea, which can make you wake up hundreds of times a night just when you enter deep sleep. The best test to determine the nature of your sleep disorder is an overnight sleep study. Consider any stimulating agents – or their withdrawal – including alcohol, decongestants, Ritalin, weight loss drugs, antidepressants and other "pep pills," bronchodilators, steroids, thyroid replacement, recreational drugs and sleeping pills which in some people have a paradoxically stimulating effect, and the most common offender of all, caffeine. If you and your doctor fail to identify a treatable cause for your insomnia, the rest of this chapter is for you.

Detaching Your Senses from their Objects

Sleep that knits up the ravell'd sleave of care.
The death of each day's life, sore labour's bath.

William Shakespeare. *Macbeth Act II, Scene III*

The ancient Sanskrit medical textbooks of Ayurveda state "A man sleeps when, with an exhausted mind, his sensory faculties and organs of action detach from their objects." This implies that as long as you are using the mind, sleep will not come. Sleep is healing, not only because it permits your body to physically rest, but also because it allows your mind to reorganize and digest your experiences and circumstances to better understand your situation and plan future action. Hence, the phrase, "I'll sleep on that."

The Vedic textbooks state further "Sleep brought on by the nature of the night itself is true sleep, called reparative sleep by the wise. Sleep caused by [dullness from foods, drink, medications and activities] is the root of misconduct and should be treated as a disease." The texts state that sleep caused by imbalances such as heaviness in the body, disease and even fatigue is not true sleep. The ancient physicians understood that the circadian rhythms induced by cycles of light and dark are the synchronizers for our best sleep and that we do our most important sleeping when we are actually rested. Just as an athlete or musician will prefer to perform when well rested, our minds and bodies are best healed by sleep undertaken when we are not exhausted.

Unfortunately, we take the same goal-oriented approach to sleep that we use to attack other aspects of our competitive lives. You think, "I've got to get a good night's sleep so I can do well in my meeting tomorrow." When you find yourself lying awake thinking about the meeting, you get anxious, further preventing the senses from withdrawing from their objects. Even worse, you start to get angry at things that seem to be preventing you from falling asleep and more anxious because you haven't fallen asleep yet. It becomes a vicious cycle.

People with insomnia may have developed the bad habit of using their bed to watch television, read, or plan their schedule for the next day and lying in bed gradually becomes associated with wakefulness rather than sleep.

Cultivating a New Attitude toward Sleep

Sleep is not something we plan or desire to do. It is the by-product of creating specific circumstances and letting nature do the rest. A proper attitude is that we go to bed to rest and not to sleep. We just lie down innocently without any expectations and whatever our nervous system needs, that is what we will get. This attitude prevents us from being disappointed at how we slept and saves us from worrying.

In this context, Edinger and his group from Duke University found that people who were given cognitive behavioral therapy for treatment of sleep maintenance insomnia, the kind most common in middle-aged and older people, were able to make long-lasting changes in their bedtime habits that translated into better sleep.[50] Treatment group subjects were given a program to change the specific thoughts, behaviors and beliefs that stand between them and a good night's rest. They were taught to **(1)** establish a standard wake-up time; **(2)** get out of bed during extended awakenings; **(3)** avoid sleep-incompatible behaviors in the bed/bedroom; and **(4)** eliminate daytime napping. This study essentially tested a critical part of the ancient Vedic approach to sleep disorders. The treatment group had a reduction of 54% in the time spent awake in the middle of the night, compared with groups getting progressive muscular relaxation or sham, placebo counseling. This is one of the most important studies to address sleep disorders because it showed that dramatic improvements in sleep could be achieved by tackling sleep habits themselves, unlike the superficial effect of sleeping pills, which are addicting and do not address the problems underlying your sleep disorder.

Stop Trying to Sleep

Most people can change several factors to improve the quality of their rest at night and to prevent age-related sleep disorders. First, change your attitude toward sleep. Stop using the word "sleep" and substitute the word "rest." Announce to your spouse, "I'm going to rest now." Take the attitude that you are simply going to put yourself in a comfortable, quiet, dark place for six to eight hours and let go. Whatever happens, fine. Take the outlook that you are just turning yourself over to God, and whatever She or He plans for you for that night is exactly what you need. Dreams, thoughts, and those moments of silence between waking, dreaming and sleeping are all as important as unconscious, dead-to-the-world sleep. Stop judging how good your "sleep" is tonight and how you "slept" the next morning. Adopt the attitude that as long as you passed your time lying down in a quiet, dark room with your eyes closed, that you are ready for your day. Asking certain yogis, "How did you sleep?" may actually be considered an insult, because sleep is considered a lower state of consciousness, barely worthy of human dignity; These yogis have cultured the ability to remain in a state of restful wakefulness even while their bodies "sleep." Keep this in mind when you retire, telling yourself you don't care about sleep, that you'll be satisfied with whatever nature presents.

Do you have Rhythm?

The ideal time for rest according to just about every tradition of wisdom on the planet (except the modern western one) is from an hour or two after sunset to an hour or two before sunrise, say around 9-10PM to 4-6AM. In these six to seven hours, more can be accomplished than from midnight to 9AM., and endocrinologists studying the circadian hormonal fluctuations of cortisol and melatonin would agree. When the lights go out, melatonin goes up, cortisol goes down and you sleep. Four AM is the onset of the *brahmamuhurta*, the period of the day when nature is beginning to stir, and the period most conducive to meditation. Take the attitude that you can get up anytime from 3:30AM. onwards, but at least get up before the sun.

The long-term health consequences of chronic sleep deprivation include the predictable depression, anxiety, poor problem solving and risk of accidents as well as heart disease and premature death. It is obviously important to learn to sleep again if you have never been properly taught. But you needn't lose sleep over a little missed sleep. Many people do fine on as little as four to five hours. Some men of great achievement (and admirable longevity) including George Bernard Shaw, Winston Churchill and Charles Darwin slept very little indeed. Thomas Edison, who lived to 84, was famous for staying up for days working in his lab, taking short naps on a cot. In case your mother never taught you, here is an elementary course on how to get your forty winks:

Establish a regular time to rise. Get up at the same time every day, whether or not you think you slept well. Studies have shown that almost everyone functions well the next day, even if they have the perception they have not slept a wink. Make your rising time early – by at least six AM. Then go to bed early enough to get the amount of "rest" you would like. If you want 8 hours, that means 10PM.

You do not need to abandon your old bedtime immediately. Many people with chronic sleep disorders end up retiring at 2AM because they are afraid to go to bed and just lie there. They call themselves *night owls* and have learned that retiring early only creates anxiety and is counter-productive. They may stay up and wait until they know sleep is coming. But two hours later, at 4AM, *brahmamuhurta* for the blue jays, their eyes pop open and they are wide awake, superficially refreshed after 2 hours of sleep. After lying awake for a couple more hours, they need to sleep in to 10AM

If this describes you, start moving your arising and retiring time earlier by ten to fifteen minutes per day. In a couple of weeks, you will have painlessly reset your biological clock to a healthier pattern. After all, you are basically on jet lag, a disorder from which we can recover at the rate of about one hour per day. The issue is not just your inner clock, but also a lifetime of lousy habits, including most importantly the habit of staying up doing things and taking in information, usually of little consequence, in compensation for a day that was less than satisfying. You can think of it as sensory bulimia, ingesting perceptions of little nutritive value from a screen or magazine. Call it a day and go to bed with the intention of making tomorrow more fulfilling.

Arise at the same time, but avoid using alarm clocks. Keep your curtains wide open to let the morning sunshine turn off your melatonin. Find someone to rouse you gently, or just set a radio alarm softly to awaken you. After a few weeks, you will be waking up without assistance at your proper time. You can have coffee or tea for breakfast, but don't take any more the rest of the day. Your late afternoon cup of joe is still in your brain when you want to be retiring that night. Avoid stimulants, including decongestants found in cold remedies, diet pills, Ritalin and alcohol.

If you spend 3 hours awake in the night, do not sleep in. Get up and get going. Above all, do not indulge in daytime sleep to make up for missed time. Stay up, but avoid using caffeine. The next night you will fall asleep more easily and awake less often. It may take some time to culture this habit, but persistence will pay off.

If you find yourself not sleeping for a while, don't let yourself think, "How will I possibly manage during my important meeting tomorrow?" Instead, just remember, "I miss sleep regularly but I always manage to get through my day just fine." This logic helps you avoid taking a rescue sleeping pill, a futile measure that has never been shown to have a significant benefit in the long-term management of insomnia. A study published in the fall of 2009 showed that changing poor attitudes regarding sleep, gave better sleep after six months than the same program combined with intermittent use of Ambien in the middle of the night if the subject felt her sleep was going poorly.[51] Using sleeping pills, even now and then, appears to sabotage both your resolve and your circadian rhythms.

A Primer on Preparing for Bed

Besides regular lights out and wake up times, eating, exercising and meditation are the three most effective pacemakers. Follow structured routines to use these biological metronomes at the same time every day to entrain your circadian rhythms, as described in the preceding chapter.

- Get plenty of exercise during the day. After a good afternoon workout, you should be ready to collapse for the night by ten PM. Don't exercise in the evening, though, as it may be stimulating.
- Use the evening hours for light, enjoyable activities with family and friends and not for exercise, work or TV. Laugh, sing, listen to or play soothing music. Avoid murder mysteries.
- Establish a bedtime routine: take a cup of hot milk (with a teaspoon of soaked poppy seeds), perhaps a hot bath or shower. Read a few verses of spiritual texts.
- Avoid sleeping pills, especially the benzodiazapene category that can quickly create dependence and tolerance.
- Use natural fibers such as cotton for your bed linens and bedclothes.
- Create a quiet environment, or if that is not possible, use earplugs or white noise.
- Avoid associating the bedroom with anything but sleep, including TV, reading or working. The bedroom should be for sleep, sex and nothing else. If you have a TV in your bedroom, move it out. In fact, move out all but the essentials. Removing the physical clutter will keep your mind uncluttered when you spend time there.
- Massage the soles of your feet with warm ghee or oil (sesame or coconut). Perhaps the ancient physicians felt that metal is a good sponge for excess mental static; they recommend massaging the oiled soles with a brass or copper pot, or sponge them with a cool washcloth.
- The best single herb for bedtime is gotukola (brahmi),[52] either as a tea or as tablets. Avoid many commercial bedtime sleep-inducing teas because they often contain diuretic herbs including spearmint and chamomile. When you finally fall asleep, you may soon be up seeking relief.

What to do in the Wee Hours: Listen to your Body's Song.

If you find yourself lying awake, avoid giving in to anxiety or anger, or succumbing to the worst mirage of lying awake: "This is boring." Your nature, after all, is cosmic, and your physiology is a reflection of the nature of the Divine. Allow your mind to innocently experience a part of the divine by interfacing with your body. Practice the exercise of body awareness from Chapter Eight. Let the mind go where it will go. Sometimes the mind will be aware of your breathing, sometimes of your heart, your limbs or your digestion, etc. Enjoy the feeling of your body resting. If you find your mind wandering to anxiety-provoking thoughts, come back to the body.

Establish a yoga space separate from the bedroom for resting during the night when you find that the body is not in a mood to sleep. Adopt the attitude that time spent in this space is just as valuable as time spent in bed. This room should have a faint night-light, a comfortable chair for meditating and listening to music, perhaps a recliner that will allow you to change positions. It could also have a yoga mat where you can go through a set of slow, soothing (vs. invigorating) postures.

If you have been awake in the middle of the night for a prolonged period and feel restless, get up for a brief period. Avoid turning on the light, which stimulates arousal by blocking the sedative melatonin secretion from your pineal gland. Place a few night-lights so you can take a walk around the house. Go to your yoga space and meditate. Or just sit in the chair and go back to your routine of projecting the awareness in the body. You can do the same technique sitting up in bed, and when sleepiness seems to be coming, slide down in bed and continue.

So why did it take so long before another study, this one from Harvard, finally found that behavioral approaches to chronic insomnia – basically a simplified form of this Vedic approach to good sleep – was more likely to produce a more normal night's repose than the prescription drug Ambien, the biggest selling sleeping?[53] Sixty-three chronic insomniacs were divided randomly into four groups receiving either Ambien, five behavioral therapy sessions, both Ambien and therapy, or a placebo pill. For eight weeks, they recorded factors such as how long it took to fall asleep and how long they remained awake during the night. After eight weeks, the group getting therapy reduced their sleep onset from 67.9 to 34.1 minutes, while the Ambien subjects only went from 71.5 to 58.7 minutes. The therapy group was better at staying asleep than the group drugged on Ambien: 83.5% of their night in bed was sleeping vs. 67.2% with the hypnotic.

Your great, great grandmother who did not have electric lights and late night TV would call these recommendations common sense. Chronobiologists call them "good sleep hygiene." If you take the time to have good hygiene by showering, brushing your teeth and wearing clean clothes, take the same care to turn your routine of resting over to nature. It's your only ticket to get the rest you need without pills.

48 The world record is now eleven days.

49 American Journal of Epidemiology (1997; 146:105-114)

50 Edinger J et al. JAMA 2001; 285: 1856-1864

51 Morin CM et al. Behavioral and pharmacological therapies for late-life insomnia: a randomized controlled trial. JAMA. 2009; 301(19):2005-2015.

52 Infuse a heaping teaspoon in boiling water for five minutes, and drink it, including the dregs. Or take 1-2 grams of gotukola powder or tablets available at most pharmacies or health food stores. See a wider discussion of this herb, including its side-benefits, in Chapter 27.

53 Gregg Jacobs et al, Archives of Internal Medicine, September 27, 2004.

CHAPTER 12

RHYTHM AND SILENCE IN THE BODY'S SONG

Every evening when my friend Narāyan arrives home from his long commute, he spends time with his young family and then devotes himself to his spiritual practice: playing the tabla. He is a quiet, unassuming civil engineer who designs highways and aqueducts. Since his teens, he has studied with the great tabla player, Alla Rakha, whose virtuosity turned the tabla from a drum accompaniment into a solo instrument. This master of the tabla presented percussion, rhythm and sound to Narāyan as the essence and expression of the Creator. For Narāyan and his teacher, the universe is pulsation and music is its heartbeat.

As a student, Narāyan was a quick study in mathematics, and engineering came easily. His day job is a simple joy, and even though he spends 9 hours a day at it, he nevertheless considers it his hobby. Creating rhythm is his profession. Narāyan delights in conceiving the elegant curve of an elevated concrete highway as it takes form, flowing across his mind as the macroscopic imitation of the shape of the curve of the protractor on his drafting table. He has a natural feel for the mathematics of a parabola and why it creates strength. For this engineer, the play of the curving forms and the magical world of abstraction that underlies them mimic the play of the Unmanifest as it manifests itself as Creation. When he comes home at night, he participates in the play in another way.

Līla in Sanskrit means play, and as in English, can be the play of a child, of a performer, or of the Creator. It is the acting out of the play of the laws of nature as they take expression in our physiology, in creation and in the events of our lives. Like a child at play, the player of a piece of music or theater reproduces the subtleties at work in the absolute: a field of intelligence interacting within itself and manifesting as a physical expression – the creation and all its parts. During my stays in India, I delighted in attending Rām Līla performances, the acting out of the epic story of Raja Rām and his heroics in trying to recapture his kidnapped queen. Sitting among the enraptured children and the elders seeing it for the thousandth time, I realized that the villagers found joy in a līla because it exposed life in all its values, from most subtle to most apparent. The children were experiencing a riveting story; their grandparents were appreciating something spiritual. The performance was the play of the Absolute within Itself.

After Narāyan tells his children a bedtime story, he sits with his tablas to play, usually from nine to midnight, and enters into a world of pure mathematics known as tala or rhythm. Literally meaning clapping hands, tala refers to the rhythmic cycle. Narāyan often starts with Jhumra, a tala of fourteen beats, 3-4-3-4, which is expressively evoked with the tabla. He touches on the beats delicately or forcefully according to tradition, since certain beats need emphasis and some need hiding. He creates a funky syncopation by not touching them as expected, creating power by the absence of emphasis.

As Narāyan warms up, meditatively feeling the heel of his hand and his individual fingers strike their notes, his attention is drawn to the moments between the beats filled with silence. As the gaps begin to appear longer with practice at a given tempo, he learns to cut them into quarters, or with more difficulty into fifths, and then once again into thirds, his fingers accelerating, even though the tempo has not changed.

Each rhythm has its character and color, and his hands weave a tapestry composed of beats with deep hues or light overtones, enlivening the character of the drama that is playing out. A tabla may look like just another drum, but it is also a melodic instrument, from which a skillful player like Narāyan can wring more than a full scale. His mood that night made him start practice with Jhumra tala, a rhythm used to accompany intensely spiritual vocal compositions that are improvised in a slow tempo, with elaborate ornamentation. Eventually he will slice the meter into odd rhythms, sevenths or even elevenths. This day, he does not need to speed up his tempo; his hands are a blur, as the tabla seems to speak with a human voice.

The Gap: Seat of Self-Repair

Narāyan's sessions with his two drums allow him to enter the gap, the place where healing occurs. Any flow of sound, whether music, speech, Vedic recitation or a mantra consists of silence and gaps. The gap is the silence between the sounds, the point where a sound dissolves before re-emerging in another form: a different note or syllable. The gap enables one continuum to take on many variations, becoming an unbounded ocean of consciousness in motion. The gap is explored in great detail by different aspects of the Vedic literature, since this is the point of pure life, the place where everything happens and all transformations occur, the literal point where the perfectly orderly field of unmanifest intelligence interfaces with the constantly changing chaos of the diverse, manifest creation.

Because the gap is the point of all transformations, it is the point pregnant with the possibility of self-repair, the place of greatest interest to patient and physician.

Narāyan is not a Vedic scholar who explores the gap by studying Veda or by reciting it. He plunges into the Veda with his mind and heart focused on music. Consciousness is the cloth and the beats he weaves are the woof and warp that outline its fabric, allowing him to penetrate into its fine structure. In his music, as in meditation or Vedic recitation, repetition gives Narāyan familiarity with the terrain, allowing him to pick out more subtle details every time he passes through it. Narāyan's spiritual path lies in the nuance, the subtle changes in the structure that come to life as he pierces the gap. Rhythm is the scalpel that cuts space-time into fragments.

Vedic musicians like Narāyan develop nuance like Bach or great jazz musicians: taking a few simple notes and repeating them slightly differently again and again.

The Heartbeat of the Universe

Narāyan's rhythms, like Jagu's, attempt to describe the heartbeat of the universe, the primordial pulsation whose defining characteristic is infinite frequency. Quantum field theory also describes such a wave, one that cycles an infinite number of times per second (or nanosecond – the period of time obviously becoming irrelevant) with a length infinitely small. Infinite frequency with infinitesimal length; this is the meaning of the phrase from the Katha Upanishad, *anorāniyān mahatomāhiyān*. Smaller than the smallest and greater than the greatest.

Because of his mathematical background, Narayan may entertain his intellect by arguing with me around concepts from set theory, but during his playing, he stirs anoraniyan mahatomahiyan in his sinews, his gut and his soul.

I met Narayan through my sitar teacher. Rajan sold me a sitar he no longer used when I started my lessons and said it could take me a year just to learn how to hold it. Rajan wanted *sa re ga ma pa dha ni*, the seven notes of the scale or *svara*, to become my constant companions, and to become so intimate and familiar that I knew each one's personality.

Unfortunately, the wire plectrum worn tightly on the fingers while playing the sitar creates pain after a few minutes of practice. Only after dozens of hours of playing do you accrue a callus thick enough to protect the finger from pain. My callus never thickened.

A year later Rajan insisted I sell my sitar back to him. He had found a student more deserving. She had promised to practice more than the twenty minutes per day I scraped together. "But Rajan, I'm a medical resident," I protested. "I work 106 hours a week."

I donated the sitar after Rajan conceded that I had learned how to hold it, and switched from sitar student to impresario, holding private concerts for my friends, giving Narayan and Rajan a chance to perform publicly and giving me an extra twenty minutes of sleep. My two musicians would arrive hours earlier than my guests to sip tea and to discuss which ragas to play.

Raga: **Flavors of Creation**

Raga is the melodic form created from a sequence of notes of the scale on which Indian classical musicians improvise using different musical styles. The word raga comes from the same Sanskrit root giving us the Ayurvedic words *rakta* (blood) and *ranjaka* (biliary fire), and literally connotes color or flavor. Each raga has a character or mood and influences the physiology based on rules of chronobiology. Certain ragas are used during different seasons to cool, warm or dry the body. Other ragas are played at different times of the day for settling the mind, or gently waking it up, in stark contrast to western popular music. Without regard to music's subtle effects, we go to early morning aerobics and spinning classes where driving rhythms and sensual lyrics stimulate the adrenal hormones and sympathetic nervous system before we are even fully awake, and then we wonder why we feel jazzed all day.

The science of raga is described in several surviving Sanskrit texts, although the most ancient have probably been lost. These texts detail the influence on the physiology of scales and modes of different notes. In general, ragas with ascending sequences of notes are enlivening. Descending sequences are settling. One well-known singer of Vedic music gave a demonstration to a group of my western physician colleagues. "Count your pulse," she instructed. "Now, close your eyes and listen." After singing, the doctors noted their pulse was slowed by about a third. She sung once more to accelerate it by a third again. "If I can change your heartbeat, imagine what I can do to your moods, your fears and your digestion."

My hired duo would wait until everyone was seated on the oriental rugs before they would take up their instruments. Tablas need to be tuned, a process that can last several minutes, but tuning a sitar takes even longer. At some vague point, my guests realized that the tuning had stopped and the raga had begun, a junction that was not well defined.

Your instrument, the human physiology, also needs to be tuned to a cosmic vibration that resonates with the universe. You and Nārāyan inhabit the same world of vibration and sound. You are both in possession of instruments that express the cosmos and which you need to tune and repair. The difference is that Nārāyan has his attention on the subtleties of musical pulsation he finds within the unified field's infinite frequency. You will likely never play like Nārāyan or Rājan; you may not even appreciate refined music. But to heal your human body when it has fallen irrevocably into disrepair requires that you put your attention on the gaps between the impulses of your consciousness – the thoughts, emotions and perceptions. Within those gaps your intention is most effective at bringing the fruit of self-repair to blossom and ripen.

Healing from the Seat of Silence

When your bodily instrument is tuned, your world is naturally imbued with more silence. The gap seems to expand and permits your attention to experience moments of pure wakefulness between thoughts. In the gap, your faint intention is translated and amplified into growth factors aimed at your inflamed cartilage, gut peptides at your sluggish intestinal muscle wall, molecules of serotonin at your blues, and a dose of GABA at your trepidation and indecision. In this book, you are learning about tools to become master of the gap. The exercises bring your awareness to the silence within and projects it into your body, turning what you previously thought was only material liver, joints and skin into a nothingness in vibration – a cosmic instrument.

By tradition, Rājan starts with the *alap*, an unstructured adagio that allows him to open his heart, gathering the elements he will put into the rāga, setting the melodic tone but only hinting at the rhythm (tala). This first movement is Rājan's moment alone in the spotlight, an opportunity he milks dry.

Nārāyan commands his tablas to bring a beat to Rājan's rhythmically unstructured melody at the beginning of the second movement, called *jor*, the real heart of the rāga. The two friends start working together to develop the melody, massaging it in different ways to evoke its different moods.

The transition from the second to the last movement, called *jhala*, is not as clearly demarcated. Both Nārāyan and Rājan become more animated with acceleration of the tempo. Their focus seems to turn from their instrument and the rāga to the other performer, a meeting of personalities.

In India today many classical musicians take the jhala movement as their chance to strut their genius and, when playing solo, Rājan flaunts his remarkable dexterity openly. Not so with Nārāyan. For him, a true virtuoso, this concert is just another opportunity to enter the gap, while being accompanied by another musician. He keeps Rājan focused on the interaction between them and on the mood in the melody. Nārāyan's master developed the participative role of the tabla player into a high art form, and his disciple learned well. Before the tempo moves from allegro to presto, Nārāyan and Rājan begin a playful series of interactions. They often start with *sangat*: Rājan improvises a short melodic phrase using the rāga's scale and then without breaking time, Nārāyan echoes it with the tabla. My guests are astounded at how a couple of hand drums can be coaxed to sound a melody.

After a few moments of relief created by simple solos with accompaniment, they begin a dialogue. Rājan, using the sitar's uncanny ability to bend notes and thus inflect a human voice, asks a question, invariably finishing with the interrogatory rise in pitch at the end. Narāyan's tablas state the answer, including a few notes of the question.

The rāga's tempo quickens as the piece nears its climax, and the sitar and tabla engage in *larant*, combat, each answering the other's volley of a phrase with a more surprising, elegant or charming variation on the rāga's underlying theme.

Although the sitar and tabla need to be tuned together, harmony does not play the important role in a raga that it does in western music. The critical elements are the rhythmical sequence, the melody and *matra* – the duration of syllables – the same elements critical to the Vedic recitation of Jagu and his partners. Narāyan's art derives itself from Veda, specifically from Sāman, the Veda that is sung.

Sound as Strategy for Self-Repair

In Jagu's world, your body's ancient song is a field of pure intelligence that he calls Veda. On its most expressed level, it is a string of syllables, some short, some long, some stressed, some unstressed. Rg Veda is a sequential flow of intelligence some 600,000 syllables long – about the size of the *Five Books of Moses*, the *Torah*. Your human physiology is a sequential expression of the most transcendental aspect of this intelligence. The body builds new DNA, RNA and the proteins they encode by playing a genetically encoded rāga using a scale of four notes, abbreviated C, T, A and G. DNA is an extraordinarily long string of these four notes (nucleotides), long enough to fill a stack of books as high as the Washington Monument. When a molecular biologist sequences a gene, she clips the nucleotides off the string-like DNA molecule one at a time, identifying each and recording it in her computer. Later, from that list of nucleotides several thousand characters long, such as CTTAGTCTGGCATAAGC etc., she can resurrect the molecule and from that, the protein it encodes.

Pure intelligence is a play, in sound and vibration, of the perpetual process of creation including creation's maintenance and its destruction, thus functioning as a constitution of the multiplicity of possible universes. A Vedic musician would say our present universe is a rāga, one of many possible flavors or colors of the expression of this intelligence. This universe has a specific character, a play between the different matter and force fields that arose from the breaking of perfect symmetry a short time[54] after the big bang. The character of the universe described by pure intelligence, in turn, after about 15 billion years, has created DNA and shaped your human physiology.

DNA has evolved over its estimated 500 million years some miraculous mechanisms for self-repair, just as Jagu's Vedic tradition has mechanisms to prevent its own distortion or corruption through the generations. His Vedic tradition describes sequences of sound to tune the human physiology that it engenders. Here are some ways sound can be used for self-repair:

Mantras: You can use specific sounds for transcending waking consciousness [55], for healing specific disorders[56], for changing the environment and more.

Listening to, or better yet, playing classical rāgas: an activity shown to create balance in the human physiology during different seasons and times of day.[57, 58, 59]

Vedic Recitation: For Jagu and his classmates, this practice is a source of energy and transformation of their physiology.

Refining your speech: The way you speak, your choice of words, pitch, melody of voice, intonation and so forth can disturb or heal, not only your listener, but also yourself.[60]

Learning, Reading and Speaking Sanskrit: Sanskrit is an ultimate refinement of speech. Reading a passage without knowing the meaning in Sanskrit has actually been shown to slow the brain waves, heart and breath rates and increase galvanic skin resistance (the opposite of failing a lie detector test), compared to reading modern foreign languages.[61] These physiological changes were similar to those seen during meditation.

Listening to Vedic recitation: Some verses create general well-being and others have specific effects including self-repair.[62]

Learn and practice Ayurvedic self pulse reading.[63] Yes, this is also an exercise in sound and vibration. An Ayurvedic verse says, "Every rāga finds resonance on the veena's strings and the subtleties of every disease reverberate in the pulse."

Yajña: Vedic performances, like Jagu and his friends were learning to perform, to effect positive change in the environment including one's own body.

Narāyan and Rājan's playful combat has given way to performing in unison in a dizzying prestissimo. They are at the limits of their virtuosity. They look to the other's eyes as each cycle of beats in the tala comes back around for the signal that the other has expressed everything he has musically to say. Magically, Narāyan ends a last rapid volley with a resounding final note on his bass tabla at the same instant Rājan twangs his sa string, the tonic, a last time with the plectrum. The rāga is over. The silence is overwhelming. My friends have never heard this music before but they are too moved to applaud. The musicians, covered in sweat, catch their breath and stare happily at each other, knowing that their listeners' physiologies have been changed for the better. Your body's ancient song floats in the sultry air.

---

54 300,00 years is only 1/50,000[th] of the length of the universe.

55 TM.org for both research and resources on meditation.

56 My research colleagues and I have found evidence that specific sounds can be used to lower blood pressure. Glaser JL, Schneider R, Robinson DK, Wallace RK, Chopra D. A stepped approach to the reduction of diastolic blood pressure using the Maharishi Ayurveda Primordial Sound Technique. Presented at the Annual Meeting of the Society of Behavioral Medicine, Chicago, May 1990.

57 *Increased Personal Harmony and Integration as Effects of Maharishi Gandharva Music on Affect, Physiology and Behavior.* The Psychophysiology of an Evolving Audience. Theresa M. Olson-Sorflaten. PhD thesis. MIU. June 1995.

58 http://www.tm.org/explore/vedic_music.html for information on Vedic music.

59 CD's with music for different times of day and season are available at
http:// mumpress.com/s_music.html [Products from Lotus Press.]

60 Speaking slowly and softly has been found to be associated with a reduction in cardiovascular reactivity, which is known to reduce risk of heart disease. Siegman AW, et al. Speech rate, loudness, and cardiovascular reactivity. Journal of Behavioral Medicine. Volume 15, Number 5/October 1992.

61 Travis, Fred. et al. Int'l Journal of Neuroscience, 109, 71-80.

62 Tapes and CD's are available at http://mumpress.com/m_audios_o.html

63 See Chapter Eight

CHAPTER 13

GETTING SERIOUS ABOUT PLAYING

Tuberosities are knobs on your bones that arise from the pulling of muscles on their sites of attachment to the bone, slowly raising the bone into a bump on which it can get more purchase. Tuberosities are the result of the body's response to a requirement: movement and locomotion.

You have been sculpted into a body that is wiry, muscular and lean or soft and mushy depending on the requirement exerted by your environment. If you walk into well-inhabited places twenty or thirty miles from the nearest road, you get a concept of the appearance of humankind during our several million years of evolution. In these communities, sedentary lifestyles and epidemics of obesity are as unknown as "working out."

In Nepal, I stayed with a family in a village with fertile terraced fields, perched on a narrow ridge 750 vertical feet above a river, the nearest water source. Every morning the mother, Archana took ten minutes to sprint with her daughter down to the river with empty four-gallon metal jugs and dirty laundry. They then hauled the jugs back up on their backs, fully loaded, suspended from a sling looped around their forehead. Depending on the load, this could take a good hour. Sometimes they repeated the ritual in the afternoon. Implausibly, Archana saw it as an outing and not a chore. She and her daughter would chat and laugh, sometimes sing, although going uphill they spent more time in silence. I never saw her without a big toothy smile. The rest of the day was not quite as vigorous: herding, cultivating, scavenging for wood. Archana was sinewy and hard and, except for her teeth, appeared in excellent health.

The Least Action Principle

Everything in nature, including living organisms, is under the jurisdiction of the Principle of Least Action. From ancient times, natural philosophers observing the smooth arc of a tossed ball or the path of refracted light have declared that nature acts by the most economical of means. Since then physicists and mathematicians have stated the principle more precisely in equations. It remains the underpinning of most of quantum physics as well as of Vedic science. The common element of every prescription in Vedic medicine is effortlessness.

Everything that makes our life easier and more enjoyable including recliners, the Segway and a sedentary lifestyle can be blamed somehow on this principle. We always choose the path offering the least resistance. The essence of a Vedic lifestyle is balancing the response to a physiological requirement with the path of least resistance.

How does this Vedic principle apply to sport, recreation and exercise? Just watch puppies, kittens and kids. Wrestling, horseplay and tussles are their work. They have no clue that they are stretching muscles, strengthening bones, sharpening reflexes and developing tuberosities, the bony attachments for their muscles. From their perspective, they're just having fun. When they get exhausted they sit out a while to catch their breath and then jump back into the fray.

Like most kids in the fifties, the dozen little boomers on our block played outside until it was too dark to see. Our games evolved: hide and seek gave rise to commandos and ditch'em, games in which Lee excelled. He possessed unusual creativity, cleverness and street smarts, despite the fact that he was pathetically unathletic. When we moved on to football no one was excluded. Lee still had a blast: calling plays, centering the ball, holding the ball for kickoffs or sneakily tripping the runner. We arrived home exhausted, never realizing that we had exercised. For us it was all just so much play. Of course, in the bigger scheme of things, this was serious work. We were not just developing our bodies, but our sense of self.

The Value of Play

Exercise done in this context is the wisest, because it is the most enduring and the safest. It is harder to push yourself to the point of injury when you have the attitude, "I'm just out playing." When we moved to organized youth football with coaches, protective equipment, conditioning exercises, incentives to win, and rules, Lee's experience with sports and athletics was over. No one would ever give him a chance again. The athletically inclined among us stopped having fun and began having injuries.

Like a newborn cub, the human body will intuitively seize on the requirement to tone, strengthen and condition itself. A cat getting up from a nap and taking a slow, long stretch is practicing the purest form of hatha yoga. In today's world, since natural play has been replaced with "exercise," you may need to rethink your attitude toward long-term fitness if you hope to gain its benefits on every part of your physiology: heart and vessels, bones, immunity, moods, sexual functioning, digestion, and metabolism.

Don't Exercise, Just Play.

A good research study showed that exercise is as effective as the anti-depressant Zoloft in relieving depression, especially in the long run.[64] More recently, it was shown in a study of Scottish adults that being physically active just once a week for 20 minutes including doing housework and gardening – is enough to lower the risk of psychological distress and improve mental health.[65] While most people are surprised by these statistics, Archana and an Ayurvedic physician would not be amazed at all. The ancient Ayurvedic Sanskrit texts describe several benefits to exercise:

> *Wholesome physical exercise helps the symmetrical growth of limbs and muscles while improving digestion and complexion. It reconstitutes energy, making the body light, firm and compact, while safeguarding against inertia and inducing cheerfulness and exhilaration.*

> Sushruta Samhitā

Ayurvedic texts that were codified over three thousand years ago seem to understand this dual role of exercise on both mind and body that many health consumers are still trying to deny today.

There is a big difference between fitness and health. Terry Fox, the teenager who was logging seventy to eighty miles a day, raising funds for a cancer foundation by running across Canada with a prosthetic leg, was the epitome of fitness. He was forced to stop halfway when he coughed up blood from a recurrence of the bone cancer responsible for his amputation. Cancer was found throughout his lungs. He was highly fit, but had terrible health. On the other hand, I know elderly people who have never been sick or needed to see a doctor. They ate meagerly and rarely walked more than a couple of blocks per week. Not fit, but excellent health.

Is Exercise Necessary?

The jury is still out on whether exercise actually makes us live longer or freer of disease. Harvard alumni who kept physically active since college live longer than their fellow students who do not, including the students who were jocks in college. This brings up a critical issue that my own orthopedist and I are highly qualified to comment upon: the only physical activity that will extend life is one that is not dangerous and is easy on the joints. If due to aggressive exercise and other adventures during youth you end up with worn out or injured joints that prevent you from being active into old age, wherein lies the benefit for longevity?

Our increasingly sedentary lifestyle is a major factor in the current epidemic of obesity, together with its resultant diabetes and other weight-related diseases. We dine in abundance on delicacies from around the world without lifting a finger, much less without the need to walk, hunt or dig in the fields to make a living as did our recent forebears. This is why every successful weight loss program emphasizes developing the habit of regular exercise – long-term success is only a matter of accounting: energy ingested less energy expended equals change in weight.

Unfortunately, most people view exercise as a way to burn calories so they can continue to enjoy their three squares plus snacks in between. However, exercise has been shown to be good for our bones, heart, elimination, endocrine glands, immune function and now our moods. Research has also shown that persisting with a boring fitness program will eventually fail. My patients confess that they push themselves to "be good" for a while, but are derailed by bad weather, holidays, a cold, responsibilities and other excuses. Soon they have lapsed back into their sedentary lifestyle. Or they reason they cannot afford or hate going to a health club. Their problem is "trying" to "exercise," two words that imply work, penance and austerity.

The ancient Ayurvedic texts stand in sharp contrast to the idea promoted by the fitness industry, that you have to work out for an hour three to four times a week. Research supports the ancients. The Cooper Institute for Aerobics Research in Dallas randomized 235 people into a group doing only lifestyle activities and another doing structured workouts in the institute's gym. The lifestyle group did gardening, playing with kids, walking, golf, dance, biking or other enjoyable activities. At the end of the study, both groups had similar improvements in muscle mass and fat loss.[66]

In addition, a Swedish study published in 2009 showed that people who increased their exercise levels from age 50 to 60 lived as long as those who had been exercising all their life. It seems it's never too late to start.[67]

Changing our Attitude toward Physical Activity

When counseling patients about getting moving, I write on a prescription sheet, "Play, ideally outdoors, about thirty minutes a day." The subtle difference in attitude this advice engenders is dramatic. "Play" implies that above all you are doing it for fun. Only then does it fulfill the Ayurvedic prescription of creating exhilaration. To make activity a life long habit you need to value the time you spend for the immediate fun factor rather than for the svelte or healthy body you may get down the road. The latter should be regarded as the side-benefit. Go out to play for the sheer joy of it.

To get started with exercise as play, you will need to invest in a few toys: walking or hiking shoes, in-line skates or a bicycle. Whatever you deem both fun and safe. Every day before your "playtime", sit quietly with the awareness in the body for a minute or two. How do you feel? Pick something fun to do based on how you feel. Too fatigued to even contemplate "outdoor play?" Try a slow session of yoga or Tai Chi, gently bouncing on a mini trampoline, or a slow nature walk. Need to get something out of your system? Fast walking, dancing, vigorous yoga, a good swim or aquajogging. Just feeling dull? Try salsa, or get on a bike and start slow, and just watch the joy come back after a mile or two of watching nature go by. Got energy but stuck in a rut? Go for something physically challenging like a long bike ride or hike.

Guidelines for Developing Fitness for Life:

Never let any recommendation for gaining fitness interfere with the joy of being outdoors. Whatever it takes to get you outdoors, having fun, year in and year out, is the most important fitness advice, because fun is the best motivator.

In a moment of languor, remind yourself that it does not take much exercise to start getting benefits, as little as 30 minutes twice a week for the body, and, at least if you are Scottish,[68] 20 minutes a week for the mind. As pathetic as this sounds, one measly hour of the 168 in a week, is more than most of the population ever gets.

Any exercise program needs to be gradual, even for a highly trained athlete. You will be happier the day after exercising having undertrained rather than overstrained.

During sport, outdoors activities, or exercise, make a habit of listening to your body, your best coach. Monitor your breathing, your heart's rate and force of contraction, your muscles and joints for early signs of pain, your level of heat and sweating, your form and technique, and your enjoyment. Changes in any of these can be a sign to back off or even knock off for the day.

Attempt to breathe through your nose when performing any sport except swimming. Nose breathing is the most natural and forces you to breathe with your diaphragm. It also ensures that you exercise within your capacity. With practice, you will be able to sustain higher levels of performance using this technique.

Don't use sweating as a measure of your level of exercise, but monitor how hot you feel. Sweating profusely may be your way of keeping your body temperature stable.

Drink before you exercise, and then drink according to your thirst if you are a person who is sensitive to your body's needs. Overhydrating, while not as common as underhydrating, can be just as dangerous. Temper your plan to follow your body's dictates with the caveat that if you are sweating and not thirsty, you may not be drinking enough.

Before you start exercising, make a plan based on how you feel. Modify the plan if your energy picks up or flags, or if you feel a discomfort. Plan to warm up with 5-10 minutes of effortless activity. If you are going on a long run, start with a walk. It should look almost like slow motion. Then spend a few minutes slowly increasing your level of performance while maintaining your heart rate and breathing at the lowest possible level. Monitor all the functions above: heart, breathing, pain, form and enjoyment.

As your activity becomes more forceful, you will reach a level of performance that you want to sustain. You can continue at this level as long as your heart is not pounding, your breathing is quiet and through your nose, there is no pain in your body, you are maintaining your form, and you are still having fun, or at least your mind is not exhausted.

Surprising levels of fitness can be gained by doing exercise in this effortless way. These are techniques used by many elite athletes; especially athletes who want to have a long career.

The Discontent of your Winter

In winter, it is easy to lose interest in playing outdoors, but from the health perspective, it is the most important season to be out there. Collective health can even threatened by the frigid winters with deep snow drifts as people hibernate indoors for four months, egged on by the gloomy banter between news anchors and meteorologists. Believing misery likes company, they tell you to stay indoors.

With cold weather gear fit for South Beach, some folks hardly poke their nose out the door, aggravating the light deprivation created by short days and long nights. The pineal gland, an important modulator of hormonal secretion, is activated to secrete melatonin when the lights go out, helping you fall and stay asleep. As nights lengthen, the pineal senses that it is time to hibernate and not to mate, using melatonin to shut down several hormones associated with the incentive to frolic and court. This primitive reflex is critical in species like deer, whose survival depends on fawning in the spring. For Homo sapiens, it can express itself as wintertime blues. Chronobiologists call this *seasonal affective disorder* (SAD), a negative shift in mood and temperament during fall and winter brought on by an inappropriate response to light deprivation and other undiscovered factors.

The best prevention is to expose yourself to bright full-spectrum sunshine for a few hours a day, ideally in the morning. The Victorians called this your daily constitutional. If you cannot get outside, or if the depression is severe, full-spectrum artificial lights are not a bad alternative. Some sufferers of SAD think they can get their daily dose just by turning on the lights as they catch the morning news, but SAD is more than light deprivation. It also involves depriving your senses, heart and limbs of their due nourishment.

When you go for a walk, the senses, mind and intellect ingest experiences and are engaged just as much as the arms and legs. There are few activities, including a walk in the woods, whereby the mind can be calmed and exhilarated simultaneously, the antidotes to both anxiety and depression. Additionally, activation of the cardiovascular and respiratory systems initiates a complex cascade of euphoric neurotransmitters, including serotonin, endorphins, and catecholamines, partially explaining why exercise has been shown to be as effective as medication at relieving depression.

Learning to Love Winter

When the first snow flies, my French-Canadian wife digs out her snowshoes, cross-country skis and ice skates. She will not hear of a winter surfing vacation in Costa Rica. There is nothing like a real winter to make a Quebecoise feel at home. The key to not just surviving winter, but truly enjoying it is to have something about it that you look forward to: snow shoeing, cross-country skiing, walks in the woods or by a river or ocean are simple, accessible and inexpensive. Skiing is a different sport than the one you knew as a kid. Rigid boots and short, shaped skies turn beginners into intermediates after barely a day and release bindings make skiing safe. While more expensive, it is eminently safer than tobogganing and sledding which have a high rate of jammed thumbs, knees and backs, yet are undertaken casually.

If you like your winter sports tamer, give curling a whirl; if you have an artistic flare, get into ice sculpture. If you do not like anything about cold and the great outdoors, try line or square dancing, followed by a cozy evening in front of a fire. Sit down and make a list of all your favorite things to do in winter so you can pick your winter passions carefully. After all, loving winter may require an investment in gear and time.

No Weather too Foul

The lift operator at the top of Wildcat Mountain looked bored as we stepped out of the aging two-person gondola that had been pelted by the wind-driven snow during the whole ride up. No one had been up to the top of the mountain for the past half hour. Instead of a snowy blast down my parka as I stepped out to put on my snowboard, I felt like I was in my living room watching a re-run of a Warren Miller ski movie of an epic powder day. My wife and I had the upper mountain and all its fresh powder to ourselves because of good goggles, facemasks and Gore-Tex. By the end of the day, we were sweating but toasty thanks to polypropylene long johns. A critical premise for anyone who wants year round fun and fitness: There is no such thing as weather too foul for sport; there is only inappropriate gear.

Getting Geared up for Walking in Cold Weather

Unless you have the freedom to fly south, find something you look forward to doing on a regular basis. Walking is the simplest, safest, and least expensive – as well as fun.

You need high top, insulated waterproof boots with a good tread.

Add polypropylene long underwear and insulated windproof pants, a fleece sweater and a waterproof windbreaker.

You will need waterproof gloves and hat, a neoprene facemask and even goggles. Use crampons if there is a risk of ice

Get a topographic map of town, available in local fishing and hunting shops. Drive eight minutes from your home in one direction. Mark the point on your map. Take a compass and draw a circle around your home with the radius being the point you can drove to in eight minutes.

Locate all the green areas on the map, including parks, woods, rivers, lakes, greenways, bike paths, rail trails, reservoirs, meadows and hills within that circle and that make nice walking areas. Within eight minutes of any given point in North America, there may be dozens. List and post them on your fridge, giving a copy to your nearby friends and family who might join you.

To make your winter day you only need to liberate less than an hour: fifteen minutes to drive back and forth, five minutes for dressing and undressing and 30 minutes to walk. Take binoculars and a guidebook to birds and trees and call it an expedition instead of exercise.

Now and then, switch to snowshoes. An inexpensive aluminum pair from the discount store works much better than the tennis racquets of yore.

Or try cross-country skis; the short ones that don't require waxing are a cinch to learn and, like snowshoes, can take you off the trail. Fifty minutes three times a week is all you need to look forward to snow.

The urban legend goes that the Inuit have a vast number of words for snow.[69] It turns out that English-speaking winter aficionados have just as many. Here are a few English words for snow that you might hear at a typical ski area, listed in order from more work to more fun: glare, scrabble, washboard, crud, granular, snowcone, slush, corn, hardpack, corduroy, freshies, powder, fluff, and champagne. The exhilaration of the feeling of a steel edge cutting through frozen H_2O has given rise to myriad expressions to describe the experience. If winter, or any other season, leaves you yawning, learn to experience exhilaration in your own way.

64 Psychosom Med 2000 Sep-Oct;62 (5):633-8

65 Hamer M et al. Dose response relationship between physical activity and mental health: the Scottish Health Survey. Br J Sports Med. Published Online First: 10 April 2008.

66 Dunn A. JAMA. 1999;281:327-334.

67 Michaelsson M. Br. Med Journal. March 2009

68 Reference 65 above

69 http://en.wikipedia.org/wiki/Eskimo_words_for_snow

CHAPTER 14

PATAÑJALI'S SONG OF YOGA

Varun and I first met at dawn as I emerged from a bath in the Ganges where it flows clear and cold out of the Himalayas. He had come for his own bath and was not used to seeing men with such white skin performing the customary riverside morning ablutions of wandering yogins. Most yogins leave for the Himalayas to get away from people but Varun was waiting for me by my shirt and pants. The sum of his entire worldly possessions besides his garments, a stainless steel pot, was at his feet.

At eighteen Varun had left his home in the crimson desert city of Jaipur with only a begrudging trace of parental blessing and the goal of becoming what yoga philosophy considers a real man. He had spent ten years wandering, without contact with his family, having sent no letters and maintaining no address. Aside from his pot he had a white dhoti and sandals. His daily routine was devoted to his practices: yoga, meditation, fasting, recitation of the Sanskrit texts, wandering and apparently discourse with strangers.

The Essence of the Yoga Sūtras

Varun's profession, a full-time occupation of becoming a man worthy of the name,[70] predates the classical Vedic times[71] and may merit the dubious distinction as world's oldest. Yogins regard a human being as a promise. We are born beasts and we become a complete woman or man through refinement of our minds and bodies. After that the body is expendable. In contrast, the Vedic and Judeo-Christian understanding is we are born men, but our body gets spiritualized so we can experience God and then spend our life enjoying his/her creation. For a yogin, your lifetime is a process of cooking or ripening and the world, with all its imperfection, is perfect just as it is because it helps hone your nervous system. If the ultimate physiological refinement does not happen in this lifetime it is not cause for concern. There will be many more chances and, anyway, becoming a complete human is inevitable. The difference between half-hearted yogins like me, a householder first and a yogi second, and a more intense practitioner, is in the haste to be freed from needing this warm-blooded frame. Even today an earnest yogin, such as Varun, does not keep or use fire, the tool of householders, and may feign insult by those who offer it to them.

Though convivial, Varun is a serious yogin. He was endowed with physical suppleness and practices extreme austerities. More importantly, he had memorized and regularly recited the Yoga Sūtras of Patañjali, the ultimate authority on yoga. Varun was almost obsessed with liberation. For a yogin to live up to Patañjali's ideals however, almost is not good enough. Patañjali prefers you be completely obsessed and Varun, as austere as his life was, enjoyed people.

Scholars know almost nothing about Patañjali (and his hypothesized team) except that he seemed to be a genius and composed his Yoga Sūtras several hundred years BC, consolidating a knowledge that had drawn hundreds of generations of Varuns from their homes to the forests, deserts and caves. The Sūtras (a suture or stitch) are a collection of 161 aphorisms,[72] a telegraphic shorthand so abbreviated that each contains only a few syllables. In those few syllables is concentrated a universe of meaning. Varun had only 161 condensed formulas comprising barely a thousand words to learn, far fewer than a student of the Vedas like Jagu or a student of Ayurveda. The Sūtras lay out the principles to guide any aspirant to Samādhī, a refined state of functioning of the nervous system in which the universe is experienced with such subtlety that everything is appreciated and anything is possible. When the yogin's mind has been freed of all its latent impressions and attachments to its objects it gains the complete purity of the cosmic self.[73] This is liberation, kaivalya, the ultimate goal.

Misconceptions about Yoga

After morning meditation Varun would drop by Maharishi's ashram where the caretakers and I were the only residents, and would take me on hikes to the caves of his yogin acquaintances. I packed in fruit from the village, something saints always appreciate. Those encounters inspired me to spend more time reading Patañjali. Considerable confusion has crept into the modern understanding of yoga. The first is over the meaning of the word yoga itself. Patañjali's second sūtra, yogas chittavrttinirodhah, states, "Yoga is the restriction of mental fluctuations." In this context, scholars trace the word yoga to the Sanskrit root [YUJ] meaning to repose, yoke or unite. Yoga is the therefore the discipline of bringing the mind to a state of repose.[74]

The third sūtra, tadā drastuḥ svarūpe 'vasthānam, says, "Thus the knower is established in his own form." When the mind is quiet, one is established in the Self. "Otherwise," warns sūtra four, "he takes on the form of the fluctuations" (vrittisārūpyam itaratra). Fewer than forty syllables into his exposition, Patañjali laid out the principle that with a settled mind free of unnecessary activity, the world is appreciated in the light of the Self, and in an agitated state, we see the world through whatever colored glasses we have put on that day.

If it is not Comfortable and Easy, it is not Yoga.

Some mornings Varun would slip into my screened gazebo at the Himalayan ashram to accompany me to the river. Witnessing me yawn and stretch in the morning darkness as I arose from the cot, he proclaimed, "You are doing what a cat does. This is the most natural form of yoga!"

On the practice of hatha yoga (the physical aspect of yoga), Patañjali has few words. Sthira-sukham āsanam, "The posture (āsana) is stable and comfortable." (YS II.46) Patañjali is codifying the general principle of yoga, passed down for generations before him that āsanas should be performed easily and without strain. Sthira-sukham āsanam implies taking postures slowly and steadily and only to the point of gentle stretch, backing off from there before holding the āsana and releasing it before any feeling of discomfort. The practitioner who attempts to do a forward bend and can only move six inches comfortably, stopping there, is a yogin aligned with Patañjali.

In the next sūtra Patañjali states, "The yogin attains the posture by relaxing in the endeavor or by identification with the infinite." YS II.47 An ancient Patañjali scholar[75] commented, "the idea is that if the posture is attained only with a very long effort, due to tremor or movement in the yogin's body, there is no steadiness in the posture." For Patanjali, the yoga practitioner who manages to touch her head to her knees after bouncing for a while is practicing calisthenics, not yoga, and no one gains, except possibly her chiropractor.

Since the 1990's there has been a proliferation of yoga schools and an unprecedented interest in hatha yoga. Still, neither yoga teachers, nor the schools that teach them how to teach, are regulated. Except for New York and a few other states, even a child without any experience, can legally open a studio and teach raw beginners to advanced practitioners. A yoga teacher is not required to have an understanding of anatomy, of a stiff spinal column or even of Patañjali.

Although there are organizations that register or certify yoga teachers, this current state of affairs in yoga instruction, regulated mainly by the dictum *caveat emptor*, is actually not a bad thing. For thousands of years seekers somehow found the right teacher without certification requirements or other government intervention. An aspirant sought out an experienced teacher, interviewed him carefully, and then once committed, became a receptive student. The teacher, authorized by his own teacher, carefully interviewed the student and laid out the requirements. The lack of official regulation can only foster greater personal commitment in the relationship.

Most yoga teachers I have met have never read and sometimes even heard of Patañjali, including many who are certified or registered. Some teachers seeking instant recognition invent yoga techniques, combining what should be sthiram-sukham (steady and comfortable) with karate or aerobics. As a result, yoga-related injuries involving the spine, knee cartilage, muscles and ligaments have increased fourfold in New England sports medicine clinics.[76] I recommend yoga to every outpatient, and many protest they tried it once and it made them worse. These people were not doing yoga as Patañjali defined it but they dismissed it for good.

The Benefits come from Regularity

Patañjali's steadiness also applies to regularity of practice. In my experience, injury occurs most frequently when the practitioner goes to a yoga class once a week, skipping practice at home. Many yoga students sign up for yoga classes because otherwise they would never practice, not unlike a wealthy patient of mine who hired a personal trainer to come into her bedroom in the morning to force her out of bed to exercise. Attending yoga classes occasionally is a formula for injury because you will have stiffened up in the interval since your last class and, intending to squeeze the most out of the session, you risk slipping your disc in the process.

A wise yoga teacher might assign her students a simple ten to fifteen minute set of progressive āsanas (five to eight poses, each to be held 30 seconds, followed by a half-minute rest) to be practiced once or twice a day without fail. Like taking pills, a habit performed routinely becomes adopted. Practicing yoga daily you will have more incentive to attend your weekly yoga class. If your time is limited, invest instead in a couple of private classes during which the yoga teacher can assess your strengths and weaknesses and prescribe your personalized daily ten-minute routine.

The terse treatment āsanas receive in Patañjali's sūtras implies that he intended āsanas to have a supporting and not leading role in yoga's ultimate aim. Some serious yogins take them to be a prelude or warm-up to meditation to prepare the body to cooperate with the mind to achieve the state of repose. Steadiness may also refer to your state of mind during the posture, with your awareness on the part being moved or lengthened, or as Patañjali says, "by identification with the infinite." In this state of mind the breath naturally takes care of itself, flowing outward when the abdomen and lungs are compressed and inward when they are expanded. Any distraction to the mind and senses (including music, kibitzing or even strong incense) that increases mental activity would make Patañjali roll his eyes heavenward.

Perfect Practice makes Perfect

Yoga āsanas are an important element of the lost art of self-repair. First, yoga is one of the best ways to bring your consciousness to attend to your physiology. This attention helps accomplish the goals of the exercises in Chapter 8; you sense your body's requirement, you detect its imbalances and you bring about change.

Second, yoga is a critical element in the prevention of chronic disorders, providing suppleness, endurance, and de-excitation of your nervous system, thus reducing high blood pressure and other inappropriate autonomic responses to stressors.

Third, yoga is the technique par excellence for rehabilitation of your aches and pains, including your joints, soft tissues and nervous system injuries. Yoga helps heal insults both to brain tissue such as strokes or MS as well as peripheral nerve trauma such as neuropathy and repetitive stress injury.

Patañjali's goal is kaivalya, singularity or oneness with pure consciousness. He is not concerned with which specific postures accomplish which purpose or how to rehabilitate an injury. Hatha yoga texts describing specific postures did not appear until nearly two millennia later. Patañjali only implies how they should be performed: slowly, with stability, effortlessly and with the awareness in the part being moved. The purpose, after all, is neuromuscular integration.

Following an injury, for example, soft tissues such as tendons, ligaments, muscles and nerves may have been traumatized, leading to stiffness and spasm. Massaging the limb, while often helpful, is not the best stimulus to injured tissue. On the other hand, creating a powerful intention to move the limb using the principles of yoga activates brain nerve impulses, invoking nerve cell growth. The yogic principle of attention to the body's requirement applies to all neuromuscular injuries from carpal tunnel syndrome to a stroke.

Like an athlete or pianist who brings total attention to her practice session to get more out of the time she spends, when your awareness attends to the body during the performance of the exercises, the effect of the physical therapy is enhanced. "Practice does not make perfect," football coach Vince Lombardi once said, "Only perfect practice makes perfect." Recent studies on patients who have recovered from a coma or from long-standing paralysis suggest that new nerve signal pathways can bypass injured nerve tissue. The new pathways develop as nerve cell axons from intact nerves, under the guidance of a protein called netrin,[77] grow toward their target. Their growth cones roll forward like a tank on its tracks.[78]

Patañjali sheds important light on physical therapy: bring your settled awareness to the limb being moved or stretched. For maximum benefit, don't exercise while reading a magazine or watching an overhead TV, whether you are in physical therapy or riding a stationary bike in a health club. Attend to your practice.

Many yoga teachers and practitioners have publicly condemned the commercial expropriation of the term *yoga* into activities that resemble dance, aerobics, martial arts and other exercise. They should applaud the movement. After all, an exponent of yoga should welcome the yogafication of all human activity, including physical activities such as sports, dance or dining; mental activities including education or enjoying music; or behavior including etiquette, relationships and sex. A better world should result from people living all aspects of their lives yogically, with a settled mind and focused attention. Classical yoga will always be available to earnest students and yoga kickboxing may be someone's entry to a serious practice.

Varun came to visit me at the medical students' hostel at the hospital in New Delhi where I was studying infectious diseases. A weekend seeker in the Himalayas had given him bus fare to Delhi. He quickly transformed my small room into his cave. "I've come to teach you how to fast." He taught me to ease my stomach into abstention without feeling its protest, to deal with false hunger in the brain, to gain lightness instead of fatigue, and to break my fast with coconut water. He had me sing Patañjali's first few verses. He slept wrapped in his dhoti in unattainable yoga poses. When he left, he gave me his parents' address in Jaipur, knowing that before I left India I planned to visit this walled desert ruby with the delicate façades.

Months later I located the house where Varun was born near Jaipur's eastern wall. His parents were cordial and insisted I stay for the night. They had received no news from Varun for ten years until I arrived. They never inquired about his health, his state of mind, what he wore, whether he begged or how he lived. I figured it was easier for them to not think, wonder and worry about him, and to simply accept that he was wandering somewhere in the world in pursuit of God and singing Patañjali's sutras.

70 Purusha is the Sanskrit word used in Patañjali's Yoga Sutras
71 Human figures in seated yoga postures have been found in artifacts from pre-vedic Harapa civilization in the Indus Valley, ~3300-2100 B.C.
72 Scholars exclude the entire fourth chapter. Its language and content indicate it is a much later addition.
73 Purusha in Sanskrit
74 Yoga-Sutra. Translation by Michel Angot. Paris, 2000.
75 The 16th century commentator of Patañjali's sutras, Vijñānabhikshu
76 Boston Globe article, 2006.
77 From the Sanskrit *netr* meaning *one who guides*
78 Argiro, Vincent. Correlation between growth form and movement and their dependence on neuronal age. Journal of Neuroscience, Vol 4, 3051-3062; and personal communication.

CHAPTER 15

BREATHING AND PRĀNAYĀMA

When I was doing research on the effects of the Transcendental Meditation technique on the physiology, some of my colleagues tested a woman who learned the technique as a child and had been practicing regularly for over twenty years. We would burden her with nose clips, masks and respiratory gauges, electrodes to her measure brain waves – plus all the other measurements of a standard polygraph lie detector test such as heart rate and palm sweating. Sitting quietly with her eyes closed prior to meditating, she breathed at ten to fourteen breaths a minute.

When she got the signal to start meditating, within minutes her breath rate would get slower and shallower. She would have moments where the breath would completely stop, sometimes for 45 seconds at a time. When she would start breathing again, she continued at her slow, shallow rate. There was no compensatory hyperventilation, like you might experience if you had just come up after staying 45 seconds underwater. She was not intentionally holding her breath. Because her physiology settled down together with her mind, her body simply did not have the same need to breathe. She was asked to press on a button when she had an experience of inner silence. Most of her button presses came at the end of a period of respiratory suspension. The researchers found forty other TM practitioners with similar breath suspension.[79]

Your body has a subtle mode of functioning where your metabolic rate slows – associated with a corresponding slowing in your breath. Perhaps you have felt quiet breathing when you are falling asleep or waking up. The research on TM shows that this softened breathing occurs not only during meditation, but also outside of it, with the eyes open. As we have seen, longevity across species has an association with metabolic rate. To add more power to your program of body renewal, you need to learn to soften the breath.

A book is no place to learn yoga, much less meditation. I will nevertheless include a simple yoga practice called *pranayama* which has the effect of refining your breath and thereby your mind and body. There are many types of *pranayama* practices, each having different effects. *Prana* means vital breath and *yama* refers to control or command. *Pranayama* entrains an intimate coordination between your nervous system and your lungs, invoking your brain circuitry that is involved in sensing oxygen requirements. *Pranayama* coordinates the brain with the stretch receptors in your thoracic cage muscles, the tension on your diaphragm, and a host of other lung functions. Some types of *pranayama* are activating and others are settling. One of the easiest and most important of the many prāṇayāmas for settling the mind and body is known as *sukha-pranayama* (comfortable *pranayama*) which refines your mind and body by refining your breath.

How to Practice Prānāyāma
(Yoga Breath Refinement)

This ancient breathing technique can be practiced for as little as a couple of minutes. After just 2-3 minutes, you will feel calmer and more clear. Even this little is enough to derive a lasting benefit if performed regularly. Five minutes makes an ideal regular practice. Prānāyāma is traditionally performed daily at the same time after your yoga asana practice and before meditation. Sukha-prānāyāma has a calming effect and can also be practiced at bedtime or during the night if you find your mind active. It is practiced sitting, never standing or lying down.

Close your left nostril by pressing your right third and fourth fingers on the left side of your nose. Exhale slowly through the right nostril. Then inhale slowly through your right nostril.

At the end of a slow, easy inspiration, release the left nostril and close your right nostril by gently pressing your right thumb on the right side of your nose. Again, exhale slowly then inhale slowly through the left nostril. Continue to alternate, first exhaling and then inhaling through the unblocked nostril, then switching again. Your respirations should be slightly deeper than usual, and the flow should be slow enough to be almost silent.

Prānāyāma is best practiced in silence with the eyes closed so your attention can fully attend to the flow of air into and out of the lungs. Avoid distractions such as music and incense. If your eyes happen to open, don't be concerned. Close them and bring your awareness back to the flow of the breath. Always use the right hand and the specified fingers. If even one of your nostrils is blocked, do not attempt to do your prānāyāma practice because it would only produce strain. Exertion, you may have gleaned by now, is not in the spirit of an effortless Vedic life.

Prānāyāma and Lung Disease

Prānāyāma is an important aid for people with chronic lung conditions. Air hunger is associated with panic and chronic air hunger is associated with anxiety. No surprise – if you've been in that situation, you fear you are going to die. Anxiety makes people overbreathe, but overbreathing occurs in many other conditions. By overbreathing, asthmatics and people with chronic obstructive pulmonary disease (COPD) can more than double the air they move in and out of their lungs in a minute. Chronic hyperventilation makes the blood alkaline and sets up a series of compensatory imbalances to keep the blood pH within its critical normal limits, but which can make wheezing worse.

Asthmatics and people with COPD are both affected by inappropriate bronchospasm, a normal contraction of the bronchi that helps properly distribute airflow, but patients quickly become dependent on bronchodilating nebulizers or inhalers. Bronchospasm is usually exacerbated by chronic hyperventilation. Asthmatics often break into a fit of coughing and wheezing with deep exhalations – as when their doctor listens to their lungs with a stethoscope. In an asthma or COPD exacerbation, patients often breathe through their mouths, losing the natural protection of the lungs that comes from nasal breathing – taking in warm, humidified air.

Prānāyāma helps people with lung disease to better deal with exacerbations of their disease.[80, 81] It encourages asthmatics to develop the habit of nasal breathing, thus humidifying their air. Regular practice of prānayāma helps prevent patients from developing panic and anxiety (taking a deep breath before going on stage has long been a remedy for stage fright). Prānayāma cultures the habit of avoiding overbreathing, and thus prevents airway collapse and alkalosis that triggers more bronchospasm.

If you have asthma or COPD, practice prānayāma regularly. Even a few minutes of prānayāma will improve the way you breathe the rest of the day. In addition to this practice of prānayāma described above, spend two minutes at the end of your practice making your breaths increasingly shallow. This will train you to avoid the airway collapse and subsequent wheezing that occurs at the end of expiration during an exacerbation of your asthma or COPD.[82]

79 Farrow JT, Hebert JR. *Breath Suspension During the Transcendental Meditation Technique*. Psychosomatic Medicine Vol. 44, No. 2 (May 1982)

80 Saxena T, Saxena M. *The effect of various breathing exercises (prānayāma) in patients with bronchial asthma of mild to moderate severity*. Int J Yoga 2009;2:22-5

81 S K Katiyar, Shailesh Bihari *Role of Prānayāma in Rehabilitation of COPD patients-a randomized Controlled Study*. Indian J Allergy Asthma Immunol 2006; 20(2) : 98-104

82 Patients who have severe COPD requiring "purse lipped breathing" or who have had elevated blood CO_2 levels should not perform prānayāma without consulting their doctor.

NUTRITION FOR SELF- REPAIR

CHAPTER 16

TENDING THE DIGESTIVE FIRE

Every September my friend Harold, a local farmer pushing ninety, shows up with three cord of fine, split hardwood that he seasons all summer in his barn. Every October a salty New England chimney sweep shows up to ream creosote out of the flue through which we burn Harold's nice, dry logs. When he finishes jamming his brushes down the vent, so much creosote has fallen to the bottom that he has to take our stove apart to take it out. As I slip a check into his soot-black hand, he gives me the same litany.

"Y've got a fine wood stove heaah, 'n nice drah logs in y'r woodpile out bayack. Withat much creosote, I'm guessin' y're puttin' a mess a logs in y'r stove 'n shettin' off the airflow evah' night so ya don' have to rekindle y'r heaaarth in the mahnin'. C'd be wrong, but t'seems we had this same discussion last yeaah."

It's the same discussion I have every fall with recently retired Paul McDermott, an overweight executive who, a dozen years ago, had the plaque in his coronary arteries reamed out and the arteries propped open with a stent. He is otherwise in good health except for some heartburn. On one level he appears to be a health nut, insisting his wife shop at natural food stores and going to a fasting retreat in Mexico once a year. From the standard perspective, when he presented to the ER that fateful day, Paul didn't look like the classical candidate for an early heart attack: he's a bit hefty, has a slightly elevated cholesterol level, and has never been a smoker. However, every evening he and his wife dine out and he is fond of rich cuisine.

Like my woodstove, Paul goes to bed with a belly full of fuel. When he lies down, the gastric juices secreted in response to the meal slip insidiously through his relaxed, wide open esophageal sphincter. The meal sits in his belly most of the night because the nerves and hormones that activate the digestive activities are shut down by the body's circadian rhythms. Like the fine, dry logs I put in my stove, all the organic, healthy food in the world will not compensate for the way you douse your digestive fire. Somehow, like my wood stove, Paul is creating his own kind of "creosote," like the deposits on my flue. His is a foamy, fatty deposit that lodges in weak areas of the arterial wall. Pathologists call it plaque; the ancient Ayurvedic physicians called it *āma*, derived from the Sanskrit *ma* meaning "to cook" or "to ripen." *Āma*, therefore, means "uncooked" or "unripened" products of digestion, since digestion in Ayurvedic medicine is understood to be the cooking or ripening of food in the stomach. *Āma* is considered such bad stuff that it is sometimes used to mean disease itself. Vedic medicine locates the critical physical factor in determining your health in the strength of your *agni*, your digestive and metabolic fires. To master the lost art of self-repair, you need to learn the Vedic arts of tending the fires. Our modern saying, "You can't have your cake and eat it too," implies that the act of eating is a sacrifice: the cake is offered onto the digestive fire. A sacrifice implies a big gain to offset a smaller loss: we give up an out for a run, or a bishop for a queen. Similarly, sacrificing the cake onto the fire of our belly, we gain not only the pleasure of the eating but also nourishment to tissues and energy, as well as a subtle unquantifiable value of biological intelligence or vital force. In the Vedic perspective, eating is a holy act and meal preparation is a part of this sacrament. In fact, this concept is invoked in the Christian and Jewish traditions such as communion or breaking bread and blessing wine before a meal. The dining table is the altar and the stomach the inner sanctum where this sacrifice takes place. It is no wonder that the digestive fire is called agni by the Sanskrit medical texts, the same as the sacrificial fire.

Digestive disorders, obesity, diabetes, and their complications such as vascular disease have become increasingly prevalent in part because this sacrament has become profane, unconscious and mundane. Once, while accompanying two Ayurvedic physicians from India on their first trip to North America, we walked by a drive-in fast food franchise where they saw cars departing – their occupants dining at the wheel. Their first reaction was backslapping laughter, which then turned to pity after realizing they had witnessed the heart of the problem underlying many of the digestive and weight-related disorders we had seen together in that day's consultations. They said the problem was not the fast food chains but modern America's irreverent attitude to the sacredness of eating, quoting an Ayurvedic verse, "Good digestion is the root of all health."

Some of my patients will do anything to get well, including making major changes in their lifestyle and diet. This includes learning not only new ways to cook and eat, but even new ways to think about their relationship with food. My experience suggests that the Ayurvedic way to eat improves not only weight but also the most common digestive problems: reflux, gastritis, bloating, gas, irritable bowel syndrome and constipation – disorders that are suffered by almost everyone.

Let us examine the elements of this Ayurvedic way of eating, which includes two aspects: what to eat and how to eat. Here we will discuss only how to eat, because what to eat could easily be the subject of a whole book. The ancient texts describe eight factors that must be considered by every conscious eater, preferably before the act of eating.

1. **Prakriti** · The properties of the ingredients. Heavy foods like meat, dairy, eggs and fried food are heavy to digest and make the body heavy. Similarly, light foods such as salad, fruit, corn, barley and soup do not tax the digestive fire and can be taken in larger amounts.

2. **Karana** · Proper preparation. Correct cooking increases the digestibility of the food. Use fresh ingredients, avoiding canned, frozen and leftover foods. If you were served these foods at a restaurant you would never go back, and your own kitchen should be the best eatery in town. Use digestive spices such as cumin, turmeric, mustard seeds and cardamom in heavier dishes and those made with oil, including stir-fry. Lightly boil milk and drink it warm to make it more digestible. Churn yogurt with water to make a light digestive drink called *lassi* (see Appendix – Recipes).

3. **Samyoga** · Food combinations. Avoid combining foods that create a product that is heavy to digest. Many people complain that they are lactose intolerant but the problem is usually taking dairy improperly.[83] Milk is best taken alone or with grains, like a cookie or cereal. Milk taken with acidic foods or vegetables may

curdle in your stomach and milk taken with meat, honey or other heavy dairy is especially heavy for your digestive fire. Avoid eating fruit with honey, milk or butter.

4. Rashi · Proper quantity. Learn your true digestive capacity, which may be an amount that is much smaller than you think. In general, start with the amount that fits into two cupped hands. At the end of the meal, the stomach should be filled roughly one third with solids, one third with liquids and be left one third empty to allow room to digest. You should also feel satisfied but not heavy, without dullness in the mind and senses, and it should be comfortable to lie down, breathe and move. Think about these ancient criteria after your next meal and if they are not fulfilled, begin to adjust your portions. Remember that the only consistent way scientists have found to increase the lifespan of a laboratory animal is to restrict caloric intake.[84] Until this is proven with human subjects as well, you can hedge your bets by restricting your dose to the amount you require to feel satisfied. See Chapter 20.

5. Desha · Place. Eat a diet that is appropriate to where you live. In New England, we eat pancakes with butter and maple syrup in the winter. It is best avoided, though, in the summer. Have you noticed that in the dry, hot deserts of the Middle East, the tradition is olive oil, rich and unctuous foods, taken in moderation? In humid tropical areas, the dishes are spicy, and in the dry, cold arctic the native food is fatty, rich and plentiful. Select your diet with consideration to your environment to create balance. In our multi-ethnic culture, think twice before ordering calzones every time you eat out.

6. Kala · Time. Vedic eating takes into account the role of time in selecting your diet, including the time of day, the season, your stage of life and even the stage of a disorder.

The Time of Day: The strength of the digestive fire follows the sun, so you should take a light breakfast and supper when your fire is low and eat a good lunch. Nineteenth century European observers of American culture satirized the tendency of shop owners to put a sign on the door, "Out for lunch, back in five minutes." Unfortunately our habits have changed little since. In many cultures it is normal to take several hours off for lunch and rest. Today most people work or study far from home and schedule their day so tightly that lunch is taken on the hoof between appointments. Try starting with the simple decision to take the time to eat lunch sitting in a quiet place (not at your desk!) where you can eat slowly and consciously. Your mind and body will be more satisfied until your evening meal. Also, unless you never gain weight, don't take a big meal at both lunch and supper! If you are not pregnant, an adolescent, an athlete in training, or working at a physically strenuous job, breakfast can be light.

The Role of the Seasons: (See Appendix 7, Seasonal Routines, for more information on this topic.) When the seasons change, consider the weather in terms of both hot/ cold and wet/dry in adjusting your diet. If it is cold and wet as in November and March, eat hot, pungent and dry fare, avoiding heavy, cold and sweet foods and take less meat and dairy. Winter is the time when the body needs more fats and calories, assuming you are not inside hibernating. In hot weather, create a cooling influence with juicy fruits, salads, cool drinks and lighter choices for meat and dairy.

The Time of Life: Youth is the phase of life when congestion is ubiquitous. Kids live on chicken nuggets and food laced with cheese, washed down with cold milk, yet we wonder why they are congested and overweight. Kids do well on lighter fare. In old age the body becomes cold, dry, brittle and stiff, as if it had been exposed to a cold, drying wind. Ayurveda therefore recommends a diet that is warm, hydrating and lubricating. But as you age, your digestive fire tends to become weaker and irregular. If you don't maintain your digestive fire, you will have a hard time tolerating the useful foods such as olive oil, milk and ghee that lubricate dry tissues and help maintain suppleness.

7. **Upayogasamstha** · Rules of eating. Most of us have never truly taken our childhood dining lessons to heart. Our great grandparents would be appalled if they saw our habits today. The ancient texts give specific guidelines for preventing *āma* formation. You may need to modify them for your modern life. They may seem obvious, but most have simply been forgotten.

• Eat only if you are hungry.

• Eat only after your previous meal is already digested because undigested food will mix with nearly digested food, slowing gastric emptying and creating a situation where part of your meal will be undigested and part over-digested or even fermented.

• Favor warm food. Besides being more satisfying (heat releases volatile aromas and tastes), warm food is also more digestible, stimulating peristalsis and secretion of gastric enzymes and secretions. Cold foods quench the digestive fires. The tradition of serving ice water in a restaurant is an effective way to assure that the patrons' digestive fires are low when the meal arrives. Try asking for cool or hot water instead.

• Ensure that your meal is unctuous, moist and lubricated, not excessively dry or rough. Even if you are on a low fat diet there are ways to accomplish this without calories. For example, if you are stir-frying start with less oil and make simple non-fat sauces. Try the Indian tradition of folding low fat yogurt into the sauce of a stir-fry at the end of cooking for a creamy texture or add a ripe, chopped tomato with Italian herbs for a Mediterranean flavor.

• Eat in a quiet place. Set the table.

• Eat from clean, pleasing dishes and utensils.

• Eat consciously. In other words, when you eat avoid doing anything else. Break the bad habit of eating while watching television or reading. Light, uplifting conversation or quiet background music is fine but don't make a habit of conducting important business, either at home or at work, while you are digesting.

• Eat when you are in a calm state of mind. If you find yourself in an anxious, angry, emotional or irritable mood, give the feelings time to pass before partaking.

- Take the time to eat leisurely and chew well but also don't eat excessively slowly. Test whether you are eating at the proper pace by noting if there is a subtle, pleasing change in the taste as you chew and whether the mind has really assimilated the joy of every bite. If you find yourself habitually eating too quickly, put down your fork between bites or correct the practice at home by eating with chopsticks.

- Take a moment of quietness before you take your first bite, as well as a moment to savor the appearance and smell of the food. Listen to your body's song. Salivation is a sign that your body and mind are ready.

- Remain sitting for a few minutes after your meal before getting up. If you are overweight, try doing this before your plate is finished and you may find that you are actually already satisfied. Take a short walk (one ancient medical text says at least 180 paces) before you go back to your activity.

8. Upayokta · Body Type and Disorders. Eat appropriately for your body type and any ongoing imbalances. If you are heavy and slow by nature or seem to be getting heavier and slower with each passing year, check your plate. Lighter foods with bitter, pungent and astringent tastes should make up 90% of the meal and heavy, rich foods the other 10%. If your body is dry, stiff and brittle, richer cuisine may be right for you.

The eight factors of how to tend your digestive fire, while commonsense, are remarkably forgotten in our busy lives. Remembering them makes eating a spiritual and therefore more enjoyable experience.

---

83 Although there may be a genetic component, lactose intolerance is virtually unknown in Pakistan, India, the Masai of Africa and other cultures.
84 See Chapter 5: The Secrets of Extreme Longevity.

CHAPTER 17

THE SENSITIVE BELLY: DISORDERS OF GI MOTILITY

Happy digesters are those who hustle their food from one end of the digestive tract to another without fanfare. All others make up the unhappy lot with the most common digestive problems. If you are a wimp about growing older, the news that these disorders increase as your gut's peristaltic muscles atrophy along with your abs and pects is not auspicious.

A Vedic physician would say that discontented digesters have a motility problem, an issue with abnormal peristalsis, sluggish emptying or even retrograde conduction of the food through their twenty-two feet of gut. From the perspective of Vedic medicine, irritable bowel syndrome (IBS), functional dyspepsia, gastroesophageal reflux disease (GERD) and constipation are all issues of motility.

Most people think of heartburn and dyspepsia primarily as issues of excess acidity (*pitta* disorders) but the underlying problem is almost invariably a motility issue. In reflux the bolus of food and secretions is inappropriately squeezed upward from the stomach into the esophagus, whose tender membranes Mother Nature never designed for chronic exposure to acids and digestive enzymes.

Reflux responds well to medications that reduce acid secretion, perhaps because it buys your GI tract time to heal itself and begin contracting normally again without being bathed in waves of acid. Unless you change the way you tend your digestive fire, you risk a lifetime of dependence on these medications.

It is important to recognize IBS and reflux as motility disorders because the cure is ultimately dependent on improving the strength and coordination of contractions of the smooth muscles of the gut walls.

Similarly, sluggish motility of the colon can account for most chronic constipation, a motility disorder that is so common that it has merited its own chapter. See Effortless Elimination, Chapter 19.

A Dietary Strategy for Disorders of Decreased GI Motility (Sluggish Digestion)

1. Eat light • If your digestion is delicate, you will do best with a light, easily digestible diet. Favor cooked dishes because raw foods require a strong digestive fire. Cooked foods are pre-digested by the fire of the pan. Cook your vegetables a little more than the "just tender" texture advised for people with strong fires. You will get better nutrition by efficiently digesting food with slightly fewer vitamins than by letting raw food loaded with vitamins sit in your belly like a rock. Your stomach senses when you indulge in heavy fats and proteins and responds by closing the pyloric sphincter at the stomach's outlet in order to delay gastric emptying. Go easy on heavy cheeses and meats and you will feel light sooner after eating.

2. Use rice • Rice is rapidly cleared by the stomach. Try brown basmati rice instead of white rice, as it may be less constipating. Bananas, pasta, potatoes and grain products cooked with fats such as cookies, cakes and chips are heavier. Plan your starches accordingly. If you have irritable bowel syndrome or reflux without constipation, you should still read the relevant points from the Thatched Hut Diet, because a sluggish colon will ultimately affect the function upstream. (Chapter 19).

3. Use olive oil and ghee • Olive oil can be used for sauteeing vegetables and dressing salads. Add ghee liberally to all grains and other cooked dishes.[86] Ghee is highly digestible and will not make your dish heavy.

4. Avoid cruciferous vegetables • Watch out for broccoli, cauliflower, cabbage, kale and Brussel sprouts unless you know they don't create gas.

5. Make soupy dal[87] • This light lentil or legume soup is highly digestible. Add vegetables such as carrots, squash, or celery to the cooked dal. Avoid all beans except mung beans and small red lentils (masoor dal), which should be made into dal soup. Black beans and large beans like kidney beans, while tasty, not only create gas but also are heavy to digest.

6. Use winter squash liberally • It can be made into squash soup, baked squash (bake it well, almost crisp, after brushing with oil or ghee) or boiled squash, which is delicious when mashed with ghee.

7. Favor sweet potatoes • White potatoes are heavier and may create gas.

8. Use khichadi • It is the lightest and easiest to digest of all whole proteins.
It is made from equal parts rice and either split mung beans or small red lentils (masoor dal). Cook together and add digestive spices at the end as described in Appendix 5.

9. Try quinoa • It is a good grain for sensitive digestion, either cooked and sprinkled with ghee or made into a soup – a specialty of Ecuador, full of protein, tasty, and fun to eat.

10. Don't forget dairy • It is the best source of calcium for someone with irregular digestion because this fickle mineral is poorly absorbed from greens and pulses. Many people digest dairy poorly. Lassi[88] is the lightest dairy food, and contains no lactose. Boil milk with some grated ginger (and at bedtime some poppy seeds to aid sleep) if you find it hard to digest. If you tolerate these, you can add light cheese such as goat cheese, ricotta, or cottage cheese.

11. Stir-fry your vegetables • Use ghee or olive oil to sauté asparagus, zucchini, endives, green beans, carrots and cucumber. These are all light and promote motility. Use only tender salad greens and lettuce such as mesclun leaves. You can wilt your salads by mixing them with your stir-fry at the end Vietnamese style. If digestion is slow, you may have difficulty with raw salad, especially when it includes cabbage, iceberg or romaine lettuce.

12. Fresh tomato soup • This soup aids digestion when it is made with sweet tomatoes, adding at the end stir-fried leeks and a little yogurt, sour cream or cream. Tomatoes are best taken for lunch rather than supper because there is less risk of nighttime dyspepsia.

13. Spices to aid motility • Cumin, asafoetida (hing – a mere pinch to take away gas), cilantro, fennel seed powder, turmeric or fresh Italian herbs. Brown the herbs and spices in a little ghee in a small sauce pan and add to the dish just before serving.

14. Pachakchurna (digestive powder) • You will need to assemble the ingredients, make a batch and keep in a tight bottle. Take a pinch with the first bite of every meal to avoid gas. See Recipes.

15. Chew dry roasted fennel seeds after meals.

16. Sip cumin seed tea • This is one of the best carminatives: it dispels gas. Boil one-teaspoon cumin seeds for 5 min., strain and drink. Add a teaspoon of coriander seeds if you tend to have heartburn.

In this chapter, we have focused on what to eat if you have a GI motility disorder. Even more important is how to eat, described in the previous chapter. Your gut also has its rhythms, shutting down and firing up in response to your lifestyle. It even has its own nervous system, called the enteric nervous system, built into the omentum, the folds that support the intestine. Structure regular routines to help support your belly's finicky motility. Strengthening your digestive fire will ultimately liberate you to eat what you like.

---

86 Learn to clarify your butter so you have a fresh supply of ghee. See Appendix 5.
87 See Recipes and Thermos Flask Lunch recipe in Chapter 21.
88 See Appendix 5, Recipes for Improving Digestion.

CHAPTER 18

Oxidation, Aging and Rust

When I was eight I performed a simple experiment in gerontology. I left my fielder's mitt out in the bright Colorado sun for two weeks one summer. What I beheld when I finally inspected my glove was hard, dry, bleached and wrinkled leather that I could barely slip on, let alone use to field grounders. It looked like my one year old mitt was seventy-five. The following morning, after applying neat's-foot oil, I was astounded: my mitt looked young again, maybe not one, but three years old. The hard, dry membranes had been transformed almost new again. Following lubrication, the gap between looking one and three was due to accelerated aging.

My mitt had been exposed to oxidation. If it had been in a vacuum, despite the sunlight, the damage would not have been as bad. Light plus dry air had been a double whammy. In the presence of sunlight, the chemical bonds between two oxygen atoms, tightly bound as the stable molecule O2 in the air, had uncoupled. Each oxygen atom was left without a mate. We call these oxygen species "free radicals" which sounds like something out of the sixties: they are free though not happy about it. Like a newcomer at Club Med, free radicals are also frenetically looking for partners with which they can couple in order to satisfy their intense need for an electron. They found them in the leather of my mitt.

The Role of Oxidation in Degenerative Disorders

We now recognize that this oxidative process plays a major role not only in aging but also in the disease process. Cancer, hardening of the arteries (think of my mitt), wrinkles, cataracts, arthritis, stroke, emphysema, Crohn's disease and looking and feeling old are only a few of the disorders attributed to free radicals. Oxygen radicals are created not only on the surface of the body where sun meets air, but also within the tissues. Fortunately, we have mechanisms for neutralizing or scavenging free radicals, but sometimes the rate at which we create them is greater than our ability to sop them up.

Free radicals come from several sources. Immune cells called phagocytes engulf bacteria, intentionally creating free radicals to literally zap them so they can be digested. Regrettably, those free radicals are left around to damage our own tissues. Sunlight and other radiation are important sources. In fact, the smooth elastic baby-like skin on an octogenarian's bottom looks supple mainly because it has rarely been exposed to sunlight. Chemicals and other drugs are important sources, including pesticides and herbicides, along with smoked and barbecued foods, the peroxidized fats in meats and aged cheeses, alcohol, cigarette smoke, and air pollution.

The Antidote to Biological Rust

You can scavenge free radicals not only with internal enzymes evolved for this purpose but also from antioxidants in plants you ingest. It is a good bet that if a fruit or vegetable is brightly colored, it is loaded with antioxidants. Pigments such as lycopenes that make tomatoes red, limonenes in citrus and carotenoids in carrots, squash and sweet potatoes are all antioxidants with activity against different free radicals.

Naturally people think, "If a few antioxidants are good, more must be better." You may be ingesting industrially concentrated antioxidants in all colors and shapes with the hopes of avoiding cancer and heart disease. The medical research, however, does not bear this out; in fact, in one study, smokers taking beta-carotene actually developed more lung cancer than those taking placebos. On the other hand, studies show that people who take more fresh fruits and vegetables in their diets have important reductions in both of these disorders.

The Fallacy of the Active Ingredient

In Ayurvedic medicine there is a principle called "the fallacy of the active ingredient" which holds that if you try to isolate the active principle from the whole you lose the benefit and you risk developing side effects. See Chapter 22, Your Bag of Supplements: the Fallacy of the Active Ingredient. An Ayurvedic physician would say that taking the beta-carotene out of the carrot isolates it from the many other elements in the whole food that may have synergistic beneficial effects.

If you want to avoid looking like my baseball mitt prematurely, shun the agents that create free radicals which are listed above like the devil. Free radicals indeed are the trident precipitating our eventual demise and yet, because they also mediate immune functions, metabolism and other healthy responses, we cannot live without them. In fact, people who take too many free radicals may suffer from fatigue because they impair the body's ability to mobilize certain metabolic pathways, according to Denham Harmon, the physician who initially proposed their connection with aging.

Ancient Ayurvedic texts recommend eating plenty of fruits and vegetables of every conceivable color. This advice had a scientific logic. Plants contain thousands of "active ingredients" such as natural alkaloids, flavonoids and terpinoids and therein resides their intelligence, their prana or life force.

I could tell you about terpenes, found in the essential oils of plants and which include the carotenoids from yellow, orange and red spectrum foods and how they have been shown to be potent membrane antioxidants reacting with singlet oxygen species and about their link to a reduced risk of heart disease, cancer and macular degeneration and cataracts. And we could talk about lycopenes found in carotenoid-rich foods like tomatoes, limonoids found in citrus fruit peels, luteins linked to eye health, saponins found in beans and quinoa, which foam when you cook them because saponins are a natural detergent. We could talk about phenols such as the 1500 different discovered flavonoids, ubiquitous in green vegetables, fruits and red wine and which block enzymes causing inflammation and allergies, keep platelets from clumping and help repair damaged capillaries. We could discuss the water-soluble anthocyandins giving berries and eggplants their dark pigments and which are helpful when there is a cascade of free radical liberation as in inflammation, exercise and trauma. We could extol the virtues of the polyphenolic catechins found in tea. We could spend a day acclaiming spices including turmeric and its putative active ingredients, the curcuminoids with their ability to inhibit the oxidative cascade and their links with protection from Alzheimer's disease, cancer and inflammatory disorders. All this dialogue would only be giving you cause to eat with your intellect – or worse, out of a bottle of supplements – instead of the Ayurvedic way, with the heart.

It is impossible to approach antioxidant ingestion intellectually because the anti-oxidants are innumerous, available in our diet due to the millions of years of relationship between mammals like us and the world of plants. The cravings for these fruits and plants are innate, coded in our DNA, the expression of the ancient song of Veda playing its refrain through your body. We only need to listen.

Already 60% of Americans think one to four servings of produce in a day are enough, obviously not listening to their body's song. The primary purpose of this book is not to tell you exactly what to eat or do for health but rather to give you the tools for self-repair. This means teaching you to listen to your body's ancient song and turning the body's requirement into a purposeful change of lifestyle over time to alter the course of chronic disorders and senescence. All you need to remember is the Ayurvedic dictum that describes a satisfying meal as one that includes all the tastes, colors and qualities of food.

Try to take your produce fresh not frozen, canned or packaged. Cook vegetables to make them more digestible, but avoid cooking out the intelligence found in their myriad phytonutrients. They may have antioxidants you need, they may even have something else you need but about which we not even aware. Until science tells you otherwise, you can feel good about picking your antioxidants the Ayurvedic way: in the produce department with your intuition and common sense and not in the drug store with your intellect.

CHAPTER 19

EFFORTLESS ELIMINATION: THE THATCHED HUT DIET

"For I am full of matter, the spirit within me constraineth me. Behold, my belly is as wine which hath no vent; it is ready to burst like new bottles."

Job 32:18-19

During my third year in medical school I went to Zululand to pursue research on tuberculosis. The British surgeon at the hospital wrote me to come in September, and several hours after stepping off the train I found out why. Most Zulu men worked in the diamond and gold mines hundreds of miles to the north and only came home at Christmas. The surgeon put a scalpel in my hand, pointed out the linea nigra, the thin, pigmented skin stripe running midline from the pubis to the navel and said, "Cut along the dotted line." We did four Caesarian sections my first day. Every Thursday he gave me a break from the incessant deliveries and took me in a van to an outlying clinic. The first week we went to a thatched farmhouse in the heart of rural Zululand where we treated local farmers and cowherders who presented with primarily infectious and nutritional disorders I had not yet even learned of. He also taught me to pull teeth, as no dentists were available. A week later we went to a clinic on the Zululand border where the villagers commuted from their huts to factories in nearby towns. There we saw diabetes, hypertension, obesity and constipation. I was now in familiar territory.

Lurching home on the rutted roads, the wise surgeon and I talked about the phenomenon of diseases of urban life. In his thirty years in Zululand, he had never seen a case of colon cancer and only rarely saw obesity and constipation at the thatched farmhouse. "Did you notice that the lady with hypertension was wearing a watch? She is paid according to how many parts she stamps per hour. Her cousin, whom we saw last week, doesn't even know what an hour is. The city cousin also eats city food – processed and salty."

One year later in India, I met a senior physician, Denis Burkitt, who had spent his life in Africa, and had described an uncommon tumor among young men and boys, Burkitt's lymphoma. He explained that he had become an astute observer of human stools because in Uganda, the great outdoors in which he loved to walk about, was the outhouse of preference. Ugandans had impressed him with their large, soft stools which have a high water content. Rural African stools resemble a cow pie more than an American or British stool he told us, and have a faster transit time, with undigested roughage from supper showing up the following morning instead of days later, as is often the case in the west. Most importantly, he concluded, the nature of the stools of rural Africans helps explain their protection from diseases of western civilization. Rural Africans rarely develop some of Westerner's most common disorders: constipation (and constipation's immediate consequences – the hemorrhoids, varicose veins and hernias that result from pelvic congestion and straining at the stool), diverticulosis, irritable bowel syndrome, diabetes, obesity, elevated cholesterol and it's consequences i.e. heart attacks and strokes. They rarely develop one of America's most common cancer's: recto-colon cancer (his logic being that there are fewer carcinogens in the stool having less contact time with the wall of the colon). During the decade after our conversation, the medical community was eager to debunk Dr. Burkitt's theory that a soft, high-fiber stool was the solution to most of our ills. In one study, adding fiber alone for a few years to the diet of Western subjects who had eaten a standard western diet all their lives did not reduce the incidence of colon cancer. These subjects did not have an African unrefined diet, nor would they tolerate one. Perhaps after a life of refined food, the carcinogenic horse had already left the barn. My own practice experience has confirmed that nearly everyone with chronic constipation, irritable bowel syndrome and diverticulosis will improve when eating what I call a "Thatched Hut Diet" – in honor of our Zululand clinic.

Constipation: a Relative Matter

Medical textbooks commonly define constipation as "a lack of fulfillment following a bowel movement," relegating the problem to the field of the subjective. Indeed some people pass a small, hard rock only once a week and are symptom free in ignorant bliss, while others have an abundant stool several times a day yet feel the world is coming to an end. Nonetheless, if you feel relief immediately after your first stool in three days, you know you have constipation. The old Ayurvedic texts profess that an easy, daily motion, like a good night's sleep and freedom from worry, is the reflection of living in accord with the laws of nature – an expression of suitable diet and exercise, and of synchrony with circadian rhythms.

According to the Ayurvedic texts, constipation is understood to be a disorder of the physiological operating principle governing transport and movement in the body, called *vāta*. More specifically, the impulse for the expulsion of materials outward and downward through the pelvis, called *apāna vāta*, is weak and irregular. *Apāna* means *outward* and creates the driving force for the elimination not only of stool but also of gas, urine, menstrual fluids, semen and babies. Indeed, because the pelvis is the center of so much movement in the body, the ancient texts call it *vāta-sthāna*, the seat or house of vāta, which, like the seat of a government or the house of a family, is the site in which vāta congregates.

Since it governs movement, vāta is likened to wind (and literally means wind) and creates a drying, shifting, cold, rough and brittle influence in the body when it becomes imbalanced, mimicking the effects of aging. In the pelvis, a vata imbalance presents itself as a drying, irregular and weakening effect on elimination. Intestinal motility becomes weak, irregular and sluggish. Since the main function of the colon is to reabsorb water from the stool, thus making elimination much more convenient and preventing dehydration, the prolonged time the stool spends in the colon makes the stool dry and hard, thus stretching the colonic tissues. In surgery I have noticed that the colons of patients with chronic constipation resemble an aging body. The colon becomes irregular, weak, thin-walled, pouched, stretched and dry, including its contents. The normally muscular walls with ample folds appear withered and smooth and are often blackened from use of stimulant laxatives like cascara and senna.

Chronic constipation is usually due to a sluggish colon or to poor emptying,[89] but both result in a vicious cycle of mischief. It may start when your stool becomes pasty and dry, as after a plane trip during which you spend the day sitting, eating starchy foods, getting dehydrated, and missing your chance to eliminate in the morning. As things slow down, your colon fills and stretches. Then, as when you blow up a balloon, the bigger the colon becomes, the easier it stretches. The muscles in the colon's walls lose their mechanical advantage and, over time, they lose their tone and strength. As a slave who is asked to shoulder an excessive burden, the effort only makes her weaker, especially if the taskmaster adds the strain of a whip, a laxative.

Relief from Constipation

This brings us to the value of the Thatched Hut Diet, a diet that mimics what you would eat if you ate only the food that you could grow on your own land, without anyone to refine, process or package the harvest. It is also similar to what the homesteading prairie pioneers must have eaten. This diet contains large amounts of raw fiber from unrefined grains, seeds, legumes and vegetables, which absorb water, functioning like a sponge. This diet also eliminates the cement we add to our usual fare in the form of refined foods. The Thatched Hut Diet breaks the vicious cycle by creating a stool with a high water content, which by definition is softer and more voluminous. Here are the practical points.

1. Avoid constipating foods. Unfortunately, most people, including people with chronic constipation, have no idea what is actually constipating! Most importantly, avoid white flour. Do you remember how you made paste as a kid? White flour and water. A few hours later your paper scraps were fused. This partly explains the high prevalence of constipation in societies that live on this staple. During the eight days of Passover when Jews eat no leavening, taking only matzo made from flour and water, they observe the tradition of eating raisins and prunes as an antidote. The word pasta, pastry and paste in fact derive from the same root; so practice moderation with these and with most kinds of bread, as well as with crackers, pretzels and cookies. Cheese, fowl, tea, potatoes, bananas and white rice can also be constipating. While you are at it, skip nearly everything that is refined, processed or packaged, except raw staples like grains and lentils.

2. Don't forget constipating medications. Ask your doctor if you are on any constipating medications including antihistamines, antacids, tranquilizers, antidepressants, antihypertensives, antispasmodics, narcotics, cough syrups and many others.

3. Go for high fiber foods. Fiber holds water and stimulates the mucous membranes. Instead of white flour, use whole wheat or bulgur wheat, and instead of wheat, substitute barley, rye, oats, brown rice, corn, buckwheat and quinoa (a delicious Andean grain high in protein). Beware of millet, however, which the ancient Ayurvedic texts describe as being potentially constipating.

4. Include nuts and seeds. Take about the amount that fit in your fist. Put them in your cooking such as in stir fry veggies and casseroles (not macaroni and cheese – the ultimate glue) and eat them for snacks. Include sesame seeds, pumpkin seeds, melon and squash seeds, sunflower seeds, etc. Use almonds with the skin instead of blanched. Avoid peanuts, which are not really nuts, but legumes and will just add heaviness and gas to an already uncomfortable situation.

5. Drink plenty of fluids. If you are chronically constipated you may unconsciously suppress thirst, get dehydrated and reabsorb water from your colon. You may need to note the glasses of fluid you drink each day. Black tea, which may be constipating, and coffee, which is diuretic, don't count.

6. Eat abundant amounts of fruit. At least four servings a day. After all, a fruit is a tree's way to trick an animal into eating its seed. The tree packages it in a sweet, enticing, aromatic container containing a good dose of natural fiber and laxatives, which hustle the seed through the animal's digestive system to get deposited a few miles away in a pile of manure. There are more pleasant ways to get your dose than the traditional prune juice. Taking fresh fruit is better nutritionally and more likely to become a permanent habit, in addition to providing both soluble and non-soluble fiber. But avoid fruits that may create gas, including pears, as well as bananas, which are constipating. One traditional Ayurvedic remedy is a handful of fresh grapes or freshly squeezed grape juice at bedtime.

7. Add other sources of fiber. The natural fibers in the Thatched Hut Diet may be all you need. You can also add flax seeds or bran. The best time for fiber supplements is with your meals, added to oatmeal or granola, for example. One of the finest sources is flax seed. Note what happens when you soak a teaspoon of seeds for a few hours: they swell with water and become mucinous. In your GI tract, flax seeds hold water and create lubrication. You can mill flax seeds fresh in your coffee grinder (for an omega-3 bonus) or use them whole. You may also drink the soaked seeds by themselves with some juice.

8. Psyllium seed husks. Psyllium is the treatment of choice if you don't get your desired results from dietary changes alone. Nearly all the psyllium in the world today is grown in India, where the Ayurvedic physicians have long prescribed it. I recommend brands that utilize the unrefined husk and leave out the sweeteners and other unnecessary additives. Add psyllium gradually to the diet, starting with a bare half teaspoon, and take it with juice or water just before the meal. If you start taking fiber too enthusiastically, you may experience bloating or gas and give up. Work up to a good teaspoon or two with each meal.

9. Granola. This can be a remarkable cure, because people actually eat it. Homemade granola provides more useful fiber with fewer calories and fat than the packaged varieties. Use whole oat, rye, barley and almond flakes, bran, flax, and sesame, pumpkin and sunflower seeds. Bake it well because these grains are harder and rougher than wheat. Mix the raw grains with a little warm olive oil or ghee (clarified butter) before baking at 325 degrees, stirring often until it turns a few shades darker. This usually takes about 45 min to 65 minutes. I spoon in some maple syrup as it is cooling. You can then add dried fruits such as raisins and date bits. A bowlful with milk or yogurt is all many people may need to conquer their irregularities.

10. Eat fresh. Reduce your use of canned, frozen, and packaged foods. In addition to making food constipating, processing and preserving removes many vitamins and minerals. When you are shopping, remember the thatched hut.

11. Get plenty of exercise. The best kinds are those that involve some bending to massage the abdominal organs and muscles. Housework is excellent as are yoga postures that involve forward bends. The easiest and most effective is the child pose: Sitting on your heels with your shins on the floor, bend your chest to your knees, hold for 15 seconds and repeat. You can almost feel the squeezing action lending you a hand.

12. Establish your colon's circadian rhythms. Use the gastro-colic reflex. Whenever you eat, nerve and hormone messages are sent by the stomach to the colon, signaling that new inventory has arrived and that room needs to be made by moving out the old. The Ayurvedic texts recommend a glass of warm water in the morning on arising. If you are leaving home early, prepare some warm water with a little salt and lemon juice to take when you awake during the night. Find a regular time, ten to thirty minutes after you awaken, to sit on the toilet non-judgmentally for a minute or two, even if you think nothing will transpire. This is akin to toilet training. Culture this habit for a month or two and your colon will begin to keep time with the drumbeat of dawn.

13. Cultivate good stool habits. Make your visits to the bathroom brief and pay attention to what is going on in your body. Leave *War and Peace* in the den. Don't strain – this is the best prevention for hemorrhoids and fissures.[90]

14. Try squatting. I once noticed that Asian visitors who had been walking barefoot outside left footprints on our toilet seat. They were using the toilet the way nature originally intended. It is not, however, the way the manufacturer intended and can result in a broken toilet. Instead, try putting two large cans or wood blocks about six to eight inches high as footrests on both sides of the bowl. Sit on the toilet regularly with your feet and knees elevated. If this position – which naturally compresses the abdominal contents and tilts the pelvis – seems more efficient, you can purchase a permanent, more elegant footrest that slides behind the bowl and out of the way. [91]

15. Avoid habitual use of laxatives. Use them only to prevent or relieve the most uncomfortable circumstances. Keep in mind that constipation is best managed through prevention. Regular use of senna, castor oil, irritant laxatives, milk of magnesia, cascara and their like can only make the problem worse by interfering with the normal tone of the colon and creating both dependence and tolerance. You will eventually need increasingly bigger doses. If people with healthy elimination find themselves constipated for several days after taking a laxative for a diagnostic test or a therapeutic cleanse, imagine what laxatives are doing to your already feeble, listless colon.

16. Triphala. One fortunate exception to the above advice is the regular use of the Ayurvedic remedy *triphala*. *Phala* means fruit and triphala is a combination of three fruits[92] that have been dried, powdered and usually pressed into tablets. Triphala is traditionally used as an upper digestive aid and as a tonic. It nourishes the skin and eyes and aids weight loss. Its side benefit is gentle laxation. You can take it in the morning or at bedtime. The usual dose is one to eight half-gram tablets. For faster effect, soak your dose in a half-cup of water for a few hours then drink, dregs and all. If you are a regular user of laxatives, don't expect much from triphala until you have implemented the rest of the program above. Triphala can be found at most health food stores.

17. Avoid enemas. They are unnecessary if you properly implement this Ayurvedic program. If, however, hard, impacted stools still develop, it is preferable to use a simple oil retention enema than to take a laxative. The oil will soften and lubricate the hardened stool, making it easier to pass without the disruption in your natural rhythm created by a laxative. The Ayurvedic medical texts recommend sesame oil but olive oil is a reasonable substitute. Avoid mineral oils which are harsh, and do not have the same nourishing effect as sesame oil on the rectal and colonic walls. Discard the contents of a Fleet enema syringe (the best thing someone with chronic constipation can do with these irritating salts) and use the syringe to administer two ounces of lukewarm sesame oil. Lie on your left side for ten minutes to allow the oil to ascend the sigmoid colon and then go about your day (with an optional disposable liner in your underwear in case you forget the oil is there).

One precious side benefit of the Thatched Hut Diet is that in improving elimination, it makes you more active, thus preventing other common serious disorders: heart disease, diabetes, hypertension and obesity. Listen to your body's song, learning to select and enjoy whole, unrefined, fresh ingredients and every aspect of your health will benefit.

---

89 Sluggish bowels and poor emptying both have many causes including other disorders and medications, so a visit to your physician may be in order. A blood test and exam, including a manual rectal exam, to rule out easily treatable causes like hypothyroidiam should be your first step if the problem is significant or new.
90 See Chapter 31: Disorders of the Pelvic Diaphragm.
91 www.naturesplatform.com
92 A mixture of the dried powders of the fruits of amalaki (*Emlica officinalis*), harataki (*Terminalia chebula*) and bibhitaki (*Terminalia belerica*)

CHAPTER 20

STAYING IN SLIM MODE:
A VEDIC WEIGHT LOSS PROGRAM

Insights from an Experienced Physician

I am a 360-pound man in a 180-pound body, give or take ten. I usually look neither fat nor thin. People say I have an athletic build or that I am built like the proverbial brick outhouse. My torso is all over the roof and walls of the Sistine Chapel. My lot is a constant vigil to my natural adiposity. When I was ten in kids' football, I had to wear a round patch on my uniform preventing me from running the ball, for fear of putting would-be tacklers at an unfair disadvantage. Instead, tackling the halfback, I fractured his tibia.

Other chapters of this book have been written with the benefit of my clinical experience and insights from Ayurvedic physicians. This chapter adds the insights of me as the patient. I present my medical history:

Case Study: JG

The patient is a middle-aged physician with a life-long weight problem. Although he descends from two parents who fought with weight issues, the cause of JG's predisposition to avoirdupois, unlike most of his obese patients, is not a cosmic mystery. He simply loves to eat! JG has also been endowed with one of the world's most powerful digestive fires. Sundaes, fries, pizza, even amoebas all tremble at his approach. He can eat lunch from the pushcarts of questionable hawkers on city squares from Tijuana to Calcutta without remorse. He hospitably harbored roundworms from either Nepal or Malawi until they were discovered ten years later in a mandatory licensing exam. When JG was a kid he would eat until he could eat no more, and then jump on a trampoline so he could go back for fifths. Had JG not gained wisdom about obesity and its consequences, his appetite would still welcome the challenge of his former gourmandise. When JG was younger, he could burn off the 7500 calories he consumed in a day with intense physical activity, including not only fidgeting but also training for extreme sports. Those immoderations have left him with several arthritic joints: two knees, a few lumbar discs and two shoulders, so JG's ability to burn calories is now disproportionate to his persistent insatiable appetite.

Conveniently, JG has been endowed with ample bones and large muscles on which to hide an extra veggie curry. His mother struggled to deliver his shoulders after his head was showing. Now, built like an inverted triangle, he can put on an extra fifteen pounds and those wide shoulders still appear to taper to the hips. This means he can buy a size 43 suit off the rack and he still needs to take in the pants. It also means his patients actually still listen to his advice about weight loss that they would not take from a doctor with a similar body-mass index but with the triangle pointed side up. Like most of his patients with weight problems, JG has two modes of functioning: fat mode and Slim Mode. In fat mode he goes about his day with a full stomach, while in Slim Mode he goes about his day with an empty stomach.

Fat mode JG serves himself a nice plate of food at home or, if eating out, he finishes the whole plate the chef dishes him up. He eats a dessert (always chocolate) even after a good meal, makes sure he grabs a snack at every possible occasion (because many of his favorite foods, like chocolate, are best taken as a snack), butters his bread and never discriminates between foods with a high and low energy content – that is, he eats them on a whim, even though he knows they are fattening.

In Slim Mode, JG's eating habits are as described in the rest of this chapter.

In both fat and Slim Modes, JG manages to feel well physically and mentally, doing the same physical activities: surfing, snowboarding, swimming, hockey, hiking and mowing his lawn. However, he feels better and healthier when he is eating lightly, even if he is stretching his pants and has just re-entered Slim Mode.

He also has a strong incentive to stay light: severe post-traumatic arthritis of the left knee from a thirty-year-old sports injury. Rubbing bone on bone, the degeneration of his cartilage causes pain with exercise, but especially if he is heavy. Most miraculously, JG can lose weight when he is in Slim Mode even without exercising, proving beyond a doubt that his weight problem is due to overeating and not due to the traditional scapegoat, "slow metabolism." Unfortunately, in spite of his experience, knowledge and maybe even some wisdom, JG cycles unrepentantly between slim and fat modes. The transition from slim to fat mode invariably begins with an extended trip away from home. Without his scale, with irregular routines, with restaurant food that is not only rich but also unsatisfying, Slim Mode is forgotten.

Fortunately, JG cycles in a controlled fashion, distinguishing him from other fat people. He has recognized the delicate status of a fat man and knows that even when he is sveltely entrenched in Slim Mode he is only one meal away from fat mode and a few months away from being fat. He has also figured out how to minimize the frequency and magnitude of the cycling, shamefully crossing the 200 pound threshold only on rare occasions. This control comprises the basis of this chapter.

Exercise: Write your own case history, noting those factors that are the causes of your weight gain:

1) Your habits

2) Your strengths

3) Your weaknesses

The Roots of Overeating

Obesity, and especially morbid obesity, is confined to humans and their pets. We do not see fat deer because even when a deer is surrounded by abundance, she will not gorge herself beyond her immediate comfort and safety. Ayurveda holds that most cases of obesity and other addictions are due to prajña-aparādha, the mistake of judgment, a universal imbalance common to everyone. Prajña-aparādha is the mistake of being aware only of the diverse, relative, changing aspects of your life and forgetting or neglecting your underlying essence, unity. We see only the manifest parts and are blind to the unmanifest wholeness. It is only natural because what is unmanifest is, by definition, hidden.

The mistake of judgment results in obesity because, untethered from life's greatest source of silence and bliss, the mind may seek fulfillment in unhealthy ways including too much rich food and too much sitting. Normal cravings are disguised because you are separated from the greatest source of satisfaction, the Self, the sweet hum of the cosmic song.

Even worse, the intellect that got you into the problem is unable to extricate you. Knowing that an elevated body-mass index increases your risk of heart disease, diabetes, high blood pressure, arthritis, depression and many other disorders – as well as premature death, not to mention its effect on your general well being – you may intend or decide to lose weight. That decision still does not prevent you from overeating any more than an inveterate smoker can be deterred by the knowledge that smoking causes heart attacks and lung cancer.

Overeating is a recalcitrant and insidious addiction because unlike dependencies on alcohol, barbiturates and cocaine, without food life is impossible. Like a member of the family that you are forced to live with, you have to maintain a permanent rapport with food, and your weight will always be a reflection of the health of that relationship. You can make the definitive decision to never let another drop of alcohol pass your lips. With food, you always find yourself in a precarious dance. Addictive overeaters who do not learn the steps put on weight with the predictability of a chronic recidivist returning to jail.

Exercise:

1) Describe the mistake of judgment in your own words.

2) List the specific imbalances in your life caused by the mistake of judgment using specific feelings: depression, nervousness, frustration, etc. For every feeling you list, describe a behavior that contributes to your weight problem (e.g. when I'm bored I rummage the fridge, when I'm depressed I...).

The Neurophysiology of Addictive Eating

Nearly everyone thinks of heroin dependence and alcoholism as obstinate addictions resistant to therapy, but if you think that overeating is not equally addicting, I have some convincing to do. Unless you deem your weight problem a serious addiction, one with as many if not more negative consequences than the others, you will have a hard time curing it. The main difference between these dependent habits is that food addiction does not land you in the clink. Food, in limited quantity, is a necessity and cannot be legally prohibited.

If you overfeed a lab animal, it will limit the self-administration of pleasure-inducing drugs, for example giving itself smaller doses of a narcotic by pushing a lever. If you starve a lab animal, it will administer itself a lot more of the narcotic than when it is satiated with food. Recent brain imaging studies in obese people show they have brain circuits with fewer receptors for dopamine, the neurotransmitter that is most implicated in the brain's reward-pleasure neural pathways. Without an abundance of these receptors, an obese person may need to eat a lot more, especially of the most rewarding foods, to feel satisfaction. This is an identical pattern seen in drug addictions. These same researchers discovered that overweight people have more activity in the brain's sensory cortex associated with the lips, tongue and mouth than people without weight problems, suggesting that they may derive more of their pleasure in life from eating.[93] In fact, when these same researchers presented food stimuli to normal weight volunteers who had been deprived of food, the entire brain lit up on a PET scan,[94] suggesting that the metabolism of the whole brain increases when these signals are processed, a reflection of a powerful conditioned response. I hardly have to remind you: when a TV commercial shows hot cheese bubbling on a pizza, you head for the kitchen.[95]

Sixty-two percent of averagely overweight, but not obese, women (body-mass index of 27 to 29) use alcohol. But the number goes down to 42% for women with a body-mass index of 40-49, and to only 35% for women with body-mass index of more than 50, the biggest of the big. The fatter the person, the less likely she will be to use illegal drugs and alcohol.[96] Most people who stop tobacco, or almost any other drug, will gain weight. Heroin addicts are typically thin because they only eat enough to live so they can shoot drugs.

Not only is the brain cortex assigned to the mouth more metabolically active in obese people, but it is also bigger.[97] Functional MRI (magnetic resonance scans) have shown that obese people have an altered response to the ingestion of glucose, permitting them to eat longer, and therefore probably more food than people of normal weight before getting the message that they've already eaten to their heart's content.

The final proof that overeating is an addiction lies in its therapies: the most useful drugs supply the neurotransmitters to create satiation without the calories.

Silbutramine (Meridia) works like anti-depressants to keep higher levels of the neurotransmitters serotonin and norepinephrine in the synapse. Dexamphetamine, like adrenalin, stimulates catecholamine receptors.

The Myth of Diet Resistance

When taking a history from a person with a weight problem, I innocently ask, "Why do you tend to gain weight?" The most common answer is "I can't understand it, I just look at food and I gain weight. Just ask my husband; he'll tell you I eat almost nothing. He eats twice as much as I and he's skinny but I can't lose a pound. I must have slow metabolism." Some people honestly answer, "I just eat too much." Some say, "I eat due to stress (or when I'm depressed)." A rare few will say, "I never get any exercise." If a patient cannot come up with a reason, I present the possibilities: "slow metabolism, simply eating too much, stress, sedentary lifestyle," the usual response after surprise and a short reflection is, "All of the above." Most patients recognize that there are many factors involved in their weight problem.

My credibility with patients who professed they could never lose weight despite sticking to diets was dramatically improved with the publication of an important clinical study in 1992. The study was performed under exacting conditions and published in the highly reputable New England Journal of Medicine.[98] The authors compared a group of overweight people, who said they were resistant to all diets and could never lose weight, with a group of overweight people who said they were able to lose weight on a good diet and exercise program, but had always ended up putting the weight back on. The researchers carefully monitored the caloric intake and energy expenditure for two weeks. The group resistant to diet over-reported their exercise by an average of 51 percent and under-reported their caloric intake by 47 percent! The resistant dieters were not pathological liars. Rather, they perceived a genetic cause for their plight. They were likely to use thyroid supplements even though their thyroids were all normal, and they described their eating behavior as normal.

People who swear they cannot lose weight despite exercising and eating almost nothing seem to be defying the laws of physics, and indeed, permanent weight loss is simply a matter of physics. Staying in Slim Mode, a Vedic approach to weight loss, makes living within these immutable laws natural and comfortable, permitting a person to effortlessly restrict total energy intake to the point where weight is lost. After prescribing this program to patients for twenty years, I have concluded that it works because it allows chronic overeaters to make a permanent lifestyle of enjoying eating, even while eating less than they thought they could.

An impressive diagram from the fifties portrayed a man next to his yearly food consumption: two cows, a pig, a lamb, several crates of chickens, twenty cartons of eggs, five barrels of milk, eight fifty-pound sacks of flour, seeming mountains of produce, two fifty-pound sacks of sugar, etc. All this food flows through us yet we somehow miraculously maintain our weight within narrow limits (albeit excessively high limits). This is due to metabolic, thermoregulatory and appetite centers in the brain, gut and endocrine organs that conspire to get us through periods of famine and cold winters and that minimize wild weight changes that could jeopardize health. Staying in Slim Mode is about learning to use these regulatory responses to our advantage.

Exercise:

Write down the reasons why you feel you are resistant to diets. Include the factors that make you feel you plateau on diets. List all the different diets you have tried and whether they initially helped. Then write down why they ultimately failed.

The Choice of Freedom or Bondage: Food as Addiction

Ayurveda is about choices, freedom, and living consciously and not about dogma, restrictions, or unconscious habits and behavior. If you adopt this Ayurvedic attitude for your weight problem,[99] it can become a path to liberation from the binding influence of ingrained responses to your senses, intellect, mind and emotions – in a word, enlightenment.

One of the underlying principles of Vedic life is the principle of karma, i.e. we reap what we sow, and the situations are rare where we experience this so directly as in our relationship with food. There is always a simple explanation underlying every case of overweight that comes down to a matter of accounting: excess revenue (calories) compared to energy expensed.

The most common excuse I hear from people with little success losing weight is that they perceive that losing weight involves a loss of freedom, but when we examine their lives, we see that in reality they have lost even more freedoms. They have lost the freedom to choose what they do: what sports they can participate in, what car they drive, what clothes they wear as well as freedom from self-consciousness, guilt and health risks. They tell me that losing weight is like being in prison and involves intolerable sacrifice. Yet when we discuss their lives, they admit they have sacrificed the most precious parts of life. Since this same issue is involved in any addiction, we need to discuss the idea of sacrifice.

Exercise:

Write down what you are willing to sacrifice to lose weight.

Yajña: the Offering of Life

A sacrifice means giving something up with the intention of gaining something more. The Vedic word for this is yajña. Yajña means action, but in a different sense than the action involved in the Sanskrit root KR that gives us words such as create or karma. In yajña, the action is supportive to life and evolutionary, leading to more well being as well as more power, influence, prosperity and health. Yajña therefore means action with the intent of gaining something in return. Marriage is an example of a sacrifice: you give up a degree of freedom to gain something more in return. Every child born thereafter represents the loss of another degree of freedom but you welcome the sacrifice because it gains you a greater joy.

Yajña has a more specific meaning as well: the precise Vedic sacrificial procedures designed to create a desired influence – the ones Jagu was learning to perform. He was learning to recite the specific verses with the proper intonation, pronunciation and rhythm. In fact, the entire Yajur Veda is devoted to yajña, hence its name.

Every yajña requires a clearly defined and outwardly vocalized intention (*sankalpa*), the goal the sacrificer is seeking in giving up something of value. It then involves preparing offerings and cooking or burning them on agni,[100] the sacrificial fire, the offerings themselves being ghee (clarified butter), cakes, rice etc.

We use the same term agni to signify the digestive fire. The process of eating is a deliberate sacrifice to this fire: we give up the cake in order to gain pleasure, energy, nourishment, and satisfaction. The proverbial "You can't have your cake and eat it, too." Eating is regarded therefore, in the Vedic perspective as a holy sacrifice. We offer food to the digestive fire and the preparation and cooking is an integral part of this sacrifice. In the expression, "the body is a temple," the digestive fire is the sacrificial altar in the inner sanctum.[101] We invoke this concept by saying grace before a meal.

Eating as a Sacred Act

Our irreverent attitude to the sacredness of eating is reflected in North American and European food habits including eating in the car, on the go, in the movies and on the job. Somehow we have lost the sacred approach to the ritual of eating and this may underlie other factors involved in the modern epidemic of obesity. While food is more abundant and our lives have become more sedentary, the primary issue is that the art of eating has become unconscious, mundane and profane.

Public health officials, pediatricians, educators, parents and even fat children are blaming the food industry for the epidemic of childhood obesity, to the point that a teenager sued her favorite fast food chain. The problem is not what children eat but how they eat it. If they unconsciously eat vegetables, rice and fish for their school lunch they will get just as fat as eating pizza with fries and soda, because they will not be obeying their brain's message telling them when they are full.

Ultimately, approaching eating as a holy act creates the biggest improvement in health when it is the by-product of bringing the sacred into our lives. I have seen pious people who never learned this, including priests and nuns, who take the wafer during Holy Communion with great reverence and then feast to the point of indigestion afterward. Vedic science describes all of life as yajña, a Holy Communion, to be lived with awareness and awe. Proper diet, exercise, rest and relationships are parts of that yajña.

Exercises:

1) Clearly define and vocalize your intention regarding your weight, and what you are willing to give up to attain it.

2) Say grace at your next meal as if for the first time in your life.

Staying in Slim Mode: Freedom through Fulfillment

The Ayurvedic approach used in Staying in Slim Mode is intended to:

1. Allow complete satisfaction from the diet.

2. Restore the sacred element to the act of eating.

3. Give you total freedom so you do not feel imprisoned in choices about food.

4. Guide you to lifelong habits that encourage maintenance of proper weight.

Let's start by analyzing appetite and the desire to eat (the two are not always the same thing!) from both the Ayurvedic and western points of view. This involves understanding the nature of the gastric and metabolic fires.[102]

The Sacred Fires

Most overweight people would be surprised to hear that a healthy appetite is one of the Ayurvedic criteria of good health. When I ask every patient, "How is your digestion?" invariably overweight people jokingly respond, "Too good!" Although they may wish they were incapable of eating anything and everything, their lot is better than underweight people with chronic digestive problems.[103] Sushruta Samhitā describes a number of agnis in the body. We will discuss how three of these must be satisfied to normalize weight and digestion.

I. The Digestive Fire (Pachaka-agni)

The first fire is the main agni, the gastric fire, commonly called pachaka-agni.[104] Pachaka can be translated the cooking fire and is derived from the Sanskrit root PAK meaning to cook. It resides in the stomach and small intestine but also includes salivation and esophageal function. Agni by nature is sharp and a proper digestive fire should be sharp. When Ayurvedic texts refer to the digestive fire, the authors of antiquity meant the physiological functions that literally burn or oxidize the food or otherwise break it down to prepare it for absorption and subsequent oxidation. Agni thus includes hydrochloric acid, biliary juices, bile acids, alkali, and enzymes.

There are three disorders of this fire: too weak (mandagni) associated with sluggish digestion; too sharp (tikshnagni) associated with too much acidity, creating burning and dyspepsia; and irregular (vishamagni) which is erratic. The sharpness of this fire is also associated with the appetite, hence our English expression, "she has a sharp appetite." Agni's sharpness should be pacified by your meal, creating a feeling of satisfaction in your stomach. Chronic overeaters will feel fullness even before the stomach has been stretched to many times its size by liters of food but there still may be no satisfaction. Scientific research has documented the important role of the stomach's stretch receptors in arresting the desire to eat. Stretch receptors in the walls of the stomach bring pleasing sensations when food fills and expands the stomach's hollow. This response is so potent that it is the basis for the most effective therapy for treating gross obesity, stapling the stomach to create a small pouch that gets stretched with a small meal, arresting the appetite.

Exercise:

Describe on paper your digestive fire, its quirks and foibles, strengths and weaknesses.

II. The Integrative Fire (Sādhaka agni) and the Desire to Eat

The second fire that must be satisfied is the *integrative fire* located in the region of the heart and diaphragm. This fire is the one that digests not the physical nutrients, but the more subtle qualities you ingest with your meal: its tastes, its aromas, its textures, its appearance, the sound it makes when it is cooking or being chewed, the ambience of the dining table including the moods of your companions, your conversations and the thoughts they invoke, the memories that arise due to the food and the surroundings, your feelings (including toward your cook) and sense of self.

For a chronic overeater, fulfillment of sādhaka agni is more important than satisfying the digestive fire, which often will not be satisfied by mounds of tasty, nutritious food. Vedic dining involves creating an atmosphere in the procuring, cooking and eating of a meal to satisfy the senses, mind and emotions. This happens by adopting the attitude that the meal is an offering.

One of the other important causes of chronic weight problems is found in the sense of self, one of the experiences that needs to be digested by the integrative fire. If a person has a fear of loss, a low sense of self worth and an ingrained fear of poverty, he may be overeating for fear of lacking in the future. You can even overeat despite a good sense of self, but with guilt about our abundance inculcated by admonitions such as "Eat your whole plate; think of the starving children in China." It turns out that in China it is customary to leave food on the plate out of politeness. The Vedic tradition of offering an abundant banquet at a wedding comes from the observation that a festive meal is the one thing you can offer to a person of any stature and make them satisfied.

Your integrative fire is responsible for processing your thoughts, emotions, and sensory impressions in a way that creates fulfillment. Traditionally it can be strengthened through gaining serenity, practicing yoga and meditation, gaining insight and wisdom into your own nature, experiencing unconditional love and culturing your emotions through greater acceptance.

Exercise:

1) Describe on paper your integrative fire. Is it strong by nature? What makes it weak?

2) How does leaving food on your plate or in the serving bowl make you feel? How can you work with your existing values (e.g. waste not, want not) to get over your tendency to not stop eating, despite feeling full, when there is still food to be eaten?

III. The Metabolic Fires (Dhātu-agni)

Our physical body and consciousness are the expressions of a pervasive reservoir of pure intelligence. We see this Vedic concept reflected in the emergence of differentiated cells from primordial stem cells. Modern biology understands that the fluids filling and bathing our cells provide nutrients for the cells' function, proliferation and differentiation. Ultimately, new cell growth comes from nutrients in these fluids. The ancient Ayurvedic treatises describe the same processes. Sap or plasma (rasa) provides the nutritional matrix for the other more refined tissues, nourishing them and providing the milieu in which they can thrive.

Tissues (dhātu – from the root DHA – meaning a foundation) are created through the action of catalysts that convert one tissue to another, starting with sap. Progressively refined tissues are created from their grosser precursors. The catalyst for this is another type of sacred fire, the metabolic fire (dhātu-agni). Modern biochemistry has described in detail how this ancient description of the metabolic fires functions within every cell to transform sugars to proteins, fats, starches – and the reverse.

Like the colorless sap of a flower which is transformed into all its colorful and varied parts – plasma is the substrate for the multiple tissues of the body.[105] Grosser tissues are converted progressively into refined tissues including bone marrow, semen or ovum and fat. Yes, you heard that right! Fat is considered refined and valuable! Fat is a necessary precursor for precious immune, blood-forming and reproductive tissue and brings lubrication, unctuousness, suppleness and flexibility to the body. It counters the drying, rough, brittle influence of aging.

Āma – Residues of Inefficient Digestion

Despite our best intentions, we fail to eat moderately of pure, nourishing fare. We eat too much, too heavily, too late, when we are still digesting a previous meal or when we are anxious, upset or rushed. The result is a weak or irregular agni and inefficient digestion with the creation of undigested residues, āma. (See Chapter 16) Āma is the predictable result of failing to properly maintain your digestive fire.

Āma, according to the scriptures, can lodge in the metabolic fires that convert one tissue to another. If āma lodges in the fire that converts fat into finer tissues, a poor quality of fat will accumulate, blocking proper lubrication of the tissues.

Just as a strong state government is critical to a strong federal government, a strong central digestive fire in the stomach is critical for strong metabolic fires in the peripheral tissues.

Exercise:

Close the eyes and allow your awareness to be in the body, listen to your body's ancient song. Note whether you feel heaviness, dullness, irritation or weakness in any areas. Could this be āma?

The Governor of the Sacred Fires (Prāna)

In addition to the belly and the heart, the other site requiring satisfaction to correct chronic overeating is in the head. There is a vital connection between the integrative fire in the heart and the seat of the senses (indriyas), mind (manas) and intellect (buddhi), called prāna. Prāna (also called prānavata) is involved with communication and movement within the nervous system, as well as between the brain and the seat of the breath in the chest.

Prāna functions as the wind that fans the flame of the integrative fire, which is seated in the heart. Without prāna, the integrative fire has no experiences to digest. Prāna must properly present the individual elements of the eater's experience to the integrative fire to allow the integrative fire to create a greater whole from the parts: fulfillment. Let us look at the functions of prāna individually: senses, mind and intellect.

Exercise:

Write down your perception of the relationship between your own mind, intellect and senses with respect to your enjoyment of food. When your nose smells pizza, can you do without and still feel happy?

The Role of the Senses in Creating Fulfillment.

The five senses (indriyas) are the gateways for satisfaction of our most basic needs: food and shelter. If taste and smell in particular are not functioning normally, it is difficult to feel satisfaction from food. Patients who suffer the total loss of taste and smell, the all-too-common complication of a severe head cold, have told me that they subsequently lost interest in food and need to force themselves to eat. They have to select their meal using their common sense because they no longer have cravings and say, "Everything tastes like cardboard." I was perplexed that rather than losing, they actually gained weight. Finally, I realized these patients tend to eat beyond the point where someone with intact senses would have stopped. Our senses, like our bellies, get full. A wise person will overcome chronic overeating by learning to satisfy the senses in a not-fattening way.

The Role of the Mind and Intellect in Creating Fulfillment

Since the function of your mind is to think thoughts, in order to eat modestly, your mind must always think the food you are about to eat looks potentially satisfying. Similarly, the function of your intellect is to discriminate and decide. Your intellect must first decide that the food is nutritious, tasty and worth eating and later decide when you have had enough. Once you have eaten, these thoughts, sensations and decisions – together with a flood of hormones, peptides and neurotransmitters coming from your now well-fed digestive organs and hypothalamus – are cooked by your integrative fire into an experience of fulfillment. Only then will you stop eating.

If an overeater makes a habit of pushing away from the table on an intellectual basis but without any fulfillment from the meal, his weight loss will be either temporary or may lead to other disorders such as anorexia nervosa or nutritional deficiency. The Ayurvedic approach to every aspect of health involves cultivating the ability to trust your feelings, intuition and cravings – your natural desires. This is the only way a person can maintain a normal weight without feeling imprisoned. The push away from the table should come from the heart feeling happy and not from the intellect enforcing rules. The latest US Dietary Guidelines, despite all their do's and don'ts, never mention that your food should actually be delicious and pleasing! Could this actually be the key issue in our race to become the world's most poorly nourished country?

A study by Swedish and Thai researchers in the 1970's looked at the difference in nutrient absorption in a traditional Thai meal of rice and vegetables laced with fish sauce, coconut milk and chili sauce. Thai women absorbed 50 percent more of the iron in the dish than Swedish men who were reported to have "liked the meal" up to a point, "but considered it very spicy." The same meal was then blended and fed to the Thai women, who absorbed 70 percent less iron from the same meal, that to them was now an unfamiliar and disgusting slop. Tasty food, finely presented, is more satisfying. A person living alone who never bothers to cook herself a fabulous meal, garnish it artistically, set the table and the mood with candles and flowers like in a good restaurant, will always be condemned to eating more calories to achieve the same level of satisfaction.

Several centers in the brain dealing with satiety (the satisfaction response that arrests the craving to eat or drink) are influenced by how you feel about things, especially your meal. The most important centers are in the hypothalamus, a neural and hormonal center at the base of the brain that regulates many autonomic functions, where cravings for hunger and thirst are intimately coordinated with neural and hormonal centers controlling libido, thermal regulation, and other critical physiological functions. The hypothalamus is hardwired through nerve and endocrine pathways to brain structures that regulate moods, explaining how anxiety, depression and grief affect our appetite. We may never intellectually understand the complex cascade of elements that creates well-being and fulfillment. But you can be conscious of the integrative fire and the prāna that governs it to master being satisfied with less.

The Role of Exercise for Staying in Slim Mode

Everyone has a Slim Mode, even people with metabolic problems. You just have to find the point at which the kilos start coming off. Most chronic overeaters with a sedentary lifestyle are surprised at how little food that actually is. Like someone with a successful gastric bypass, they may even feel that their life has become a permanent fast. This perception is all relative. To a reasonable eater, a 600-calorie supper may look like a banquet and to a chronic overeater, it looks like the appetizer. One of the most important roles of exercise is to make Slim Mode less austere by changing the point at which your caloric balance sheet runs from the red into the black.

In Chapter 13 we examined the primary role of exercise in creating exhilaration in mind and body, and saw that exercise was as effective as antidepressants in dealing with melancholy. With exercise, you are less likely to overeat. Although exercise may make you put on a pound or two of firm muscle, you will look and feel better.

How to start losing weight

First, prepare the mind

1. Create an intention (sankalpa). With weight loss, unlike some addictions where it is best to quit cold turkey, it is not necessary to set a start date. It is only necessary to start to create an intention. Avoid making that intention, "I intend to lose weight." Just think, "I am going to put myself in Slim Mode." Weight loss is the by-product of staying in Slim Mode.

2. The Gut Check. Learn a simple technique for testing your hunger before eating. I call this the "Gut Check." All three satisfaction centers crave to be satiated. Listen to your body's song, bringing the awareness to each center individually: **1)** the seat of the digestive fire in the stomach; **2)** the seat of the integrative fire in the heart; **3)** the seat of prāna, which governs movement of the senses, mind and intellect with the vital breath and which is located in the head and respiratory tract. If possible, take a moment to close the eyes and allow the awareness to project to these sites for a few seconds each. Start with the gut: project your attention and your awareness innocently to the stomach area. Check to see whether there is fullness or emptiness, whether there is a true gnawing hunger caused by a void or whether your hunger is false. In the heart, check to see if there is emptiness caused by the emotions. Maybe you are just feeling blue, angry, frustrated or unfulfilled. Note your mood. Move to the head. Check to see if your desire for food is due to deprivation of the senses, or an imbalance in your mind or emotions.

3. Understand your hunger and cravings. Learn to decipher the messages you receive from your body, mind and heart. After the gut-check, decide if you are truly hungry, or if you just want food to satisfy the emotions, senses, and mind or to ward off boredom.

4. Discover non-fattening ways to be satisfied. Keep all three satisfaction centers satiated. The only one that needs physical food is your stomach's fire. The others require a different type of nourishment. Try sipping hot water to ferret out false from true hunger.

5. Learn to enjoy being empty. Staying in Slim Mode is a spiritual path as well as a simple way to lose weight. This program is a means to gain liberation over an aspect of our life that was dictating limitations. Slim Mode is a mode of functioning in which you perform best physically, mentally and spiritually.

Here is what the 14th century Sufi mystic, Rumi, said about lightness in the belly:

There's hidden sweetness in the stomach's emptiness. We are lutes, no more no less. If the sound box is stuffed full of anything, no music. If the brain and the belly are burning clean with fasting, every moment a new song comes out of the fire. The fog clears, and a new energy makes you run up the steps in front of you. Be emptier and cry like reed instruments cry. Emptier, write secrets with the reed pen. When you're full of food and drink, an ugly metal statue sits where your spirit should. When you fast, good habits gather like friends who want to help. Fasting is Solomon's ring. Don't give in to illusion and lose your powers, but even if you have, if you've lost all will and control, they come back when you fast, like soldiers appearing out of the ground, pendants flying above them. A table descends to your tents, Jesus' table. Expect to see it, when you fast, this table spread with other food, better than the broth of cabbages.[106]

Exercises:

1) Take a very light diet or even a liquid fast for a day, if it is comfortable.

2) Write down all the ways you feel well-being while your stomach is empty. Post it so you can re-read it frequently.

Second, arm yourselves with tools you will need

1. Get a scale. It does not matter if the scale is accurate because you do not have a target weight. The scale is to measure changes in your relative weight. Your weight will end up being the weight at which you feel best and which is do-able with the amount of exercise you can comfortably incorporate into your day.

2. Weigh yourself to get started. Do not write it down or keep a diary. You will not forget where you started and where you are going.

3. Weigh yourself regularly in a non-judgmental fashion. Weigh in the morning, after elimination, in the same way. The only purpose of weighing is to see whether you are in Slim Mode. In Slim Mode, you will lose 1/4 pound every few days. At the end of a week you will have lost 1/4 to 3/4 of a pound. If you see that you have gained over the last week, you may need to reconsider what it means to be in Slim Mode. (You may be like the people in the study above who underestimated how much they were actually eating). Do not forget that even in Slim Mode, you can gain weight. Fluid retention caused by extra salt, elevated progesterone levels during the last week of the menstrual cycle, nonsteroidal anti-inflammatory drugs like ibuprofen or other medications, or extra fluid intake can add weight without gaining fat. You can also gain muscle mass if you increase your exercise level, and thus gain weight even though you are losing fat. The idea of weighing is not to see how close you are to your goal. Keep in mind the purpose of the daily weighing: a verification and correction of our concept of what it takes for you to be in Slim Mode, nothing more. If you see that you have gained weight the day before, think about your day and the meals and snacks you ate. If you stay the same after one week, this simply means that you are not yet in Slim Mode. If you gained weight during the previous week, this likely means you are still in fat mode. This is why you need to be nonjudgmental during the daily weighing. If you still are judgmental, hold a heavy rock with unknown mass in your hands as you weigh yourself, thus rendering the reading relative.

4. Learn how to cook quickly the things you love most. See Chapter 21. This might include a fresh 3-minute soup, 10-minute stir-fry or steamed vegetables, a 3-minute salad, a protein dish such as lentil soup, or broiled fowl or fish.

5. Organize your life to eat a light supper.

6. Contact the source of true fulfillment. See Chapter Eight. Practice prayer, meditation, prānayāma, yoga, and the exercise for awareness in the body. These make the mind and body more attuned, and the mind more likely to sense your body's needs. Research demonstrated that Transcendental Meditation normalized weight in several hundred people instructed in the practice who did not expect weight loss to be a benefit of the practice.[107]

Exercise:

List the dishes you can realistically cook for yourself to make nutritious meals that will make you satisfied over the long haul.

Third, learn how to eat consciously.

1. Learn how to enjoy your food. "What?" you say, "I already enjoy food too much!" In reality, if you are a chronic overeater like me, you do not enjoy your food enough, and that is why it takes so much of it to satisfy you. When you truly learn to eat, even one bite can satisfy you. I am an inveterate lover of fine dark chocolate. However, I can eat chocolate and still maintain my weight – eating one square with total involvement. One piece of Swiss or Belgian dark bittersweet chocolate with 86% cocoa content, containing 25 calories, eaten slowly gives me more satisfaction than a whole candy bar. Suppose you do the Gut Check and decide you are not hungry enough for a meal. Your heart, mind and senses simply want a piece of chocolate. I am going to teach you how to eat chocolate or any other food for which you have a yen.

2. Eat with all your faculties awake. Take the square of chocolate and put it on a plate. Sit by yourself without any distractions. Take a moment of silence; bless the food, as you would a meal. Use you eyes. Check out the sheen – maybe a confectioner made a design in it you had never appreciated before. Enjoy the roasted aroma. Cut it into 6 to 8 pieces. Put the first piece in your mouth. Notice the texture as you bite into it or feel it melt, move it around your palate. Eat it as if it were the first time you ever tasted chocolate – without any expectations. Or savor it like it might be your last. Notice the tastes (*rasas*) and aftertastes (*uparasas*) and how they blend. It may take you 5 minutes to eat that one square of chocolate but you just saved yourself 25 minutes because the alternative, the 200-calorie candy bar, would take a half hour of sweating to burn. When you finish, your emotions and perceptions should be pacified and your boredom eased (don't forget – you really were not hungry, malnourished or lacking energy, you just wanted a snack and only chocolate would do). The hankering rarely comes back soon when you have given yourself what you really craved – the experience of chocolate for entertainment.

As long as you keep listening to your body's refrain, you can eat a little of anything you desire. Slim Mode is about moderation, not deprivation. You will also discover that many foods you thought you liked just don't do it for you. Remember which and you are done with those cravings for good. Use this technique of conscious eating even when you crave low calorie foods such as a fresh papaya or minestrone, and you will find you become satisfied with increasingly less. Most importantly, use this technique not just when eating a snack but especially a whole meal.

3. Cultivate a refined palate. Learn about the different ingredients in food and practice detecting them as you eat. If it is a soup, try to determine if the cook added sautéed onions or garlic; taste for turmeric, cumin, nutmeg or fine herbs. If it's a salad, eat each leaf separately and note if it is iceberg, spinach or arugala. Discriminate between foods that are steamed, stir-fried, leftover, frozen and canned and notice the pleasure value that comes with eating the freshest foods prepared with care.

4. Avoid distractions. The Vedic approach to eating consciously is identical to the Vedic approach to doing everything else in life: one thing at a time. Avoiding eating with the television, newspaper or a book, like I used to do. When the news was over, so was my meal, and I hardly remembered eating it. My belly was full, but my senses, mind, intellect and heart had not even begun to feast. You can play calming music softly in the background (especially Samaveda)[108], but not if it will distract you from your meal. Similarly, conversation should be lighthearted and pleasant. As you first start this program, occasionally try to culture the habit of eating consciously by eating the Vedic way – in silence.

5. Always sit when eating. This helps you eat consciously and slowly in order to savor your food. Even if you just grabbed a few raisins out of the cupboard as you walked by, put them on a plate, sit down, check your three satisfaction centers, and then eat them one by one, consciously, joyfully. A good part of North America eats lunch standing by a lunch wagon or crossing the street with a hot dog or burrito, while European bistros are generally completely lacking seats at all, a ploy to get their patrons to eat quickly and move on, making room for more customers. Worse, the workers who sit for lunch are often working at their desk or driving their car.

6. Eat slowly and chew well. Put your fork down between bites. You are trying to satisfy the integrative fires and this cannot be rushed. The thousands of people who present themselves in the emergency room every year with chicken and fish bones stuck in the esophagus are not even chewing. The Heimlich maneuver is only necessary for people who are in fat mode, eating unconsciously.

Exercise:
Take a small amount of something you love to eat and eat it as I eat chocolate.

Fourth, allow conscious eating to affect your intake: less is more.

1. Check your satisfaction centers. Before every meal verify that you are hungry in your gut, heart and head. If you are hungry in your gut, eat consciously until the hunger is gone. If you are not hungry, you do not need to eat.

2. Organize your mealtimes. The goal is to satisfy your natural hunger with the least total energy intake. If your daily routine requires you to eat a meal before your natural mealtime, consider putting the meal off until you are truly hungry.

3. Eat until you feel 2/3 full. You should leave the table feeling light but satisfied, not full. The proper amount of food in the stomach leaves space for digestion.

4. Start with a small first serving. Later you can always take a little more. The traditional amount to eat for most people is the amount that fits in your two hands cupped together to make a bowl.

Exercise:
Find a bowl that is about the same size of your two cupped hands and fill it with your dinner, not heaped too high. Put the meal on a plate so you can visualize how your properly served plate should look. Take a photo of your plate and put it on your refrigerator door. Serve your plate thereafter to look like that picture.

5. Don't eat after supper. You can sip beverages, but stop taking food. For many, this will cut out a third of their daily energy intake.

6. Repeat your Gut Check. You never have to eat what is still on your plate. In fact, one key to permanent weight loss is the ability to not feel guilty about wasting food. The chef's assistant who dished up your meal didn't know you are watching your weight. If you still feel hungry and not yet 2/3 full, wait a few minutes. You will be surprised how often hunger at the end of a proper meal will resolve after a few minutes. If, in spite of your wait, you are convinced that you are truly hungry, take a bit more. Avoid repeating this process ad infinitum. Limit yourself to a small second portion. Ask yourself why the first serving was not satisfying. One of the six tastes (rasas) may not have been satisfied. Take the small second portion with a twist of lemon, some extra salt or spice. Add a spoonful of a spicy chutney, salsa or pickle.

7. Be discriminating. In this Vedic weight loss program, you can eat what you like, but it will only lead to permanent weight loss if you consume fewer calories. You are not a receptacle for food that would otherwise be wasted. Wasting food is a hard habit to break if, as a child, you were expected to polish off every scrap.

8. See the glass as half empty. This is just the way you want it. When you leave the table and go about your day, notice how good it feels to have a light stomach. You should feel this lightness even though you are still hefty. Compare this feeling with the way you felt in fat mode: bloated, slow and lethargic. The difference in these two ways of feeling is one of the main incentives for maintaining Slim Mode. The feeling of lightness is true well-being and is the main reason to follow the Vedic weight loss program. Staying slim is the by-product.

Fifth, and lastly, put attention on what to eat.
(Lastly because it is the least critical factor)

1. Eat what you naturally like. Any other advice is doomed to failure because it will never give you a dietary program that you can follow for the rest of your life. Staying in Slim Mode considers weight loss lasting less than 3-5 years to be temporary, a failure. If you decide that you naturally need fettuccine Alfredo, unless you plan to take up long distance running, to stay in Slim Mode you can only eat small quantities. A chronic overeater who naturally likes soup, salad and cooked vegetables will be more satisfied with the feeling in her belly after a meal than the lover of fettuccini Alfredo because she can eat nearly to her heart's content. (Do you remember the integrative fire located in the heart?)

2. Learn what you naturally like. "Eat what you naturally like" means not eating the foods that you take out of habit, comfort, stress or convenience or even because you think or have been told they are good for you. "What you naturally like" does not include foods that most intelligent adolescents and adults find distasteful on their first taste and for which you eventually cultivate a taste, like beer.

3. Keep your dietary limitations minimal. If you can lose weight you will have done the biggest favor for your overall health. The key to weight loss is satisfaction, and you are learning to effortlessly sacrifice one of the biggest sources of satisfaction: calories. You can therefore forget almost all the other advice dispensed with other restrictive diets. This is not a time to be on restrictive diets such as macrobiotics, yeast-free diets and the like.

4. Favor a light diet. If the body is heavy it is helped by its opposite quality: lightness. Assuming you like them, your choices should emphasize fresh vegetables, salads, fruits, legumes and bitter grains. Bitter grains happen to be the ones with the lowest glycemic index, the measure of how long it takes a food to turn into sugar in the blood. The fastest foods to appear in the blood, besides sugar itself, are grains with little fiber and lots of starch such as puffed rice or white bread. The slowest, those with the lowest glycemic index, are the bitter, rough grains that Ayurveda traditionally promotes for creating lightness: barley, millet, buckwheat, quinoa, amaranth and rye. While these grains are not sweet like wheat or rice, they happen to be among the tastiest. Because of their high fiber content, they may take longer to cook, but no more time on your part if you plan ahead. These grains are much more nutritional than wheat or rice, leaving out the calories and providing fiber, essential amino acids and fatty acids. See Chapter 26.

5. Restrict carbs to reduce your fats. A light diet restricting the major source of calories, the carbohydrates and fats, is ideal for the person wishing to stay in Slim Mode. Foods that promote energy storage as fat include bread, pasta, potatoes, pastry, bananas, corn crackers, pretzels, bagels and rice. Avoiding starches eliminates the most important source of calories in the diet. Since every gram of carbohydrate contains 5 calories, most North Americans consume a good half of their daily energy in the form of starches. Even worse, we have devised ingenious ways to prepare these starches that incorporate plenty of fat, bearing 9 calories per gram, such as French fries, buttered popcorn, muffins and other pastries, bagels with cream cheese, bread with butter or peanut butter, etc. Carbohydrate avoidance is the easiest way to reduce total calories. A study of 53 women randomized either to eat ad lib from either a very low carbohydrate diet or to eat an equivalent number of calories from a low fat diet showed that the women on the low carbohydrate diet lost more weight after 6 months (19 vs. 9 lbs). Neither group had any measurable ill effects.[109] While many weight loss programs say simply, "a calorie is a calorie," leaving out the starches makes it much easier to restrict your calories to the point where you lose weight over an extended period.

6. Keep your dietary plan simple. Many people equate Ayurveda with the three doshas and rigidly follow a diet to pacify kapha. Staying in Slim Mode is a plan based on the essence of Vedic medicine, effortlessly creating fulfillment.[110]

7. Handle cravings without food. Use non-dietary means to deal with imbalances in your nervous system. Try structured daily routines, meditation, yoga, prānayāma, exercise, music, and removal of stressful influences.[111]

8. Choose nutrients over calories. Select a diet you enjoy that is rich in nutrients and low in energy. This is not a contradiction of terms. In our affluent society calories are not the issue. We need to restrict energy-rich foods and take foods that supply small molecules and minerals that our bodies cannot manufacture: anti-oxidants, vitamins, essential fatty acids and amino acids, co-enzymes and trace elements. These nutrients are best taken as food – and not as manufactured supplements without the dietary cofactors which help them to be assimilated. The proper symphony of nutrients can be called "biological intelligence," distinguishing these nutrients from starch and simple sugars. One of the few ingredients starches supply is fiber, but fiber can be found in many other foods without the calories.

9. Emphasize fresh produce. Fresh fruit and vegetables should be the base of your food pyramid. Your ideal staples are cooked vegetables, salads, soups and fresh fruits. Your pyramid should have a few well-selected starches and fats at the peak.

10. Don't skimp on critical nutrients. Include dal soup (lentils, split peas, and cooked mung beans) and other legumes. Also, include dairy with its important nutrients (vitamin B12, fatty acids and calcium). The tastiest way to take dairy without a lot of calories is in milk (1% or skim) and lassi (yogurt mixed with water about 1:4, with a touch of salt and cumin. See Recipes.) Many overeaters have a craving for cheese. Use feta, low-fat mozzarella, low-fat soft cheeses, Middle Eastern string cheeses, ricotta cheese, cottage cheese and low-fat goat cheeses. Non-vegetarians can include lean cuts of broiled, baked or grilled fowl and fish (both without the skin).

11. Use fats to your advantage. Pay careful attention to the quality of fats you eat. Fats are the most fun of all the foods we consume, even though they are relatively tasteless. Food marketers call their value "mouth feel." A well-managed fat intake can make the difference between success and failure. Fats are the hardest nutrients to digest and require the activation of bile acids from the gall bladder and special enzymes from the pancreas, stomach and intestines for absorption. Fats create satisfaction and are effective in arresting hunger, probably by stimulating the secretion of small gut peptides that simultaneously put your digestive system into high gear while discouraging further consumption. Take small doses of the fats that make your meal satisfying. For some, it may be olive oil on a salad. For another, butter on toast. Or perhaps cream on berries or whole milk in a cup of coffee. Only you can know what makes your mouth happy.

12. Don't overdo breakfast. Breakfast in North America has become a lot of fast, empty calories. These starches, including bagels, most cereals, hash browns and toast enter the bloodstream quickly, giving you a quick rush to go with your caffeine, but may create mid-morning cravings because they provoke an insulin response that drives down your blood sugar. The morning meal needs to be one that will stay in your belly a while and be absorbed slowly. A small bowl of granola or quinoa will leave you feeling light but satisfied for hours.

Exercises:

1) Write down what you naturally like. Pick up your list every week for the next four weeks and make modifications based on your changing tastes with Staying in Slim Mode.

2) Draw your new food pyramid based on what you have discovered about the foods you naturally like.

93 Wang GJ, Volkow ND, Thanos PK, Powler JS. *Similarity between obesity and drug addiction as assessed by neurofunctional imaging: a concept review* J Addict Dis 23:39-53, 2004.

94 Positron emission tomography – an imaging technique that has allowed researchers to correlate a brain function with a part of the brain's anatomy.

95 Wang GJ, Volkow ND, Telang J, et al. *Exposure to appetitive food stimuli markedly activates the human brain's anatomy.* Neuroimage 21:1790-1797,2004.

96 Kleiner, KD, Gold MS, Frost-Pineda K, Lenz-Brunsman B, Perri MG, Jacobs WS. *Body mass index and alcohol use.* J Addict Dis 23:105-118, 2004.

97 James, GA, Gold MS, Liu Y: *Interaction of society and reward response to food stimulation.* J Addict Dis 23:23-37, 2004.

98 SW Lichtman, K Pisarska, *Discrepancy between self-reported and actual caloric intake and exercise in obese sublects.* et al. New England Journal of Medicine. Volume 327:1893-1898, December 31, 1992.

99 I use the term overeater or chronic overeater throughout because it describes the most common cause of being overweight and this chapter is written for this person. There are other clinical causes, including endocrine problems like hypothyroidism and Cushing's syndrome (excessive cortisol) requiring therapy in addition to the advice given here.

100 Discussed in greater detail in Chapter 16, Tending the Digestive Fire.

101 The Judeo-Christian counterpart to this understanding is found in the contemporary custom of treating the family's dining table as an altar since the destruction of the Temple in Jerusalem in 70 A.D., because sacrifice, as described in the Bible, can only be performed at that holy site. Therefore salt, which was used in purifying the sacrifice, is traditionally kept on every dining table.

102 The common underlying cause of our modern epidemic of obesity is multifactorial, especially involving appetite responses resulting from stress. From a classical Ayurvedic perspective, being overweight involves disorders of the three doshas (the physiological operators – vata, pitta and kapha described in Appendices 1-3) and three gunas that govern the mind. Kapha means structure and its principle quality is heaviness. Obesity would logically seem to be a kapha imbalance, the imbalance resulting from chronic overeating coupled with a sedentary lifestyle. However it is not sufficient to treat obesity by simply putting a person on a fat-free, kapha-pacifying diet. Chronic overeaters have invariably tried that under so many other names. Anxiety, anger, depression, frustration and lack of fulfillment are root causes of overeating and under–exercising and need to be addressed first.

103 Obesity surgery in essence induces a chronic digestive problem, so the person feels full after only a few bites.

104 Pāchaka pitta is called pachaka-agni by Sushruta, elsewhere it is called jatharāgni (the principle fire), showing that the ancient authors made no distinction between pitta and the different metabolic and digestive fires they called agnis.

105 See Appendix 4.

106 The Essential Rumi – by Coleman Barks.

107 *The Transcendental Meditation Program and normalization of weight.* Weldon JT, Aron A. Collected Papers. Scientific research on the Transcendental Meditation program, Vol. 1. ed. Orme-Johnson D, Farrow J, MERU Press, New York, 1977.

108 See Resources.

109 Brahm B, Journal of Clinical Endocrinology and Metabolism. April 2003.

110 A kapha-pacifying diet restricts total energy intake by emphasizing light, bitter and astringent foods. If you can minimize calories you will lose weight. No other element of a kapha-pacifying diet is important, including the oft-repeated injunction against foods that may appear to be laden with water, such as melons and grapes, or "heavy" foods such as tofu. Grapes, which are prohibited by other Ayurvedic authors because of their water content are in fact excellent diuretics and their consumption has the effect of reducing fluid retention. Tofu (bean curd) is not described in the ancient texts, yet is categorized as kapha-aggravating by other authors, together with other curdled foods such as yogurt and cheese. Tofu is free of fat, is mostly water, full of protein, easy to digest and therefore helpful for overweight patients.

111 The most common vāta disorders involve the nervous system: anxiety, tension headache, insomnia, hyperactivity and ADD, etc. These problems are best treated using lifestyle changes other than diet. The rich, heavy, unctuous (vāta-pacifying) diet promoted by some Ayurvedic authors is a secondary consideration, and clearly contra-indicated if you have a weight problem. You need to reduce total calories to lose and maintain weight, and a rich diet may splurge your whole day's allotment of energy in one meal. A diet with more fat content is still sometimes advisable if you have a weight problem, especially if you have a disorder characterized by internal dryness such as constipation. In most cases, losing weight while treating another vāta disorder is most effortlessly accomplished with a light diet to which you add unctuous nutrients like ghee and olive oil.

CHAPTER 21

HOME-COOKIN' FOR A BUSY LIFESTYLE:
INDISPENSABLE FIVE-MINUTE RECIPES

Research has shown that one critical factor you can control for gaining disease-free longevity is keeping off the weight over the long haul. This requires training the connections between your stomach and your appetite center in the hypothalamus to be satisfied with a nutritious, tasty meal of moderate portions.[112] You need to eat exactly what you like, the way you like it, and when you're hungry – especially when your meal is cooked with fresh ingredients and love. We're talking home cookin'. Restaurants, however, are making it big – serving us big portions of rich food.

The Sanskrit texts prophetically recognized the importance of the emerging science of chronobiology dealing with biological rhythms, correlating the strength of the digestive fire (agni), with Old Sol. The digestive fire is low in the morning and evening and strongest at noon. As such, there is an ancient logic behind the rest of the world's tradition to take the main meal at noon. In France and Quebec, known for their appreciation of good cuisine, the noon meal is called *dîner*, to dine, contrasted with lunch, which implies a mere trifle. The English supper comes from the Old French *souper*, to take soup, which – chronobiologically – is all you need after sundown. Even the French rarely need many calories to get through an evening and something light and liquid, like soup, is rapidly cleared by the stomach, making it unlikely to trigger the frequent midnight lament, "I can't believe I ate the whole thing."

A good lunch, on the other hand, lets you opt for something light in the evening. For too many working people, however, lunch is a sausage stand, a sandwich at your desk, a cold pizza delivered to the office, or frozen corn and canned tuna at the company cafeteria. No wonder we want a big, stick-to-the-ribs meal in the evening. Unfortunately, scientific research shows that sticking is just what it does. In a study using normal weight subjects, weight loss occurred when a single daily meal was ingested in the morning, but there was minimal weight loss, or even weight gain, when the single meal was taken for supper.[113] So let us rethink the three meals, finding wholesome recipes for anyone needing to watch their weight, sugar, fiber, salt or cholesterol and with the criteria that they can be prepared in less than five minutes and use only one pot for easy cleanup.

Breakfast - Stewed fruit

When you hear the cereal marketers from Cedar Rapids and Kalamazoo tell you that breakfast is the most important meal of the day, don't fall for it unless you are a lumberjack. The stomach, having been empty all night, is quite easily satisfied with meager fare. That is a useful tip for the majority of North Americans who need to seriously restrict calories in these days of abundance and an increasingly sedentary lifestyle. Here is a seriously nutritious meal that is easy to digest:

1 apple and/or pear

1 handful of raisins or other dried fruit

Optional sweet spices (cardamom, cinnamon, clove, nutmeg)

Chop the fruit into quarters or eighths and simmer it for 5-6 minutes in a small pot, adding a few tablespoons of water, raisins and optional spices like a clove (helps mucus), cinnamon (good for cholesterol) or nutmeg (settles the brain activity). The fruit does not need to be cooked thoroughly, just slightly tender. Sugar is not generally needed. Eat it warm, adding a handful of granola or muesli if desired, or even a dollop of yogurt or cottage cheese. The logic behind stewed fruit is that it is easy to digest while the fire is low and aids elimination (the basis behind the "apple a day"). From a scientific perspective, apples and pears contain soluble fiber (pectin), insoluble fiber (cellulose), flavonoids with their oxygen free radical absorbing capacity, and trace minerals.

Lunch - Khichadi - Thermos Flask Meal

A complete, hot, tasty feast, khichadi is the ideal lunch for anyone who wants to eat well at work while avoiding cafeteria and restaurant food. A grain with a legume constitutes a complete protein because they contain all the eight essential amino acids that the body cannot manufacture. Khichadi also contains fiber and all your vitamins and minerals in the fresh vegetables. So this satisfying dish can be taken day after day, swapping different legumes, spices, and vegetables for variety. In fact, a good part of the world eats grains and a legume as their staple – such as bean burritos or black beans with rice. With practice, you will find that it takes only 5-10 minutes out of your morning, less than the waiting time at the restaurant. In addition, it saves $6 a day or $1500 a year for both you and your spouse – with interest, not much less than what you'll get from Social Security.

1/4-cup split yellow mung beans, small red lentils (masoor dal) or small brown lentils (all available at whole-food stores, or at Indian and Mediterranean groceries).

1/4-cup basmati rice – less if watching your weight

1/2 to 1 cup fresh vegetables cut into small pieces to fit into a thermos

Whole or ground spices to taste (salt, pepper, cumin, ginger, turmeric, curry powder, etc.)

1 tablespoon olive oil or clarified butter (ghee)

2-3 cups boiling water

A one-half quart to one-quart wide-mouth thermos

Boil the water in a teakettle while you chop the veggies and then sauté the spices in a 2-qt. pot for 15 seconds in the oil or ghee. Add the washed beans or lentils, rice and chopped vegetables to the pot. Cover with the boiling water and boil for three to five minutes. While it is still boiling hot, quickly pour the mixture into the thermos (you may need to ladle it in, but don't let the mixture cool). Close the thermos quickly and leave it closed for two to four hours. Your lunch will cook and be fresh and tasty, the vegetables just slightly crispy, when your digestive fire is ready for something hot.

Notes:

• Try this for the first time at home on a weekend or take some lunch money on your first attempt. The biggest mistakes are choosing large beans that require a long cooking time, putting the mixture into the thermos when it is not boiling, or having an inefficient thermos.

• You may need to experiment with quantities and cooking times to get the best result. The cooking time in the thermos depends on how well your thermos retains heat and the type of lentil. If you take a late lunch, only a few minutes cooking in the pot may be required. If you will take your thermos feast within 2 to 3 hours, then five to seven minutes may be needed.

• Since mung dal and rice swell up substantially, you will need a generous amount of water to get to get the proper consistency. Soupy khichadi is traditional and much better than having undercooked rice and beans due to lack of liquid.

• Firm vegetables like carrots need one to two more minutes of cooking with the rice and dal, while leafy greens like spinach can be added just before pouring the whole mixture into the thermos.

• You can substitute black beans and large green lentils for the smaller beans, but they should be soaked overnight and will need extra cooking in the pot.

You can make this meal for several people at the same time. With a piece of fresh fruit and a cup of yogurt, there are almost no missing nutrients.

Supper - Simone's Five-minute Soup

Let's learn to cook supper. In most two-breadwinner households, this meal has to be quick, light and easy to clean up. I recommend my French-Canadian mother-in law's soup. She cooked for eight kids. My wife is so good at it that she has soup on the stove and is already on the floor doing her evening yoga before I have even finished unloading the car.

Fresh vegetables
Olive oil or clarified butter
Spices and herbs
Water

Bring the teakettle to boil while you rummage through the fridge for your favorite vegetables, including tomatoes, asparagus, broccoli, green beans, and zucchini. Pick veggies of all different colors for broad-spectrum free radical scavenging[114] and a dramatic visual effect. Chop them while you are sautéing leeks, scallions or onions, and celery in the bottom of a two-quart pot. Throw in the vegetables and add the boiling water. You can add a handful of small brown lentils or split mung beans. Don't forget the spices, especially fine herbs, plenty of black pepper and a little salt. Cover the pot and let it simmer while you practice your 15-20 minutes of evening yoga or meditation. Soup's on! At the last minute, add tender vegetables such as spinach, bean sprouts, cilantro or zucchini, or perhaps a handful of rice vermicelli, ramen noodles or angel hair pasta. Nothing much more is needed.

Avoid a rich dessert.
When you are done enjoying this complete meal, throw the leftovers away.

Good nutrition is more than the right vitamins and minerals. It involves biological intelligence or vital force (prāna), a value that is lost when food turns stale. With practice, it will only take five minutes of your time to make something equally fresh tomorrow. You deserve better than soggy veggies and would likely never return to an eatery that served you yesterday's soup.

Master these three simple recipes and as long as you keep the ingredients on hand you will never hesitate to make your busy family a satisfying, healthy meal.

---

112 See Chapter 5, The Secrets of Extreme Longevity; Chapter 16, Tending the Digestive Fire and Chapter 20, Staying in Slim Mode.

113 Hirsh, E., Halberg, F., Goetz, F.C., Cressey, D., Wendt, H., Sothern, R., Haus, E., Stoney, P., Minors, D., Rosen, G., Hill, B., Hilleren, M. & Garett, K. (1975) Body weight change during 1 week on a single daily 2000-calorie meal consumed as breakfast (B) or dinner (D). Chronobiologia 2 (suppl 1): 31-32.

114 See Chapter 18, Oxidation, Aging and Rust.

CHAPTER 22

Your Bag of Supplements:
the Fallacy of the Active Ingredient

At bedtime I dutifully press a few "vitamins" out of their blister pack, wash them down, and think of Dr. Margaret Barker and the natural supplements – mother's milk – that she insisted on slipping into her patients' diets.

I am taking my vitamins for the only valid reason known to medical science for a person who is in good health: as a guinea pig in an experiment to see if vitamins are actually good for anything. Despite many experiments on cells, mice and humans, there is little evidence that the vitamins and hundreds of other chemicals marketed as nutritional supplements have beneficial effects. Yet, supplements can be manufactured by anyone and marketed without government regulation thanks to the DSHEA Act of 1994. Caveat emptor. Most evenings as I feel them pass my gullet, I wonder if the other 7,000 physicians who volunteered with me in this Harvard-sponsored research are similarly skeptical. As I toss the pills back, I toast Oliver Wendell Holmes who stated that if the whole materia medica would be sunk to bottom of the sea it would be all the better for mankind and all the worse for the fishes.

Can Humans improve on Mother Nature?

"Why is it that nursed Zulu babies seem to do fine and the ones taking cow's milk or formula are somehow doomed to death?" I asked British pediatrician Margaret Barker as she held a dark Zulu baby up to the window's light for a better look. "She just won't grow and keeps coming down with diarrhea and colds despite all my treatments." "Find this wee one a wet nurse and she will blossom," Dr. Barker replied, "it will be better than a boatload of antibiotics." Her predictions always worked. She had spent her life practicing in Zululand.

Breastfeeding was an unusual practice on the obstetrical wards of the Denver hospitals where I had been working as a medical student in the early 70's, something only practiced by hippies and backward folks, and far below the dignity of modern women. Like the rest of my medical school class I had been brainwashed by specialists who told women to make life easier for themselves. "Don't allow your breasts to swell then sag; be liberated, it's the twentieth century." As Denver mothers checked out of the delivery suite, nurses handed them formula samples from big multinationals and told them they were superior to their own milk and more convenient.

"If ever there was a panacea for babies, it is Mum's milk," Dr. Barker countered. "The magic bullet for digestive disorders and infections. The gut and the lung form the boundary between the hostile world of African microbes and baby's immature tissues. From the moment they take their first breath of African air, these babies are assaulted with pathogens their tender immune systems can't handle without the antibodies in Mum's milk. And it's so much more digestible."

My first rotation when I returned to my Colorado medical school was pediatrics and I rankled a few feathers as the high apostle of breastfeeding. I was told to shut up or flunk. Twenty years later, science has discovered that Mum's milk is complete, containing growth factors and fatty acids necessary for brain development. Breastfed babies have higher IQ's as well as lower rates of ear infection, meningitis, respiratory infection, sudden death, diarrhea and diabetes. Mum ends up with less breast and ovarian cancer, better weight loss and stronger bones. What's not to like?

You, dear reader, may well be chuckling derisively at the stupidity, arrogance and stubbornness of the post-war pediatricians and obstetricians knocking breastfeeding. But if you are gobbling unproven snake oil in the form of vitamins, anti-oxidants and other supplements, you are just as guilty, believing you can improve on Mother Nature by swallowing the supposed active ingredients while ignoring the simple, natural panacea that is right under your nose – wholesome food. This panacea is prescribed by your inner physician, Dhanvantari, with access to a 500 million year old database, your genetic code, on which is written what heals and what you should crave. This sequence of nucleotides is only the most recent refrain of your body's ancient song.

Antioxidants out of Context

One of my research study tablets is red. I was told it contained beta-carotene – a potent antioxidant – or an inert placebo. The logic goes that neutralizing the influence of oxidative damage on cell membranes and DNA should reduce cancer and heart disease. At some point the researchers wrote me to stop taking the red capsule containing either beta-carotene or placebo. The committee monitoring the study computed that even after several years, there was no difference between the placebo and active beta-carotene groups in the incidence of heart attacks, strokes, cancer, prostate problems or any other discernible problems. By the way, they told me, I had been taking the active beta-carotene.

The designers of the study may have included beta-carotene to put to an end to a lot of hopeful thinking. Observations had already shown that people who consume beta-carotene through their choice of abundant amounts of fruits and vegetables had less cancer and heart disease. However, when 22,000 doctors meticulously took this pigmented extract of orange vegetables (such as carrots and squash) for twelve years, they had no less disease than the ones on the placebo. Apparently, you have to actually eat carrots and squash, a radical finding confirmed by my several thousand colleagues and me obediently swallowing our pills. In spite of that unfruitful report and several others, including two large studies of tens of thousands of subjects showing that beta carotene actually increases the risk of lung cancer and heart attacks in smokers, sales of beta carotene do fine along with sales of everything else promising benefits with a good logic behind it.[115]

Similarly, in 34,000 women there was a reduction in heart disease for those that had the highest consumption of vitamin E, but only if it was taken as part of their diet. Taking it as a supplement did not make any difference.[116]

The Harvard researchers sent me a letter telling me to stop taking the brown capsule containing Vitamin E or placebo oil. Again, no benefits, despite wishful thinking it might help heart disease. Later, a letter arrived telling me to stop taking the orange pill containing Vitamin C or placebo after I'd swallowed it for seven years. Ditto: no harm, just no benefits to be found after 7000 diligent docs reported on hundreds of measures of health every six months. Now my fellow lab rats and I are down to one silver-grey capsule containing B vitamins or placebo. There is no hint, it appears, that we would not have been better off if we had disposed of them as Holmes had suggested.

The Bag of Pills

Patients intent on natural approaches to healing arrive in my office with a plastic bag of chemicals cleverly disguised as "natural" nutritional supplements, eager for my opinion on the value of each. We line them up on my desk and I read the ingredients of each, commenting, "That's said to be good for the liver (heart, kidneys, joints)." From the patient's perspective it is important that her physician acknowledges and understands what she is doing to help herself. Unfortunately, despite the fact that 62-65% of Americans take supplements,[117] my fellow physicians are only grudgingly beginning to drop the inflated illusion that our patients unwaveringly follow only our advice.

The bag of pills is not always benign. As a third year medical student at the Veteran's Administration Hospital in Denver in 1971, I had the good luck to shadow an old-school British cardiologist. An elderly nurse from the First World War pulled twelve western medications from her brown paper bag for dealing with hypertension, heart failure, constipation, insomnia and assorted other problems. The cardiologist started to walk out, leaving me to deal with the patient. I desperately asked, "So, which medications should she continue to take?" "You decide," he responded, "but only two." The look of trepidation on my patient's face at the prospect of giving up her laxatives, sleep aids and tranquilizers was as anguished as mine was. He had given me a demanding but rewarding exercise in therapeutics, challenging me to determine which underlying disorders were leading to the other complicating symptoms and which medications were causing side-effects that required her previous physicians to add even more. She returned to the clinic two weeks later with two pill bottles in her purse and feeling fine.

The Trajectory of the Remedy

There are two influences of any remedy: the action at the end organs and the Trajectory or path the remedy takes to get there. The end-organ action is the subject of intensive pharmacological study but wise medical management of the Trajectory can turn an ordinary drug into an effective cure.

The Trajectory is the path by which the medicine flows – a path the patient and the doctor can consciously manage for an optimum outcome. That path, depending on how it is managed, can be negative or positive. The Trajectory is an integral part of the Vedic practice of medicine. Charaka describes how to take medication:

> "If the patient, after cleansing the mind of its impurities like passion, doubt or other inauspicious sentiments and concentrating his mind on the treatment, takes this dose, it brings about the most desirable results."

Charaka Samhitā

I have capitalized Trajectory because for a Vedic physician, the subtle aspects of healing make her profession a sacred one. She spends her workday in the realm of the development of consciousness if she takes the time to consider her patient's mindset when determining the best way to aim the remedy. Prescribing medicine is merely a trade. Giving the medicine a healing Trajectory is a sacred art.

A renowned Boston cardiologist, Bernard Lown, MD, who pioneered the coronary care unit and other innovations, taught me the value of managing the remedy's Trajectory when he came to my hospital as a visiting consultant for our difficult cardiac cases. We presented a patient who was too feeble to tolerate a coronary artery bypass but could also not tolerate his angina medication because of its common side effect, headaches. Dr. Lown told us, "You warn your patient, 'Nitroglycerin frequently produces side effects like headaches and flushing,' but that just gives him a negative expectation for the inevitable experience. Instead try approaching the disclosure like this: 'If ever you feel pain in the chest from angina just put this nitro under your tongue and within seconds it will dilate arteries all over your body. You will feel the warmth of more blood flowing into your skin and even into your head. This is the sign that the nitro is working and taking some load off of the heart. Your heart's vessels will also be filled with that same flow of blood and within moments you will be pain-free." Dr. Lown understood the Trajectory.

Yatha pinde tatha brahmande. As is the individual, so is the cosmos.[118] The human physiology is an expression of the underlying intelligence governing the Totality. A staggering variety of bioactive therapeutic substances are found in plants, minerals, fungi, molds, animal or human urine, milk or serum, mussels, leeches, animal glands, venom, and many other inconceivable sources that are used today in modern medicine; every aspect of human physiology has a complement in nature.

Most chronic disease begins as a distortion in the expression of nature's intelligence. A well-conceived therapeutic program reconnects life with its source in this intelligence, enlivening the link between changing, error-prone values of the physical body and their unchanging origin. Herbs and other phytonutrients are small packets of "software" that supply an essential "patch" to compensate for or restore integrity to the body's faulty source code.[119]

The Fine Line between Wholesomeness and Toxicity

Botanical medicine is becoming increasingly aware of the importance of synergy and balance in herbal formulations. Ayurveda sometimes uses whole plants or parts of plants to maximize the therapeutic response while avoiding harmful side effects. In many preparations, the expert compounder includes the leaf, flower, bark, stem, fruit and root. When Charaka writes, "The worst poison can be a remedy and the best remedy a poison,"[120] he is asking us to consider the nature of toxicity. Strychnine, digitalis and the most abundant mineral in your cells, potassium, are all remarkable remedies derived from nature that in the wrong route or dose can function as potent poisons. Meanwhile, the most common deadly poison in the American diet is excessive calories in any form, from tofu stir-fry to cheeseburgers.

Nature often provides a remedy in the geographical location where disorder or imbalance exists. The native medicinal plants in any locality are held to be most effective for maintaining health for the people of that region. For example, the cinchona bush from which quinine is derived grows best in the hot, humid areas where malaria is prevalent. The Ayurvedic texts pioneered thinking global, eating local. Unfortunately, over the last century overharvesting and the exportation of invasive species, often as ornamental plants, have changed the botanical population in many locales. Medicinal plants are now much less abundant in the wild.

The Fallacy of the Active Ingredient

Conventional medicine, with its focus on isolating and treating symptoms of disease, has approached botanical pharmacology by attempting to isolate the plant's active ingredients, giving us many antibiotics, cancer chemotherapy agents, digoxin and a good portion of the rest of our modern drugs. When the active ingredient is disconnected from the balancing power of the whole plant, side effects can occur, a phenomenon known as the *fallacy of the active ingredient*. For example, an alkaloid in carrots, taken by itself in a sufficient dose, can provoke colic in an infant.[121] Yet infants love and thrive on carrots, which every mother invariably cooks and purees whole.

Plants contain hundreds of bioactive substances, all of which have a biological purpose in the life of the plant, protecting it from light, decay, insects, and mold. Some pigments make the plant colorful to attract pollinators like bees and birds; others make it tasty enough to be eaten and its seeds disseminated. Some molecules make it disgusting and poisonous to protect it from being eaten. If you are trying to identify a new active ingredient among the hundreds or thousands in every plant, your best candidates are alkaloids, flavonoids, terpinoids and steroids.

Most hormones, drugs, neurotransmitters and herbs act by binding to receptor sites on cell membranes. These relatively small molecules have specific conformations and function as a key, fitting into the receptor site to activate or inhibit a protein's action, thus creating a specific effect. Most drugs and herbs mimic the effects of the body's natural molecular keys called *ligands*. Narcotics mimic endorphins; tranquilizers mimic GABA;[122] nicotine mimics acetylcholine, etc.

It is alluring to find one compound in a medicinal plant that can explain it's principle effects. Scientists are bred to find elegance in simplicity. While simple explanations are the rule in physics, in medicine they are exceptions. Boiling things down – i.e. reductionism – usually means overlooking an important relationship.

In the 1930's, beside diuretics that were often made from mercury, there were few good antihypertensive medications.[123] German and Swiss pharmacologists visited India in search of useful Ayurvedic medicines and heard of a small bush used since antiquity as a tranquilizer for treatment of hyperactivity, anxiety and mania, and known in Sanskrit as *sarpagandha*, meaning the smell of a snake. The Latin name for the bush is *Rauwolfia serpentina*, and it provided the first truly effective medication for hypertension. Ayurvedic doctors traditionally prescribe powders or decoctions boiled from a handful of rauwolfia branches, leaves and roots. The Swiss chemists isolated a mixture of alkaloids that potently lowered blood pressure, and which can still be prescribed today in a dose of about 50 mg. Going a step farther, they isolated *reserpine*, the most potent of the alkaloids for hypertension, requiring barely a couple of milligrams. Reserpine has an extremely narrow therapeutic window: an extra milligram or two causes depression and fainting from sudden drops in blood pressure. This otherwise safe and useful herb was rendered toxic by reducing it to a few intense milligrams of potent alkaloid, a classic example of the fallacy of the active ingredient.

From the Vedic perspective, we are violating the same law of nature when we consume vitamin C without the orange, soy isoflavones without the tofu, and beta-carotene without the squash. Ayurveda deems vitamins and minerals important, but au naturel, right off the tree.

Risks of using Active Ingredients

When you take the vitamin C out of the orange and take it in concentrated amounts you are exposing yourself to the same type of dubious logic as taking reserpine out of the rauwolfia plant: only the active ingredient is important. Fortunately, with two-thirds of Americans taking supplements and low levels of reported serious side effects, we assume that most active ingredients are harmless. My 7000 physician colleagues and I altruistically agreed to swallow these unproven supplements to do our part in definitively burying or resuscitating these assumptions.

Here is a short list of supplements that can be toxic:

• Vitamin A – Safe up to 10,000 IU daily but toxic to the fetus at 20,000 IU and to adults at 50,000 IU.

• Beta-carotene – As above.

• Vitamin B6 – Peripheral nerve toxicity at doses of 100 mg/day over 6 months or 2,000 mg/day over a few days, giving numb feet and problems walking.

• Vitamin C – Higher doses (10 grams per day) can cause indigestion and diarrhea.

• Vitamin D – The milk alkali syndrome, including damage to the kidneys and heart, occur with doses over 5,000 IU/day.

• Vitamin E – High doses interfere with zinc elimination and can mask pernicious anemia (Vitamin B12 deficiency), leading to nerve damage.

• Niacin – Taken in large doses can cause liver damage and in therapeutic doses for reducing cholesterol commonly causes rashes, flushing and tingling.

• Iron – One of the most toxic. Too much can cause liver and heart toxicity and interferes with absorption of other minerals. Even a little can be constipating and cause a bellyache. Unless you are anemic or pregnant, iron is best taken as food.

• Potassium – Death in infants, usually from arrhythmias.

• Zinc – Supplementation has been shown to inhibit copper and iron absorption, and increase[124] urinary tract problems. Zinc lozenges and nasal sprays taken as a cold remedies can cause permanent loss of smell.

• Amino acids – Eosinophilic myalgia syndrome – see below.

• Antioxidants – Even these wonderful gems if taken in quantities can cause fatigue.[125] After all, they inhibit oxidation and burning fuel is how you make energy.

Your Body Manufactures Supplements without Impurities

Another major problem with taking manufactured vitamins and supplements in addition to those in your diet, beside the potential toxicity of the purely refined active ingredient itself, is the noxious potential of the by-products that are generated in manufacturing the supplement. Even if your vitamin B6 is 99.999% pure there are still ten parts per million of unknown substances that could be noxious, a level of purity rarely tolerated for other toxins like lead or mercury. In 1989, for example, 1500 people began to have fever, rashes, muscle aches, malaise and high levels of inflammatory cells in the blood. In all, 38 people died of the eosinophilic myalgia syndrome. One bad Japanese–manufactured batch of tryptophan, a naturally-occurring amino acid promoted as a sleep aid, was responsible for the epidemic. The batch had a higher than normal level of impurity from the manufacturing process.

You play Russian roulette not only when you take medications and drugs, but also when you extract active ingredients out of what should be your diet. In the United States, unlike medicines, supplements can be manufactured and marketed by anyone without a license or supervision, imported from any backwater lab from any country on earth by unscrupulous companies with no interest in your health but only in their bottom line, and further adulterated with fillers at best or other chemicals at worst, including potent anti-inflammatory drugs, sedatives, Viagra and others. When you take your vitamins as food, the quality control is supervised by the laws of nature as well as by the USDA. The only law regulating the shelves of health food stores is caveat emptor.

Analyzing your Own Bag of Supplements

Fortunately for the 2/3 of Americans who swallow supplements, we know that vitamins and other supplements, while not documented to be of any benefit, are mostly harmless. Dieticians, naturopaths, government regulators, pharmacologists, consumers and physicians bicker over their relative merits. Don't expect the controversies to be resolved soon. These issues get little research funding. Worse, research designed to identify any long-term benefits require following large groups of healthy people over long periods. Epidemiologists wisely decided to recruit tens of thousands of doctors and nurses as research subjects to resolve the issue, reckoning that medical professionals would sympathize with the vitamin conundrum and volunteer as compliant guinea pigs. Thank me and my fellow lab rats for the answers that are starting to flow in, but don't blame us when today's dogma ends up on the scrap heap of abandoned practices tomorrow. The appropriate use of supplements, more than any area of medicine, remains an educated guess. If these experts cannot agree what is best policy for populations, certainly you, who know your body best, are competent to make that guess yourself. The Trajectory a remedy takes to get to its site of action is a frequently overlooked part of the remedy's value. Even the most useless, inert capsule filled with straw can be a powerful medicine if it follows the proper Trajectory. The Trajectory is determined by the flow of attention, the patient's consciousness. It is intensely affected by the physician's attitude, the price, the route of delivery and many other factors.

At a clinic where I volunteered in Zululand, the village folk held a remedy's medicinal value to be proportional to its cost. Unfortunately, the best medicine for the ubiquitous malnutrition, powdered milk, was dirt cheap and regarded as such. The clinic charged for any remedy – even a penny. For a Zulu, an injection is better than a pill, and an IV – or better yet, blood – has unparalleled healing power. Funnily, in the twenty-first century I spend time talking sophisticated Americans out of risky infusions when a simple pill is just as good. The most healing Trajectory is always relative to an individual and her culture.

To be a healer, a doctor must adopt a supportive or at least a neutral attitude when a patient walks in with his bag of self-selected supplements. I am honored when my patients share their bag with me because to 72% of doctors it is concealed.[126] The physician needs to inform patients of those rare instances where a contraindication to a particular herb exists.[127] Otherwise the physician should step aside and allow his patient to choose based on her own beliefs.

Dealing with your own bag of supplements is an exercise in using the Trajectory. You may grab the bottle off the health store shelf because the rationale with which it was promoted sounded logical. Female hormones from estrogen to the pill are manufactured from diosgenin sterols found in the Mexican yam (Dioscorea villosa). Shouldn't a cream or pills made from these yams help a menopausal woman manufacture more of these hormones? It turns out that for women who volunteer as experimental subjects, dioscorea neither changes hormone levels nor reduces menopausal symptoms any better than sham dioscorea powder.[128, 129] Nor can diosgenin be converted by the body into a hormone. But when an individual woman on a mission to find a solution to her night sweats massages wild yam cream into her thighs, her rubbing takes a Trajectory that somehow passes through her cerebral cortex and from there to her hypothalamus and pituitary where thermoregulatory processes are mediated. Depriving her of yam cream will predictably increase her hot flashes.

Harvard researcher and acupuncturist Ted Kaptchuk has shown that not all remedies without active ingredients are created equal. In 2006 he reported that patients with chronic arm pain who received sham acupuncture had more improvement in their pain than those receiving an inert pill.[130] In 2008 his group showed that a therapeutic ritual (sham acupuncture treatments for patients with irritable bowel syndrome) could be augmented by a patient – practitioner relationship that added warmth, attention and confidence to the therapy. Twenty-eight percent of patients on the waiting list to receive therapy got adequate symptom relief, compared to 44% getting limited sham acupuncture and 62% getting practitioner-augmented sham acupuncture, a stunning success rate for this obstinate disorder.[131] These Harvard researchers confirm the advice of Charaka above: *cleansing the mind of doubt and concentrating on the treatment brings about the most desirable results.*

Becoming Master of the Remedy's Trajectory

Everyone needs to learn to control and use the Trajectory because the Trajectory makes herbs, supplements, standard medications and even food more effective and tolerable. Blessing your pill, like saying grace before a meal, is a good way to empower the remedy. Close your eyes and feel where it needs to go. Listen to your body's ancient song. The self-pulse reading and body awareness exercises in Chapter 8 will be useful in allowing you to use increasingly subtle means of healing. In Vedic science, the Sanskrit name reflects the herb's effect. Reciting its name aloud, or even better – within – has such a beneficial effect on the Trajectory that the herb itself may not be needed.

First class medicine uses consciousness to prompt the cure. Meditation, yoga, a healing sound or mantra, listening to a specific verse of the Veda or to healing music, the use of a gem, the Sanskrit sound of an herb, and the powerful intention to direct one's healing attention[132] are powerful active ingredients requiring no swallowing because they manage the Trajectory.[133]

Start with your own bag of supplements. Give it a good cleansing, first with your intellect, then with your common sense and finally with your heart. Toss the bottles that no longer fit with your growing consciousness and appreciation of your body's capacity for self-repair. Apply the Trajectory to the keepers, acknowledging without a doubt that they are right for you.

115 For a discussion of these research studies and their references see the editorial by Greenberg and Sporn: Antioxidant Vitamins, Cancer, and Cardiovascular Disease. Greenberg ER and Sporn MB. NEJM, Vol 334:1189-1190. May 2, 1996. Number 18.

116 Kushi LH, Folsom AR, Prineas RJ, Mink PJ, Wu Y, Bostick RM. *Dietary antioxidant vitamins and death from coronary heart disease in postmenopausal women.* N Engl Med 1996;334:1156-1162.

117 Ipsos-Public Affairs survey funded by the Council for Responsible Nutrition, with 1,002 respondents in a telephone survey and 2,022 participants in an online survey, 2003-2005.

118 Yajur Veda

119 Maharishi Mahesh Yogi, Personal communication with the author and other physicians, 1987.

120 Charaka Samhitā 1.41

121 Dr. PJ Deshpande, Benares Hindu University, personal communication.

122 Gamma amino butyric acid.

123 Franklin Roosevelt met his untimely end because of uncontrolled hypertension – he had a massive stroke.

124 Johnson AR, et al. *High-dose zinc increases hospital admissions due to genitourinary complications.* J Urol. 2007;177:639-643.

125 Denham Harmon, MD, PhD, personal communication, 1999. Dr. Harmon first described the influence of free radicals on the aging process in 1952.

126 Eisenberg DM et al. *Unconventional Medicine in the United States – Prevalence, Costs and Patterns of Use.* New England Journal of Medicine. Volume 328:246-252. Jan 28, 1993.

127 For example St. John's wort taken before surgery or with antidepressants, willow bark with warfarin, etc. These conflicts and contraindications are rare but important.

128 Wu WH, Liu LY, Chung CJ, et al. *Estrogenic effect of yam ingestion in healthy postmenopausal women.* J Am Coll Nutr 2005;24(4):235-243

129 Komesaroff PA, Black CV, Cable V, et al. *Effects of wild yam extract on menopausal symptoms, lipids and sex hormones in healthy menopausal women.* Climacteric 2001; 4(2):144-150.

130 Kaptchuk T, et al. Feb. 1, 2006 British Medical Journal.

131 Kaptchuk T, et al. *Components of placebo effect: randomized controlled trial in patients with irritable bowel syndrome.* BMJ 2008;336:999-1003 (3 May),

132 Intention is translated *sankalpa* in Sanskrit. See Chapter 20 for a longer discussion.

133 "First class medicine" was discussed in the Prologue.

DODGING THE DEADLIEST BULLETS: CANCER, HEART DISEASE AND THE BRAIN

CHAPTER 23

CANCER: A BUG IN THE SOFTWARE

Staring down the barrel of a microscope at the fresh smear of Pamela Rizzi's blood, I saw white blood cells with big blue nuclei instead of their usual shape like a string of lapis. *Undifferentiated* was the word going through my mind. Like the fellows down on their luck bumming quarters a block east on Montreal's St. Lawrence street while hiding Molson beer bottles inside paper bags, the cells had lost their purpose in the society of cells. They lacked the organelles to do anything more useful than divide. Although I was just a resident, the only doctor that night at the small Royal Edward Chest Hospital (aptly dubbed the RECH), my suspicions had been confirmed: acute myelocytic leukemia, not exactly the type of patient who could best benefit from a pulmonary hospital.

The ER doc who admitted her to the specialty hospital must have been in a hurry to go home, I thought, when Pamela Rizzi told him she had left chest pains just a few weeks after being given an inhaler for mild asthma. To me she looked pale and I found a large spleen causing her "chest" pain. Pinpoint brown hemorrhages on her legs hinted she lacked platelets and that I should peek at a blood smear. Now I had to go face her with the news that rebellious, undifferentiated cells were dividing purposelessly in her bone marrow, crowding out the ones she needed to properly produce her blood elements.

The Role of Biological Intelligence

Modern medicine understands cancer to be distortion of the sequence of base codes determining the structure of the DNA molecule that holds our genetic information. The intelligence in DNA guides a cell to develop and perform its different functions, including growing from an undifferentiated, primordial stem cell into a cell with specific structures to carry out its role. For example, an undifferentiated bone marrow cell can develop into the precursor of a red blood cell, a white blood cell or a platelet. All cells are ultimately derived from a stem cell, which itself is a field of all possibilities. Liver cells, blood cells, kidney cells, breast cells – all are easily identified under a microscope because they have differentiated and taken on unique, specific forms. In cancer, the information contained in the DNA has been somehow altered or mutated. Radiation and sunlight are known to create free radicals that alter the genetic information through oxidation. Toxins, pollutants and even cosmic rays may do the same. Viruses are known causes of certain tumors such as cervical cancer, while a predisposition to colon and breast cancer may be inherited. Aging is associated with the accumulation of intracellular debris, promoting errors and impairing the cell's self – repair mechanisms. In 2009, new evidence emerged that aging and cancer are just two sides of the problem of DNA damage, and that weakened repair of damaged DNA are a potential cancer cell's Achilles heel.[134]

In cancer, distortion of the genetic information is inevitably involved. Oncogenes that promote cancer are activated, permitting the cell to grow and divide recklessly.

The cell loses respect for tissue boundaries and escapes its programmed cell death. The cell's tumor suppressor genes are somehow turned off, so its normal cell replication cycles are ignored. It escapes detection by the immune system and starts to tap into the blood supply. The rogue cell gains a foothold and begins to divide.

We previously examined the properties of the unified field which gives rise to all matter and force fields. DNA is the first biological expression of this field. *Yatha pinde tatha brahmande*, says the Yajur Veda: the physiology is the expression of cosmic intelligence. Vedic medicine locates the cause of cancer as a distortion of this repository of intelligence. Cancer is regarded as a tissue (*dhātu*) that has lost the memory (*smriti*) of this field of intelligence, which normally guides its functioning and growth. Like the cloudy reflection of the sun in a glass of muddy water, the physiology loses its ability to express this infinite order without distortion. The cell ceases to evolve according to its natural role in the society of cells.

Cells, too, have a Dharma

The word dharma was generally used in Vedic society to express the idea of universal natural order. For you as an individual, it expresses your role in that order, one which is effortless and evolutionary. In some societies, it is customary for one's role to be tied to a family tradition: a tailor wants his daughter to be a tailor; a mother wants her progeny to carry on the family business. Parents provide the knowledge for the child to effortlessly take her role in society. A broader understanding regards dharma as a support on which Veda, the field of pure intelligence, guides one's evolution, or even is the source of order itself. One can become whatever one wants to become in life, but certain paths are effortless and natural. Similarly, cells have rules. They need to divide and proliferate, but are programmed to stop the process when they arrive at boundaries.

Modern science understands cancer as something that is localized and then becomes generalized (that is, metastasizes to lymph nodes and other sites). In Vedic medicine, cancer is seen as something that is generalized – i.e. the weakness or imbalance that has given rise to the distortion of the information – and then becomes localized as a cancer.

From the Vedic perspective, the modern understanding that cancer is due to lack of self – repair mechanisms from accumulation of intracellular debris is the old story we discussed in Chapter 16. Āma (residues of inefficient digestion and metabolism that block self – repair) accumulates in the cells and the channels (srotasas) between the cells – and is a common root of the most serious chronic disorders. Cancer in the Vedic perspective is a degradation of information that is passed from mother to daughter to granddaughter cell. A cancer cell has lost touch with its tradition, its dharma. It has become a rebel, oblivious to its surrounding environment. Charaka Samhitā sees cancer as a software problem.

Vedic approaches to Cancer Prevention

The Ayurvedic approach to cancer prevention is to correct bugs in the software by restoring the cell's memory of how to differentiate into a purposeful cell. This is done in several ways:

First, eliminate residues that might obstruct the flow of the body's inner intelligence. The Ayurvedic diagnosis of cancer focuses on determining the digestive or metabolic imbalances responsible for creating āma.[135] Strengthening the digestive and metabolic fires, as discussed in Chapters 16 to 21, is the most important factor in long-term prevention. By tradition, a healthy person should perform an Ayurvedic program for rejuvenation and āma elimination twice yearly (panchakarma). This is ideally performed in residence (See Resources). If this is not possible, see Appendix 6: A Home Program for the Elimination of Āma. While panchakarma has not been scientifically documented to prevent cancer, its other benefits for body renewal should be your motivation.

Second, restore your body's connection with the field of pure intelligence – of which it is an expression. Quantum physics describes a field of perfect harmony, orderliness, balance and integration, exactly the qualities of the Vedic medicine's understanding of pure intelligence, the blueprint of the cosmos and your own human body. Conscious experience of these qualities is the essential basis of the restoration of health, because it is the basis for ultimately bringing these qualities into your physiology. Refer to Chapter Eight.

Third, follow an Ayurvedic lifestyle. I will refrain from giving you much advice on preventing cancer, because this entire book is about living a life that will keep your body's intelligence intact, and prevent the accumulation of āma, the intracellular debris now well shown to prevent self-repair of DNA. The recommendations in the preceding chapters – for eating fresh produce of many different colors, using spices, avoiding heavy foods that create āma,[136] playing outdoors, practicing behavioral tonics, yoga, learning to boost your immune system and other chapters about the lost art of self-repair – are themselves your plan for preventing cancer.

Lastly, use turmeric. If you feel you have a higher risk of cancer – e.g if you have already had one cancer, have a family history of a genetically-related cancer such as breast or colon cancer or have a condition like ulcerative colitis that predisposes to cancer, you should certainly follow modern guidelines for cancer prevention. In addition, take extra large amounts of turmeric on an ongoing basis. Make your life easy and take turmeric as tablets or capsules, one gram twice a day. See Chapter 29.

Because Nature herself is the most elegant source of intelligence, researchers have been evaluating the entire world of plants for cancer remedies, including herbs that have traditionally been used in Ayurveda as immune modulators. Many researchers, myself included, have tested their efficacy in test tubes, animals and humans for preventing carcinogenesis and neutralizing free radicals. The results have been encouraging: a number of published studies suggest that several Ayurvedic preparations may have roles in cancer prevention and in scavenging the oxygen radicals generated during cancer chemotherapy. One hundred twenty-three women receiving chemotherapy for metastatic breast cancer were randomly divided into a group ingesting an Ayurvedic herbal mixture with potent antioxidant effects and a control group getting a similar – tasting placebo paste and tablet. The group getting the active herbs had significantly fewer side effects from the treatments as well as a better outcome.[137]

Pamela Rizzi had come to the ER alone, thinking she only had asthma, and now she was trying to make sense of some devastating news. At my request, the ambulance from the Royal Victoria Hospital was coming to pick her up without its flashing lights. I attached the microscope slide with the rebellious, undifferentiated cells to her chart and put the chart in her hands as if to emphasize that now she was part of the battalion. It was one of the first of many times I would have to be the bearer of bad news and every time has been just as hard. I saw Pamela two years later when she was still hanging on after getting a remission with chemotherapy. I try to remind myself that as a physician, like a cell, I have a tradition to follow and boundaries to respect. As spiritual beings, we strive to experience the boundless aspect of life, even while living within the boundaries imposed by physics and biology. Nature takes care of the rest.

134 Hoejmakers, JHJ. *Molecular origins of cancer: DNA damage, aging and cancer.* NEJM Oct. 8, 2009

135 See Chapter 16 for an extensive discussion of āma.

136 Numerous articles in large populations (such as Seventh-Day Adventists) suggest that reducing meat consumption reduces the risks of several common types of cancer, even after controlling for the reduced use of alcohol, tobacco, caffeine and hot spices seen in vegetarian populations.

137 Misra NC et al. *Antioxidant adjuvant therapy using a natural herbal mixture (MAK) during intensive chemotherapy: Reduction in toxicity.* In: RS Rao et al eds. Proceedings of the XVI International Cancer Congress. Bologna, Italy. Monduzzi Editore, 1994: 3099-3102.

CHAPTER 24

Taking Care of your Heart

He who is in the sun and in the fire, and in the heart of man, is One.
He who knows this, is one with the One.

Maitreya Upanishad

The endothelium is probably the most important tissue in the body you never heard of – and one of the most amazing. It lines every vessel: artery, vein and capillary. Stretched out, your endothelia might cover a tennis court. Endothelium cells permit your blood, thick with red and white blood cells, to flow frictionlessly, yet the endothelium can expand or contract within seconds. The endothelium can patch itself nearly instantly when rent asunder, keeping you from exsanguinating from every little cut, yet it remains amazingly free from obstruction. Unless, of course, you don't take care of it properly.

In 1799, Caleb Hillier Parry[138] was examining a heart during an autopsy when he felt something brittle and hard in the coronary arteries. Instinctively, he looked to the crumbling ceiling of the morgue, thinking that perhaps plaster had fallen into his dissection. He soon realized that the arteries themselves were the source of the calcium. Parry's was the first modern description of atherosclerosis, hardening of the arteries, the burden carried by a quarter of Americans and the scythe that will be carried by the grim reaper when he comes to collect more than 40% of us.

In brief, the walls of the vessels that nourish the heart, brain, kidneys and even the legs become choked with deposits composed of rancid, foamy collections of fats, platelets and fibers. Foamy cholesterol deposits enter the vessel wall at weak areas, like barnacles clinging to defects on the smooth hull of a boat, and their presence is aggravated by the body's response. The artery, sensing it is being damaged, activates the same survival mechanisms that occur in moments of trauma and stress: inflammation and clotting. Tens of millions of years of evolution have taught primates that it is better to be safe than sorry, so even though the vessel was not really pierced in combat, the body dispatches cells and other molecules to initiate clotting and inflammation in response to the perceived injury. The result is thickening, hardening and eventually calcification of the deposits. Like your dentist, physicians call it plaque. By now, you know that Vedic physicians call it āma.

To make matters worse, in moments of stress, just like the muscles that cause goose bumps and clenched fists, the muscles in the vessel's wall contract and the artery goes into spasm, further narrowing the passage for blood to flow. Think "white knuckle syndrome." Angina and heart attacks are largely a matter of accounting: when the heart muscle cells' demand for blood exceeds supply, the deprived cells may be injured. When your cells get an inadequate blood supply, it is called *ischemia*. When the muscle damage is severe and cells die, it is a heart attack or *infarct*.

Identifying the Risks for Endothelial Disease

Heart disease and stroke are the first and third most common causes of death, and yet are almost completely preventable. Recent research has shown that over 90% of heart attacks are caused by nine modifiable lifestyle factors. Coronary artery disease declined by 57% due to improved habits between 1968 and 1990 in the U.S., a trend that is unprecedented in industrialized countries, and one of the most impressive health achievements of the 20th century. In fact, heart disease is continuing to rise in Russia and other Eastern European countries.

Yet experts do not know exactly why heart disease is declining. In fact, until 40 years ago there was no clear understanding about the different factors that contributed to heart attacks and strokes. At that time an experiment was conceived by Harvard physicians: "Let's interview and examine a big chunk of the population of a typical town, follow them for a decade or more, and see what the people who develop heart disease have in common."

These epidemiologists picked Framingham, a blue collar town west of Boston. Eight to ten years later the answers began to appear. The researchers coined the term "risk factors" to delineate those behaviors or conditions that predisposed to heart attacks. They are now known to include tobacco exposure, blood lipid elevations, high blood pressure, low HDL cholesterol, diabetes, hyperinsulinemia and diabetes, obesity (especially abdominal), a sedentary lifestyle, and perhaps (it's not clear) stress or a stressed personality. Some risk factors cannot be modified: being male, elderly, and having a family history of early coronary disease.

The Vedic Medical Poets and a Healthy Heart

Since prevention was conceived and refined to a high art by the ancient Ayurvedic physicians, if we examine the heart from their perspective we may gain insight into this riddle, as well as a practical program for avoidance and treatment of this scourge.

The Sanskrit root for heart is *hṛd*, from which we get the Greek (kardia) and the English and German words (Herz). In Sanskrit, the root hṛd is used to convey the idea of feeling or emotion, the essence of the person as well as the physical organ. A wealth of recent research has shown the important role of the emotions in the development and healing of coronary heart disease. One study suggested that one of the most important factors determining whether a man admitted to a coronary care unit with an acute heart attack would survive was whether he felt his wife loved him. A poetic passage in Charaka Samhitā, describes the heart in terms of its subtle functions, and gives insight into how to protect it:

> Ten great vessels of great consequence are rooted in the heart.....The body with its six limbs (two arms, two legs, trunk and head), the intellect, the sensory faculties, the five sense objects, the Self and its qualities, the mind and its objects reside in the heart.[139]

The ancient anatomists counted ten great vessels, the number you come up with if you include the pulmonary artery and veins. The qualities that we associate with the brain, spinal cord and cranial nerves are also located by the Sanskrit text in the heart. The heart in Ayurveda is felt to be the root of the vital essence – ojas – the cream of the nutrient fluid of the body, in which resides the vital breath.

> One who wants to protect the heart, the great vessels and the ojas should particularly

avoid the causes of mental suffering. That person should adopt measures beneficial to the heart and ojas, and that cleanse the channel, and should zealously strive for serenity and knowledge. [139]

It appears that the ancient physicians and anatomists understood that the heart is both a tough physical pump, capable of contracting over three billion times over your lifetime, as well as a delicate organ with subtle functions, and that good maintenance keeps it free from obstruction.

The Multifactorial Causes of Coronary Disease

Spasm of muscles in arterial walls, excessive fats in the blood and the stress responses of clotting and inflammation are the principle pathological mechanisms responsible for hardening of the arteries and are fortunately biological responses that allow us to get a handle on coronary disease using natural methods.

Many other diseases have been shown to have a single principle cause like a virus, bacterium or toxin. Spina bifida is nearly completely prevented by giving pregnant mothers folic acid; emphysema by stopping smoking. Arterial disease, on the other hand, is a complex disease with many contributing factors: dietary, emotional and behavioral. The heart and vessels are subject to an exquisite balance for their health: too much or too little exercise, fat, passion, salt or rest upsets its delicate equilibrium and, if prolonged, turns into disease. It is important to understand the interconnected risk factors for vessel disease and how we can modify them.

The role of stress in the development of coronary disease is still an area that is widely disputed by physicians. During the 1970's some preliminary studies of personality factors in heart attack victims impelled doctors to write "Type A personality" on their examination notes, implying that their patient was intense, goal- and time-oriented, and impatient, and presumably more prone to heart disease than a comparable laid-back Type B peer. This theory has since been shown to be not altogether valid. Yet many connections between atherosclerosis and stress have held up through time.

During stress, blood pressure, the tendency of the blood to clot, cholesterol and other blood fats all increase. Lipids in the blood are entirely appropriate when we need a surge of energy together with the ability to synthesize cortisol and other stress hormones in a hurry. Race car drivers were found to have elevated levels of fatty acids and other lipids as race day approached, peaking interestingly just before the race and not in the thick of it, showing that the anticipation of stress is actually more stressful than the stress itself. Israeli researchers reported that high cholesterol and even normal cholesterol are lowered by the practice of Transcendental Meditation[140], thereby confirming that stress reduction joins a low fat diet, exercise and weight loss as behavioral ways to lower your coronary risk without drugs.

Your ancestors needed to initiate clotting quickly in response to a stressor such as a predator. These days the predatory threats are fangless (bills coming due, rush hour, mutinous teenagers, estranged spouses, demanding bosses) but our nervous systems interpret their threat in the same way, making our blood more prone to clotting. In fact, one of the best triggers for platelet aggregation, a key event in clotting, is adrenaline, the ultimate stress hormone.

Insulin resistance and diabetes are endothelial goons because the increased blood sugar, simplistically stated, caramelizes the lining of the vessels not only of the heart but also of the eyes, kidneys and extremities. See Chapter 26 for a discussion of diabetes.

Blood pressure rises to pump blood more forcefully into muscles being used for fight or flight, but today as we flee mainly our demons, the response is inappropriate. Since the late 1960's, researchers had observed that stress management reduced high blood pressure, another of the major whammies promoting vessel trauma and subsequent hardening.

Young people who have a heart attack do much better than the elderly with the same amount of muscle damage. No surprise. But when you hear that an otherwise healthy person keeled over dead from a massive heart attack without any warning, it is more likely to be a young person, typically a male between forty and fifty years old, who has an isolated major blockage near the origin of a coronary vessel feeding the heart's most critical muscle. That fellow got up in the morning with the vessel half open, enough to get by, but the rupture of vulnerable plaque and spasm of the surrounding artery brought blood flow to a halt.

On the other hand, the elderly tend to have developed plaque throughout their coronaries arteries over a prolonged period. Sections of their heart muscles, being deprived of blood, signal the coronary vessels to supply them by building detours around the areas of blockage. The result is the development of collateral circulation, natural bypasses that circumvent the obstruction. New vessels can grow from the watershed of healthy vessels to supply blood on the side with a drought. Exercise accomplishes this effectively in a process called ischemic preconditioning. It stresses the heart muscle to the point of oxygen deprivation and thus stimulates repair. Interestingly the elderly are not as adept at this as the young are, but exercise and caloric deprivation have both been shown to be highly effective at reversing heart damage even in this population.

Testing the Vedic Approach to Heart Health

The effectiveness of the Vedic principle quoted above for preventing heart disease, "striving for serenity" and "avoiding the causes of mental suffering," was recently tested by Amparo Castillo -Richmond, M.D., a Colombian researcher working in a team from Iowa.[141] Their group, together with researchers from UCLA and a grant from the National Institutes of Health performed a randomized, controlled clinical trial on a group of elderly, inner city African Americans with hypertension. They compared subjects practicing 20 minutes of TM twice a day with a group who were given a health education program on heart disease prevention and were told to spend 20 minutes daily in a leisurely activity like reading or exercising. After five months, the TM group had a reduction in the thickness of the artery walls of nearly 1 millimeter, corresponding to a reduced risk for heart attack of 11 percent. During the same period, the control group increased the fatty buildup in their artery walls, increasing their risk of having a stroke or heart attack. Dr. Castillo-Richmond called the find, "better than I ever dreamed of."

A group at UCLA recently found that TM reduced insulin resistance, blood pressure and heart rate variability, a measure of heart health, in older overweight patients. Insulin resistance, hypertension and obesity are the major components of the feared quintuple whammy, dubbed the metabolic syndrome, giving people with major risks another way to beat the odds without drugs other than intensive exercise and a large weight loss.[142]

Researchers at the Buffalo VA Hospital in the 1970's had shown that patients with angina, when taught TM, were able to exercise longer and perform more work on a standard treadmill test before pain or the ECG changes of angina appeared.[143]

Established blockages in the coronary arteries have also been shown to be reversible by a regimen incorporating many of the elements of an Ayurvedic lifestyle. Dean Ornish, MD did imaging studies of the coronary arteries of patients who had had angina or heart attacks.[144] All patients were then given the usual medications for heart disease patients. One group of 28 patients, however, was given intensive counseling to follow a demanding program consisting of a vegetarian diet with less than 10 percent of calories from fat, daily exercise, yoga, meditation and group counseling. The other 22 patients were provided with "usual care" for patients with coronary disease including instructions on a low fat diet, daily exercise and the importance of quitting smoking. They were not asked to make lifestyle changes but were free to do so. The intensive treatment group, when imaged one and four years later, had progressive improvements in their vessels; the usual care group got progressively worse.

Many physicians vested in high tech approaches to heart disease are critical of Ornish's approach, calling it drastic. When an interviewer brought up this question, Ornish replied, "I don't understand why asking people to eat a well-balanced vegetarian diet is considered too drastic, but it is medically conservative to cut people open."

Get Started now to Reduce your Heart Disease Risk

On a practical level, here is an Ayurvedic program for heart disease. It can be followed by virtually anyone with heart disease, but it is always wise to consult with your physician when making changes in your diet and exercise. Almost anyone who has had a heart attack or angina needs a few medications (usually a daily aspirin, beta-blocker, and lipid lowering agent). The Vedic lifestyle program below should complement but not replace these standard approaches.[145]

1. Adjust your attitude. There is nothing fixed or mechanical about coronary and cerebral artery disease. It is a reversible process. The endothelial cells lining the arteries resemble the epithelial cells of the skin: they are constantly remodeling themselves. Just as you slough off the old cells and grow a new skin every 28 days, you remodel the lining of the vessels. This understanding belies the attitude of mainstream medicine, that sick vessels tend to continue to degenerate. It explains the research findings cited above that heart disease is reversible using natural Vedic methods.

2. Let your attitude change your life. If you have developed significant vascular disease, some aspects of your life are probably due for a drastic change. Take an inventory of your diet, exercise, and behavioral or emotional habits in the light of your heart stats (blood pressure, weight, sugar and lipids).

3. Stay happy and serene. "Eat your heart out, baby!" This expression commonly used to evoke envy, is exactly what will happen if you compare yourself with others or are unhappy with your lot. If you are depressed, anxious, chronically pessimistic, irritable or angry, your chances of developing a major illness are doubled,[146] and that illness is commonly heart disease. Even if you are grumpy, acting happy may protect your heart. In an NIH funded study reported in 2010 of 1700 people without heart problems followed for ten years, the happier people were less likely to have developed a heart problem.[147] Remember also that there is no conflict between serenity and a healthy, competitive drive to get ahead.[148]

4. It's more what's eating you than what you eat. Change those areas of your life that create negative emotions. Fix your relationships or consider a more fulfilling career. Simplify your life, including your time commitments, your expenses and your needs.

5. Rethink your life. Re-evaluate the two qualities of your heart: emotional and physical. Your profession thus becomes living life fully; your job becomes your hobby or avocation, a place you go to amuse yourself while attending to the serious profession of rehabilitating both qualities of your heart.

6. Make time for the neurochemistry of health. It can be as simple as five to ten minutes of yoga and fifteen to twenty minutes of meditation, followed by prayer, singing, martial arts or a walk. I recommend Transcendental Meditation as it is extensively researched and is so simple it can be learned by anyone. Research has also shown that its medical benefits are side effects of its even greater value of nervous system integration – enlightenment.

7. Get serious about reducing animal fats. They are the only source of cholesterol. Start first with red meat, then with fowl and eggs. Reduce unhealthy dairy sources of fat, substituting reduced fat milk for whole milk, light cheese for Camembert, and frozen yogurt for ice cream.

8. Think like a vegetarian. Instead of planning a meal around a meat dish, think in terms of different staples. Reconstruct your food pyramid with salad and vegetables at the base, fruit and grains in the middle, dairy near the top and meat at the very tip.

9. Favor fruits and vegetables. They are rich in antioxidants, the molecules that fight inflammation. Strive for a colorful plate of food: dark green leafy vegetables, yellow and orange as in squashes and fruits, blues and reds as in berries. See Chapter 18.

10. Use grains and legumes to increase fiber. Dietary fiber lowers cholesterol by reducing its absorption. Especially helpful are oats, bran, flax seeds and psyllium, pumpkin and sunflower seeds. Add them into granola and start your day with cereal and fresh fruit.

11. Eat fresh garlic. It is renowned by the ancient physicians as useful for the heart, a finding supported by modern research. Add a fresh clove to the cooking to avoid the oxidized, rancid oils in garlic powder.

12. Use turmeric. It is a potent anti-inflammatory and antioxidant (See Chapter 18). It has been traditionally prescribed in large quantities for heart disease and recently has been shown to protect the endothelium from the plaque-forming effects of cholesterol.

13. Choose olive oil. It is rich in mono-unsaturated fats as opposed to other vegetable oils, margarine, butter and shortening.

14. Don't just eat light fare, eat lightly. If you are even a little overweight, restrict your calories. Easily reproducible research has shown that caloric restriction prolongs the lives of lab animals See Chapter 5.

15. Go out every day to play. Follow the advice you would give to a heavy, mopey child. This can be walking, biking or swimming. It can be basketball at the gym, or gardening in your yard. Just make it fun. This accomplishes the main purpose of changing your neurochemistry of stress and is the best way to insure that you make it a lifetime habit. See Chapter 13. Walking on a treadmill can indeed help your heart, but the same time spent outdoors has a double value. Grab binoculars as you go out the door and think, "I'm going bird watching," and not "I'm going to exercise."

16. Take care of other sources of inflammation. These may play a role in triggering an inflammatory response that accelerates vascular disease. See your dentist about gingivitis; deal with festering infections of the nails, skin, lashes or sinuses. Statin drugs, used to reduce cholesterol, help to reduce heart disease risk through their potent anti-inflammatory actions. They reduce the risk of heart disease and stroke even in people with favorable cholesterol profiles, probably through their anti-inflammatory actions. Because they are anti – inflammatory, they even help in the middle of a heart attack. Reducing your body's inflammatory burden using the advice in the first half of this book may well have a similar effect.

17. Use three Ayurvedic herbs. These herbs used since ancient times for circulatory problems have been shown to improve heart disease. Someone with established coronary disease can be advised to take all three. Bear in mind that many cardiac medications interact with other drugs (e.g. coumadin, statins, nitroglycerin and antihypertensives) and may require dose modification, so always check with your physician before adding these to your regimen.

1) Arjuna. The *Arjuna myrobalan* tree soars to 90 feet high and has a thick grey bark that peels off in thin sheets, allowing the brittle cortex to be harvested without destroying the tree, whose shade is precious in the hot Indian sun. The bark has been shown to have potent antioxidant and cholesterol reducing effects.[149] It kills bacteria and prevents carcinogenesis in test tube models.[150] Arjuna is traditionally used by Ayurvedic physicians for its effect on the both the emotional heart, including depression, and the physical heart for angina, heart failure and arrhythmias.

Arjuna was found to improve the left ventricular ejection fraction, the usual means of quantifying the heart's efficiency, in ten patients with congestive heart failure due to ischemic heart disease.[151] Arjuna was compared with a commonly used medication for angina (isosorbide mononitrate) in its ability to improve exercise tolerance on a treadmill in 58 men with chronic stable angina (NYHA class II-III). Both groups were equivalent and better than placebo, and the patients on the Arjuna extract tolerated it well.[152]

2) Guggulu. A traditional Ayurvedic herb, guggulu, has been shown to lower total cholesterol and raise the good HDL cholesterol. Guggulu is a resin similar to myrrh, and comes from the bark of a bush, *Commiphora mukkul*. Fractions of guggulu have been shown to attach themselves to receptors in the liver responsible for cholesterol synthesis. Guggulu is also a good anti-inflammatory and its principle traditional use in Ayurveda is for joint disease. It is also traditionally used for weight management and control of fat and sugar metabolism, making it an important herb for people with coronary disease.[153]

3) Ashwagandha. Literally meaning *smell of a horse*, ashwagandha (*Withania somnifera*) is one of the most commonly prescribed adaptogens, or balancing herbs for dealing with the effects of stressors. Studies have shown that it protects the heart muscle from the damage of ischemia (blood flow deprivation).[154]

Take 500 mg of each herb as a tablet or as a powder twice daily. Tablets are easier to swallow. You can instead buy all three herbs as a bulk powder and take a half-teaspoon of the mixture twice daily with water. Because this is bitter, some people may opt to put the powder mixture in capsules for convenience and taste. Bulk powders are much less expensive than tablets. See Resources for a list of capsulation suppliers.[155]

138 Caleb Hillier Parry. *Inquiry into the Symptoms and Causes of the Syncope Anginosa, Commonly Called Angina Pectoris*, Illustrated by Dissections (1799).

139 *Charaka Samhitā*. Ni.30.3-14.

140 Cooper M, Aygen M. Journal of Human Stress, 5, 24-27, 1979.

141 Stroke. March 2000.

142 Merz NB et al. Archives Int Med. June 12, 2006.

143 Zamarra J et al. Am J. Card 77:10;867-870.

144 Ornish D, Brown SE, Scherwitz L W, Billings JH, Armstrong WT, Ports TA, McLanahan, SM, Kirkeeide RL, Brand RJ, Gould KL. *Can lifestyle changes reverse coronary heart disease? The Lifestyle Heart Trial.* Lancet. 1990 Jul 21;336(8708):129-33.

145 If you have significant coronary risks, see your physician about whether you may need a statin or aspirin as part of your preventative program.

146 University of California at Riverside, Prof. Howard Friedman.

147 Davidson K et al. European Heart Journal. Feb. 18, 2010.

148 Friend and Frew found in the 1970's that executives who learned TM in a corporation, compared to the control group, reported that they felt less pressure to climb the company ladder, but were rated by their colleagues as more likely to be promoted. Acad Mgmt Journal 17:362,1974

149 Gupta R, Singhal S, Goyle A, Sharma VN. *Antioxidant and hypocholesterolaemic effects of Terminalia tree-bark powder: a randomized placebo-controlled trial.* J Assoc Physicians India. 2001 Feb;49:231-5.

150 *Terminalia arjuna*. Altern Med Rev. 1999 Dec;4(6):436-7.

151 Dwivedi S, Jauhari R. *Beneficial effects of Terminalia arjuna in coronary artery disease.* Indian Heart J. 1997 Sep-Oct;49(5):507-10.

152 Bharani A, Ganguli A, Mathur LK, Jamra Y, Raman PG. *Efficacy of Terminalia arjuna in chronic stable angina: a double-blind, placebo-controlled, crossover study comparing Terminalia Arjuna with isosorbide mononitrate.* Indian Heart J. 2002 Mar-Apr;54(2):170-5.

153 Guggulu is usually compounded with other herbs depending on the purpose. Kanchanar guggulu is a good formulation for heart disease. It can be purchased plain, in bulk, and mixed with other herbs as described above.

154 Mohanty I, Arya DS, Dinda A, Talwar KK, Joshi S, Gupta SK. *Mechanisms of cardioprotective effect of Withania somnifera in experimentally induced myocardial infarction.* Basic Clin Pharmacol Toxicol. 2004 Apr;(4):184-90.

155 Bazaar of India carries vegetarian capsules.

CHAPTER 25

TREATING HYPERTENSION WITHOUT DRUGS

As a medical student, I did an elective rotation at a major medical center in New Delhi and attended rounds in two cardiology clinics: the valve clinic and the coronary clinic. In the valve clinic, I needed an interpreter because the patients could not speak English. They were mostly young, poor, and undernourished, and came from farm villages complaining of the symptoms of heart failure. Years before, they had acquired a streptococcal infection and, without easy access to penicillin, had developed rheumatic fever that destroyed their heart valves.

In the coronary clinic every patient spoke perfect, cultured English with a hint of a British accent. They were from business and professional families from the city and well fed. I never needed an interpreter. It didn't take me long to conclude that our modern epidemic of vessel disease and its primary risk factors (hypertension, diabetes, obesity, smoking, lack of exercise and high cholesterol) could mostly be eliminated if we could somehow abandon our overfed, sedentary and stressful lifestyles.

A large national survey reported in the New England Journal of Medicine showed that less than a quarter of the population with high blood pressure had adequate control.[156] Other studies have demonstrated that half of people who start medications will have stopped them in a year, allowing their blood pressure to rise because they could not tolerate the side effects. Half of the hypertensive patients consulting me for Vedic medicine will also have stopped their medication – but their pressure will be controlled without drugs.

Ayurveda has a long history of treating hypertension, even pre-dating the invention of the blood pressure cuff. In fact, the first antihypertensive medication was an Ayurvedic plant, *Rauwolfia serpentina*, known as *sarpagandha* in Sanskrit.[157]

Aggressive treatment of blood pressure dramatically reduces the risk of the commonest diseases you least want to get, starting with strokes and heart attacks. It is never too late to start; in the elderly, careful control of blood pressure has been shown to reduce the onset of dementia by half. Even white coat hypertension has documented risks. In rush hour traffic, your vessels undergo the same stresses as when the nurse takes your blood pressure. Your vessels constrict in response to adrenaline. This increases the resistance to the easy flow of blood through your arterial beds, stressing your heart muscles and placing shearing forces on the delicate endothelium that lines the vessels of your vital organs – especially your brain, kidneys and heart. Too many traffic jams and thirty years later you have the makings for a sudden, often unheralded, vascular event. Not a good moment for people who are wimps about growing older.

However, aggressive lifestyle changes can reduce or even eliminate the need for pills. People who make these changes and who no longer require their medications are probably even better off, because in addition to reducing their blood pressure, they have made dietary and lifestyle changes that improve their well-being and reduce the risks of many other diseases, including diabetes.

Owning your own blood pressure cuff is the ticket off your pills, because when you see your doctor your blood pressure will be always be higher than it is at home (white coat hypertension), especially if you are motivated to get off your medications. Show your doctor a diary with 20 to 30 home readings each time you get checked. A reliable electronic cuff that you apply to the upper arm (not the wrist or finger) is a good investment because these cuffs are easier to operate and will not fudge the reading. Calibrate your cuff with your doctor's reading. Record the date, time of day and comments about your frame of mind, diet and lifestyle next to the reading so you can identify factors that raise or lower your pressure.

Besides herbs, there are other scientifically documented ways anyone can reduce their blood pressure without drugs.

Here is my short list:

1. Avoid salt. Add it only in moderation while cooking and refrain from reaching for the saltshaker at the table. Especially avoid packaged and prepared foods that are high in sodium such as snacks, frozen meals, macaroni and cheese and other convenience meals. Use more spices, lemon juice or shavings from a good, smelly cheese for extra flavoring. Good for a systolic reduction of 3-5 mm Hg.

2. Lighten your diet. Cultivate a taste for a diet that focuses on fresh produce, whole grains and low-fat dairy. Favor fruits and vegetables in abundance and reduce meat and other high fat foods. This ancient Ayurvedic prescription for long life has now been dubbed the DASH diet (Dietary Approaches to Stop Hypertension). Combined with salt reduction, it's good for another 5-10 mm Hg.

3. Lose extra pounds. Today's high blood pressure epidemic is partially related to our epidemic of obesity. Extra pounds increase the resistance to blood flow and make your heart pump blood through a few more miles of capillaries. This can be good for 1 mm Hg for every pound lost. A drug free way to knock off another 5-10 mm Hg.

4. Get fit. Exercise promotes the flow of blood to muscles and other organs, thereby lowering the resistance to blood flow that causes hypertension. It's that simple. 3-4 mm Hg.

5. Stop smoking. Have you noticed how smoking makes your hands and feet feel cold? This is the result of constriction of your blood vessels. Count on 3-5 mm Hg.

6. Potassium supplementation. Adequate potassium can lower blood pressure by 20 points according to a Duke University study. In a twelve-year study of 859 hypertensives published in the New England Journal of Medicine, the 24 people dying of stroke had a significantly lower dietary intake of potassium even after adjusting for caloric intake. Forget potassium supplements.[158] The large doses of potassium in the fruits (mangoes, pears, strawberries and melons) and vegetables (cucumbers, tomatoes, legumes) this book recommends as antioxidants for preventing cancer, aging and other problems should be equivalent.[159, 160]

7. Extra magnesium. Adequate magnesium levels lower blood pressure by up to 11% (or about 15 points) in only two months for people with mild hypertension.[161] Again, why take supplements when fruits and vegetables are nature's perfectly balanced food, as well as much more fun to swallow. Go for spinach, artichokes, beans, figs, nuts, and seeds.

8. Calcium. Taken in a dose of 2000 mg per day (about double the recommended amount for the average postmenopausal woman for preventing bone mineral loss), calcium can have a modest effect on systolic pressure. The best source of calcium is dairy.[162]

9. Garlic. Only fresh, never powdered or extracts, which quickly become rancid and are often socially distasteful. Several studies have shown garlic can knock off 2-3 mm Hg.

10. Meditation. Twelve published studies, the most recent sponsored by the National Institutes of Health, have shown reductions of 8-10 mm Hg in practitioners of Transcendental Meditation not seen in control groups doing mindfulness meditation and progressive muscular relaxation. Several studies were done in the most resistant types of blood pressure including elderly, inner city African-Americans. Transcendental Meditation even lowered blood pressure in inner city black adolescents at high risk for hypertension.[163] Groups doing Transcendental Meditation had a reduction in the thickness of the lining of their carotid artery, reflecting less deposition of plaque.

11. Deal with stress. Avoid traffic jams, needless confrontations, unreasonable deadlines and other behaviors that make you irritated. 2-5 mm Hg depending on your burden.

12. Chocolate. Yes, fellow chocoholics, you read right! Researchers from Cologne analyzed ten studies that met stringent criteria of reliability, including five randomized trials, and concluded that consumption of chocolate, but not tea, lowers systolic blood pressure by an impressive 4.7 mm Hg – what you might expect from some medications.[164] Phenols in cocoa may dilate arteries and increase endothelial production of nitric oxide, the same mechanism that causes vessels to dilate in erections and other vascular responses. If you eat 3 oz of dark chocolate containing beneficial polyphenols,[165] keeping your total caloric consumption the same, your risk of stroke would be reduced by 20% and mortality from all causes by 8%. Your low pharmacy bills could pay for all that chocolate. No wonder chocolate was worshipped by the Mayans! Be conservative and lop off 3 mm Hg.

13. Herbs. Beside 70% Theobroma cacao disguised as fine Belgian dark chocolate, the most important single plant that anyone with hypertension can take is *punarnava (Boerhaavia diffusa Linn.,* aka spreading hogweed). *Nava* in Sanskrit means new and *punar* means again. This creeper was held by the ancient physicians to make you new again. It is known to have potent anti-inflammatory properties and has been shown to relax the coronary arteries of goats due to a direct vasodilator effect. The roots and leaves have a mild diuretic effect and are used in many kidney disorders.[166] The dried whole plant can be purchased in tablets or loose powder, and is taken in the dose of 250 mg twice daily. When taken together with Arjuna tree bark (See Chapter 24), punarnava is a simple herbal supplement for people with hypertension and another coronary risk. It should be used in this way after consulting your physician. Easily good for 3 mm Hg.

Add them up and knock off some points just to be realistic. I rarely find a patient on blood pressure pills who cannot reduce or sometimes even discard them within a year. As you change your diet, lose weight, exercise and meditate, your blood pressure will trend down and your doctor may taper your dose. If, in spite of your best efforts, you still need your pills, the lifestyle changes will make you feel better and reduce other risks for stroke, heart attacks and cancer.

156 *Characteristics of Patients with Uncontrolled Hypertension in the United States.* Hyman DJ et al. N Engl J Med 345(7): 479-486 August 16, 2001.

157 See Chapter 22, Your Bag of Supplements, for a discussion of reserpine in the context of the fallacy of the active ingredient.

158 Unless you have been prescribed potassium to replace that which is lost with diuretics.

159 See Chapter 18 for a diet rich in antioxidants.

160 If you have kidney insufficiency or certain adrenal problems, ask your doctor before taking a diet high in potassium.

161 Am J Card 2003, Sep 15;92(6)665-9.

162 See Chapter 28, discussing calcium supplementation in osteoporosis.

163 Barnes V. American Journal of Hypertension, April 2004.

164 Taubert, D et al. Arch Intern Med. 2007;167:626-634.

165 Researchers have identified the highly bioavailable flavonoids catechin and epicatechin in cocoa and tea as active in blood pressure in animal models. Cocoa, however, possesses many procyanids that may be active antihypertensives. In any event, Ayurveda regards consuming the active ingredient of a plant to be risky and not holistic. See Chapter 22 for an extended discussion of the fallacy of the active ingredients.

166 If you have renal insufficiency, consult your doctor before taking any diuretics, herbal or otherwise.

CHAPTER 26

INSULIN RESISTANCE AND THE ROYAL HORMONE

In 1973, when I first met Eddie Mason, he was in his eighties and still practicing endocrinology in Montreal. I was a lowly intern. He had started his practice soon after the discovery of insulin.

The first afternoon I saw patients in the diabetes clinic with him, I knew this was going to be a unique experience. Diabetic patients always have thick charts, but on the front of his typical patients' thick charts, was scrawled "Volume 6 of 6." The patients in the waiting room were almost all elderly and the nurse told me many had been with Eddie for fifty years.

My first patient was a seventy-five year old woman who was thin and spry. The summary in the chart said she had been diagnosed with juvenile diabetes at the age of eleven and was referred to Dr. Mason. She told me, "Dr. Mason is the toughest taskmaster I have ever known, but that is why I am still here. He had me check my sugar six times a day when I was a teenager. It took half an hour to check your sugar. You had to boil up a mess of chemicals after putting the blood drop on a filter paper, then wait for it to develop. We didn't have long-acting insulin then, so he'd have me give myself regular insulin six times a day based on what my sugar was. That wasn't easy either without disposable sterile syringes and sharp needles. I'd boil my syringes and needles while I cooked the lab reagents. We'd sharpen the needles over and over. If we weren't willing to cooperate with Dr. Mason's tough approach, he said we could just get another doctor. But take a look at this old gal. Dr. Mason says my vessels are like a young spring chicken's and I can see just fine."

I assessed the diabetics before Eddie Mason walked in. Whether they had juvenile or adult onset diabetes, his patients were generally in remarkable shape for people who had lived with the disease for so long. They all pulled out a blood glucose diary for Eddie to examine and held their breath to see if he would praise or scold their efforts before adjusting their insulin schedules. Few of his patients were on the oral hypoglycemic drugs we had available then; he called them "second-class treatments" reserved for the non-compliant. "If you want to prevent complications in diabetics, insist on strict control with insulin."

It took another twenty years for the medical establishment to prove with scientific research what I learned in three hours with Eddie Mason: strict control of blood sugar prevents long-term complications. From the discovery of insulin in the 1920's until the early 1990's, it was felt that insulin could prevent a person from having acute complications such as acidosis and infections but it was not proven that strict control of blood sugar made a difference in chronic complications. In 1993 a landmark study was completed showing that 1,440 insulin dependent diabetics, whose physicians followed guidelines to achieve better control, had fewer complications than patients whose regimen was less strict, including 70% less damage to their retinas.[167, 168] It was easy for me to be convinced because I was observing patients who had been subjected to a defined experimental protocol – Eddie Mason's demanding prescriptions – and compared them to the "control" diabetics I had seen in other clinics whose doctors were more forgiving.

Insulin – the Royal Vedic Hormone

Insulin resistance is the result of a defect in the biological mechanism that allows us to eat when it is convenient, sparing us from constantly needing to consume food. A hummingbird spends a good part of her day foraging for sugar because it has a high metabolic rate due to its tiny body that easily loses heat, together with its rapid wing beat. The life of a hummingbird is made easier because of insulin, and insulin makes a lion the king of the jungle. Insulin stores the glucose from the gazelle in the lion's muscles, liver and fat, so he can make a kill, eat to his fill, and relax for a few days until the next hunt.

By now, you have grasped that effortlessness and the refinement of consciousness are the soul of a Vedic life. Insulin is the quintessential Vedic hormone, storing energy in moments of plenty to set us free to be creative, regal, spiritual beings with time to enjoy the song and play of the universe.

The body's mechanism for storing nutrients and slowly releasing them in response to activity is an elegant display of the expression of intelligence in the physiology. Blood sugar remains within relatively narrow limits through feedback loops that sense changes in its level and adjust its release or storage accordingly.

When insulin's function breaks down, either because it is not secreted (e.g. insulin-dependent diabetes and juvenile onset diabetes) or because it is impotent at its site of action (non-insulin-dependent diabetes including many people with adult onset), the sugars from the meal are not stored and therefore inappropriately remain in the blood, circulate throughout the body and attach to proteins. This is the root of the long-term complications. Sugar is sticky. This stickiness allows sugar to attach to proteins when it is concentrated, in effect caramelizing the body's proteins. Most critically, this occurs in the lining of the vessels of the kidneys, where sugar concentrations are highest. Sugarcoating of the proteins in the vessels, called "glycation," is what leads to premature vessel disease, and the eventual damage to the heart, retina, kidneys and toes. Your vessels' linings have essentially turned into Fruit Loops.

The ancient Ayurvedic physicians recognized diabetes and named it *madhumeha*, or "honey in the urine." Charaka describes the laboratory test, "crawling of bees and ants on the body or the urine."[169] The medical treatises also describe the presenting symptoms in lyrical Sanskrit: 'always drinking, yet always thirsty; always eating, yet always hungry, they waste away in a stream of their own urine.' This is a textbook description of the way some undiagnosed patients present to their doctors even today. Indeed, during World War I, before the discovery of insulin, Elliot Joslin wrote, "the food which the untreated diabetic patient wastes in a week would feed a soldier for a day."[170] Without the hormone insulin, like a hummingbird, you would have to spend nearly all day eating.

Wherefore Insulin Resistance?

Maturity onset diabetes is so prevalent that one is led to wonder if there might be a logical explanation, especially since it is found in nearly half of the Pima tribe of Native Americans and other populations. It may be that this type of diabetes is nature's way of insuring that a population will survive famine. Diabetics' cells are resistant to insulin's message to take up sugar and convert it to starches and fat, a condition that is dramatically improved by weight loss. Diabetics therefore thrive in conditions of famine, where, with meager food resources, diabetics lose their fat stores and maintain normal blood sugars, while non-diabetics may succumb to the ravages of starvation.

Perhaps a distant population of our ancestors was wiped out in a famine and among the survivors were a few individuals who were on the verge of becoming diabetics. They thrived because they could maintain normal glucose levels while performing high levels of activity, scavenging the countryside for a few meager morsels of food, and easily convert their body's stores of fat and starch (glycogen) to glucose. These same individuals, however, in times of abundance, are at a disadvantage since their cells are resistant to insulin. We are now in an age of abundance and diabetes takes its place as one of the major disorders of the new millennium. Some evolutionary theorists have proposed that, as a species, we have just not had time to adapt to the newly imposed stress of abundance and leisure and that natural selection will soon weed out those who can't keep fit and eat less.

In the Vedic texts, diabetes is described as a disorder of contrasts. The tissues and blood become sweet, sticky and heavy (a kapha imbalance), and then the sticky tissues dry out, becoming stiff and brittle (a vata imbalance).[171] In essence, this is a modern understanding of the premature hardening of the arteries underlying a diabetic's complications.

The solution from the Ayurvedic perspective is straightforward: impose the conditions of famine and diabetics are in their element. A meager diet and lots of exercise mimics a day foraging. Most doctors have had my experience of witnessing patients who have followed this advice for adult onset diabetes. The patients lost weight, became fit and no longer required any medication. Others have reduced their medication requirement. Almost everyone, if they follow this program, will reduce their risk of future complications.

A Vedic Program for Insulin Resistance

Charaka describes the benefits of this Ayurvedic program in poetic terms:

Diabetes approaches like a bird to its nest-tree the person who is greedy for food and who dislikes bathing and walking. Death, in the form of diabetes, takes away the person who is sluggish in activities, obese, over-indulgent in fatty foods and is a voracious eater. The person who takes food which maintains the equilibrium of tissues and also practices various physical activities enjoys a happy life."

Charaka Samhitā
Ni.4.50-52

Followed more casually, this is a preventive program for anyone who is at risk of diabetes: anyone who is overweight, has had a borderline fasting blood sugar test (95-125 mg/dl), or has someone in their immediate family with adult onset diabetes, especially if that relative is not overweight. This program may also be added to any non-insulin-dependent diabetic's current regimen, with the caution that as your blood sugar begins to drop, you may need to consult your physician to adjust your medications accordingly. Inform yourself about diabetes. This is one of the diseases where you need to know almost as much as your doctor. Don't count on your doctor to be as aggressive as Eddie Mason in controlling your blood sugar, because most doctors do not have the time or inclination in the exam room to do the scolding, educating, pleading, cajoling, sympathizing and hand holding that is involved in good diabetic care. During the years when I was espousing the strict approach of Eddie Mason, many doctors were making their patients happy telling them they could be relaxed about diabetes, to get a life and eat more or less what they wanted. With this program, you can get an even better life, and in a few decades, when the complications of diabetes usually begin to appear, you will be happy you took care of yourself.[172]

The Essence of Maintaining Insulin Sensitivity[173]

1. Watch your glycohemoglobin. If you have insulin resistance or frank diabetes, follow your glycohemoglobin (hemoglobin A1C level) as if it were the Holy Grail. This blood test is the best indicator of the effectiveness of your overall program – diet, exercise and stress management – because it reflects the average sugar level during the previous three months. The glycohemoglobin is a measure of how much the sugar in your blood has attached itself to the proteins in your red blood cells, reflecting what is going on in the walls of your arteries. If you keep your levels equivalent to non-diabetics, i.e. under 6%, your diabetes will not reduce your longevity. If you have diabetes, repeat the test three times a year. If you have high normal sugar levels (90-100mg/dl), ask your doctor to order this test yearly.

2. Measure your body fat and your weight. Keep yourself lean. If you lose muscle, the best burner of sugar, you may be losing ground; so keep yourself both lean and fit.

3. Be regular with exercise. Plan on a good session of exercise daily, but think of it as your time to play. Because exercise has to become a part of your everyday lifestyle – for the rest of your life – devise ways to make it fun and something you look forward to. See Chapter 13. Find recreation that works for you in all seasons. If it seems like drudgery, you have adopted both the wrong activity and the wrong attitude. Stay active; burning sugar and fat is a daily issue. You are permitted days off, but when you take time off for extra rest, reduce your food consumption. In this spirit, the ancient Ayurvedic texts suggest that diabetics avoid daytime naps.

4. Walk after meals. It can be short and leisurely, and even for just five to ten minutes. This stimulates the digestive fires and increases metabolism.

5. Eat foods with a low glycemic index. Foods with a low glycemic index, i.e. the foods that take a prolonged time to be absorbed as glucose and other sugars are the ones recommended by the Ayurvedic texts. White bread, a food with a high glycemic index of 70, appears in the blood as sugar in a matter of minutes. Foods that require a longer time to be broken down and absorbed, like beans (glycemic index of 32), will raise the blood sugar level rather slowly. Adopting the diet you would follow if you were living in a third world country, without processed, refined and packaged foods is a good way to start because fiber rich foods, in general, have a low glycemic index. A study following 40,000 black U.S. women for eight years found that those women who consumed a diet low in fiber and having a high glycemic index were more likely to develop diabetes.[174]

6. Eat foods that are bitter, astringent, rough and light. This Ayurvedic recommendation will automatically select the foods with a low glycemic index.[175] This index is a way to quantify what the ancient Vedic physicians had learned thousands of years before the discovery of insulin. By avoiding blood sugar spikes and keeping insulin levels low, the Vedic diabetic diet controls appetite, promotes weight loss, does not tax an overworked pancreas, and may prevent insulin resistance. In a study of thirty-six thousand Australian men and women followed for four years, those that ate the most white bread and starch had the highest risk of developing diabetes.[176] Women participating in the huge Nurses' Health Study who were insulin resistant or overweight, and who ate a high glycemic index diet, were found to have a higher risk of developing heart disease than similar women taking lower glycemic foods.[177] In a study of 129 overweight young Australians, high carbohydrate diets with the lowest glycemic loads were best at lowering the bad low-density lipoprotein cholesterol level (LDL) associated with risk of coronary disease.[178, 179] A high glycemic index diet has also been seen to damage rats' pancreases.[180]

7. Follow your palate. Rather than focus on the glycemic index, keep your joy in life by following your palate and intuition – the Vedic way to bring about self-repair. Your staples should include "bitter" foods such as salad, vegetable soup, cooked legumes such as lentils or beans. Take low-fat dairy and lean cuts of meat and fish. The Vedic diabetic diet can also be spicy. The most important item this list leaves out is starch. Avoid grains that are "sweet" such as rice and wheat, and favor grains that are "bitter" such as rye, barley, buckwheat, millet, oats and quinoa. Corn is a good grain if it is not refined, so include corn tortillas or whole grain corn chips. Use brown rice rather than white rice or basmati, and avoid products made from white wheat flour, which have a high glycemic index, appearing quickly in your blood as sugar. Instead of pasta, white bread and couscous, favor instead bulgur wheat, wheat berries, and bread and crackers made from rye or whole-wheat.

8. Eat a wide variety of fresh produce. Your diet should contain dark green, leafy vegetables (the prototype of a bitter food, according to Ayurvedic texts), as well as produce with blue, red, orange, and yellow pigments, the antioxidants that combat the damage of accelerated aging of vessels. Therefore don't avoid fresh fruits simply because they are 'sweet' and may have a high glycemic index. Fresh fruit contains so many useful ingredients such as natural antioxidants, flavonoids, vitamins and other essential nutrients, that it is better to forego other carbohydrates, such as starches, so you can eat plenty of fresh fruit.

9. Use bitter melon. Bitter melon looks like a wrinkled cucumber. Consumption of this tasty vegetable, known as *karela* in Asian markets across the country, actually lowers blood sugar levels, but more importantly for diabetics, it helps you to not miss sweets. Karela has a delicious, but bitter taste you quickly adjust to. It can be chopped finely or grated and added to soups, stir-fry vegetables, and other savory dishes. At first, try it as a garnish, crispy-fried in a non-stick pan with a little olive oil and salt. It may be eaten cooked or raw, juiced or whole – just eat it.

10. Use turmeric. This bitter, astringent spice is useful for diabetics and for deliciously flavoring the vegetables and legumes that make up a large part of the diabetic diet. Similarly, fenugreek seeds are good for diabetes. Sprinkle the whole or powdered seeds (available at Asian markets) into your sauces. Both of these spices should be used abundantly if you have associated weight problems or arthritis.

11. Use gymnema. The most important herb that can be taken by any diabetic, juvenile or adult, fat or thin, brittle or stable, without the need for consultation with a physician, is *Gymnema sylvestre*. This herb regulates appetite, weight and sugar metabolism. One of its Sanskrit names is *gurmar*, meaning, "destroyer of sugar." It attaches itself to sugar receptors, reducing sugar cravings and your appreciation of sweet tastes. Suck on a tablet for ten to twenty seconds and the craving soon passes. It also blocks sugar uptake from the gut and reduced glycohemoglobin in non-insulin dependent diabetics.[181]

Eddie Mason had remarkable insight and inexhaustible patience.[182] He still lives within generations of medical residents, and through us, in our patients with a predisposition to insulin resistance.

167 NEJM 329:977-986

168 Recent research that was unpublished at the time this book is going to press has shown, however, that aggressively lowering sugar levels and HbA1C through tighter insulin administration in middle age and older diabetics with established complications like heart disease may not reduce complications and mortality. After all, insulin works by converting sugar into fat and starch, and then storing them in the body. Insulin and other diabetes drugs, while lifesaving, generally make you gain weight if not accompanied by gastronomic moderation and exercise. In addition, excessively strict control introduces the risks of hypoglycemia including sudden death, strokes, heart attacks and falls.

169 Charaka Samhitā Ni. 4.47

170 *The Treatment of Diabetes.* Elliot P. Joslin. 1917.

171 Refer to Appendices 1 and 3 for a discussion of the doshas.

172 This is an Ayurvedic program for non-insulin-dependent diabetics. It is not for juvenile onset diabetics. While simple to understand, it is not necessarily easy to follow, and could be deemed "arduous." The Sanskrit word for an arduous life is *tapas*, whose root implies "ascetic ardor," and invokes "burning" negative impressions, stresses or actions (karma) in the fire of penance. Similarly, from a vaidya's perspective, this program "burns" unnecessary nutrients and metabolic residues (āma) to keep the vessels and channels (srotamsi) clear.

173 Juvenile onset diabetes may benefit from some of these recommendations, but because of the brittle nature of their disease, they should always talk to their doctor before making changes.

174 Krishnan S, et al. *Glycemic Index, Glycemic Load, and Cereal Fiber Intake and Risk of Type 2 Diabetes in US Black Women.* Arch Intern Med. 2007;167(21):2304-2309.

175 Low glycemic foods are found in the Ayurvedic kapha-pacifying diet. Kapha, being structure or solidity, has the qualities of heaviness, sweetness, coldness and unctuousness and is therefore pacified by the opposite qualities in the diet.

176 Hodge, A. Diabetes Care, November 2004; vol 27: pp 2701-2706.

177 Nurses' Health Study. Simin Liu et al. Am J Clin Nutr. Sep 1999.

178 Archives of Internal Medicine, July 24, 2006, Arch Intern Med. 2006;166:1438-1439, 1466-1475

179 Women in the study lost more weight when their low glycemic index diets also had high levels of protein.

180 Ludwig, David S. Boston Childern's Hospital. Quoted in: *Don't Play a Numbers Game, Experts Say, Just Eat Your Vegetables* By Mary Duenwald. New York Times. September 14, 2004.

181 Baskaran K, et al. Ethnopharmacolocy 30:295-305, 1990

182 Dr. Mason outlined the essence of this approach in his 1927 paper, *The Treatment Of Diabetes Mellitus Through Office Practice*, which appeared only a few years after the discovery of insulin. (Edward H. Mason, M.D., Can Med Assoc J. 1927 February; 17(2): 175-179) The article is available online at http://www.pubmedcentral.nih.gov/picrender.fcgi?artid=406960&blobtype=pdf

CHAPTER 27

MAINTAINING BRAIN FITNESS

My rotations as a resident at the Montreal Neurological Institute always seemed too short. Its ornate halls, steep amphitheaters and hidden murals depicting the great figures in the annals of neurology who had passed through its doors were conducive to the study of the human brain. Some of those early pioneers, like Wilder Penfield, who mapped the brain's cortex, still walked its halls. Every Wednesday afternoon the neurology residents would take a break in a lounge where, like the Thanksgiving turkey, a brain was sitting on a wooden carving plate next to a sharp silver carving knife. The brain invariably belonged to a patient who had expired during the past week and whose family wished us to gain whatever information we could from its examination. As we hovered around it trying to peer inside, the chief resident would make vertical slices from front to back. I soon noticed that the older the patient, the more space we would see between the folds of the brain (sulci) or in its ventricles, the clear fluid-filled cavities inside.

With time, your brain risks undergoing the same processes as your aging skin. The plump, white, moist tissue that fills the skull becomes shrunken, dry, fibrous and yellowed and its normally small, fluid-filled ventricles become enlarged to replace the lost mass of the fleshy neurons. In 30-80% of people getting an MRI, the margins of the ventricles, which are composed of the fibers responsible for rapid conduction of thought and movement, become fibrous and degenerated.[183] Sometimes these visible changes are so dramatic when I view a patient's scan that I marvel, 'How can this person act so apparently normal?' The answer is *brain plasticity*. Your brain is endowed with an astounding capacity of self-repair, and can create new neuronal electrical pathways around or through an area of obstruction or slowing. This flexibility is one of the keys to brain fitness.

Preliminary studies suggest that people who make a lifelong habit of doing *neurobics*, lifestyles that promote new connections between brain cells, such as being adventuresome at trying new things, engaging in life-long learning, doing exercise and playing physical games may preserve brain function. Strength training has been shown to improve memory. It is simply not true that you can't teach an old dog new tricks.

It is neither possible nor desirable to maintain your brain in its younger configuration, because the brain, like your bones,[184] is always remodeling itself. Change is inevitable and necessary. Just as you clean out your house, change the walls and replace the belongings, our brain regularly dumps most of its contents, retaining important bits, of course, but probably not in the same anatomical arrangement. Remodeling and change within the brain is the basis of its plasticity and its ability to withstand the ravages of aging, while remaining functionally intact. The Vedic approach to brain fitness aims to maximize the brain's natural flexibility and faculties of self-repair.

Researchers at the Salk Institute in San Diego recently discovered a protein responsible for scavenging and eliminating beta-amyloid residues, the same ones that are the main culprit for the multiple, dreaded cognitive problems of Alzheimer's disease, the most common cause of dementia.[185] Everyone accumulates beta-amyloid; it is a part of aging. In Alzheimer patients, however, it builds up as plaque inside the brain neuron cells and clumps on their surfaces. When Andrew Dillin altered a gene that has long been known to determine worm lifespan, worms in the laboratory not only lived longer, but also had a reduced buildup of the toxic amyloid, and fewer neurological problems, the worm-equivalent of dementia. The researchers feel their worms improved because the cellular cleanup mechanisms that dispose of amyloid, or that clump it into non-toxic packages, were spared the usual age-related decline.

This research gives us, as therapeutic optimists, reason to be hopeful despite the nihilism surrounding the constant sobering barrages of news about brain decline. Are you getting used to the idea that, for a Vedic physician, the aging process for all organs is due to plaque, called *āma* in Sanskrit, the residue of inefficient digestion and metabolism? Indeed, gerontologists have confirmed that as we age, all our cells – not only our neurons – accumulate debris that cannot be cleared and which ultimately interferes with function.[186]

Four Ways to Lose your Marbles

From the perspective of a physician who is a wimp about his nervous system growing older ungracefully, there are four likely ways I could lose access to my brain's hard drive and CPU:

1. Treatable causes. The treatable causes of brain dysfunction, while relatively rare, are common enough to be worth ruling out with a few simple tests. Hypothyroidism and other hormonal imbalances, normal pressure hydrocephalus, remote untreated infections, vitamin B12 or folic acid deficiency, medications and drugs, and stress and depression are examples of a few. Doctors are occasionally embarrassed when they miss a treatable cause later diagnosed by the patient's sister-in-law. If you feel your brain is slipping, see your doctor. Sometimes just doing the blood tests, including a scan to see if there is atrophy or other brain changes, is enough to relieve your mind of its chief distraction, the fear of losing your intellect. Few diagnostic tests are as therapeutic!

2. Simple aging. The loss of short-term memory is usually due to aging for no good reason (Amnestic Mild Cognitive Impairment, aMCI). This is the memory loss middle-aged adults and seniors laugh about when they get together and which they fret about in private. aMCI fortunately does not decline into severe dementia, nor is it usually accompanied by other important mental disabilities. For aMCI, you need to follow the simple recommendations in this chapter.

3. Vascular dementias. These are largely preventable brain disorders caused by blockage of vessels or bleeding from vessels deep within the brain, causing mini-strokes. They account for 25% of dementia. They are preventable because they are found in people who have the same risk factors as for heart disease including high blood pressure, diabetes and smoking. To avoid these, follow the advice in the three previous chapters.

4. Alzheimer's disease. This represents 60% of serious dementias. Standard medicine says your main risks are a family history (10% of cases), being female and perhaps being mentally idle. Many neurologists still tell you that the main prevention is crossword puzzles and other activities that enhance mental sharpness. Sounds good; don't buy it. Ronald Reagan did not spend his life being mentally idle. Alzheimer's disease is a problem of āma accumulation, as understood from both the western and Vedic perspectives and requires drastic, long-term prevention through lifestyle modification and āma elimination. In this chapter, you will learn an Ayurvedic approach to Alzheimer's prevention that, although it requires some time and effort, is part of a bigger program for general health. This program is for people who have a strong family history of Alzheimer's disease or who feel they are mentally slipping in their thirties or forties and cannot afford to lose a single neuron.

A short list for keeping your spouse as a bridge partner

1. Attend, without distraction, to things that matter.
2. Meditate.
3. Don't worry, be happy.
4. Avoid hypertension and vascular disease.
5. Avoid unnecessary medications.
6. Eat your vegetables.
7. Take your herbs and spices.
8. Eliminate āma.

We should analyze these one at a time before your partner dumps you because you can't count trump.

1. Attend, without distraction, to things that matter. In several cultures, well-designed studies that followed older populations prone to mental decline show that some leisure cognitive activities reduce the expected deterioration. Mental activities like reading, and challenging games such as chess, checkers and bridge are helpful, but not enough. One physical activity, dancing, has proven even better, perhaps because it involves more focus. At McGill University, tango lessons were better than an equivalent time spent walking for improving motor coordination as well as cognition. When you dance you have to synchronize your movements with the music, coordinate with your partner and remember the steps. Some more passive activities, however, including watching television, writing[187] and group discussion did not help. [188, 189] From the Vedic perspective, the critical ingredient to maintain brain youthfulness is engagement of the whole brain in complex, novel activities requiring an intention. You have to do new things to lay down new nerve pathways. Activities that simultaneously engage the brain's motor areas, emotions and intellect such as playing music, singing or dancing may be the best at this integration. Another study showed that people with rich social networks had a decreased risk of dementia. Participating in engaging activities with friends or family may be the best way to get your daily dose of meaningful cognitive exercise. More importantly to someone with an active healthy brain, however, is to culture the habit, while you are still young, of attending to one thing at a time with involvement of your senses, feelings and intellectual faculties.

2. Meditate. A group of Harvard researchers led by Ellen Langer randomized nursing home residents into groups that learned Transcendental Meditation (TM), mindfulness training, progressive muscle relaxation or no treatment at all. At the end of five years, the group practicing TM had improved word fluency, associated learning and cognitive flexibility, and had a higher survival rate.[190] Proper meditation allows intense impressions, which overshadow the mind, to be released. For a Vedic neurologist, forgetting is the critical link to achieving a better memory because dementia is not an issue of poor memory or recall. The issue is registration. Some people are astounded when demented 92-year-old Aunt Ida recounts events from 80 years ago as if it were yesterday, but neurologists see this phenomenon daily. The tougher mental task of registering or imprinting the impression was accomplished when Ida was twelve.

The first ability seniors lose is registration of new memories, like where you put your keys five minutes ago. Registering the new event involves new learning. Proper meditation improves the ability to forget, a critical function that liberates your mind from its preoccupations that prevent new registration. Like rebooting your computer to purge or free occupied RAM memory for new content, proper meditation frees us from useless impressions (*samskaras*) and preoccupations – the useless attention the nervous system devotes to those impressions. Without the natural tendency of the mind to reboot, such as in sleep or dreams, our awareness would soon be hopelessly cluttered. Even before our brains have aged, stresses and preoccupations make us lose the ability to shake off our unneeded impressions. Our brain is not free to register anew. Proper meditation has a physical effect on the brain itself, settling it to its quietest state, even while it remains alert. This state of restful alertness is different from sleeping and dreaming, and allows the brain to throw off or reorganize its impressions – both good and bad – more efficiently. The key to brain orderliness, like maintaining a home or office, involves constantly throwing out the old, and reorganizing the contents. Dreaming and grief help us reorganize, but only correct meditation helps us learn to properly forget. If you are feeling wimpy about one day finding yourself with a brain cluttered with impressions, like the house of a person with compulsive hoarding, learn meditation properly[191] and make it a regular practice.

3. Don't worry, be happy. Since registration of new impressions is the first and most critical cognitive faculty to go, avoid habits that prevent new imprinting. After intoxication and distractions (discussed above in #1 such as multitasking, distracting music, or conversations), the next best way to interfere with registering critical data is by being mentally preoccupied. Anxieties, complicated relationships, obsessions, compulsions, experiences of hopelessness and fears – all these are powerful distractions to our ability to imprint new data. The New England Centenarian Study has suggested that the ability to deal easily with stressors, i.e. getting over a problem and getting back to living, was one quality the oldest old have in common.[192] How do you gain this ability if it is not part of your natural makeup? Throwing off overshadowing impressions (samskaras) is the natural result, and even purpose, of yoga and Vedic medicine. This topic is openly addressed, or hidden like a child's medicine in ice cream, in nearly every chapter of this book.

4. Watch your blood pressure. Be vigilant about your risks for vascular disease. Every other part of your body can withstand considerable blood deprivation and survive just fine, such as when your leg "falls asleep" from a pinched blood flow. Your brain, unlike most other organs, will quickly die without a constant flow of nutrients and oxygen. Its blood flow gets priority over all the other organs including the heart muscle itself. In addition, the brain's delicate arteries and tissues are perfused with a head of pressure[193] that is lower than the mean arterial blood pressure in your body's other tissues, around 80 mm Hg. Any sustained blood pressure elevations can damage vessels, producing blockages and microbleeds deep within the brain tissue. Over time, this can cause nervous system damage that goes beyond memory problems. This is another reason to take seriously the three previous chapters on the prevention of endothelial disorders, controlling blood pressure and blood sugar.

5. Avoid unnecessary medications. Despite their frequent negative effect on mental clarity, medications are often necessary. Treating depression, even with drugs, often helps improve memory and focus, despite some initial experience of feeling spacey. Medications can prevent vascular diseases in people at risk, and this includes the vast majority of people over 50, despite their best intentions. Anti-hypertensive medicine, cholesterol reducing statins and aspirin are not only beneficial, but generally do not make you feel dopey. You, with your doctor, have to pick the lesser evil. When the jury will finally be in, however, some medications may prove to be harmful in the long term for brain function.

> **Here is the short list:**
> • Acetaminophen (Tylenol, etc.) depletes glutathione, one of the most critical brain anti-oxidants and perhaps one of our best defenses against brain cell plaque. Use it when necessary, but otherwise sparingly.
>
> • Drugs that deplete coenzyme Q10, critical for brain function: beta-blockers (atenolol, metoprolol, etc.), sulfonylureas (glipizide, etc.), phenothiazine antidepressants (amitriptyline, etc.) and statins (Lipitor, simvastatin, etc.). While I generally do not advocate taking vitamins and many other supplements casually, you can fortunately compensate for the CoQ10 depletion by taking a supplement of 60 mg daily.
>
> • Drugs that raise homocysteine levels, a promoter of inflammation in the brain and heart. Metformin, H2 blockers like Zantac and Pepcid, and diuretics are in this class. The simplest way to know if you need B vitamin supplementation is to have your physician order a blood homocysteine, folic acid and B12 level. If they are low, take a low dose B vitamin supplement with at least 1 mg of folic acid.
>
> • Cholesterol-lowering drugs – friend or foe? These highly useful medications are one of the best defenses against vascular disease and reduce the risk of both heart attacks and strokes in the short term. There is cause to believe that their anti-inflammatory effects may help reduce the plaque seen in Alzheimer's disease, but to date they have not been shown to decrease the risk of any cause of dementia. Their action, however, reducing cholesterol, has been thought by some good neurologists to possibly impair the formation of the fatty myelin sheath that insulates nerve cells – and which is made from cholesterol. This could prevent formation of this insulating lining and slow conduction of the electrical impulses involved in mental activity. Anecdotal cases of people who claim they act demented on statins is

currently being assessed with a double-blind study.[194] Fortunately, the available published research on thousands of people taking statins for long periods has shown neither harm nor benefit. As this book goes to press, an unpublished study following over 17,000 Finns over 60 showed that 18% of the 1500 people developing dementia had taken a statin, but 37% of those who were dementia-free had taken a statin, a significant difference.[195] Therefore, take a statin in good health if you and your doctor have decided, despite a good diet and exercise, that they are needed, with a CoQ10 supplement for good measure.

• Most psychoactive medication, including recreational drugs. Benzodiazepines like Valium, Ativan, Xanax, etc. are famous for compromising antegrade memory – preventing registration of new impressions from the time you take them until they wear off – sometimes a day or more later. Marijuana has been well documented to impair learning. Pain medications, anti-depressants and tranquilizers of all varieties and even stimulants can weaken your mental faculties in subtle ways. If a patient has the new onset of symptoms of dementia, the first diagnostic (and therapeutic) step is to stop all medications. Caffeine, however, as long as you are not addicted to it, appears to have no harmful affects on your brain.

6. Eat your vegetables, oils and spices. Because inflammation appears to play a seminal role in many dementias and is one variable we can partially control, be sure to optimize your antioxidants, best accomplished naturally through your diet. People with higher consumption of vegetables[196], fish[197] and olive oil, and reduced consumption of saturated and trans fats appear to have a greater decline in mental function.

7. Take brahmi – now and later. There are dozens of herbs used in Ayurveda for prevention of mental decline and regaining lost function. One of them, *brahmi*, is so outstanding that we will focus exclusively on it. Its name derives from Brahman, Totality, because the herb makes the nervous system so refined that it promotes the experience of Brahman. Its use is described extensively in the Ayurvedic texts. A curious thing happened during the course of time, probably because not every plant described in the ancient texts could be found growing in all climates. In different parts of Asia and the Middle East (the extent of the Vedic civilization's range), two different plants became known as brahmi. One, *Bacopa monnieri*, can be grown just about anywhere, even in my kitchen. It is the most important brahmi, and in ancient texts is known as jal brahmi. The other, *Centella asiatica*, also known as gotu kola, demands a lusher environment free from pollution. Both plants have been subjected to many scientific research studies and found useful and free of adverse effects, even if their exact mechanism on brain function is not understood.

While both brahmis are good for both prevention and mental clarity, their effects are different. Gotu kola brahmi settles the mind, eliminating distracting thoughts and allowing the task at hand to dominate in your awareness. It can be used at bedtime. Bacopa brahmi is more activating and energizing, creating focus and attention and is used in the morning. With the two plants, you have a complete brahmi.

For gotu kola and bacopa to work, their constituents must penetrate into your brain tissue. With most psychoactive herbs and many medications, brain penetration is not automatic because a blood – brain barrier (BBB) protects the delicate brain tissue from many natural toxins. The blood – brain barrier is an ingenious creation of nature composed of tightly packed glial and endothelial cells. It protects our brains from our own ignorance and excesses, preventing passage of molecules that are not lipid-soluble, but permitting lipid-soluble ones like CO_2, oxygen, steroids and, obviously, alcohol. The ancient Vedic physicians accounted for the blood-brain barrier and compounded most herbal preparations for the nervous system using vehicles that could penetrate the brain's lipid-rich membranes. While both brahmis can be taken as a powder, tablet or tea, the best vehicles are whole milk or ghee (clarified butter).

You can purchase both brahmis as powder and tablets. The powder of the whole plant is best. Many Ayurvedic companies sell brahmi compounded with other herbs, and it is generally impossible to determine what proportion of the formula is actually brahmi. For this reason I recommend the pure herbs. See Appendix 8 (Resources) for vendors of brahmi. Bacopa, in addition, is available as herbalized ghee, the best possible preparation because ghee, consisting of short-chain fatty acids that penetrate membranes easily, is its most effective vehicle. There are few suppliers of brahmi ghee.[198]

Start with only one of the brahmis at first so you can note any effects. Gotu kola brahmi taken at bedtime is a good start. Use only a small dose, about a quarter teaspoon of powder (roughly 350 milligrams, the weight of an aspirin). Stir it into half a glass of warm milk and be sure to drink the dregs containing the bulk of the herb. You may add a half to one teaspoon of ghee to increase digestibility and absorption. A small amount of sugar can be added to taste.[199] Hot milk with ghee at bedtime is considered a tonic by itself in Ayurveda and a delicacy even today for Indians and Pakistanis. Slowly increase the dose over a month to a heaping teaspoon, or 1-2 grams of the powder. Then start taking bacopa brahmi in the morning in the same way. If it is not convenient to take your brahmi with warm milk, just take it any way you can. It is better to take it with minimum fuss – as a tablet, or in capsules[200] and washed down with water – than to not continue this useful remedy because it was inconvenient.

Remember that taking brahmi for retaining your memory is a long-term proposition with short-term benefits.[201, 202] My patients have reported sharper focus and attentiveness, improved registration and recall, remaining cool under stress and more settled meditation, as described in the ancient books.[147 148] Gotu kola is held by the ancient texts to be an adaptogen – reducing the influences of stress – and is held to nourish brain tissue. Both brahmis are antioxidants. Bacopa is a stimulator of several of the body's natural antioxidant systems and as such is an important ingredient in Ayurvedic wrinkle creams. The long – term use of these two herbs appears to have side benefits for more than the brain.

8. Eliminate accumulated āma (plaque)[203]. The brain is one of the most lipid-dense organs in the body and its plaque is poorly soluble in water. Just as you cannot remove an oil-based paint from your brush with water, it takes a lipid-based solvent to penetrate the brain's blood-brain barrier and to dissolve the poorly water soluble amyloid plaque in its tissues.

If you feel you are losing your registration and recall and your physician cannot find a treatable cause, you may get desperate. Many people facing mental decline turn to unproven remedies. In Appendix 6 you will find a Three-Step Home Purification Program which has been used by Ayurvedic doctors for hundreds of generations for regeneration of a flagging mind and body. Unlike taking other herbal preparations in this book, this program demands time and attention. It is best undertaken as an in-residence program, and I encourage you to look into this option. See Resources, Appendix 8. Since an in-residence program is not always an option, this home program is the best alternative.

As a scientist, I must admit that this program has been tested only by time, and has not yet been subjected to a series of randomized controlled trials. There is a small body of research supporting the ability of Ayurvedic panchakarma programs to reduce toxins, however. For example, fifteen subjects undergoing an in-residence program had a reduction in blood levels of thirteen out of the fourteen common agricultural fat-soluble toxins which were measured, including polychlorinated biphenyls (PCB's) and pesticides.[204]

If your brain is doing fine, you have a busy life and simply want the advantages of an herbal tonic to support your mind as you grow older, in addition to the first six points above, commit yourself to taking brahmi on an ongoing basis. If you feel your brain needs a major cleansing of plaque and a deep infusion of brahmi, turn to Appendix 6 where the program is described.

183 We call this deterioration *periventricular white matter changes,* referring to the margins of the ventricles.

184 See Chapter 28

185 Andrew Dillin et al. Science. August 10, 2006

186 See Chapter 5 for more information on theories of aging, Chapter 15 and Appendix 4 for a more elaborated discussion of āma, and Chapter 22 for a discussion of the connection between aging and intracellular debris causing errors in DNA replication.

187 Some study participants may have reported writing casual content like shopping lists.

188 Joe Verghese, MD; Aaron LeValley, MA et al. *Leisure Activities and the Risk of Amnestic Mild Cognitive Impairment in the Elderly.* Neurology. 2006 March 28; 66(6): 821-827.

189 J.Y.J. Wang, MD, PhD, D.H.D. Zhou, MD. *Leisure activity and risk of cognitive impairment: The Chongqing aging study.* Neurology 2006;66:911-913

190 Alexander, CN, Langer, EJ et al. *Transcendental Meditation, mindfulness, and longevity. An experimental study with the elderly.* Journal of Personality and Social Psychology. 57, 950-964, 1989.

191 See Chapter 8.

192 Silver, M.H., Jilinskaia, E., Perls, T.T. *Cognitive functional status of age-confirmed centenarians in a population-based study.* Journal of Gerontology, Psychol Sci 2001;56B:P134-P140.

193 The cerebal perfusion pressure or CPP.

194 A study in which neither the doctor nor the patient knows whether the nightly pill is a statin or a placebo.

195 Alina Solomon. University of Kuopio, Finnland. Poster presentation at the International Conference on Alzheimer's Disease. Vienna, 2009. After controlling for baseline cholesterol, BP, and other factors this represented a 57% risk reduction.

196 Morris MC et al. Neurology Oct. 26, 2006

197 S. Kalmijn, MD, et al *Dietary intake of fatty acids and fish in relation to cognitive performance at middle age.* Neurology 2004;62:275-280

198 One of the few suppliers of brahmi ghee is Herbs of Ayurveda, herbsofayurveda@yahoo.com, www.herbsofayurveda.com. They keep supplies of bacopa brahmi ghee for shipping and compound special orders on request.

199 Avoid honey, however, which is never taken with milk in Ayurveda.

200 Capsule fillers and vegetarian capsules are available online at bazaarofindia.com

201 C. Stough, J. Lloyd, J. Clarke, L. Downey, C. Hutchinson, T. Rodgers, P. Nathan (2001). *The chronic effects of an extract of Bacopa monniera (Brahmi) on cognitive function in healthy human subjects.* Psychopharmacology (Berl).

202 S. Roodenrys, D. Booth, S. Bulzomi, A. Phipps, C. Micallef, J. Smoker (2002). *Chronic effects of Brahmi (Bacopa monnieri) on human memory.* Neuropsychopharmacology (Wollongong).

203 For a complete discussion of the Ayurvedic concept of āma or plaque, see Appendix 4.

204 John Fagen, PhD, Robert Herron, PhD. *Lipophil-mediated reduction of toxicants in humans: an evaluation of Ayurvedic detoxification procedure,* Alternative Therapies in Health and Medicine, 2002;8:40-51.

WHEN THE FLESH IS WEAK

CHAPTER 28

DEM BONES, DEM DRY BONES: OSTEOPOROSIS

One of the most important factors behind our perpetual aggravation by our bones and joints is that we see them as mechanical, fixed structures instead of as evolving, living tissue. It is only natural, since many people have seen and touched a skeleton in a biology class and have seen that it is articulated and functions like a tinker toy set. I am one of the worst offenders, having broken most of my bones and beaten up my joints before I even finished college. Until medical students enter practice and observe first-hand how the supposed mechanical frames of their patients evolve over the years, they usually regard the skeleton as a structure on which to hang the rest of the body. Let us contemplate bones in a non-linear light instead of in terms of pulleys, levers and hinges, the domain of classical Newtonian physics.

My first clear understanding of the human skeleton came when I was working in a remote area of the Philippines on a public health project. On a day off I borrowed a mask and snorkel and drifted along the coast, fixing to float a mile or two with the current. The world I witnessed gliding over a coral reef during next few hours would change my understanding of biology. The reef was not unlike a human bone: solid, yet full of holes. It had two distinct surfaces. One was soft, colorful, complex and living and the other was bare, white and dead. The dead coral created the foundation on which the living coral thrived. It was so thick that it comprised the actual bed of the ocean. The sand appeared to be mostly dead coral that had been broken off and pulverized by the waves. The sand was littered with the shells of crabs and mollusks, as well as with dead bits of the reef. The living coral covered the dead foundation, its multicolored polyps waving in the current, visibly ingesting plankton that were illuminated by the sun. As you touched the polyps, they would recoil and close, then reopen when they thought the danger was gone. Miniature fish, barnacles, stars, anemones, fans and mollusks were hiding in the coral's crevices, while bigger fish lurked, ready to gulp down any prey. "Where did this reef come from?" I wondered. "Where did it get all the material to build itself up?" I continued to drift. Hours seemed like minutes. My skin became wrinkled, as the otherworldly flora and fauna paraded before my drifting form.

When I finally crawled out of the sea, I had begun to fathom my experience. The old coral and abandoned shells were a repository of calcium that kept calcium dissolved in the sea water, from where it was taken up by the living coral polyps and turned into new coral skeleton. I was witnessing a massive recycling of calcium by countless tiny polyps that were creating a huge living organism miles long. Over hundreds of years, the coral's backbone had accumulated and organized itself into a matrix of honeycombed caverns and tunnels that harbored this unthinkable diversity of far-fetched creatures, which in turn would attract food for the coral. My reef was a non-linear, self-referral system, nourishing itself by nourishing all that lived around it. And the backbone that held the whole system together was calcium. I also saw village fishermen dynamiting the reef, stunning fish to float to the surface where they could be scooped up. This ancient, living creature with its delicate ecology was being destroyed.

Disrupting the Ecology of Bone

Years later, when Leora appeared in my office complaining that her period had stopped, I remembered my afternoon in the Philippines. She was a young woman who had been on a diet, to end all diets. A little overweight all her life, she had begun to lose weight and then could not stop. She had learned to control her natural hunger and the weight kept coming off because she still thought she was fat. Her ribs were showing. Even her pelvic bones could be seen where one expected buttocks. She had no breasts and her eyes were sunken. "I haven't had a period for a year," she complained. A bone density test revealed early osteoporosis, an uncommon finding in a woman this young, as well as other metabolic and hormonal abnormalities. Basically, this troubled young woman had lost all the fat stores that held her estrogen, and without estrogen, not only did her periods cease, but her body's bone-dissolving cells were working unopposed, turning her bones into soluble blood calcium where it would be redistributed to muscles and other organs.

Leora's bones were just like the coral reef, a precarious, constantly changing structure in dynamic equilibrium with their milieu, constantly being remodeled, reabsorbed and reconstituted. Leora was stealing timbers from the house to feed the stove, without replacing them. Thinking of the skeleton as a river instead of a structure is the key to healthy bones. Our bones change so quickly that astronauts returning from a week or two in space, where their skeletons have virtually no stress, lose substantial amounts of bone mineral – and even the ability to stand due to muscle weakness.

The Vedic Perspective on Bones

Unlike our own view of bones, the ancient Sanskrit texts regard bone (*asthi* – related to our root *osteo*) as a fluid, highly refined tissue and the precursor of the bone marrow and immune system, which is not far from the current understanding of embryology. Nails, teeth, skin and hair are seen as the byproducts of the formation of bone, and the health of the bones is estimated by examining these tissues.

Your body is constantly calculating its demands and its resources. Your parathyroid glands need to keep the blood calcium level within narrow limits to prevent seizures and cramps. Your body knows it needs a certain amount of new calcium from the diet to replace calcium lost in the urine. Otherwise, its most available source is your bones. Since bone mineral is in constant flux, it is important to keep the balance sheet in the black.

Here are a few ways to do that:

1. Measure your height yearly. If your doctor doesn't do it, do it yourself. Pick a doorjamb and make a mark, like when you were growing up. If you see you are starting to grow down, see your physician.

2. Get a bone density measurement. For women, the first should be during the peri-menopausal period, but men should get one by age 60, especially if they have been on steroids or used tobacco. A DEXA scan of the hip and spine is the gold standard. When you book the scan, ask if the imaging center plans to upgrade their equipment soon, because you should repeat the scan 2-3 years later on the identical equipment in order to detect a small change in bone density. If bone density changes, you will not know if it is due to a difference in equipment. You need two measurements to know whether the density is going down, and if so, how quickly. A urine test for byproducts of bone breakdown (hydroxyproline) can help monitor your progress in between DEXA scans.

3. Walk. Every time we take a step, the stress on the bone creates a small piezoelectric current along the shaft of the bone and functions as a stimulus for bone deposition. Lifting weights and swimming will help the bones in your arms and shoulders, but you need weight-bearing exercise like walking, tennis or jumping rope to avoid hip fractures, the most common cause of disability from bone mineral loss. The amount of exercise required to improve the bones is surprisingly little. I write on my prescription pad (so patients take it more seriously), "Rx: Take 40 minutes of progressive exercise two times per week." Studies have shown that this little exercise will help most sedentary people regain nearly all the bone lost to osteoporosis. In addition, this little exercise increases strength by 50-75%, increases energy levels 27%, increases balance, decreases the risk of a fall, decreases weight and makes people look both thinner and younger. However, studies have shown that exercise will not help people who take less than 1000 mg of calcium a day, and calcium will not help people who are not moderately active. Therefore:

4. Take plenty of calcium. The best source of calcium is in your diet, preferably as dairy. Milk is rich in other ingredients such as magnesium, potassium and vitamin D that make the calcium more absorbable. Make no bones about it, the mineral is so finicky that it is poorly absorbed in forms other than dairy, and most women get less than 70% of what they need. There is lots of calcium in spinach, but its oxalic acid reduces absorption. The calcium in wheat bran is so tightly bound that your gut cannot pry it out before you excrete it. Meat also reduces absorption. If you cannot tolerate a cup of skim milk (302 mg), use cheese (218 mg/oz), cottage cheese (212 mg/cup) or yogurt (400 mg/cup!). Try a yogurt shake with equal parts yogurt and water, adding a little sugar and fresh fruit. Take your dairy by itself if you have sluggish digestion. Boil your milk with a pinch of fresh grated ginger root if it gives you gas or mucus and do not take it with meals, since meat, fish, vegetables and salad make it curdle and harder for your stomach to digest. Taking dairy instead of supplements has a fringe benefit according to a study in the New England Journal of Medicine: a drop in blood pressure of 5.5 points if the person also takes healthy doses of fresh produce, a reduction that equates with a significant drop in heart disease. For patients with hypertension the drop was 11.4 points, equivalent to medications. The cow is sacred in Vedic medicine, and for a good reason!

5. Take calcium supplements to make up for what isn't in your diet. The irony for women is that calcium is most helpful when there is plenty of estrogen to stimulate its deposition. After menopause, when estrogen levels are low, a much smaller fraction of ingested calcium ends up in your bones. Yet most women who start calcium supplements begin only after menopause, or worse, once bone demineralization has become advanced. As you age, your calcium requirement goes up not simply because calcium is more rapidly leached from your bones, but also because it is not being absorbed as efficiently.

Picking a calcium supplement is easy. If you have sluggish digestion, use calcium citrate or calcium gluconate, because calcium carbonate, otherwise known as chalk, is more difficult to absorb. If you have acid indigestion, if you cannot swallow big pills, or if you are on a budget, use calcium carbonate (marketed as Tums or Rolaids) but consider looking for a product without the artificial flavorings and colorings used in the name brands. Avoid "natural" sources like bone meal and dolomite, which may contain mercury. Take calcium with your meal to enhance its absorption by 10% and you will be getting magnesium and other minerals that are otherwise included in many calcium supplements. Most women need 500 mg of calcium with two meals a day, more if you are older, pregnant or nursing or have rapid bone loss.

6. Get plenty of sunshine. Walking outdoors accomplishes this and is much more fun than a treadmill. Your skin needs sunlight to make vitamin D for proper bone metabolism and calcium absorption. If you are over 50, you will need more than 15 minutes per day, but 5-15 minutes is fine for younger people.

7. Use medications prudently. Remember that ultimately you want to reduce your risk of fracture and loss of height, and that bone density is not the only determinant of bone strength. The other factors are the quality of the bone crystals and their architecture. The most effective bone, like a Gothic cathedral, bears stress along arches, buttresses and beams, thus lightening the bones and providing space for the precious marrow that forms our blood elements. Some drugs that increase bone density, such as Fosamax and Actonel, do not improve the risk of fractures to the same degree as the increase in density, probably because they lay down new bone tissue in a haphazard way. This is like nailing extra two by fours onto a house to reinforce it without asking an architect exactly where to put them. The house would be denser, but no stronger. Consult your physician about what medications are needed.

8. Replace hormones. If you are a postmenopausal woman and not taking hormone replacement, take plenty of phytoestrogens in your diet. Estrogen helps create a higher quality of bone than other medications, perhaps because it prevents the loss of strong bone rather than by making new bone. Bio-identical estrogen and progesterone are available for women whose bones are losing density rapidly and who have no contraindication to estrogen replacement. Options to hormone replacement include soy products like tofu, tofu dogs or burgers, miso, soy sauce as well as soy isoflavone or citrus bioflavinoid supplements. One study showed improvements from topically applied progesterone supplements available in health food stores. Other options include the Ayurvedic herb, nirgundi (Vitex nirgundi), which is taken in the dose of 300 mg twice daily on an empty stomach.

9. Add a seed crystal. Ayurvedic medicine recommends a tiny amount of a highly refined quality of calcium to function as a seed crystal for new bone. Pearl, coral, conch shells and mother of pearl are all used, but the latter three are the least expensive. These minerals can be ground into a fine powder in a clean coffee or pepper grinder.[205] Take one sixteenth of a teaspoon in addition to your usual supplement. Ayurvedic herbs that can be taken with calcium to improve its absorption include heartleaf moonseed (guduchi), licorice, and asparagus root (shatāvari). A mixture of equal parts of the three herbs can be taken in a dose of 300 mg with your calcium. Sesame seeds are also held as excellent for bones. They can be taken roasted and rolled into delicious snack balls with a little honey or maple syrup, or taken as sesame butter (tahini), which can be used as a tasty spread in the place of butter or peanut butter.

Remember the coral reef. Your bones are alive and changing, and soon you will have a nearly new skeleton.

205 This is a tradition in many developing societies. I have observed village women in Ecuador bringing sacks of sea shells they have gathered to be ground by a man with a hand grinder mounted on a cart in the village plaza. The women take the fine powder with their meals.

CHAPTER 29

DEGENERATIVE ARTHRITIS

The labour we delight in physics pain.
Shakespeare. Macbeth Act ii Sc. 3.1

"Wear and tear" is what your physician proclaims when you ask why your knees ache while she reads your x-ray report that diagnoses degenerative arthritis. "Degenerative" implies wear and tear, like mechanically grinding down the enamel on your teeth. While wear and tear plays a supporting role, it is often a lame explanation. Osteoarthritis is found in pashas who never use their fingers for anything more strenuous than playing cards or their knees for more than walking in the garden, and it can leave untouched roughnecks who for decades employ their hands as a hammer and their legs for running marathons.

Osteoarthritis, one of the most prevalent chronic disorders,[206] is an ongoing process that can lead to failure of the cartilage of the bone-joint surfaces. It is associated with inflammation, which results from the interaction between a person's nature (both his genetics and his body-build), metabolism, sex hormones, and biomechanical factors. Not only the cartilage but also the bone, joint capsule, and muscles are involved in the breakdown and an attempt – often inappropriate – at self-repair. The cell in the starring role in this drama is the chondrocyte, the main cell of cartilage tissue found imbedded in a supporting matrix that it secretes about itself. In osteoarthritis, the chondrocyte inappropriately synthesizes proteins and inflammatory molecules, proliferates or even self-destructs in a maladaptive response to a major injury to the cartilage, like when you jump from a height, or when you sustain many little injuries, as during a long run.

Interestingly, Vedic medicine understands arthritis as a digestive/metabolic disorder resulting from inefficient tissue synthesis and the deposition of residues in the joint space, which is then converted into by-products (āma) that create inflammation, swelling, dryness of the joint, and pain.

Balanced Exercise and the Prevention of Arthritis

The most important role of both ancient and modern medicine for an arthritic patient is prevention, because self-repair is at best long and arduous. We need to explore the cause of arthritis. Research suggests that osteoarthritis is dependent on the balance of many factors. Chondrocytes in test tubes secrete more of the protective protein matrix about themselves when they are stimulated with a moderate amount of "exercise" than with a little, or with a lot. If a limb is put in a cast so it cannot be flexed, within a month you find some of the same severe degenerative damage in the unmoved joint that you see in arthritis, and these effects are reversible when the joint is flexed again.[207] And following an amputation, the cartilage in the joint above the amputation becomes thin, even if it is moved,[208] due to lack of weight bearing. Finally, joints adapt their remodeling to the stresses of progressive exercise to avoid damaging cartilage surfaces.

If you have normally aligned joints, too little exercise or repetitive, high impact exercise can put your joints at risk. If your joints are out of line or are anatomically abnormal, even moderate, low impact exercise can increase your risk for developing arthritis.[209, 210] This research on exercise confirms the Vedic principle of maintaining balance: underutilizing or abusing your joints may impede your plans to age gracefully.

Your nature (prakriti) also plays a role in whether you will develop osteoarthritis, with higher risk from both your genes and a solid (kapha) body type. You have a two-fold risk of developing arthritis of the hand if your sister has it, and that risk is 5-7 times greater if her arthritis is severe.[211] If you are built solidly, your risk is also increased. Obesity increases your risk of arthritis of the knee and hand but, interestingly, not necessarily of the hip, suggesting that the risk is not all due to the increased stresses of weight on the joint. That risk goes away with weight loss. If you have solid bones without much osteoporosis, you still have an increased risk of arthritis of the hip.[212] Even strong muscles, like a firm handgrip, can confer you a greater risk, even if you do not use your hand as a vise,[213] but weak muscles are a risk, too.

Pain pays the income of each precious thing.

The Rape of Lucrece. Shakespeare

How you use your joints is important, because problems have been found in cyclists (kneecaps), ballerinas (heel joints), boxers (knuckles), wrestlers (elbows and shoulders) and other athletes, including sled dogs (hips and shoulders) and racehorses (forelegs),[214, 215, 216] as well as in certain professions.[162] Still, the major risk is to competitive and not recreational athletes, so unless you are involved in a sport that exerts major stresses on your joints and you do it many hours a day, you are probably justified in continuing. Just remember: prevent arthritis by maintaining balance in exercise and weight.

Treatment of Osteoarthritis

Besides preventing its onset, the Vedic approach to arthritis is focused on preventing its progression, because controlling your pain and swelling and can be accomplished with anti-inflammatories. These recommendations should be used with an arthritis management program prescribed by a physician because they depend on the joints involved, your age and disabilities, associated disorders and biomechanical factors. You may not even have arthritis but rather a bursitis or other condition.

You may have initiated your cartilage loss due to genetic and metabolic problems, but once the process gets started, simple mechanical factors can conspire to grind the rest of your cartilage off. You therefore have to consider your weight, exercise, biomechanics, cushioning and other factors that can put off the day when you find yourself rubbing bone on bone.

The Conundrum of Exercise, Rest and Weight Loss

Arthritis of the knee, spine, hip and even hand respond nicely to weight loss. Even ten pounds lost over ten years can prevent arthritis of the knee. If you are overweight, the benefit is linear: a few pounds help a little and many help a lot.

Rest, like exercise, plays an important role in healing a joint if you have overused it. Let it heal before you start to exercise vigorously again. Non-steroidal anti-inflammatory drugs (NSAIDS) such as ibuprofen (Motrin, Advil and others), naproxen (Aleve and others), diclofenac (Voltaren and others) have never been shown to reverse – much less prevent – cartilage destruction. However, when your knee is aching after a long trek and you're wondering how much longer you can continue to hike without a joint replacement, there's nothing like a hefty dose of NSAIDS to get you feeling positive again.

This brings up the conundrum of degenerative arthritis. You need to lose weight, but exercise immediately makes your worn out joint ache – and rest helps, so you sit around eating pretzels.

Enter Vedic medicine, a health science dedicated to choices and to making you self-sufficient in your (multiple) life-long projects of self-repair. Vedic medicine is not a compendium of healing remedies, but a science to think creatively, intuitively, and with sensitivity to the needs of your body and environment. It gives you tools to find a pleasurable way to stay fit that is in accord with your talents, disabilities and laws of nature.

If your arthritis involves knees and hips, you can row, kayak, cycle, lift weights, swim and practice aqua-aerobics, ice-skate, in-line skate and do tai chi and yoga. Let yourself be inspired by the elite level of fitness of the competitors in a wheelchair marathon, realizing that some of the competitors do not even have legs. Moderate exercise has been shown to be good not only for arthritic joints, but also in preventing osteoporosis, heart disease and depression.[217] Home exercise has been shown to be just as good as supervised exercise in helping patients with arthritis,[218] and may even be better because it is convenient and less expensive.

For any person suffering from arthritis of a major joint, membership at a warm swimming pool open year round is one of the best investments in your long-term health. The buoyancy of water sets you free to move without impact and joint compression. You can sweat without the aches, yet you stay cool and feel light. When you need to rest, you are already lying down and never have to struggle to get up. A pool can save you from obesity, depression, and therefore from hypertension, diabetes and heart disease. Best of all, there's few things as fun as a pool full of people.

Keep Your Joints Warm

Recent research has documented the increased pain experienced by arthritis sufferers with changes in weather and especially with a cold, damp climate. Vedic texts state that cold exposure not only makes the pain worse, but also contributes to the progression of arthritis by decreasing the metabolism in cartilage undergoing trauma. Stay warm all day and keep the humidity out in damp weather by heating a sealed house. When you go out in the cold, bundle up your affected joints in extra layers with gloves, long underwear or a neoprene knee warmer.

Yoga (Physical Therapy)

Every person with progressive arthritis needs a consultation with a physical or occupational therapist to work out the mechanics of walking and other activities that create pain. Never forget that pain is your joint's best friend; it signals that you have gone too far, potentially creating inflammation and mechanical stresses that rob your joint of its remaining cartilage.[219]

A good physical therapist will analyze and treat the factors that create shearing forces on your knees, hips, and spine. For example, she can equip you with wedge insoles to shift your ankle alignment so your weight is distributed to the uninvolved compartment of your knee. An appropriate brace to realign a knee or kneecap can be useful if you can tolerate it – especially when you are exercising or working around the house. A physical therapist can recommend proper cushioning insoles or elastomere soles to cushion your knee from the impact of every step. She will give you exercises that strengthen the typically weak muscle groups surrounding a joint to stabilize the joint and to help you absorb the impact of walking on uneven surfaces. She will manually stretch or prescribe stretching exercises for spastic muscles around an arthritic joint, reducing pain and improving function. Your physical therapist may know nothing about yoga, but for a person with arthritis, a good physical therapist is your best yoga teacher, because she unknowingly practices the essence of hatha yoga, the art of effortless movement.[220]

Diet

Western scientists have studied the effect of diet in arthritis mainly by looking at the content of antioxidants like vitamins C, E and D in the diet of a population, and found that while antioxidants may help prevent its onset, they do not seem to halt its progression once arthritis has started.[221, 222] Researchers in this field address only what their subjects generally eat and not whether their subjects were digesting their food, overeating, constipated, bloated or dyspeptic – all of which Vedic medicine regards as a principle cause for the creation of the metabolic problem behind osteoarthritis. Consult the relevant chapters to normalize your weight and manage digestive problems.

Your diet should include an abundance of fresh fruit of every color,[223] cooked vegetables, tender salads and bitter grains (barley, buckwheat, amaranth, quinoa, brown rice). Avoid heavy foods including yogurt (lassi is fine), deep-fried foods, and heavy meats and breads.

A Vedic arthritis-busting diet also should include an abundance of five pillar ingredients for arthritis: ginger root, turmeric, fenugreek, ghee and almonds.

1. Ginger. This tasty root is one of the best therapies for osteoarthritis, and has been found to reduce pain from arthritis of the knee in six weeks.[224] Ginger should be taken as the fresh root for optimal treatment of significant arthritis pains. The best way to get the dose you need is to put fresh ginger root through a juicer[225] and to drink at least 3 to 6 tablespoons per day, either plain – if you have the courage – or diluted in vegetable or fruit juice. You can also add a teaspoon of honey to 1-2 tablespoons of ginger juice and take it before three meals a day to get a therapeutic dose. Taken before the meal it also increases the digestive fire and reduces āma.

2. Turmeric. This valuable root related to ginger has many different active ingredients that have been identified as potent anti-inflammatory agents in addition to its properties as an antioxidant and anti-allergic agent. Turmeric can be added to any savory dish, but your family may stop raving about your cooking if you use therapeutic doses. Give them a break by buying turmeric tablets or filling empty cellulose capsules[226] with fresh bulk turmeric powder purchased at an Indian food store. Take one or two with each meal.

3. Fenugreek seeds (*Trigonella foenum-graecum*). These seeds are a bitter, delicious spice used in stir-frying and lentil dishes. The easiest way to take them is to soak one teaspoon of seeds overnight in a quarter cup of water and to drink the water, swallowing the seeds, in the morning. Fenugreek is held by Vedic physicians to help the quality of cartilage.

4. Ghee. Clarified butter is not only delicious but also useful for many disorders. Chemically it is unique because it is composed of very short-chain fatty acids. This may explain why the ancient Vedic texts describe ghee as being *subtle* (able to penetrate deeply into tissues). Ghee is felt to be the best substance for dissolving residues accumulated in the tissues and to be a building block for the formation of new cartilage. If you have significant arthritis, be sure to take several teaspoons with each meal, using it instead of other oils or fats. It makes a delicious cooking oil and will not scorch like butter, so it can even be used for making popcorn. It cannot be used on salad. Do not worry about its effect on your cholesterol: patients taking large quantities of ghee have been shown to have lower total cholesterol levels and improved levels of the good HDL cholesterol.[227] Reduce your intake of carbohydrates and other fats to compensate for the extra calories and recheck your lipid profile after two months on a good dose of ghee.

5. Almonds. These wholesome nuts are prized in Ayurveda and are considered by Ayurvedic practitioners to be one of the best foods for arthritis – owing to their bitter quality. They have been shown to favorably lower total cholesterol levels by 9.4% and they contain no saturated fats. Take one to two handfuls a day, including especially the bitter skin. Raw almonds are best, but roasted and salted are fine.

Ayurvedic Herbs for Osteoarthritis

The three wise men from the East bearing gifts to the Christ child must have known something about Vedic medicine, because myrrh and frankincense are two of the best herbs for the treatment of osteoarthritis. Known best as *guggulu*[228] and *boswellia*, these precious resins scraped from small, bushy trees have been found in numerous scientific studies beginning in the 1950's to improve signs and symptoms of arthritis both in the laboratory and in human studies. Whole guggulu resin was serendipitously found to reduce cholesterol in patients taking it for arthritis because it is also traditionally used for reducing body fat. In the west today, guggulu has become popular for lipid control and consumers may incidentally note that they feel less achy.

1. Guggulu (*Commiphora mukul*). Because the plant and its resin are relatively rare and the therapeutic benefit depends on the quality of the resin, be sure to purchase guggulu from the most reputable suppliers and expect to pay a little more.

Good guggulu always uses the whole resin and never an extract. Good guggulu is dark, bitter and pungent. If the tablet is hard (which may happen with good guggulu that has not been properly crushed or properly compounded with another herb) it may not dissolve and might be eliminated intact, so check by putting a tablet in water for an hour. Guggulu is useful for all types of osteoarthritis, but the herbs it is mixed with can vary. It is more important to get good quality guggulu than to worry about the formulation. Yogarajaguggulu, which combines the guggulu resin with digestive herbs (since guggulu is only effective in the absence of constipation), is the easiest to find in high quality. Its pungent nature makes it spicy, so avoid taking it with anti-inflammatory medications like ibuprofen, naproxen, aspirin and the like. Take one 375-500 mg tablet before meals three times daily.[228] Guggulu is useful for any painful musculoskeletal problem.

2. Boswellia (Boswellia serrata, or frankincense) is an extract from the gummy resin of a small tree growing in dry, hilly regions. Boswellic acids isolated from this extract shrink inflamed tissue by increasing the blood flow and repairing damaged vessels. Boswellia is generally marketed as a pure boswellia tablet of 250-350 mg. It should be taken twice daily before meals, and can be taken with guggulu but not with anti-inflammatories.

3. Castor oil. This useful remedy for osteoarthritis is taken every bedtime for several months – not for its colonic stimulant effect – but because Vedic medicine holds it to repair cartilage. Since it is distasteful, most patients abandon the nightly ritual before they can evaluate if it will help them. If this valuable remedy interests you, consider finding castor oil capsules and take the equivalent of one teaspoonful (usually about 5-6 capsules) with a little hot water, reducing the dose if your morning stool is loose.

4. Rasna (*Pluchea lanceolata*) is an orchid that roots on other trees. The dried leaves are rich in anti-inflammatory glucosides. Take 300 mg of the rather bitter powder twice daily as a capsule or tablet.

In summary, appropriate strengthening physical therapy, range of motion exercise, rest, weight loss, an arthritis-suitable diet, herbs, avoidance of the side effects of NSAIDS, and application of the lost art of self-repair should keep your joints lasting longer than your orthopedist may have predicted.

206 Present in over 80% of people over 55 and 97% of people over 65. Lawrence, JS, Bremner, JM, Bier, F. *Osteoarthritis prevalence in the population and relationships between symptoms and x-ray changes.* Ann Rheum Dis 1996;25:1.

207 Grumbles, RM, Howell, DS, Howard, GA, et al. *Cartilage metalloproteases in disuse atrophy.* J Rheumatol Suppl 1995;43:146.

208 Palmoski, M, Perricone, E, Brandt, KD. *Joint movement in the absence of normal joint loading does not maintain normal articular cartilage.* Arthritis Rheum 1980;23:325.

209 Lane, NE. *Exercise: a cause of osteoarthritis.* J Rheumatol Suppl 1995;43:3.

210 Buckwalter, JA. *Osteoarthritis and articular cartilage use, disuse, and abuse: Experimental studies.* J Rheumatol Suppl 1995;43:13.

211 Jonsson, H, Manolescu, I, Stefansson, SE, et al. *The inheritance of hand osteoarthritis in Iceland.* Arthritis Rheum 2003;48:391.

212 Hart, DJ, Mootoosamy, I, Doyle, DV, Spector, TD. *The relationship between osteoarthritis and osteoporosis in the general population: the Chingford Study.* Ann Rheum Dis 1994;53:158.

213 Chaisson, CE, Zhang, Y Sharma, L, et al. *Grip strength and the risk of developing radiographic hand osteoarthritis.* Arthritis Rheum 1999;42:33.

214 Panush, RS, Brown, DG. *Exercise and arthritis.* Sports Med 1987;4:54.

215 Helminen, HJ, Kiviranta, I, Saamanen, A-M, et al. *Effect of motion and load on articular cartilage in animal models. In: Articular Cartilage and Osteoarthritis*, Kuettner, KE, Schleyerbach, R, Peyron, JG, Hascall, VC (Eds), Raven Press, New York 1992. p.501.

216 Panush, RS. *Does exercise cause arthritis? Long-term consequences of exercise on the musculoskeletal system.* Rheum Dis Clin North Am 1990;16:827.

217 Biddle, S. *Exercise and psychosocial health.* Res Q Exerc Sport 1995,66:292.

218 Chamberlain, MA, Caree, G, Harfield, B. *Physiology in osteoarthritis of the knee.* Int Rehabil Med 1982;4:101.

219 People with disorders that keep them from feeling pain in the joints quickly develop massively swollen joints because they unwittingly beat them up.

220 The Arthritis Foundation strongly recommends hatha yoga for flexibility, reducing stress and increasing patient confidence.

221 McAlindon, TE, Jacques, P, Yuqing, Z, et al. *Do antioxidants micronutrients protect against the development and progression of knee osteoarthritis?* Arthritis Rheum 1996;39:648.

222 McAlindon, TE, Felson, DT, Zhang, Y, et al. *Relation of dietary intake and serum levels of vitamin D to progression of osteoarthritis of the knee among participants in the Framingham study.* Ann Intern Med 1996;125:353.

223 See Chapter 18.

224 Altman R. Arthritis and Rheumatism 2001:44:2531-38.

225 Put a large piece of fresh ginger root through your clean juicer, enough to make 8 oz of juice. It will keep well in the refrigerator for several days. After the ginger, you can use your juicer to make a glass of "gingerized" fruit or vegetable juice before you clean it.

226 Bulk tumeric, capsule fillers and empty vegetable-based capsules are available at www.bazaarofindia.com.

227 Waldschutz R. *Veranderungen physiologischer und psychischer Parameter durch eine ayurvedische Reinigungskur.* Erfarhungsheilkunde (Acta medica empirica) II, 720-729, 1988.

228 Myrrh is slightly different from guggulu (*Commiphora mukul*) and is called *Commiphora myrrha*.

CHAPTER 30

RADIANCE: THE KEY TO BEAUTIFUL SKIN

She was a Phantom of delight
When first she gleamed upon my sight;
A lovely Apparition, Sent
To be a moment's ornament;
Her eyes as stars of Twilight fair;
Like Twilight's, too, her dusky hair;
But all things else about her drawn
From May-time and the cheerful Dawn;
A dancing Shape; an Image gay.
To haunt, to startle, and waylay.

William Wordsworth. 1770-1850

The essence of beauty in the Ayurvedic understanding is embodied in the idea of luster or radiant light. When we say, "She was radiant!" we imply a quality coming from deep within that emanates contentment, joy and accomplishment. Cultivating this luminosity, as expressed by the Vedic words *tejas, ojas* and *jyoti*, enhances beauty.

Tejas is the elemental fire or light and the major constituent of agni, the metabolic and digestive fires critical to good health. Without tejas, the bodily fires that create health are weak, and hence, no luster and beauty. Tejas, as light, is also the primordial element associated with vision.

Ojas is the essence of the tissues, the dhātus, and is created only when tissues are properly formed. Ojas functions at the threshold between your body and its finest expression – consciousness – permitting effortless communication between the body's metabolism and its underlying intelligence. Associated with moonlight, ojas, the texts declare, gives the radiance that comes from culturing and orienting the body's physical, sexual and immune strength into refined thought and action.

Jyoti is "inner light," the light value of consciousness that arises when human awareness touches and functions from the level of its most silent state, without noise and stress. Jyoti gives a radiance that evokes the joy of someone in possession of knowledge and wisdom. This aspect of beauty is timeless and glows more brightly with age. To enhance beauty, according to Ayurveda, you need to culture tejas, ojas and jyoti. They are the wave values through which light expresses the hum of the universe, your body's song.

To begin rejuvenating your skin, you first need a diagnosis. There are three main skin tendencies:

1) excessive dryness and wrinkles[229]

2) inflammation, redness, or sensitivity[230]

3) oiliness with large pores.[231]

1. Dry-type skin – with tendencies to wrinkle

The Vedic principle governing movement (called *vāyu* or *vāta* in Sanskrit) means literally "wind." Dry-type skin looks as if it were left in the wind: it is rough, appears aged, wrinkles easily and will look dull, even when you are young. It can even get flaky. Dry-type skin needs to be cared for with attention to creating more lubrication, both inside and out. Avoid dehydration by drinking enough fluids (except coffee and other beverages that have a diuretic effect) and enjoy juicy, sweet fruits or their juices. Avoid excessive washing with strong soaps and other products with fragrances and chemicals. Dry-type skin requires a heavier moisturizer with more sealing effect. Natural oils that can be used include almond oil, avocado oil or sesame oil (cold-pressed and without odor – not the dark, strong sesame oil used in oriental cooking).

A nightly face wash with whole milk or cream is good for dry-type skin. Instead of washing the skin with strong soaps, just rinse it, or use a mild soap such as clear glycerin soap. Then bathe your face and neck with milk or cream, using a soft, natural sponge or cotton balls. Let the milk dry and rinse it off before applying your moisturizer. Milk and cream have natural fats and minerals including magnesium and calcium as well as proteins that have a toning, astringent effect. These ingredients tighten and nourish the connective and elastic tissues.

2. Fair skin – with redness and inflammation

The Vedic principle governing metabolism and the digestive fires is called agni (or *pitta*) in Sanskrit. When this principle becomes excessively sharp, it may create inflammation. Fair, pitta skin is called Type 1 and Type 2 by western dermatologists the kind that is easily sun-damaged and carries the highest risks for skin cancer.[232] Fair skin is by nature warm and soft. It is sun-sensitive and when overexposed, becomes flushed and ruddy. If you have blonde or reddish hair and lots of freckles or moles, you likely have pitta skin.

People with fair skin types may blush easily, making their skin prone to sprout vessels and rosacea over time, especially if they have not avoided the sun and other influences that make the skin flush (alcohol, spices, etc.) While vāta-type skin may wrinkle from sun exposure, fair skin is prone to inflammation leading to pre-cancerous lesions and skin cancer. On the other hand, fair, pitta skin is a delight to behold because it readily reflects the tejas quality of light, giving a natural glow and the expression "a ravishing redhead." Most significantly, in all skin types, inflammatory skin conditions, including acne, hives, psoriasis, eczema and pigment disorders such as liver spots, angiomas and spider veins respond to treatments that reduce heat in the body (called pitta pacifying; see Appendix 3). Avoid sun exposure and tanning booths meticulously. Reduce foods that exacerbate flushing such as spices, cayenne, vinegar and alcohol. Avoid products that contain chemicals, fragrances and preservatives. Remarkably, these ancient prescriptions for pitta pacification are advocated by modern dermatologists, who may otherwise deny the idea of accumulation of heat in the body or the validity of Ayurvedic three dosha theory.

Pitta skin does not need as much moisturizing as vāta skin, but the product used should be cooling. One good natural moisturizer is coconut oil, which can be applied in the evening after washing and a milk bath (see above). In the daytime, pitta skin needs sun protection more than a moisturizer. Use a barrier sunblock instead of sunscreen, such as zinc oxide or titanium oxide. If this does not work for you, use PABA-free sunscreen with a high SPF rating.[233] People with pitta skin often need to try many brands before finding one that is not irritating.

Pitta skin requires turmeric in the diet, and lots of it: the curcuminoids act as natural anti-inflammatory, antioxidant and anti-allergy agents. Add the savory spice to soup, vegetables, rice and lentils. If your skin is dark, you can also put a pinch of turmeric in the milk bath (above) or even use it in the facials below, but people with fair skin who try this may look like they have been dyed yellow.

3. Oily skin with large pores.

Kapha is the physiological principle of cohesion, and kapha skin tends to be firm and oily. This skin type is thick, soft, lubricated, and cool to the touch. People with oily skin tend to have larger pores, and less of a tendency to wrinkle, thus naturally appearing to age more gracefully. Oily skin accumulates sebum, our natural oils secreted by sebaceous glands. Sebum becomes irritating and toxic as its oils become rancid or oxidized. This can result in deeper, cystic-type acne with whiteheads and abscesses, as well as unsightly oily skin.

Kapha skin requires more cleansing and exfoliation of the outer layers of cells that hold in the sebum. Soaps are usually well tolerated. People with oily skin can also do a milk massage as described above, but should use low fat or skim milk and never cream. Oily skin also requires frequent masking for more intensive exfoliation. Use clay for a base, adding one-half part mung bean flour or chickpea flour and one quarter part sandalwood powder (soothing, cooling, astringent and delightfully fragrant). You can procure these products in Indian grocery stores. Mix the flour with skim milk and if desired, a little rose water. Massage gently and leave it on until it dries. Kapha skin may still need a moisturizer. Try three parts of aloe vera gel with one part cold-pressed sesame seed oil (use less sesame oil if your skin is very oily). With kapha skin, like with obesity and other kapha imbalances, it is important to follow a diet that avoids excessive fats and starches.

Avoiding Wrinkles and Loss of Elasticity

If beauty is important to you, no matter what your skin type, avoid the influence of oxygen free radicals generated by sunlight, chemicals and other harsh influences. These tiny, short-lived molecules rob your skin's connective tissue of electrons, essentially denaturing the skin's collagen and proteins, and making them lose their elasticity. Take plenty of fresh fruits and vegetables for their antioxidant content, including all the different colors: reds in berries and red peppers, blues in blueberries and blackberries, yellow peppers, carotenoids as in squashes, yams and carrots, and dark green leafy vegetables.[234] If you need to be inspired to eat your veggies, remember that this prescription has some solid research behind it. When dermatologists looked at Greek, Australian and Swedish subjects, they noticed that those who ate diets highest in antioxidants had the highest degree of protection from sun damage on the back of the hands.

The Nightly Day Spa

Sometimes your skin may simply need extra nourishment, even if you are doing your nightly milk wash. If it needs only moisturizing, try an oatmeal mask.[235] For skin nutrition with an astringent to tighten the skin, use yogurt (mixed with one-half part water if it is too thick or if you simply want a quick wash). If you have inflamed (pitta) skin, try a watermelon puree for a rinse or cucumber puree with a dash of rose water. Honey is astringent, and therefore makes a good facial for oily, kapha skin. One of the best facial masks that can be used by people with any skin type is the juice or pulp of fresh cherries. They are astringent as well as unctuous and leave the skin both clean and plump. Leave it on for ten minutes.

Dry, Itchy Skin

Young and old can be bothered by dry skin conditions. Consultation with a physician is important to make sure you do not have a disorder requiring specific therapy. For stubbornly dry skin not responsive to usual measures, try the following program. Always test any new approach on a small patch and wait a day or two to see the effect before using it all over.

1. Wear natural fabrics. Favor cotton or rayon. Silk is acceptable in winter but may be sticky in hot weather. Avoid synthetic fabrics and wool, which may make you itch and scratch.

2. Avoid long, hot baths. Bathe by showering briefly in warm or cool and not hot water. Use gentle glycerin soap only in the groin and underarms. Otherwise use mung bean flour, barley flour or chickpea flour instead of soap, available in Indian groceries (mung bean flour is usually best, but you can try them all). Keep your flour in a dry container near the shower, moisten it in your fingertips and gently apply it to areas to be cleansed. Be careful that the flour does not block your drains. Mung bean flour is soothing and will not dry your skin.

3. Use ghee as a moisturizer. Apply ghee before a shower. It is especially useful if there is associated inflammation, as in eczema and psoriasis.

4. Coconut oil or shea butter. Try this if nothing else has worked, 1-2 times per week. If you find it helpful, you can use it daily. Apply while your skin is wet to trap the water in the skin's outer layer.

5. Avoid scratching.[236]

6. Fresh cherries. Use the fresh cherry mask over any affected areas. (See above.)

7. Turmeric. Add turmeric to the cooking, or take 1-2 tabs or capsules of turmeric daily with a meal. It is the best spice for itching and allergies.

8. Sweet, fresh fruit. Take ample amounts to correct internal causes of dryness.

Beauty Rest?

> *rūpam gunam vayastag iti subhanga karanam. (Transforming the body into auspicious splendor requires culturing outer, inner and perpetual beauty.)*[237]

> Charaka Samhitā

Beauty is accomplished, above all, by staying well rested. The actress Catherine Deneuve, who is radiating beauty as an active actress at an age when most leading ladies are long retired, once credited her beauty to going to bed early and getting all the sleep she needed. Practice meditation, prānayāma and yoga in addition to and not instead of, a good night's sleep. *Yogas chittavrittinirodhah*, the second of

Patanjali's Yoga Sutras, states that through these techniques, the fluctuations of the mind are brought to complete rest. In 1992, I published a study together with Norman Orentreich, MD and his colleagues from a large New York dermatology and cosmetic surgery practice that catered, among other clients, to models and actors. We found that a population of several hundred long-term practitioners of Transcendental Meditation, recruited from a large meditating community, had higher levels of DHEA sulfate, a hormone that declines with age. The meditators' DHEA sulfate levels were typical of people in his practice who were 10-15 years younger.[238]

In an Ayurvedic beauty prescription, tejas, ojas and jyoti, the fundamental aspects of beauty, are enlivened on deep as well as on surface values. The luminous type of beauty they create is not simply a cosmetic glow or a side benefit of good health. This deeper beauty is actually healing for those who behold you. In the Vedic tradition, it is incumbent on everyone in society to exude orderliness and luminosity into the environment in order to promote harmony and prosperity throughout creation. So, pitch in for world peace by making yourself radiant!

229 a vāta imbalance
230 a pitta imbalance
231 a kapha imbalance
232 Type 1 skin is porcelain and Type 6 skin on this scale is black. Type 6 does not burn and has a low risk of skin cancer.
233 This is not a Vedic approach, but the best advice to someone with an active, outdoor lifestyle.
234 See Chapter 15 for a more extensive discussion of free radicals and aging.
235 Available commercially as Aveeno® and others.
236 Consult your physician about the use of non-sedating antihistamines such as loratadine or cetirizime to relieve itching and to break the itch-scratch cycle. Ask about the use of mild steroid cream in areas of intense itching, but use sparingly.
237 Translation by author.
238 Glaser JL, Brind JL, Orentreich N et al. *Elevated serum dehydroepiandrosterone sulfate levels in older practitioners of the Transcendental Meditation and the TM-Sidhi Program.* Journal of Behavioral Medicine, Vol. 15, No. 4, 1992. (Reuters coverage including USA Today, December, 1992).

CHAPTER 31

DISORDERS OF THE PELVIC DIAPHRAGM:

INCONTINENCE, HEMORRHOIDS, PREMATURE EJACULATION, ERECTILE DYSFUNCTION, VAGINISMUS, UTERINE PROLAPSE AND PROSTATE PROBLEMS

Before the sport was forever banned due to high accident insurance premiums, in my junior year in high school I enjoyed a brief career as a trampoline artist on the gymnastics team. My fellow competitors had two main complaints regarding the home team's trampolines. Wiry types, who garnered points stringing together triple and quadruple twisting flips, grumbled when the bed and springs were tight and could not be sufficiently flexed to gain height. Athletes like me, with more meat on their bones, could impress judges by maintaining height and grace, so we complained when the trampolines were too loose.

Like the classic trampoline every gymnast loved that was simultaneously strong and supple, your health as you age will be much better, and life a lot more fun, if you can maintain the same qualities in your pelvic diaphragm. In addition, overcoming many common disorders of the pelvic diaphragm, including urinary incontinence, hemorrhoids, premature ejaculation, erectile dysfunction, vaginismus, prolapse of the uterus, prostate problems and disorders of the urethra and rectum is dependent on keeping the diaphragm's spring-like muscles toned and firm. This chapter is critical if you intend on maintaining a healthy sex life as you grow older, so read it before jumping ahead.

Apāna, the Eliminative Operator

Apāna is the Sanskrit word referring to the physiological operator that expels products downward and outward from the body, including urine, stool, gas, menstrual fluids, semen and babies. We discussed this operator earlier with respect to constipation in Chapter 19, Effortless Elimination. Since the uterus, urethra, vagina, rectum and prostate are all supported by the pelvic diaphragm, apāna's well-being depends on the health of the body's "trampoline." Vedic science holds that because apāna governs all the pelvic organs, if it is not balanced, you may suffer from multiple eliminative problems. Indeed, modern epidemiology has shown apāna problems do flock together: a person with urinary incontinence is much more likely to also have fecal incontinence and pelvic organ prolapse.[239]

Ancient Vedic medicine states that pelvic diaphragm abnormalities come in two flavors corresponding to the two main problems with Denver's public high school trampolines: most commonly, too loose and weak (the old trampolines that had been stretched out) and less commonly, too stiff or in spasm. Weakness of the pelvic diaphragm, according to Vedic medicine, is due to the pelvic diaphragm straining against obstructions that resist natural elimination. The biggest offender is the tearing and stretching of childbirth. The second is chronic straining against a hard, constipated stool. For men over forty, the resistance is often a large prostate. Other stresses like the weight of a pregnancy, obesity or chronic cough weaken the muscles themselves. The muscles can also be weakened by the effects of aging or neurological disorders. On the other hand, too much tone in the pelvic diaphragm is usually due to an inappropriate response to stress, creating muscular spasm.

Strengthening the Pelvic Diaphragm

Levator ani means, in Latin, the anal lifter, and this large muscle group is stretched and suspended on both sides, like a trampoline, from the pubis in front, to the pelvic walls on the sides, to the coccyx in the rear. The levator ani muscles comprise the bulk of the pelvic diaphragm. Their health can make the difference between a life of effortless continence with easy elimination and great sex or a life of organizing your life around your bodily functions. For this reason, a chapter on the levator ani begged to be included in this book on self-repair. With levator ani exercises, you can learn to prevent and manage nearly all the pelvic diaphragm disorders.

The levator ani muscles are different from the anal and urethral sphincter muscles responsible for relaxing and permitting evacuation. So different, in fact, that early Sanskrit yogic texts make clear distinctions between the practices that lift the pelvic diaphragm and those that merely contract the anal and rectal sphincters. The anal contraction, *ashvini mudrā* (horse gesture, named in Sanskrit, because of the characteristic way a horse puckers its anal sphincter) can be learned by squeezing your anal sphincter against the tip of a finger. The urethral sphincter contraction, called *vajroli mudrā* (contraction of the phallic sphincter) or *sahajroli mudrā* (for women) can be learned by feeling which muscles are used to stop the flow of urine in mid-stream.

The levator ani muscles that raise and descend the entire pelvic diaphragm are distinct from these sphincters and were considered important to health and enlightenment by the ancient sages. Control, tone and endurance of these muscles are most effectively developed using a yogic technique called a *bandha* or lock (the Sanskrit root for bind, band). For a woman, the technique is *yoni bandha* (womb lock: *yoni* means a sacred place, receptacle or womb). For a man, it is *mūla bandha* (root lock: *mūla* refers to the root of the *lingam* a term for penis or phallus that carries meaning of the organ for its reproductive, purification and spiritual functions.).

Perfect Practice makes Perfect

Modern appropriations of these yogic techniques (commonly called Kegel exercises), differ from *mūla* and yoni bandhas by omitting the essence of yoga: effortlessness, conscious awareness, coordination with the breath and systematic practice. Kegel exercises are taught to strengthen the urethral sphincters. The patient is commonly advised to forcefully contract the urethral sphincter, to do the exercises during commercial breaks on TV or at stop signs, and to attempt one hundred repetitions a day. Taught in this way, the exercises do not strengthen and tone your levator ani, they do not connect your awareness to the practice thereby permitting you to isolate the sphincters from the pelvic diaphragm, and they do not foster regular and systematic practice. Remember, practice doesn't make perfect, perfect practice makes perfect.

You must first learn the techniques for developing the pelvic diaphragm and sphincters so you can apply them to the treatment of your pelvic diaphragm disorders.[240] Yoni and mūla bandha should always be practiced without distraction, ideally on an empty stomach. If you already practice yoga, they can be a part of your daily postures (āsanas). Sit on the floor in samāsana (Equal pose), women with the left heel on the perineum (which is located between the anus and the vagina) and the right heel just in front of it, with the outer bump of both ankle bones (lateral malleoli) on the floor. Men put the right heel on the perineum (between the anus and scrotum) and the left ankle in front of the right. If you are among the many people who are unable to put your heel in the proper position due to arthritic knees, large thighs or stiff tendons, you may sit in any comfortable position – ideally on the floor, or on a firm chair – and put a small, soft ball of cotton fabric in the place of the heel. A rolled up pair of cotton socks is about the right size. The heel or cotton ball accomplishes several purposes: bringing your awareness to the perineum, acting as a lever to make the retraction of the pelvic diaphragm easier, and relieving congestion in the rectum and engorgement of blood and edema in the perineal tissues.

Place your arms on your thighs, close your eyes and bring your awareness to the perineum. Listen to your body's ancient song. Women will place attention on contraction of the vaginal muscles. Men put the attention on contraction of the scrotal sac, attempting to elevate the testes.[241] Exhale fully and contract the pelvic diaphragm, bringing it to about 90% of maximum tension and holding it for 4-5 seconds. Release the muscles slowly but completely as you inhale. Rest about the same interval as the duration of your contraction and repeat – at first three to eight times. Take a 30-60 second rest and then complete one more set. Remove the heel or cotton ball and complete one set bringing the awareness to the contraction of the urethral sphincter.

If this technique feels uncomfortable with the pressure of your heel or the cotton fabric ball in the perineum, which is often the case with prostatitis, prostatic enlargement or other conditions, do the exercise without the pressure. For hemorrhoids or rectal prolapse, move the heel or cotton ball closer to or even onto the anus.

At first, you may find that you are unable to isolate the levator ani muscles alone and are instead contracting the urethral and rectal sphincters. This is normal and even good, because ultimately you need to strengthen both the sphincters and the trampoline. Be certain you are not squeezing the buttocks or thighs together or sucking in the abdominal muscles. When yoni bandha is done properly, a woman will feel a squeeze on a finger inserted in the vagina. A man will feel the base of the lingam squeezed and raised upward. Do not perform yoni or mula bandha while eliminating urine or stool. Be patient and persist. With diligence, these practices are highly effective. Women had 63 to 81 percent fewer incontinent accidents when properly coached and encouraged to practice regularly, and the techniques were more helpful than the most effective medication.[242, 243] A scrawny baseball player needs to lift weights for many months to improve his chances of hitting home runs. Similarly, yoni and mūla bandha should be done with regularity and continued for at least six months before evaluating whether they are effective.

Bandhas as Spiritual Techniques

Mūla and yoni bandha have a value that transcends their benefits for disorders of the pelvic diaphragm. Their principle intent in the yogic tradition is the culture of *pratyahara*, turning the senses away from the outer world of change, differences and boundaries and directing them inward toward the Self, the field of non-change, unity, boundlessness. Both fields are real and both are valuable, but because the world of objects and change is always in your face and the Self so subtle, we neglect the inward and get lost in the dramatic display of the world of change. Ayurveda calls this a mistake of judgment, *prajña-aparādham*, and the root cause of disease. The practices associated with yoga (kriyas, bandhas, yāmas, niyāmas, meditation, samyama, etc.) settle the mind, turn the senses inward and enliven the inner Self.

Ayurveda adopts the terminology of the Vedas and Upanishads, describing the upward moving vital breath (prāna)[244] as governing the strength and stability of the nervous system.[245] Apāna, the eliminative operator, is the support for the prāna, thus explaining why you are lethargic and depressed when afflicted with disorders like constipation and menstrual problems, and why TV commercials for Ex-Lax show a smiling, energetic woman the morning after her dose.

Yoni bandha is effective when it is done as yoga, with your awareness drawn to the organ of concern for the purpose of self-repair. Your consciousness, awake in the Self from your daily spiritual practices, flows to the requirement in your physiology, guiding the nervous system to relax muscles and increase blood flow, increasing the influx of anti-inflammatory molecules, cytokines, immune cells and hormones. This is self-repair. Let us now see how these spiritual exercises can be used to prevent and treat different disorders.

Urinary Incontinence

Whenever a woman's urethral sphincter muscles cannot maintain a pressure greater than the bladder pressure during brief increases in abdominal pressure such as coughing, sneezing, laughing or exercise, accidents are bound to happen. This is stress incontinence. With a healthy pelvic diaphragm, when the abdominal pressure increases, the urethra is forced down onto a stable base formed by the vaginal wall, squeezing the urethra flat to keep it closed. When your pelvic diaphragm is weak, the urethra cannot be pinned firmly and compressed when the abdominal pressure rises and you leak like an old faucet. Urge incontinence sufferers, in addition to having weak pelvic floors, have bladder detrusor muscles that contract when they should not, and sometimes on cue, such as when they get the key in the door to their home.

If you are a woman with urinary incontinence, in addition to starting this program in every case, an evaluation by a urologist specializing in the problem is critical, because skilled analysis of your anatomical problems and contributing factors may identify other treatable causes such as diabetes or medications.[246]

Many foods and drinks have been reported[247] to contribute to incontinence, especially alcohol, coffee and tea (including decaf), acidic fruits and juices, tomatoes, pungent spices, carbonated beverages, artificial sweeteners, food colorings, MSG, and even water. Take plenty of fluids during the day, but restrict them in the evening for a less interrupted night's sleep.

Vedic medicine prescribes strict obedience to natural urges, which in the case of the pelvic diaphragm, includes never suppressing the passage of urine, stool, semen and flatus.[248] This principle gives us a logic for treatment of incontinence: taking a holiday from the soaked panty liner by preemptively emptying your bladder before it gets so full you might leak. If you should feel a sudden urge, instead of rushing to the bathroom, often a recipe for an accident, sit or stand quietly with your awareness on the pelvic diaphragm, perhaps gently performing yoni bandha until the sensation dissipates, then go to void.

A useful remedy for incontinence is shilajit, 250 mg of which can be crushed and placed in a 12 oz. sports bottle of water and then sipped throughout the day. Shatāvari (one gram twice a day) and āmla (one gram twice a day) may help strengthen pelvic musculature.

Premature ejaculation (PE)

Don't believe the old tale that premature ejaculation is due to feelings of guilt or shame. While emotional and mental conditions play an important role in the problem, premature ejaculation is usually the result of hypersensitivity of nerves in a reflex pathway involving the lingam, pelvic diaphragm, spinal cord and brain. Sometimes it is simply due to an ardent desire.

Also, don't be fooled by reports that most normal males are marathoners: Kinsey's report in the 1950's showed that 75% of men ejaculate within 2 minutes of penetration in half of their sexual encounters. Many men have a normal ejaculation latency of five to ten minutes (after the usual false starts of a novice) and then develop the problem after an infection such as an STD that inflames the nerves. While many men can delay ejaculation only seconds, endurance of 30 minutes or more is neither common nor necessary, and five to ten minutes can usually satisfy both partners.

Forget the squeeze and pinch technique promoted by many therapists, wherein the glans of the penis is pinched by the partner when ejaculation is imminent. It is not only a waste of time, but even dangerous because it can lead to retrograde ejaculation and inflammation of the prostate. Forget also the use of topical anesthetics. They are highly effective at numbing your partner. Also, why would you try thinking about the Superbowl instead of the beautiful woman in your arms. After all, why are you having sex? To be totally connected, or to be somewhere else?

The basis of the long-term management of this problem must be the toning of the pelvic diaphragm, which supports the prostate and seminal vesicles, bladder and lingam. Techniques resembling mūla bandha are found in other medical traditions beside Ayurveda, including Chinese traditional medicine, where it is called the deer exercise.[249] Mūla bandha can strengthen these muscles to such a degree that when you perform the technique during sex at a moment of excessive stimulation, the pressure on these over-inspired structures arrests the nerve stimulation and milks the semen from the ejaculatory ducts back into the prostate and seminal vesicles, allowing you to settle the process down and start over.

Learning this technique requires a patient partner who will allow you to slow down or stop moving altogether. Above a waterfall, there is always a pool of still water. Try to stay in this pool, occasionally moving out into the current that takes you toward the waterfall. Before you go so far that you are carried over the edge, stop all friction, apply your well-practiced mūla bandha and return to the safety of the pool.

The SSRI antidepressants commonly delay orgasm in both men and women. Women call it a side effect, men a side benefit.[250] Its use for premature ejaculation is considered an off label use of these medications, not one approved by the FDA. For most men with premature ejaculation, the other side effects such as somnolence, nausea and insomnia make them not worth taking because they adversely affect the quality of the 99% of your life not engaged in sex. However, for many men who have a considerable amount of performance anxiety associated with what they consider an inadequate gig, SSRI antidepressants can restore confidence and start them on the pathway to healing.

The most useful herb for premature ejaculation is chandraprabha, a mixture containing shilajit (mineral pitch) as one of its chief ingredients.[251] Take one to two 500 mg tabs twice daily for its benefits on general strengthening of the genitourinary system as well as for premature ejaculation. Don't bother to take a big dose before a romantic evening.

Besides mūla bandha, frequency of sex is the best remedy. This can involve a second round of love-making in the same day, or many times a week. The benefit of frequency of sex for premature ejaculation is another reason why a committed relationship with a patient partner is critical to making progress. Single men without a partner who are looking for help in random brief encounters should instead envision a steady relationship as part of the cure.

Erectile Dysfunction

Living a rejuvenating life is the key to preventing and treating erectile dysfunction. This involves balance in diet, exercise, daily routines, behavioral tonics, meditation and yoga. ED is often caused by physical causes requiring diagnosis, including endocrine problems like low testosterone and diabetes, so start with a consultation with your physician. Maintaining mental and physical youthfulness and virility are the subjects of two of the eight branches of Ayurveda, and a complete discussion is therefore beyond the scope of this chapter, but are discussed briefly at the end of Chapter 34. [252]

Practice mūla bandha. It is extremely useful for both the prevention and treatment of erectile dysfunction and promotes virility into extreme old age. It promotes blood flow and tones the vessels in the corpora cavernosa of the lingam that engorge with blood during erection. It is not paradoxical that mūla bandha is useful for both continence and virility: Vedic medicine is about choice and when you maintain health of the pelvic diaphragm and lingam, you increase your choices. Mūla bandha is so important to the treatment and prevention of erectile dysfunction that it is being included in this chapter instead of the Chapter 34: Restoring Passion to the Bedroom, which is also critical reading for someone with erectile dysfunction.

Viagra and similar drugs are the first effective medicines for dealing with this common problem. They may some day be credited for saving endangered species by reducing the demand for the useless tiger bones, rhinoceros tusk, bear gall and other products touted by some traditional Chinese and Oriental practitioners for increasing virility. Before going the medication route, read these chapters. Also, try a few simple Ayurvedic treatments:

Massage. Apply sesame oil or mahanarāyana oil (a specially herbalized sesame oil) to the lower abdomen above the pubis, to the perineum, and to the root of the lingam daily before the morning shower and massage gently.

Lingam tea. Take a heaping teaspoon of the following formula at least twice daily in hot water or milk. Drink the dregs. Mix equal parts of the powder of gokshura (caltrops, Latin: *Tribulis terrestris*), ashwagandha (winter cherry, Latin:

Withania somnifera) and vidari-kanda (Latin: *Ipomoea digitata*). Store the mixture in an airtight container. Let the mixture soak in the water or milk for a minute or two before drinking. You can add brown sugar for taste.

Garlic is one of the best Ayurvedic remedies for erectile dysfunction. One of its many Sanskrit names means *that which is hated by the renunciates*, because it enhances sexual power just when the yogin may be trying to forget about sex. Unfortunately, garlic on the breath may be one of the biggest turnoffs for your partner, so make sure she takes some, too. Try swallowing a fresh clove of garlic whole or cut in half, in the form of a capsule, together with your hot milk – herb mixture.

Take hot milk with 6-7 threads of saffron at bedtime for increasing *shukra* (semen) and ojas (the finest essence of the tissues).

Hemorrhoids

In susceptible people, both internal and external hemorrhoidal pillows fill with blood under the pressure of straining at the stool, during childbirth, or at other times, and the blood then clots. I learned this the hard way, during a mountainous half-marathon footrace, when I ducked off the trail and strained to finish my business quickly so as not to lose too many precious seconds. The next morning I awoke to a large, painful, clotted external hemorrhoid – and the seconds I saved would not have affected my standings anyway.

Analysis of my acute problem illuminates the cause of most hemorrhoids. In my haste, my pelvic diaphragm had pushed some of the mucosal tissues out of the rectum (a condition called a prolapse) and engorged them with blood. Not concerned with pushing them back in or even tidying up, I ran the rest of the race, giving the blood in the tender, swollen hemorrhoidal pillows plenty of time to clot. Even while running, my distended, clotted tissues became firm and later, when I got around to caring about them more than the race, could not be pushed back in (i.e. reduced) to their proper place, a vicious cycle.

Prevention of Hemorrhoids

Strengthening the levator ani, which supports the rectum and anus, is the best prevention for hemorrhoids. The story of hemorrhoid prevention can be abridged to the management of constipation and the imbalances in the brain that make us so impatient that we strain to finish our business too quickly. We also need to correct poor habits such as spending too long on the throne not accomplishing much, thereby allowing the anal tissues to prolapse. It is important to avoid acute external hemorrhoids, because they are the harbingers of internal hemorrhoids, the ones that bleed, prolapse and end up face to face with a surgeon.

After passing a stool and wiping well, use a finger to tuck any prolapsed tissues back into the rectum. Now is the time for your horse mudrā, the contracting of the anal sphincter (see above), which will pull the tissues deeper into the rectum and drain them of any engorgement of blood that could be the seed for an incipient hemorrhoid. You can perform horse mudrā sitting for a moment, or standing if sitting is not convenient.

Managing Hemorrhoids

For acute external hemorrhoids, hot sitz baths, topical witch hazel and an ointment of two parts ghee and one part turmeric powder are the mainstays of therapy.[253] For large internal hemorrhoids, the ounce of prevention described above is easier than trying to make them disappear.[254] Try making suppositories by mixing two parts ghee with one part turmeric. Keep the mixture at about 60 degrees Fahrenheit so it becomes firm but not hard. Roll the ghee into balls or bullets about the size of an almond and put them into the fridge where they keep well and become hard. Insert a suppository into the anus at bedtime, allowing it to melt in the anal canal where your hemorrhoid is located (and not to slide past the sphincter into the rectum where its medicinal effect is wasted). Wear old underwear if you use turmeric suppositories, because turmeric stains yellow if it leaks. If you are not motivated to be surgically rid of your hemorrhoids due to prolapsing, pain, or bleeding, putting off an operation occasionally gives them a chance to clot and scar on their own, a spontaneous self-repair.

Vaginismus

Vaginismus, or painful spasm of the muscles of the vagina during sex[255], can be improved by yoni bandha, which increases muscular blood flow, the antidote to the reactive constriction of the vessels of the muscles of the vaginal walls that accompanies pain and its associated anxiety. Vaginismus is a vicious cycle because pain begets spasm, which begets more pain and anxiety. Yet vaginismus is eminently treatable: 99% of women with the problem ultimately find relief. Yoni bandha, behavioral therapy[256] from a competent sex therapist, a patient and gentle partner who can aid in developing relaxation of the pelvic diaphragm and vaginal walls after they have been strengthened, and copious lubrication are the pillars of therapy.

After improvement using the above, yoni bandha can also be practiced with a lingam stone[257] or another object with a soft lingam shape. Yoni bandha can also be performed with a patient partner whose only concern is your healing and well-being. This yogic practice is so effective for both vaginismus and incontinence that it has spawned a new specialty of modern physical therapy known as pelvic relaxation therapy. A consultation with a therapist trained in these programs is often the best way to start, even if your therapist may not have a clue she is actually practicing an ancient yogic art. She can diagnose other associated conditions and individualize your program. Pain during intercourse (dyspareunia) associated with vaginismus can be associated with many physical conditions including a tilted or prolapsed uterus (both often related to a weak pelvic diaphragm), cysts, masses, menopausal conditions such as thinning and dryness of the vaginal membranes and others.

Prostatitis

Mūla bandha is critical for the prevention of prostatitis because the contractions create a natural massage and milking action, preventing stagnation of the prostatic secretions and subsequent infection. The ball of cotton cloth positioned carefully on the perineum to squeeze the prostate without creating pain is useful in preventing recurrences.[258] It should not be used during an acute episode of prostatitis. Sipping shilajit as described above (for incontinence) is also useful for all prostate problems.[259]

Benign Prostatic Hypertrophy (BPH)

If you are a man over 50 when you start to develop a weak stream, frequency, hesitation, dribbling, and retained urine, don't count on mūla bandha to reverse decades of overgrowth of tissue due to high androgen hormone levels.[260] You likely have BPH. Because the prostate sits in the bladder like the mound in an orange juicer with the urethral opening on the top, your urine pools at the bottom and simply cannot get out. Regular practice of mūla bandha allows you to raise and contract the bladder at the end of urination for more complete elimination, as well as to relax the smooth muscles in the prostate and bladder walls, a beneficial response that otherwise can only be accomplished by medications,[261] with their attendant side effects. Use a cotton fabric ball or your heel judiciously at first, leaving it in place for only a minute or two per day until you determine that the effect is beneficial.

Prolapsed uterus

The stresses of a delivery on the uterus's supportive tissues are the principle cause of prolapse. Prevention using yoni bandha before and after delivery is far more useful than starting the practices when the cervix is beginning to peek through opening of the vagina. If you have established uterine prolapse and you do not notice any benefit after six months of practice, and, if you do not plan on further pregnancies, having a hysterectomy while you are still relatively young and healthy is an option that is rarely regretted.

Daily Attention to the Pelvic Diaphragm

It is better to think of your yoni and mula bandha practice as a yogic or spiritual technique rather than as a cure for your disorder because that attitude dissociates the exercise from its fruits. This encourages you to practice it with attention, increasing its benefits and fostering regular, long-term practice.

239 Jackson, SL et al. *Fecal incontinence in women with urinary incontinence and pelvic organ prolapse.* Obstet Gynecol 1997;89:423

240 Acknowledgment to Mukunda Stiles for generously sharing his notes on the practice of bandhas and mudras. His book, *Ayurvedic Yoga Therapy* (See Resources), is highly recommended.

241 *Gheranda Samhitā.* Rendered with Commentary. by Robert L. Wisehart Based on the 1914 translation by Rai Bahadur Srisa Chandra Vasu and on other authoritative sources. http://www.classicyoga.org/texts/Gheranda-1.html#Chapter-3-Mudra

242 Burgio, KL, Locher, JL, Goode, PS, et al. *Behavioral vs drug treatment for urge urinary incontinence in older women: a randomized controlled trial.* JAMA 1998;280:1995.

243 Burgio, KL, Goode, PS, Locher, JL, et al. *Behavioral training with and without biofeedback in the treatment of urge incontinence in older women: a randomized controlled trial.* JAMA 2002;288:2293.

244 The five aspects of vāta (vāyu) are prāna *(vital breath, nervous system), udāna (upward movement in the head and neck governing speech, coughing, movement of secretions, etc.), samāna (gastric and intestinal motility), apāna (pelvic functions and elimination) and vyāna (movement about the body of circulation and energy).*

245 There are many Vedic ways beside the Ayurvedic one to understand the interaction between the nervous control of the muscles and visceral functions of the pelvis and the other divisions of the central nervous system. A more recent Vedic science, kundalini yoga, describes apāna as a lower energetic plexus or chakra, and is focused on the transmutation of its energy to higher chakras in the heart, neck or head. Without the attendance of a proper teacher, kundalini is best left alone and not learned from a book.

246 For many women with incontinence, life began anew with a surgical procedure, allowing them to travel, exercise, and attend social events and other activities that were impossible before. Newer procedures such as the tension free vaginal tape (TVT) are less invasive and more effective. They should be considered in consultation with a urologist if there is little benefit after practicing yoni bandha for six months without results.

247 There has been no definite proof of this connection, but most of these foods are held by Ayurveda to be intensely pitta aggravating, and therefore potentially irritant to the mucous membranes.

248 The other urges you should never suppress are sleeping, belching, sneezing, yawning, hiccupping, coughing, spitting, vomiting, hunger and thirst. See Appendix 4.

249 Steven Chang, *The Tao of Sexology.* Tao Publishing, 1986.

250 The most effective SSRI (Selective Serotonin Reuptake Inhibitor) for delaying orgasm is paroxetine (Paxil and other generics), but it is also one of the more sedating. The SSRI needs to be selected by your physician based on your medications, temperament and mood. The effect takes several weeks for its full effect, so you can't take an SSRI, like medication for erectile dysfunction, an hour before you expect to perform. Also some people, especially women, report the SSRI medications reduce not only sexual responsiveness but also libido. For men, improved performance generally improves libido in spite of the medication.

251 Chandra (moon) + prabha (light) in Sanskrit refer to the influence of the herbal preparation in promoting continence, thereby increasing shukra (semen) and ojas (vital essence of the seven dhātus which gives radiance to the body). It is therefore used by men seeking to practice brahmacharya (Brahmanic or spiritual continence).

252 *Vajīkarana* and *Rasayana* are the names of these Ayurvedic specialties.

253 Topical local anesthetics and hydrocortisone are the active ingredients in most useful OTC remedies. Vaidya PJ Deshpande, with whom I studied Ayurvedic anorectal surgery at Benares Hindu University Hospital, promoted the use of tumeric in anorectal disorders for its anti-inflammatory properties. These adaptations for western lifestyles are my own.

254 First, be sure what you think is an internal bleeding hemorrhoid is not cancer; do not hesitate to see your doctor.

255 As well as during pelvic exams or the insertion of tampons, etc.

256 Aqueous lubricants (Astroglide, KY gels, etc.) are most widely recommended by gynecologists. Ayurveda also recommends the use of sesame oil for its positive benefits on the vaginal mucous membranes.

257 A lingam stone is a prosthetic lingam made from stones of different weights that are used as physiotherapeutic aids in the practice of yoni bandha. By tradition, they are inserted with adequate lubrication into the vagina while lying on your back. Using yoni bandha, you push the lingam stone upward and outward. The weight of the stone is incrementally increased. This practice is also useful for incontinence and uterine prolapse.

258 Research on internal rectal prostate massage and myofascial release therapy, which is closely related to this treatment, has shown benefits in symptoms and reduces electromyographic evidence of pelvic spasm in prostatis. (1999 Selected Abstracts from American Urological Association Annual Meeting. Myofascial Release Therapy for Category III Chronic Prostatitis. RU Anderson; D Wise; and M Meadows; Stanford, CA).

259 Don't avoid seeing your physician for treatable infectious causes of prostatitis, because antibiotics are frequently curative and neglecting the condition can lead to chronic prostatitis.

260 Medication and surgery are the two main medical options for benign prostatic hypertrophy. Prostate cancer as a cause for the symptoms should always be ruled out by an exam and prostate specific antigen (PSA) level.

261 Alpha adrenergic blockers, oxybutinin, etc.

CHAPTER 32

MENSTRUATION AFTER THE EASY YEARS

"O swear not by the moon, the fickle moon, th' inconstant moon, that monthly changes in her circle orb, Lest that thy love prove likewise variable."

Shakespeare's Juliet to Romeo II,2

Part One: Monthly Rhythms and Routines

Let's start with men. They have never enjoyed the physical pleasures of menstruation and childbirth to test how manly they really are. After the easy years, when the period begins to become unpredictable, tedious and extravagant, many women would like to forego the ritual as well. Men are encouraged to read this chapter because they have been physically deprived of the glory of a healthy menstrual cycle in renewing and purifying the mind and body and therefore don't appreciate the role of cyclicity in creating a balanced life. Men also need to understand some dominant forces that shape the behavior of the other 51% of society.

A highly motivated Danish endocrinologist, Dr. Christian Hamburger, wondered if men also have monthly rhythms. He began collecting his urine daily and amazingly continued for fifteen years, analyzing it for levels of 17-ketosteroids, the metabolites of testosterone that substituted for today's modern testosterone measurement. He noted a monthly fluctuation that persisted even after his wife went into menopause, suggesting that a man's hormonal cycling is not a rhythm imparted to the husband through his partner's female pheromones[262] or other subtle signals that change with her monthly cycle. This normal, healthy man, who did not have a unique endocrine problem but was simply a committed researcher (and subject!), appeared to have a monthly burst of testosterone, just as women have monthly bursts of estrogen and progesterone. This finding was recently confirmed using salivary testosterone levels sampled every other day in 31 healthy young men.[236] Monthly variations in the male body have been recorded since 1657, when Santorio wrote about a healthy man who practiced extreme moderation in his lifestyle, yet whose body weight fluctuated by several pounds and followed a monthly cycle.[264]

If these observations had been with respect to women, your reaction would be, "Big deal, what else is new?" So why are we so surprised that men also have cyclical changes that coincide with the phases of the moon? After all, a moon, including the moons of the other planets, can make oceans rise and induce shifts and tides of the magma within their host planet. The full moon somehow precipitates deliveries and brings "lunatics" to the emergency psychiatric units, and rashes of suicides, homicides, crime, accidents and other lunacy to police departments.

Yet with the advent of the solar-based Roman calendar, we are increasingly less conscious of the moon's phases, together with the traditions and festivals that revolved around it. And women have become oblivious to the functions and routines whose names derive from the same root: *menses*, about a month.

The Two Phases of the Vedic month: Inward and Outward

Vedic science places importance on physiological cycles because it sees physical creation as the concretization of the flow of abstract intelligence (natural law) that functions as a constitution of the universe. Human physiology is an expression of the harmonics that arise from the play of this pulsation. Like it or not, humans are subject to inward and outward phases corresponding to cycles of rest and activity. Sleeping and waking, exercise and leisure, Sabbath and the workdays. If we feel the need to go inward, we may take a day of fasting or go on a retreat. Meditation is the most powerful inward phase of all, because during every sitting, although sometimes only for a moment, mental and physical activity nearly cease, time is suspended, the outer world dissolves, and only the Self remains.

Similarly, in the Vedic way of looking at things, for a woman (and some research suggests also for a man), the month can be divided into an inward and outward phase. The inward phase, like meditation, sleep, Sabbath or a retreat, is a time to prepare for dynamism, for gaining potential energy. It is a time for taking more rest and avoiding creating strain. This is a time of month to balance your body and mind, to contemplate and reflect on your upcoming activity or on spiritual matters. It is a time for dwelling on the Self. This part of the month, lasting from one week before the onset of flow until about a week after, corresponds to pulling the arrow back on the bow.

The outward phase is a time for dynamism, for turning potential into kinetic energy, for letting the arrow fly. It lasts from the end of your flow until a week before the next. This is when the uterine lining (endometrium), under the influence of estrogen, is becoming thick and rich, a fertile field for implantation of an embryo. The peak of the outward phase is the middle of your month, the day of ovulation, when the vaginal mucus becomes copious and clear like a raw egg white, and the uterine lining's loam is most fertile. The peak of the outward stroke is when nearly all women are feeling the most sexual.

Although a woman might dream of a life free of any influence from her cycle, if she learns to value the entrainment of her routines with her natural rhythms, she gains freedom because she can plan and choose for better health, success and pleasure. Life loses its naturally effortless, regal and joyful nature when you are stuck toiling on a critical project while you are also dealing with cramps, bloating and shifting moods.

The inward phase for most women corresponds to the recognition by the body that an embryo has not implanted and the corpus luteum, the abandoned shell of the released ovum, begins to secrete progesterone. The uterine lining ripens and breaks up as a menstrual flow.

A Woman's Month

Let's take a guided tour through a woman's month, bearing in mind that women are so varied in their rhythms and behaviors that what is normal for the majority may not apply to every woman. In fact, over the course of your menstruating life, you can expect to have longer or shorter cycles, longer or heavier flows, a longer inward phase or a different day of ovulation. It is even natural for a woman to have a day of mild spotting in the middle of a cycle. One woman may feel the exact moment of ovulation while another has no inkling. In all of these instances, you should not think that something major is wrong with your menstrual health. If changes happen, it is useful to note whether they relate to any changes in the season, your diet, medications, exercise, travel or other stressors. You should take remedial measures, including seeing your physician if you have persistent discomfort, either in your body or your emotions, if you saturate a super-absorbent maxi more than once an hour, if you recurrently miss periods, or if you have more than one period per month. Problems with your periods requiring proper diagnosis include fibroids, cysts, polyps, endometrial tumors and hormonal imbalances including thyroid problems. However, if a woman adopts the Vedic habits described here, her cycle will invariably become more comfortable and will naturally tend toward a 29-day month if it is longer or shorter. [265]

Day one:

The Vedic month for a woman commonly begins with a spontaneous, large bowel movement heralding the onset of flow. When I describe this to my patients, they often respond, "Yes! That happens to me every month!" Menstruation and evacuation of stool are intimately linked in the understanding of Vedic medicine. Apāna, we have analyzed in the preceding chapter, is the eliminative movement downward and outward, responsible for expelling menstrual tissues and stool, but also urine, gas, babies and semen. Contracting the perineal muscles squeezes the vagina, the urethral sphincter and the anal sphincters, thus blocking all the different functions coming under the influence of apāna.

Well begun is half done is the logic behind the Ayurvedic prescription to take extra rest during the first two days of heavy flow. These days are the culmination of the inward phase. During the first two days, take the attitude that you are on retreat, even if you have to go to work. If possible, put off for a day or two any activity that creates engorgement of your pelvic organs, or that creates a harsh influence if your nervous system is feeling delicate. These are the days to build cooperation between your mind and body, when nearly every function – hormonal, nervous, circulatory and sexual – may be yearning to be left in peace.

Stress and exertion during these first two days of flow negate the restorative effect that menstruation has on both your uterus and your nervous system. Stress creates vasoconstriction – as in the fight response – inappropriately constricting the smooth muscles in the walls of the blood vessels, vaginal walls and uterus – just when they need to relax and let blood flow. The result is cramping; a dark, coagulated, scanty flow; and the retention of endometrial debris and clots. In this scenario, when the endometrial lining begins to proliferate a week or two later, it does not have a clean basis on which to build, leading to spotting or breakthrough bleeding. Well begun is truly half done.

In a modern world, your days of resting or retreat must necessarily include going to work and dealing with all your otherwise unavoidable activities. Procrastination, delegation, and learning to say "no" can make your day more like being on retreat. In the meantime, you can spend more time horizontal (as in a long, warm bath), reading (especially spiritually uplifting texts), meditating or doing gentle yoga (asanas that don't strain the pelvis – including gentle forward bends – can relieve pressure and expel clots). Take a walk instead of a run or tinker in the garden (the bending and kneeling can be beneficial.

Try to retire early, and save your sexual energy because apāna needs to flow downwards and in a few days, you will enter your outward phase where you will appreciate that energy more. Some women, nevertheless, find that the uterine and vaginal contractions of orgasm help relieve pelvic congestion, and their libido is aided by the knowledge that these are the days that it is impossible to get pregnant. Many women are too sensitive both in the pelvis and in the nervous system for sex. Some women describe being irritated just brushing their hair. The important rule is to respect the dictates of your mind and body. Listen to your own body, rather than to advertisements implying that a modern woman can work out daily, or to admonitions against sex or other activities that you find make you feel more balanced.

If the idea of taking it easy during your first two days of flow sounds old-fashioned, it may be because it is a several thousand year-old tradition that women have found works, making periods more comfortable and easing gynecological symptoms in later years.

There are nevertheless obligations that you simply cannot put off. German physician Uta Pipig had an obligation to herself (and her trainer) to try to win the Boston Marathon in 1996. With one mile to go, she was 100 yards behind leader Tegla Louroupe. Millions of viewers watched her live on TV as she squeezed a last burst of energy from somewhere within to pass her opponents and break the ribbon. Her legs were coated with menstrual blood and diarrhea. An intense competitor, the value of that moment for her was worth all the suffering and self-conscious indignity she had to endure. However, when there is a choice, try to opt for long-term reproductive system health and align yourself with nature.[266]

Ayurveda holds these days of purification to be a unique opportunity for the elimination of āma that is pitta-charged, i.e. having a heating quality. This āma is different from the heavy residues or plaque caused by inefficient metabolism and digestion (discussed in Chapter 16). Pitta-charged āma is held to be the byproducts of inflammation and detoxification that have not been efficiently cleared by the liver and reticuloendothelial systems. Ayurvedic physicians maintain that efficient menstruation detoxifies a woman's body and mind of impurities that cannot be released by the kidneys, GI system and sweating. For example, releasing these heating residues during menstruation is held to prevent acne and other inflammatory disorders, anger, and mood changes during the rest of the month, and to purify the blood. For this reason, the menstrual blood is called – among many other Sanskrit names – *pushpa*, a flower, which heralds the coming of the fruit of fertility. The color of the flower determines the quality of the impurity that is being released. Note the quality of your flow to help determine the nature of your other imbalances or impurities. (See Appendices 1-4 for more information on the Ayurvedic tridosha understanding of impurities and imbalances.)

An irregular (vāta-predominant) pushpa is scant, dark and thick with clots. The flow will start and stop, and arrive off schedule. The flow lasts fewer than five days and may be accompanied with cramps.

The heating (pitta-predominant) pushpa is bright red, abundant, and lasts 5-8 days. It may be associated with sweating, a feeling of heat or migraine and a distinctive odor from sweating in the groin, the powerful pheromones of a pitta quality menses.

The watery (kapha-predominant) pushpa is characterized by edema or fluid retention. The pushpa may be frothy or streaked with mucus. The flow lasts 4-7 days and may be associated with lethargy, breast fullness, bloating in the lower abdomen, hands, and feet. Your rings may fit tightly and your varicose veins will swell.

Note the nature of these signs and symptoms during your days of flow, as this helps diagnose the causes of other symptoms like PMS, cramps, bloating, spotting, and irregularity.

By tradition, the pushpa is best absorbed in a clean, cotton cloth. Modern disposable pads and tampons have a highly absorbent polymers in addition to cotton and rayon, as well as surfactants and lubricants. They are so absorbent, as well as inexpensive, form fitting and adhesive, that their convenience outweighs any subtle advantage over pure cotton. However, it is important to avoid obstructing the natural flow downward and outward from the uterus created by apāna. If you use tampons exclusively, an Ayurvedic gynecologist would advise you to restrict their use to lighter days or occasions when a pad just won't do. I have never met an Ayurvedic doctor who herself admitted to using tampons. If you find residual clots in the vagina when you remove a tampon, the downward flow of apāna has been restricted, meaning that you should use tampons mainly on lighter days.

Days three to six:

When the initial flow has begun to slow, there is no need to restrict activities, even the more strenuous ones. You are still technically in the inward phase, so keep that in mind as you plan your exercise, work and social activities. Strive for effortlessness. If a jog on the beach will be easy and joyful, it will renew your body. This is a time for an "inward" type of spontaneity: more time for yoga, meditation, artistic endeavors, playing with children, visiting your family, planning and preparing for your outward phase.

Days Seven to Twenty-two:

I don't have to give you any creative ideas about maximizing your life during the outward phase of the month. Now is your chance to spend the energy you banked during the inward phase. Let the arrow fly. Crack the obstacles in your path toward greater progress. This is the time to be a little crazy, to permit yourself some immoderation, perhaps a challenging outdoors expedition, a night on the town. It is a time for enjoying your sexuality in its full blossoming, keeping in mind that it is also the period of your greatest fertility.

Ovulation Day (Somewhere between Days 12-16)

The release of the eggs from the ovarian follicle may fall somewhere between the twelfth and sixteenth day, depending on the length of your cycle. Many women are aware of the exact moment, experiencing a twinge or even a frank pain known as mittelschmerz (German for *pain in the middle of the cycle*). These women may be intimately connected with the inner functioning of their bodies or have serosal membranes that are sensitive and richly endowed with nerve endings. The importance of ovulation day for your monthly routine is that it signals the onset of a major shift in hormonal balance from the two weeks before. The active follicles form the progesterone-secreting corpus luteum. Technically you are still in an outward phase, but many women are immediately plunged into a two-week period of PMS (premenstrual syndrome). Also, if you are trying to get pregnant, bear in mind that ovulation day is the most favorable day for intercourse with the two days preceding it being next best, but the day after yielding very few pregnancies.

Days Twenty-three to Twenty-nine.

You are entering the inward stroke of the month. It is completely natural at this time to feel a more inward-directed consciousness – the desire to take more time alone – perhaps even an instinctive inclination to avoid intense social situations. If this natural tendency is exaggerated and you feel frank depression, irritability or radical mood swings, it is no longer normal. This is PMS. It is better to recognize and respect the usual emotional changes that naturally accompany the days before the appearance of the flow and which are in part related to your big dose of progesterone and diminishing dose of estrogen. These moods must have a natural reason, perhaps having to do with what is in a woman's best interest if she had just gotten pregnant – to be inward – or not gotten pregnant, i.e. to give her partner a period of abstinence to make him more ardent in a couple of weeks. If you are not feeling sexual and do not want to be touched, remember, you are in an inward phase – it is normal. If this natural inward trend feels uncomfortable or you are frankly depressed, don't miss the longer discussion regarding the treatment of PMS later in this chapter. Just as you analyzed the quality of your pushpa during the days of flow, now is the time to analyze any pre-menstrual symptoms to determine what may be contributing to your discomfort.

Day Twenty-five to Twenty-six.

Your flow will be starting in three days, assuming you are on a 29-day cycle. It is time to prepare your apāna for the coming flow, directing it downward and freeing the pelvis of its burden of stool while the ovaries and uterus are swollen and engorged. The technique recommended by Vedic medicine is purgation.

Monthly Virechana (laxative purgation)

Interestingly, pre-menstrual purgation is a tradition that seems to be practiced by other traditions besides Ayurveda. My French-Canadian mother-in-law had a Native American mother, from whom she must have learned this practice. She kept a calendar with the menstrual dates of her seven daughters. Three days before each was due, she would serve them a heaping tablespoonful of castor oil. Castor oil purgation prior to your period is the technique Vedic medicine recommends for any woman who has irregularity, heavy flow, cramps, endometriosis, or PMS. If you have had ten years of easy menstruation, don't bother to fix something that ain't broke. Otherwise, this simple ritual can often accomplish miracles.

I recommend the purgation be performed once per month, about three days before the period. You can do it in the evening at bedtime to have a good motion in the early morning, or you can do it in the early morning to have a good motion in the late morning. However, do not attempt the latter on a day when you have to go out. If the third day before your period falls in the middle of your workweek, take your castor oil at bedtime. Three days is not a magic number, so you can pick a Saturday or Sunday morning if that will allow you to comfortably do the purgation one to five days before your period is due. Remember that if you tend to be late, the purgation, because it stimulates apāna to move downward, may trigger the onset of flow. You can benefit from the castor oil purgation even if you are never constipated. The purpose is to stimulate an easy flow from the uterus by encouraging apāna to press downward and by emptying the abdominal and pelvic cavities.

Take your castor oil on an empty stomach. If you plan a bedtime dose, have an early light supper such as mung dal soup (see recipes) or oatmeal. Take a hot tub bath, enough to make you sweat, or apply a hot water bottle to your lower abdomen. This increases the circulation in the abdominal organs before taking the castor oil.

The oil from the seeds of *Ricinus communis*, the castor bean plant, is more than a simple laxative. For thousands of years this oil has also been widely used in many different medical traditions. Castor oil has many different properties including anti-inflammatory, so it is prescribed by Ayurvedic physicians for other problems, such as arthritis. Castor oil can preempt the need for anti-inflammatory and pain medications for menstrual cramps. It is widely used topically for pain and inflammation and can be rubbed on the lower abdomen if you get cramps. Called *eranda* in Sanskrit, castor oil steadies, strengthens and soothes apāna. Its laxative nature is reliable but gentle, and although it functions as a colonic stimulant, it does not create cramps or significant next-day constipation like other stimulant laxatives.

Castor oil's nature when taken internally is heating, so it can be taken with an optional 2-3 tablets of triphala ("three fruits," see Effortless Elimination, Chapter 19). Triphala has a cooling influence, as well as aiding the action of the castor oil. Purchase only fresh castor oil; check the expiration date on the bottle, because when the oil becomes rancid, it is less palatable and less effective. The tasteless variety may go down more easily, but it takes more of it to do the job. With the Painless Castor Oil Recipe (see the box in Appendix 6), the oily consistency and bitter taste of standard castor oil shouldn't discourage you. If castor oil has been hard to swallow in the past, you can substitute either castor oil capsules[267] or two to three standard tablets of senna alkaloids.

After swallowing the castor oil, you only have to wait for the result. You may feel and hear some activity in your belly as the castor oil does its work. You may make many trips to the bathroom or only one. Women who have used laxatives frequently in the past may get no effect from three teaspoons. In this case, you can repeat the process the following night using six to eight teaspoons of castor oil.

Once the laxative effect has worn off, avoid eating for a few hours. Sip hot ginger water and take kanji (see Recipes). Your first meal after a laxative should be extremely light: ideally just mung dal soup. Continue to eat lightly, taking khichadi (see Recipes) with steamed vegetables for supper if you are hungry. The following morning, ease yourself back to your regular diet.

We have completed our tour of the monthly routines for a woman living a Vedic life. Your period will start in a few days, and hopefully more predictably and comfortably due to the respect you have given your body during the previous twenty-nine days.

Part Two: Chronic Menstrual Symptoms

It is time to consider how to manage menstrual symptoms of long duration. As you will see, it is often as simple as using the tools we have discussed above in more specific ways.

Cramps and pain (dysmenorrhea)

Menstrual cramps, affecting 90% of 19 year olds, are understood by Vedic medicine to be caused by the restricted downward flow of apāna.[268] This creates uterine contractions (which we now understand is due to the release of prostaglandins) and lack of blood flow to the uterus due to constriction of uterine muscle blood vessels. Conventional medicine is trying to finger the pituitary hormone vasopressin as the culprit in this vicious cycle. Similarly, Ayurveda maintains that restricted movement downwards creates spasm and cramps due to the muscular contractions of a swollen uterus; from the stretching of a stiff, unyielding cervix (unsoftened as it becomes at the end of pregnancy) while the uterine muscles try to push a thick, clotted pushpa through the cervix; and by the inflammation created by these events. The ancient Vedic physicians clearly had remarkable insight.

Like most other pain symptoms, menstrual cramps are eased by measures that have a lubricating and soothing influence (vāta pacification – See Appendix 3). Specifically, the uterus and cervix have to be made more compliant and flexible, the cervical passage has to be lubricated, the pushpa has to become more fluid, and pressure on the uterus from above has to be relieved.

If you suffer from menstrual cramps, in addition to the measures outlined above for a woman's monthly routine, adopting some additional preventive strategies will save yourself a lot of agony, as well as save you the time you spend curled up with your hot water bottle and ibuprofen. Most doctors will want to start you off on a number of hormonal approaches including birth control pills, progestin implants, androgens and the like. Save them for the last resort. Also, don't neglect one important Vedic remedy for dysmenorrhea that has been confirmed by a crossover study vs a placebo pill, a low-fat vegetarian diet.[269]

Preventive purgation for cramps

For the most definitive non-drug solution to cramps, the tradition of monthly virechana (laxative purgation) has helped more women than any other remedy in the Ayurvedic doctor's bag of tricks. A good purgation creates vigorous contractions of the colon that hustle the stool through the colon. The rush downward through the pelvis becomes a flood that carries everything with it, as the alluvial tides in a river's delta drains the swamps and backwaters to the sea. During purgation, the intensity of the downward movement of apāna triggers an efficient descent of the menstrual flow. In addition, shifting a couple pounds of stool out of the pelvic cavity relieves pressure on the swollen uterus and ovaries.

Cervical Lubrication (Yoni Pichu)

Cramps are also helped by *yoni pichu*, an Ayurvedic technique for softening and lubricating the cervix to allow the easy elimination of the pushpa. This is especially important if the pushpa is dark, scanty or clotted (a vāta pushpa). It involves putting the proper oil next to the cervix during the night. There are two methods: traditional and a modern, more convenient one.

The oils that can be used are ghee, sesame oil, and coconut oil. For cramps, I recommend ghee (see Recipes), which is traditionally herbalized. Since plain ghee is nearly as good, and because ghee is difficult to herbalize and nearly impossible to procure in North America, stick with the plain.

Traditionally ghee is introduced into the vagina at bedtime on a strip of new cotton gauze. Cut a length of about twelve inches and put one teaspoon of ghee along a six-inch length. Roll the ghee-impregnated cotton into a ball, and introduce it deep into the vagina, leaving the remaining length as a tail that will protrude about an inch to permit easy removal in the morning.

An alternative way to introduce the ghee to the cervical area is to make small balls of ghee the size of an almond. Store them in the fridge and keep three or four of them cool, about 60 degrees, to use prior to the flow. At this temperature, you can introduce them deep into the vagina when you retire. The ghee will be melted by your body's heat and pool around the cervix through the night.

The yogic technique called yoni bandha, performed during the 24 days of the month when you are not menstruating, is also useful for dealing with cramps. These pelvic floor exercises increase the tone of the neuromuscular reflexes arising between the nerves and the smooth muscles of the uterus that they activate. The vaginal, rectal and urethral sphincters that are toned and strengthened when you perform yoni bandha share some common nerve pathways with the muscles of the uterus that produce cramps.

By sequential tightening and relaxing the muscles of the pelvic floor, yoni bandha increases the tone of the vaginal wall muscles, strengthens the urethral sphincters (with less likelihood of urinary continence) and gives stronger orgasms with better muscular control of sexual tension. See the extensive discussion of these important techniques in the preceding chapter.

Irregular periods

For most animal species, the time of estrus, corresponding to the few days of fertility a woman experiences ending on the day of ovulation, is the only time the animal shows any interest in sex. Fortunately for the uninterested female of nearly every other species, nature has organized her suitor's libido to rally and flag with her own desire. A bull can graze contentedly next to a dozen cows without a trace of the craze that overtakes him when a cow is ovulating. Understanding the reason why an animal's estrus cycles with the seasons is important to making your own erratic cycle regular. It is critical for a doe to fawn in the late spring. She can't fawn too early because tender, nourishing leaves may not yet have emerged or may be covered with snow or worse, the fawn may become stuck in deep snow and severe weather. The doe can't deliver too late because the fawn will not have time to grow to survive the following winter. Deer get their signals to rut and mate in the fall when the days get short. Similarly, birds get their signals to fly north and mate when the days get longer. The rest of the year, they don't care about sex.

Humans on the other hand, can be willing any day of the month or year. Like other mammals and fowl, your pineal gland is exquisitely responsive to nerve input that is triggered when light strikes the retina. The pineal secretes melatonin, a hormone responsible for not only the response to deactivate the business of the mind to let you sleep, but also plays a role in libido, mood, ovulation and other functions. This explains how American women in a college dormitory began to menstruate synchronously by manipulating their light exposure, keeping an incandescent light on at night, for example, to create a phase shift through stimulation of their pituitary's secretion of sex hormones. It explains the ability of Pakistani women in a village to menstruate synchronously using a traditional Islamic lunar calendar, as was observed in a 1970's experiment of communal birth control where the villagers were encouraged to be abstinent at mid-month.

Regularity through the body's pacemakers

The practical key to menstrual irregularity is to re-establish the body's metronome. The brain's pacemaker centers in the pineal gland observe both a structured daily routine (as described in Chapter 10, the Rhythms of Life) and a structured monthly routine as described above. If a woman keeps late hours, the combination of fewer hours of sleep and more hours of light exposure can change the delicate balance between melatonin and sex steroids.

Entrain your rhythms by becoming conscious of the moon. Keep a calendar to make yourself aware of where you are in the lunar month. Try observing a traditional Ayurvedic moon ritual, held to create a cooling influence on the mind and body. On the full moon night, place a bowl of milk (or rice/soy milk) outside in the full moon's light and drink it at bedtime. Gaze upon the moon's reflection in the milk and connect the softness of the light with your sexuality: the time in your cycle, your libido, your emotions.

Follow the moon in its phases. Remind yourself what the moon will look like and where it will be when your period comes. Observe the monthly routines described above for the inward and outward phases of the month. Above all, don't forget the monthly purgative that will prepare your pelvis for your period to start. Within a few months you will find yourself menstruating on time.

Excessive bleeding (menorrhagia)

Excessive pushpa, including both heavy bleeding and longer periods, is commonly due to an excess of estrogen over progesterone, but can be caused by intrauterine devices (IUD's), fibroids, polyps and other problems. In addition to a good monthly routine, heavy bleeding needs to be treated with herbs during the rest of the monthly cycle. To stop heavy flow, drink the milk from a fresh coconut twice daily, or if this is not available, make coconut balls from fresh coconut meat or dried shredded coconut that has been soaked in milk to soften it. Canned coconut milk is widely available as an acceptable option. Hibiscus and raspberry leaf tea as well as fresh raspberries can help decrease the flow. The single best herb for menorrhagia is the bark of the ashoka tree. Take 500mg twice daily with milk or coconut milk. Organic bark powder is easily available.

PMS

Physicians call PMS premenstrual dysphoria, implying an uncomfortable change of mood. From the Vedic medical perspective, the treatment of PMS requires proper diagnosis of the nature of the mood. To make it simple, the spectrum of the problem can be classified as follows:

1. Vāta PMS symptoms: A woman with vāta-type PMS may feel constipated, anxious, or awaken frequently in the night. Her skin or limbs may feel tingly or crawly. She may have mood swings and feel spacey.

Remedy: See Chapter 19 for dealing with constipation. Give yourself a warm sesame oil massage every morning. Practice prānayāma (Chapter 15) and slow yoga asanas.

2. Pitta PMS symptoms: Classically, if you feel anger or irritability, these are pitta symptoms of PMS. You may also have intense cravings for food, flare-ups of acne or rosacea, malodorous vaginal discharges, or migraine-like headaches.

Remedy: Spend time outdoors, take long walks or go for a swim. Brighten your home with flowers. Perform slow prānayama. Drink lassi (See Recipes). Avoid heating or spicy foods.

3. Kapha PMS symptoms: Swelling of the abdomen and breasts, bloating, lethargy, and melancholy are the symptoms suggesting that your PMS has its basis in a kapha imbalance.

Remedy: Go for a lot of exercise. Sweat. Be with uplifting people. If your swelling and edema are confined to this time of month, you do not need diuretics to reduce it. Sweating and exercise alone should help. If your swelling is persistent, see your physician.

The remedial measures to balance the mood changes that occur during the week before the period should be initiated 3-7 days before their usual onset, or to be safe, even with ovulation. They should be continued until the flow begins, at which time you should follow the balancing program focused on making the period of flow more comfortable, e.g. dealing with cramps or heavy bleeding. All types of PMS benefit from adherence to the monthly routine as described above and from regular, vigorous exercise such as a long daily walk in which you come back sweaty enough to need to shower.

In addition to the monthly routine and the specific measures outlined above, each type of PMS is helped by a specific set of herbs that you take during the last half of your cycle, but especially when you have symptoms. The best way to take them is as an herbalized water or tea, which you prepare fresh in the morning and sip throughout the day. Drink it hot from a small thermos or cooled from a 12 oz sport water bottle. Boil the herbs for 5 minutes and strain the cooled decoction into the bottle. For convenience, prepare a large supply of the ready-mixed blend so you only have to spoon out the desired quantity into the boiling water.

Pitta PMS: 1/2 tsp fennel seeds, 1/2 tsp cut sarsaparilla root or root powder, a pinch of cardamom powder (or a dozen seeds) and a few petals of edible rose.

Vāta PMS: a pinch of licorice (provides sweetness), a pinch of cardamom powder (or a dozen seeds), a pinch of cinnamon, 1/2 tsp fennel seeds, and an optional 1/2 tsp of cumin seeds if you have abdominal bloating or gas.

Kapha PMS: a pinch of licorice root powder (a gentle diuretic to reduce the edema), 3-4 slices of fresh ginger root (or 1/2 tsp of ginger powder), 2 cloves, a pinch of black pepper, a few strands of saffron.

Make the Most of Your Days of Flow

There are many reasons why women generally live longer than men and why there are so many widows competing for the few eligible widowers. One of these may turn out to be the value of woman's cleansing during the first half of her life. Take the opportunity to make the days of flow a spiritual, purifying and healing experience, an inward retreat, and a sabbatical from your routine and you will reap the benefits now as well as later.

262 Secreted chemical compounds that influence the behavior or physiology of other animals through smell or other mechanisms.

263 Biological Rhythm Research. Taylor & Francis. Volume 34, Number 3/ July 2003.305-315. *Circatrigintan Cycle of Salivary Testosterone in Human Male.* Peter Celec, Daniela Ostarníková, et al.

264 Cyclical variations in mental and physical functions that are about thirty days is called a circatrigintan rhythm, meaning *around thirty.*

265 If this is not the case, I feel it is not worth taking the extreme measures advocated by some to synchronize the onset of flow with phases of the moon, because the benefits are subtle and the trouble significant for what is often a temporary change. Theoretically, from the Vedic point of view, this moon phase synchronization is useful, but it takes many months to change the cycle and most women find themselves soon out of phase. There are many easier ways to regain menstrual balance.

266 My Ayurvedic clinic had a policy that if her co-workers would cover for her, an employee could take two days off with pay when her period started. All the women opted in.

267 You can procure castor oil capsules. Just remember that a capsule contains 400-600 mg of castor oil inside a sizable shell of gelatin, so it may take 30 capsules to accomplish the same efficient elimination as a tablespoonful of oil. If you use capsules you can just swallow them with the triphala tablets, skipping the teacup, hot water and orange wedges designed to eliminate the unpleasant experience swallowing castor oil reported by many people.

268 If you develop fibroids or endometriosis, cramps often get worse as you grow older.

269 Malmstrom K, Kotey P, Cichanowitz N, Daniels S, Desjardins PJ *Analgesic efficacy of etoricoxib in primary dysmenorrhea: results of a randomized, controlled trial.* Gynecol Obstet Invest 2003 56:65-9

WHEN THE SPIRIT IS WILLING

CHAPTER 33

THE UNEXPECTED JOYS OF MENOPAUSE

Waves are fascinating phenomena in nature; we can watch them for hours. Surfers are happy sitting all day on their board, meditatively watching breakers approach, feeling the rise and fall as the surge rolls under. Some people are fascinated to the point of listening to recordings of waves. Vedic science is a science of waves, imparting the wisdom of utilizing cycles in life. The universe, according to field theory and Vedic science is a wave function – a song. Daily and seasonal cycles are its notes, waves of the earth's rotations. Biologists have documented a thirty-day (circatrigintan) cycle in nature, corresponding to the waxing and waning of the moon, that are found in creatures from plankton and plants to menstruating humans. When a girl enters puberty she gives herself over to this rhythm, riding up a wave that some day must also pass.

Katrina is a blossoming opera diva who laughed heartily as she showed me her "girly soup," an international concoction consisting of dong quai, evening primrose, Siberian ginseng, citrus bioflavinoids, Mexican wild yam, shitake mushrooms, soy isoflavones and black cohosh. I couldn't make myself tell her that a 2006 review of 70 studies on alternative therapies for hot flashes had shown they were no better than placebos. The sugar pills, however, were surprisingly effective, giving a 50% reduction in hot flashes.[270] In one of the studies on black cohosh, six women showed liver side effects and some women on isoflavones (plant estrogen analogues) had thickening in their uterine linings. I hardly needed to tell her the "girly soup" was useless or worse. At forty-eight she is still menstruating, but sits at her day job drenched in sweat.

Lynn, on the other hand, is fifty-five, petite, and came to see me because she felt her three glasses of wine every night together with recently starting smoking were becoming an irresistible habit to deal with stress. When asked about menopausal symptoms, in stark contrast to Katrina, she said it was the best thing that ever happened to her, "a gift from heaven." It brought a sudden deliverance from forty years of cramps and changing pads ten times a day for eight days a month plus seven days of PMS with bloating before she started over again. That was the easy part. For the last fifteen years of her menstruating life, she had had intractable migraines every month two days before her flow. "My life began with when my periods ran out."

Lynn is not alone. Most women over fifty report that the experience of aging is better than they expected according to a nationwide poll by researchers at Brandeis University. Seventy percent rated their health as good or excellent, and of women over 80, fully 90 percent called their emotional health good or excellent.

A Worthwhile Sacrifice

Women are creatures of the moon; it is no accident that the menstrual cycle is 29 days. For thirty to forty years the waxing of the moon dictates the ebb and flow of the hormones that ripen the lining of the womb. A woman will have more periods than there are days in a year. After so many new moons, the girl who started out with 45,000 follicles capable of secreting precious estrogens and progestins finds herself with only a few and her relationship with the moon must change.

Reading the ancient Sanskrit texts of Ayurveda, one senses that they are a ship captain's handbook, devoted to navigating the waves of life to gain maximum progress. The captain of a racing sloop teaches his mates to hold the bow hard to the wind as they tack up the windward side of large waves and to turn the boat off the wind so the hull can surf down the lee side. Similarly, we teach our children to use cycles to get ahead. Study when your mind is fresh; get fresh air when it's sunny; eat hot meals in winter; exercise and meditate on an empty stomach. Every culture has traditions marking stages when these life cycles change: first communions, bar mitzvahs, marriages, graduations. These transitional events are sacrifices: we give something up to gain something greater in return. With a bat/bar mitzvah you give up not being responsible for your actions to gain acceptance as an adult in the community. With marriage, we give up independence to gain a relationship and a family. The Sanskrit name for this sacrifice is *yajña*.

Menopause is an important *yajña*: we change our relationship with the moon and its incessant cycles, together with the limitations, burdens and risks it imposes on our lives (the vigilance to vaginal hygiene, the risk of pregnancy, the burdens of child care) to gain the greater joy that only a woman can feel. But the sacrifice must be performed properly, modulating into a different rhythm.

The Role of Estrogen for Arterial Suppleness

Unfortunately, most women don't see menopause in this light. They only see what they are losing: youthfulness and estrogen. By the time menopause arrives, most women don't miss childbearing, but they miss their estrogen for other reasons. Estrogen, after all, is a remarkable hormone, responsible for creating suppleness in many tissues, most importantly the cardiovascular system. Nature has cleverly endowed a woman with abundant estrogen during pregnancy, permitting her to increase her vascular volume by 50%. As a result, she can lose nearly a gallon of blood during delivery and still live to raise her kids. The arterial suppleness bestowed by estrogen is a principle reason women are protected from hardening of the arteries for the first 50 years of their lives, while heart attacks in men in their forties are regrettably too common.

Incomplete Research Taken as Gospel

Due to this known effect of estrogen and its benefit on cholesterol, most doctors were surprised by the results of the Women's Health Initiative's randomized trial investigating estrogen as a prevention for heart attacks in healthy women. Sizable doses of equine estrogens were not only ineffective at preventing heart disease but actually slightly increased the risk. One week after this study hit the front page, many physicians, like myself, were inundated by phone calls from women who stopped their hormones on their own and were seeking alternatives for relief from hot flashes.

The study had several limitations, so although many doctors and patients are acting as if the verdict is in, the hearing is not yet over. First, 40% of the women on hormone replacement therapy (HRT) did not adhere to their regimen, and 10% of the controls switched to HRT.

Second, the mean age of these subjects was over 63, ten to thirteen years older than the usual perimenopausal woman contemplating HRT. With respect to HRT preventing coronary disease, these women started on the program fifteen years after the horse had left the proverbial barn. The study was therefore hardly a true test of estrogen's preventive effect, because it did not measure what happens to women who start HRT soon after menopause. Preliminary studies appear to show an effect that is quite positive on the heart and other organs in these women.

Third, the study did not look at the newer low dose regimens using bio-identical hormones, including progesterone, i.e. a HRT regimen that recreates a woman's premenopausal hormone levels.

Estrogen has many beneficial effects in addition to improving hot flashes and vaginal dryness: preventing bone resorption, reducing the risk of colon cancer, relieving depression, and improving cognitive functions like memory and concentration during perimenopause. There are also clear cosmetic benefits – estrogen's actions in making tissues supple also maintain the elasticity of the skin's connective tissues.

Another important concern of any treatment for menopause is the risk of breast cancer. I like to help women making the decision about HRT by enlisting the Gail model risk assessment tool to predict the likelihood that a woman will develop breast cancer. It helps put your risk in a personal perspective, and is accessible by anyone.[271] A 51 year-old woman with an average risk has a 1.1% chance of being diagnosed with breast cancer in the next 5 years. It is important to present the statistics the other way, too. Without HRT, she has a 98.9% chance of not being diagnosed in 5 years, and 98.6% if she opts for it.

Both health consumers and physicians tend to make blanket judgments regarding the benefits of treatments as controversial as HRT, exaggerating or misinterpreting the established risks without considering individual risk assessment. As a result, many women who could benefit from HRT may now be deprived of its benefits. For Katrina, like for many women, the symptoms were so debilitating she stopped functioning effectively and lost her usual joie de vivre.

Estrogen Alternatives

Because for millions of women estrogen is a miracle hormone it would be nice to be able to recreate its effect in the body without side effects. Many women of menopausal age are more aware than their physicians regarding the spectrum of options for dealing with menopausal symptoms. From most synthetic to most natural these include:

1. Selective estrogen receptor modulators (SERM). These are designer hormones, like raloxifene (Evista).

2. Standard estrogen replacement and synthetic progestins, like the Premarin and Provera (Prempro) used in the Women's Health Initiative study, using equine estrogens or estradiol, the most potent human estrogen.

3. Bio-identical hormone replacement.[272] This uses the three estrogens present in every woman, including large amounts of the weakest estrogens like estriol, which may block the more potent forms from the estrogen receptor sites. Bio-identical HRT also uses natural bio-identical progesterone. When a woman needs HRT, or fails to control symptoms with natural approaches, I prescribe bio-identical HRT. It is possible that some day bio-identical HRT may be shown to have similar risks to standard approaches – but there is preliminary evidence that it may not have the risks of Prempro. In my experience, it is better tolerated. Because natural hormones are assimilated more irregularly, they require more communication between the woman and her physician – not at all a bad thing. More research on this approach needs to be done before the risks and benefits of HRT are considered a closed case.

4. Phytoestrogens which mimic the action of estrogen such as soy isoflavones and black cohosh. The most effective products are concentrated extracts.

5. Natural dietary, herbal, and lifestyle programs focused on specific symptoms.

Katrina and Lynn are worlds apart in their symptoms of menopause. Lynn, although she feels fine, is a petite smoker and needs something to deal with her bones as well as her wrinkling skin. Katrina is also happy now, her hot flashes have been made tolerable without hormones; she has lost weight with exercise, a treatment that with herbs and diet has resolved her issue of heat regulation.

Natural Approaches to Specific Complications of Estrogen Deficiency

Most health problems caused by the loss of estrogen can be helped by lifestyle programs that go beyond the simple prescription of a pill. They are discussed separately in specific chapters of this book:

Heart and vessels – Chapters 24, 25

Memory and concentration-Chapter 27

Weight gain – Chapter 20

Sleep – Chapter 11

Skin – Chapter 30

Bones – Chapter 28

Perimenopausal bleeding – Chapter 32

Incontinence, uterine prolapse – Chapter 31

Sexual dysfunction (libido, vaginal dryness and vaginal atrophy) – Chapter 34

Herbal Approaches to Menopause

If your menopausal symptoms are not mild, in addition to these chapters, you may need some Ayurvedic herbs.

The best herb for hot flashes is the seed of the tulsi plant, known as holy basil (*Ocimum sanctum*). It looks similar, but is a different variety from common basil. Tulsi augurs good omens and is planted around Indian homes and auspicious places such as temples and sites of pilgrimage. Holy basil seeds can be purchased in most Southeast Asian groceries, where they are labeled *Takmaria Seeds*. The seeds are popular as a delicacy in sweet beverages and their medicinal value is not well known. Put one to two teaspoons of the seeds in juice[273] or in water for five minutes and drink. The seeds swell, becoming soft and tasty. The seed is known as refrigerant, creating a cooling effect in the body, and is used in the hot season by both sexes. Tulsi seeds work by modifying the body's thermoregulatory system rather than acting as a phytoestrogen. Takmaria seeds can therefore be used by any woman, including those with a contraindication to taking estrogens, such as women with fibroids, endometriosis, breast cancer or a family history thereof. Men can benefit from them in hot weather.

In addition to takmaria seeds (and the herbs recommended for any specific menopausal problem in the appropriate chapters above), any woman can gain balance from two herbs useful for menopause in general, and which are also helpful for hot flashes. Make a mixture of equal parts of shatāvari[274,] and vidāri.[275] Take one teaspoon of the mixture twice daily on an empty stomach with water.

Women in menopause who compare their sacrifice to their gains almost invariably find out they come out in the black. In England, a poll of over 1,500 middle-aged men and women compared symptoms including weight gain, forgetfulness, waning libido, depression and wrinkles, etc. and found that the only symptoms for which women differed were vaginal dryness and hot flashes. So, count your blessings, ladies and gentlemen, and dive into menopause and andropause headfirst.

270 Archives of Internal Medicine, July 24, 2006
271 http://bcra.nci.nih.gov/brc
272 Estradiol is the strongest natural estrogen, present in small amounts. Estrone is next most potent, and estriol is the weakest stimulator of the estrogen receptor. In bio-identical HRT, the pharmacist and physician work together to prepare a formulation that would mimic a woman's physiological requirements.
273 The most cooling effect comes from sweet pomegranate juice.
274 Shatāvari in Sanskrit means *one hundred husbands*.
275 Vidāri is in the yam family, and is a rich source of sterols needed for hormone synthesis, but its traditional usage for menopause likely is related to other properties.

CHAPTER 34

RESTORING PASSION TO THE BEDROOM

"This is the monstruosity in love, lady that the will is infinite and the execution confined; that the desire is boundless and the act a slave to limit."

Shakespeare's Troilus, before making love to Cressida.

With respect to sexual desire, the discrepancy between one's aspirations and the reality often underlies its waning. Stated succinctly in marketing terminology, when a product doesn't match its stated hype, demand falls.

Nowhere in medicine does a symptom have so many delicate and nuanced inputs as fading libido. I always remember patients who defy this general rule, like a 35 year old woman whose periods suddenly stopped for no good reason. One month later, she found herself watching a steamy movie and was surprised to feel absolutely nothing. "Like a preadolescent girl," she told me, "I understood what was happening between the actors, but didn't feel the usual stirring in my pelvis. My husband's affections didn't evoke any passion." Women are endowed with 40-50,000 ovarian follicles at birth, and hers had simply run out. Within one month of starting estrogen and progesterone replacement, her love life was fine. If only every patient with a libido problem had such an easy solution!

Balanced sexual desire is subject to so many contributing factors that in Vedic medicine it is used to assess general good health, along with energy, mood, easy elimination, normal weight and normal menstruation. A balanced libido is a reflection of these factors: when mood or energy is depressed, libido will flag. A physician can use a question about libido as part of a medical history to gain insight into the healthy functioning of the body and mind.

A balanced libido means that the desire will be strong when wanted and will leave a person alone when it is not. Feeling randy when there is no partner, or worse, with an inappropriate partner, while not as much a reflection of physical disease as a low libido, can often cause more suffering. Every healthy person needs to master both how to develop and to control sexual desire.

The Joy of No Sex

In the presence of a balanced libido, the conscious decision to be celibate is not only normal, but indicative of good health. It is an option that a person can choose at different times in life for greater fulfillment and growth. Adolescents and students, people in transitions from previous relationships, people recovering from physical or emotional trauma, people undergoing regimens focused on physical rejuvenation, and people desiring to channel their energies into spiritual development are examples of individuals in whom sexual desire might be sublimated to gain something more precious. Without this greater gain, the fruit of your sacrifice could end up being the dubious enjoyment of privation. In many spiritual traditions, celibacy is honored as the ideal path for the most serious of aspirants.

The benefits of celibacy are many, but the main one is a simple life without cares. You don't have to spend time or mental energy nurturing, cajoling, whispering sweet nothings, being considerate to, being offended or hurt by, dreaming about or even desiring a lover.[276] Like an alcoholic who has made the decision to never have to be faced with the choice of whether he will drink at a function, and how much and in what circumstances, the decision to be celibate saves the heart the agony of deciding.

The secondary benefit of celibacy is the transformation of the subtlest quality of physical matter and energy into rejuvenative, cognitive and spiritual purposes. *Shukra* is Sanskrit for semen or ovum,[277] recognized as the finest physical tissue (dhātu), as well as the hormones, follicles and secretions that support their functioning. Ovum and semen are so subtle, yet potent in nature, that they can engender a human being. In the case of semen, one lovin' spoonful has the potentiality to generate a hundred million souls. When shukra is abundant and of high potency, it gives rise to *ojas*, the essence of all the tissues and the subtlest of substances. Ojas is created spontaneously when semen and ovum are properly formed from the action of the metabolic fires – through proper diet, lifestyle, routines, rest and spiritual practices, in other words, a holistic life.

Ojas is seen as so subtle that it does not qualify as a tissue, yet it still has a material value, being slightly more manifest than the level of pure intelligence itself. It has been described as located in the gap between pure intelligence and the body and permits frictionless communication between the body and its source of intelligence. Ojas permits pure intelligence to express itself as the material body and is responsible for physical and mental strength, radiance and beauty, immunity, and well-being.

Many spiritual traditions hold that preservation of sexual energy through abstinence enhances the development of these qualities. This assumes, of course, that there is little stress involved in remaining sexually continent. If you are torturing yourself, or if your partner is frustrated or feeling rejected and in turn torturing you, the subtle benefits of celibacy are outweighed by the loss of energy dealing with your unhealthy relationship.

Creating a balanced sexual desire can only be understood in the proper cultural context. In western civilizations, highways are lined with sexually themed billboards, while in some traditional societies a square inch of bared flesh is hard to find. I have visited prisons, worked on construction crews, and attended Dartmouth before it admitted women. In these male-only environments, sexuality is pervasive. Yet among male celibate aspirants with whom I have lived – who are healthy, virile men – sexuality is a consciously neglected part of their environment. Since each aspirant shares the group's devotion to yoga and other spiritual practices, women and sex simply do not arise as topics of conversation. Likewise, among a similar group of women. Even without imposing on themselves a group injunction against sexual topics, these spiritual aspirants naturally take the attitude that whatever you put your attention on grows in your life; and allowing yourself to think about women/men/sex at any time of day or night makes the time you spend practicing yoga or meditation less enjoyable and productive.

Brahmacharya – A Life Focused on Brahman

The Vedic understanding of celibacy is found in the word *brahmacharya*, i.e. practices for Brahman, or routines devoted to culturing a neurophysiology that can comprehend and experience one's nature as Brahman, Totality. While brahmacharya is most often used to denote sexual abstinence, its derivation implies that it refers more to an attitude than a behavior. Constant thoughts distracting from the experience of the divine are the biggest block to a spiritual aspirant. For most people, they may be more of a hindrance than having sex in moderation and then not being bothered by distracting feelings – both emotional and physical – the rest of the week. A brahmacharin or brahmaracharini simply does not have the time or energy to waste on anything more trivial than Brahman itself. Living in a society that constantly bombards us with sexual themes requires more focus on your life's bigger purpose.

Celibacy – not for Everyone

Celibacy is a problematic option when we are in a loving relationship with someone who doesn't want anything to do with sexual continence. The decision by one partner to be celibate can present the same conflicts within a relationship as lack of libido – except the other partner may feel even more rejected. There is a difference in the effect of such a denial upon men and women.

The ancient Talmudic rabbis analyzed the Biblical commandment to "Be fruitful and multiply," considering the grammar and context of the ancient Hebrew and concluded, in their wisdom, that the words apply to men rather than to women. In this 2000-year old enlightened interpretation, it is not incumbent upon women to submit to their male partner and to endure pregnancy after pregnancy. Rather, the learned rabbis proclaimed, the man must satisfy the desire of the woman. Perhaps they understood that testosterone is the hormonal engine for sexual desire in both women and men and that the latter naturally have a lot more of it, are less sensitive to small changes in mood, atmosphere, time of day or month, and are generally more ready to oblige. In this light, the decision to embark on a path of celibacy, while rewarding for singles, is a path that requires good communication and mutual agreement for a couple.

The Nature of Love

Shakespeare's succinct diagnosis of most problems with sexual fulfillment lies in the divergence between the infinite and unbounded nature of the soul and the confined and limited nature of the act. The nature and purpose of life, for a Vedic physician, is the expansion of happiness. Life is about change, and as long as it seems to be in the direction of progress, we perceive it to be satisfying and easy.

Many people sense that the most profound experience of infinity can ultimately only come from a spiritual connection with the boundless itself – unity with the Divine. Because spiritual experiences are elusive and abstract, on the path to the Divine you may not only content yourself with, but even crave more concrete experiences. These may include absorbing yourself with material expressions of infinity such as art, music and relationships. The most intimate of these surrogate experiences of infinity is the losing of your body's physical boundaries as it merges with another. Sexuality, our most primal desire, as compelling as eating and sleeping, is the expression of our need to progress and expand. More pleasure plus more progeny. Making love with your partner or even entering into a brief but torrid affair, as much as we hate to admit it, comes from the same primordial impulse for expansion of happiness that motivates us to attend church, to meditate, or to give to charity.

It is recorded that Yajñavalkya, a seer and devoted husband, before leaving his dutiful wife for the life of a recluse, asked if he could answer any last ardent questions. She asks, "What should I do with something that cannot make me immortal?" Her spouse replies, "You have always been dear to me... The husband is dear to the wife not for the sake of the husband, but it is for her own sake that he is dear. And the wife is dear to the husband not for the sake of the wife, but it is for his own sake that she is dear." Similarly, Yajñavalkya explains, for children, parents and wealth.

Whenever we love, it is always the Self that is loved: a higher Self, not the small finite self of our flesh-covered frame. The object of love (spouse, kids, friends) is the medium through which the Self is reflected. When you fall in love, your lover is allowing you a glimpse into the infinite nature of the divine within yourself. Caring for your child out of love, as exasperating as it may be at times, is a vehicle for you to experience the unboundedness of the Self. "It is the time you lost on account of your rose that makes your rose so important," the fox tells Saint-Exupery's Little Prince.

Depending on the clarity of your own nervous system, the value of love is reflected everywhere differently. If you are anxious or depressed, even a handsome, attentive lover will be seen in that light, and precious little of your infinite Self will be appreciated. The nature of the relationship is also a filter for the infinite. You may pick someone who is not available, whom you see once a month or always has a bone to pick. The Self becomes diluted to a wisp of its cosmic status.

In the circumstance when the lover, the beloved and the relationship between them are in harmony, the three become as one. The physical and emotional understanding of this paradox, how multiplicity can also be unity,[278] is the spiritual experience of love. The experience starts unconsciously; we do not comprehend what is happening within, we just feel more freedom.

Restoring Passion to the Bedroom

Sexual union is the rite in which this experience of the juxtaposition of diversity and unity becomes intensely concrete and available to our awareness. It can be had by just about anyone with a human physiology, albeit usually only fleetingly. Flirting, courting, romancing, seducing, caressing and flattering are powerful primal impulses that bring us to the moment of unity. For a brief moment, everything about the changing, decaying nature of our body and life dissolves in an experience of oneness, silence and power. Our partner is the path. We look in her/his eyes and we see our Self reflected there. We have become all That.

"Good sex" is when this experience is profound and effortless and leaves us changed, wiser, and stronger. In reality, something is always missing. Things do not lead to our expectations. The problem invariably is that we have expectations. In other words, we are looking for infinity in something finite, which can often come close – but never quite be – infinity.

Regarding any experience, including a sexual union, an expectation is a preconceived notion of what we want to happen or feel and unfortunately, it can never be the same twice. We anticipate something specific, and in looking for it, we miss a sweet, subtle sensation that may be equally pleasurable, but is different from our predetermined plan. We are left unsatisfied, and with time, we get frustrated and even angry at the partner who cannot satisfy us. We see them as unresponsive lovers. This leads to a decrease in desire that in turn produces the seeds of physical dysfunction. A little disappointment may result in weak erections. Women may lack their usual arousal with its resultant lubrication and relaxation of the pelvic muscles, leading to a conditioned, uncomfortable spasm of the vaginal muscles (vaginismus) resulting from recurrent painful sex. This overshadows any pleasure, and enjoyment in the union goes from waning to gone. The vicious cycle spirals downward.

"Good sex" also implies that you have to be able to lose yourself temporarily, to lose yourself in your partner. This requires trust. Like riding on the back seat of a tandem bicycle, you turn your fate over to your partner. When trust is not a firmly established part of the relationship, any insignificant breach of confidence or loyalty makes repulsive the prospect of submitting your body to another. In short, letting go can best happen when you feel good about your lives together. Alcohol and other similar "lubricants" increase sexual desire by making us throw this discretion to the wind.

Making Love for the First Time Every Time

Youthful innocence makes every experience fresh. Older scientists prefer working with naïve minds that attack their problems from a new perspective. Innocence allows people to bring fewer expectations to sexual encounters. Youth helps, but any familiarity breeds expectations. The only cure for familiarity, other than changing partners, is learning to always make love as if for the first time. Meditation, yoga, spiritual texts[279] and other spiritual practices help culture the attitude of innocence and turn a sexual experience into a spiritual event.

Youth helps sex in other ways: tissues are suppler, strong, and elastic, including not just genital organs but also joints. Youthful libido doesn't turn on at nine and off at ten PM. As we get older on the other hand, we are less self-conscious, but we also accumulate more physical issues to be embarrassed about such as weight, wrinkles and cellulite, and with these, more barriers to letting go.

The Finest Aphrodisiac: an Exhilarating Partner

With respect to stimulation of the appetite, Benjamin Franklin wrote, "Hunger is the best pickle."[280] Likewise, for men with declining interest, an Ayurvedic medical text, states,

"The best of aphrodisiacs is the exhilarating woman. The favorite sense objects even individually are so pleasant, they become manifold more tempting where they are located collectively in a woman's body....."

Charaka Samhitā, CiII,4-6

Caraka describes how one partner grows in beauty and other attractive qualities, i.e. becomes a better aphrodisiac for the other, upon finding the other.

"She gets into the heart quickly, is a celebration of the heart, gets into the same frame of mind, anticipating her partner's desires, and with her excellent qualities becomes like a noose for his five senses; separated from whom one feels as if the world is devoid of women and the body as deprived of perception. And when one meets her, one feels both consoled and exhilarated, and with whom every sexual encounter, even frequent, is as if always fresh because of an urge so powerful that one can never be fully satisfied. This is the best aphrodisiac."[281]

Charaka Samhitā, CiII,4-15

Hearty Sexual Appetite: a Relative Thing

Normal sexual yearning has a remarkably great range depending on your culture, age, body type and even, as we saw above in the section on celibacy, your spiritual orientation. In one Nigerian society, older women return to abstinence, whereas in one quarter of primitive societies, older women become more sexually active, less inhibited and are regarded as more attractive to men.[282] Obviously, your culturally imposed preconception of your sexual role at any time of life can greatly influence your libido.

Two partners may also differ in their perceptions of their sex life. In Woody Allen's comedy, Annie Hall, Woody and Annie (Diane Keaton) are simultaneously talking to their therapists, who each ask, "How often do you make love?"

Woody responds, "Hardly ever. Maybe three times a week." Annie: "Constantly. I'd say three times a week."

The Value of Hormones

If you are in the throes of andropause or menopause and have lost your sex hormones, appropriately prescribed testosterone (for both sexes) or estrogen (for women) can often be the silver bullet that restores the sex life you had before. For a peri- or postmenopausal woman, estrogen deficiency is often the principle culprit. For the young female patient described above, it was all she needed to restore desire. Studies have shown that estrogen replacement alone increases frequency, enjoyment, and fantasies. [283, 284] There is nothing as efficient as estrogen for improving painful vaginal dryness, sleep deprivation caused by hot flashes with its related fatigue, and menopausal mood changes – all of which can squelch libido.

While psychosocial reasons for a sluggish sexual appetite are most common, be sure to get a good medical work-up if you cannot explain your problem from obvious things like problems with your marriage, work, or mental state.[285] Half of postmenopausal women secrete no testosterone from their ovaries while the other half continue to churn out enough to make a functional difference,[286] but which is still only half of the testosterone a young woman produces.[287] It is worthwhile to have both estrogen and testosterone levels measured if you are a woman with unexplained loss of libido.

The truth in the adage "use it or lose it" with respect to menopause and andropause has been well documented. A postmenopausal woman who maintains an active sexual life will have a slower deterioration in the structure and function of her pelvic organs. This includes less thinning and atrophy of the tissues and mucous membranes lining the vagina, bladder, urethra and external genitalia, and improved maintenance of tone of the pelvic muscles, and better blood flow to the vaginal tissues with improved arousal.[288] A lack of estrogen prevents the estrogen-dependent nerves to the clitoris from responding, so orgasm – if it occurs at all – may be diminished. There can even be painful uterine contractions in women over sixty.[289]

Because libido is related to so many factors including the health of your relationship, the attractiveness of your lover, your general energy (which is directly correlated with your job, responsibilities and habits), your hormone levels, and the suppleness of your genital organs, any of these factors can be responsible for the cascade of events that results in the decline of meaningful sex.

A postmenopausal woman may have a defunct sexual desire simply because estrogen deficiency has made her vagina atrophic and sex painful. The Rx is simple: vaginal estrogen.[290] On the other hand, in spite of healthy reproductive organs, there could be a dearth of testosterone, the hormone that previously fueled your healthy sexuality. See your physician for a testosterone level test and to see if replacement would be right for you. [291, 292]

It is critical to determine if deficient hormone levels underlie the problem, especially if the loss of libido is sudden in a person who is otherwise healthy mentally and physically, because hormonal deficiency is one cause where exhaustive efforts toward a natural, healthy lifestyle generally makes little difference. While this book is about body renewal and self-repair, holistic remedies have not yet proven their role as a substitute for sex hormones, and I would be irresponsible if I did not describe your options. In one-third of older couples, erectile dysfunction and a man's dwindling interest is responsible for the decreased frequency of making love. The other two-thirds are due to menopause.[293] Psychological factors, fortunately, are much less important in older couples.[294] As you gain in wisdom, you lose your hang-ups – if only the flesh were willing.

When it's a Guy Thing

Premature ejaculation and erectile dysfunction (ED) are male problems that end up, for obvious reasons, contributing to waning libido in both partners. Both problems merit a visit to a physician because they may have causes that are physical and not psychological, and because therapies are available for both. Sildenafil (Viagra)[295] and similar medications have proven so useful that they are laced into traditional herbal aphrodisiacs sold by disreputable sources. Erectile dysfunction and premature ejaculation are so common that they have been treated in their own sections in Chapter 31, Disorders of the Pelvic Diaphragm. They are discussed in that section because their cure requires some attention to yogic practices designed to strengthen the involved muscles.

Vedic HRT?

Hormonal deficiency symptoms are often most pronounced at the onset of menopause when the contrast is greatest, even though absolute hormone levels may still be detectable. With time, the ovaries or adrenals may begin to make testosterone, as evidenced by the increased facial hair that bothers postmenopausal women. If a woman can keep the vaginal tissues thick and flexible, she has a good chance of maintaining her love life without replacement.

The ancient physicians had nothing against hormone replacement as evidenced by their ubiquitous prescriptions for drinking or preparing herbs with the urine of bulls, cows and mares, which are rich sources of estrogens and testosterone. Premarin is indeed made from and derives its name from pregnant mare's urine.

Sometimes hormone replacement, especially the most commonly prescribed form using equine estrogens and estradiol, may paradoxically result in decreased desire. These potent estrogens can stimulate production of sex hormone binding globulin (SHBG), which binds to estrogen and testosterone and reduces their availability. This creates not only diminished desire, but also reduced tissue hormone levels and more hot flashes.[296]

Although we generally prefer a non-pharmacological approach to any medical problem, a lot can be accomplished with tiny amounts of topical estrogen[297] and testosterone. For example, only about 10% of a dose of vaginal estrogen is available throughout the body (breasts, heart, etc.), and half the milligram equivalent to a daily oral dose of estrogen can be used twice a week to maintain the youthful state of the vaginal, vulval and urethral tissues. Strong vaginal tissues can thus be regained by any menopausal woman with only 1/70th of the systemic estrogen exposure sustained in usual oral estrogen replacement therapy. Moreover, the vaginal membranes can be maintained with the weakest form of estrogen, called estriol, which is only about one fourth as potent as estradiol, the principle human estrogen. Yet, in the name of health, I see many holistically-oriented women let their love life slide, and thereby their marriage or relationship, out of fear of estrogen.

Drugs and Libido

You also need to resolve whether the mood changes and depression that might accompany a weak yearning for your lover is its result or its cause. After all, the hallmark of depression is lack of interest in everything, and sex is the first to go, because it takes both mental and physical energy, which need to be saved for mere survival. If the blues are due to problems in your relationship and sex life, an antidepressant is just going to make things worse, especially the selective serotonin reuptake inhibitors (SSRI).[298] These mood elevators make sexual responsiveness and orgasm difficult, a side benefit for men suffering from premature ejaculation, but a big drawback for women. If on the other hand depression is the cause of the lack of interest in sex, they may help in spite of their infamous side effect. Other drugs that can interfere with interest, arousal, and orgasm include antihypertensives, oral contraceptive pills, tranquilizers, narcotics, alcohol and marijuana. The latter two may render a lover less inhibited, but embarrassed in his ability to perform despite his bravado.

Yoga for the Pelvic Muscles

The most important exercise for most people interested in a good sex life, beside a well-rounded routine of yoga asanas, has been known for centuries as bandhas (locks). See Chapter 31, Disorders of the Pelvic Diaphragm for a more thorough discussion of this topic.

The Most Enjoyable Diagnostic Test You'll Ever Undergo

If adequate sexual energy is a problem in your life and relationship, you and your partner deserve a therapeutic test to diagnose whether your libidinal shrinkage is due to a specific physical cause or due to non-specific, general fatigue, aging, or the blahs. You may have already diagnosed yourselves; good nocturnal erections, or sexual function that is good now and then suggests a lifestyle issue. To resolve the issue, plan a three-week period of celibacy, during which you and your lover sleep in different beds and save your sexual energy. During the three weeks, go to bed early and take a walk in the morning. Eat lightly; do not allow yourself to feel heavy after a meal. Court and charm your lover by bringing her/him flowers or helping your lover in little ways. At the end of the three weeks, take a short honeymoon, just a weekend getaway – without kids or friends. Choose somewhere romantic but don't plan on doing anything exhausting or complicated. Avoid alcohol and heavy foods. Remain celibate on your first night. The next day after you are settled in and fresh, allow the sparks to fly.

This is a diagnostic test, so don't judge your performance, orgasm, or satisfaction. Just note your desire and your body's response to it. If the urge is strong and you feel responsive with blood pumping into your pelvic organs even once, the issue is probably general and involves your lifestyle, attitude, and habits. When you get home, permanently implement the changes of the past three weeks and your love life should be fine. If, on the other hand, despite the ideal circumstances, nothing has changed over the three weeks in your desire and the feelings in your pelvic organs, the issue could be specific. See a gynecologist, urologist, or endocrinologist, because blood tests and other exams may show a treatable cause. Feel free to modify how you carry out this test as long as your changes will not interfere with your ability to interpret the results.

Erections Beget Erections

It is no surprise that regular sex protects against erectile dysfunction. In a Finnish study of men 50-75 without any sexual dysfunction, those having sex at least weekly had half the chance of developing erectile dysfunction compared to those having it less than weekly, and the more frequently a man had sex, the better he fared.[299] Erections may improve circulation and oxygenation. Since frequency has been shown to maintain better function in both men and women, once you have rebooted your sex life, you should try to sustain a frequency of love making that will continue to enhance it. Your sexual activity, according to the ancient texts, should be proportional to your energy, appetite, and age. If as a woman your sexual interest is infrequent, don't be surprised if your lover, deprived of ejaculation for months at a time, cannot delay orgasm long enough for you to be satisfied. If frequent sex makes him a better lover, you naturally will desire him more.

Aphrodisiacs

The branch of Ayurveda dealing with libido and sexual potency is called *vājīkarana*, from the word *vājī*, a horse, whose intensity in the act is symbolic of healthy desire. The text describes many mineral and herbal formulas for increasing both psychic and physiologic imbalances in sexual functioning. Formulating and dispensing these mixtures is a subspecialty for many Ayurvedic physicians. The texts also emphasize changes to be made in lifestyle including techniques for creating a romantic ambience that are not unknown to our own century: fragrances, flowers (such as jasmine and water lilies) and scented baths, oil application and massage, suitable music, soft evening breezes, good food and drinks (but not too much), fresh attire and bed linens, adorning the body with jewelry and ornaments, pleasant conversation, and a mind free of worries. [300]

The best single herb for general sexual strengthening any man can take is ashwagandha (winter cherry), whose name evokes the proverbial horse (ashwa). Take 1000 mg twice daily before meals. The best single herb for any woman is shatāvari (asparagus root), whose name implies she could accommodate one hundred husbands. 1000 mg twice daily before meals.

For most of us, besides an exhilarating partner, the best long term aphrodisiac is *Body Renewal*: exercise to increase energy and stamina; weight loss to improve your self image and endurance; yoga and stretching to keep your pelvis and back supple; meditation for the brain to regain its youthful innocence; prānayāma; listening to your body's song; an early bedtime with, perhaps, the prospect of romance; and finally, respect and consideration for your partner during the 99% of your time together that you aren't making love.

276 The decision to be celibate when you are in a committed relationship is one that should involve both partners. In these circumstances, many of the benefits of a single celibate person are lost, because the same time and attention are required to continue to nourish the relationship.

277 *Artava* is often used to specify ovum in Ayurvedic texts.

278 The lesson of the boy, Jagu, in Chapter 3.

279 *Tantrāloka* and other ancient texts are not so much how-to manuals but spiritual treatises, guiding us in how to make sexual union an experience of merging with the divine.

280 *Little Richard's Almanac*

281 *Caraka*, Ci II, 8-15. The text reads as if for the effects of women on men, but some passages are neutral, implying it applies to both sexes.

282 Bajulaiye O, Sarrel PM. *A survey of perimenopausal symptoms in Nigeria.* In: Notelovitz M, van Keep PA, editors: The climacteric in perspective. Proceedings of the Fourth International Congress on the Menopause, held at Lake Buena Vista, Florida, October 28-November 2, 1984. Lancaster, Boston: MTP Press Limited; 1986. p. 165-75.

283 Keep PA van, Kellerhals JM. *The impact of socio-cultural factors on symptom formation. Some results of a study on ageing women in Switzerland.* Psychother Psychsom 1974;23(1-6):251-63.

284 Hällström T. *Sexuality in the climacteric.* Clin Obstet Gynaecol 1977 Apr;4(1):227-39

285 Interestingly, sexual responsiveness, and perhaps sexual appetite may have a genetic as well as cultural component. Many women report that they rarely or even never achieve orgasm and they can partly blame their DNA. British researches surveyed thousands of pairs of twins. Fully one third of women reported that they never or rarely have an orgasm during lovemaking. On further analysis, genetic factors like differences in hormone levels, anatomy, predispositions to depression and anxiety, and responsiveness of the pleasure pathways in the brain accounted for 30-50% of a woman's chances of having an orgasm. If lack of orgasm accounts for your lack of libido, consultation with a sex therapist is often successful at initiating normal function. Ref: Spector, Tim et al. Biology Letters. June 2005.

286 Lucisano A, Acampora MG, Russo N, Maniccia E, Montemurro A, Dell'Acqua S. *Ovarian and peripheral plasma levels of progestogens, androgens and oestrogens in postmenopausal women.* Maturitas 1984 Jul;6(1):45-53.

287 Botella-Llusia J, Orio-Bosch A, Sanchez-Garrido F, Tresquerres JAF. Testosterone and 17 beta-oestradial secretion of the human ovary. II. *Normal postmenopausal women, postmenopausal women with endometrial hyperplasia and postmenopausal women with adenocarcinoma of the endometrium.* Maturitas 1997 Jan;2(1):7-12.

288 Masters WH, Johnson VE. *Human sexual response.* Boston: Little, Brown; 1966.

289 Goldstein MK, Teng NN. *Gynecologic factors in sexual dysfunction of the older woman.* Clin Geriatr Med 1991 Feb;7(1):41-61. Sarrel PM. Sexuality and menopause. Obstet Gynecol 1990 Apr;75(4 Suppl):26S-30S; discussion 31S-35S.

290 Systemic hormone replacement through a pill or patch can also be indicated in this situation, but is an issue that is beyond the scope of this book. Both vaginal and systemic estrogen therapy need to be carefully considered in the context of one's medical history and exam with a qualified physician.

291 Graziottim A. *Loss of libido in the postmenopause.* Menopausal Med 2000 Spring;8(1):9-12. Davis SGR. Androgen treatment in women. Med J Aust 1999 Jun 7;170(11):545-9.

292 Many physicians are not familiar with the use of low dose topical testosterone in women, a product that can be compounded at a compounding pharmacy or used off-label in similar doses from topical products for men. Consult a physician familiar with bio-identical hormone replacement.

293 *Great sex: what's age got to do with it?* [Results of AARP/Modern Maturity Sexuality Survey conducted by NFO Research, Inc]. Modern Maturity 1999 Sep-Oct:41-5,91.

294 Barber HR. *Sexuality and the art of arousal in the geriatric woman.* Clin Obstet Gynecol 1996 Dec;39(4):970-3.

295 The usefulness of these drugs was discovered serendipitously when male heart patients, who were subjects in a failed clinical trial to evaluate the use of seldenafil (Viagra) in alleviating angina pectoris, did not respond to a request to return their unused medication to the researchers, while the control subjects complied.

296 Nachtigall LE, Raju U, Banerjee S, Wan L, Levitz M. *Serum estradiol-binding profiles in postmenopausal women undergoing three common estrogen replacement therapies: associations with sex hormone-binding globulin, estradiol, and estrone levels.* Menopause 2000 Jul-Aug;7(4):243-50.

297 Handa, V.L., K.E. Bachus, et al. (1994). *Vaginal administration of low-dose conjugated estrogens: systemic absorption effects on the endometrium.* Obstet Gynecol 84(2):215-8.

298 These include fluoxetine (Prozac), sertraline (Zoloft), citalopram (Celexa) and others, and are used off-label as therapy for premature ejaculation, discussed in the Chapter 31.

299 *Regular Intercourse Protects Against Erectile Dysfunction: Tampere Aging Male Urologic Study.* Koskimäki, J et al. Am J Med. 121;7 208.

300 Caraka Samhitā. Ci II, 20-30.

EPILOGUE – CHAPTER 35

LIVING IMMORTALITY IN DAILY LIFE

A poor Brahmin boy a little older than Jagu had a father who decided he could make greater spiritual progress by breaking the bonds of attachment to everything worldly. The father made an impulsive decision to sacrifice everything he owned, which wasn't much. The boy, Nachiketās, thought to himself, "A man who offers only a dried up old cow will surely end up in an afterlife without joy!" Unable to contain himself, and wanting to add value to the sacrifice, the son blurted out, "And to whom do you give me, father?" Taken by surprise, the father made another rash decree, "To Mrtyu!" In one impetuous moment, the boy found himself irretrievably bequeathed to the impulse of intelligence that brings about transformation and change.

As a bud is destroyed for the flower and in turn, the flower for the seed; or as a lily sprouts out of the decay of the mud in a bog, transformation from one state to another is the characterizing feature of the matter fields and force fields that comprise the smaller manifest (vs larger unmanifest) portion of the universe. Mrtyu is the name given to this quality to change and transform. Mrtyu could also be called Death, because the reactants are destroyed in the creation of the products. Mrtyu is ancient Sanskrit from which we inherit the word *mortal*.

Nachiketās found himself, quite literally at Death's door, and Death happened to be away. The boy waited patiently until Death returned after three days. Upon seeing the boy, who, even as an apprentice like Jagu, had been twice born and had dedicated his life to the Vedas, Death realized he had offended and not properly respected a custodian of the Vedas. "Please forgive me for keeping you waiting. I grant you any boon." "I accept your offer," the boy requested, "tell me about death."

"No, that is the one boon I can never grant. No one can know about death while still in a human body. Pick any other boon." "This is the only boon I want," replied the boy. Death would not yield. "Pick health and a life as long as you choose, with riches, children, pleasures and comforts, and sovereignty over all the land. Pick any boon but this." Nachiketās stood firm. "Knowledge of death is the only boon worthy of you. If you don't grant me this request, you can just consider your offense against the Vedas forever unpardoned."

Death was pleased. Nachiketās had proven himself worthy of the knowledge of what lies beyond because he was willing to sacrifice everything worldly to have it. You, dear reader, must be eager to hear Death's account. If Death was wise enough to test the boy before revealing what everyone else must pay with their life to know, then surely I would be negligent if I simply gave you an abbreviated version of his message. Your test may be finding the initiative to go to the library or Internet to read the conversation between Mrtyu and the boy as revealed in the Katha Upanishad. It is compact but meaningful and full of life.

Vedic Engineering

The teaching Death gave to the boy reminded me of Wim, a Brazilian father of Dutch descent who was an engineer's engineer. He had founded a company of 250 civil engineers that designed and built huge projects, such as dams and bridges over the Amazon. Wim came to our health and retreat center twice yearly to recover from the stress of completing his huge contracts under budget. He would receive our Ayurvedic purification treatments, meditate and take long walks in the New England woods. The other guests rarely saw him and invariably dubbed him *the phantom*, because he spent his time inwardly in retreat. At his first visit, Wim was 59 but looked much older. Ten years later, he looked about 59.

Once I lent him tapes of Maharishi describing the organization of the Veda into stanzas and chapters. He left that week saying, "The pylons of my new bridge need to have the same structure as the Rig Veda: ten bundles, with the First and Tenth bundles holding all the weight and the other eight acting as support. We can anchor them in the river more easily than one big one."

Four months later, Wim was back. "You're not due for two months, Wim, what's up?" "We underbid the competitors for the bridge by thirty million dollars. Now we're bidding on a tunnel and my senior engineers need me to solve a technical problem. They sent me to find inspiration." His routine exam revealed a lump in his armpit. The surgeon who excised it told me it was dark blue, a sure sign of metastatic malignant melanoma. I searched every cranny of his skin and membranes with a Wood's lamp without finding a primary lesion. Wim had some scars on his trunk. "A curandero (South American traditional healer) removed some moles a year ago with moxibustion." The proposed interferon to prevent further metastases gave only a 15% chance of success but a 100% chance of feeling more horrible than the worst chemotherapy. He went home and opted for a milder treatment, launching himself into his tunnel with the same structure as the Vedic literature. He came back six months later with his wife and best friends knowing it would be his last trip.

The Physics of Immortality

Wim had always been serious about immortality. He knew I subscribed to a medicine based on the unified field and was always inquiring regarding the anatomy of that part of nature not subject to transformation. He felt that if his designs were based on a physics of immortality they would last longer, even if they were still just cement rotting in river water. Even before his diagnosis, he would repeat a Sanskrit phrase, *anor aniyān mahāto mahiyān*. "Smaller than the smallest and greater than the greatest." It was Mrtyu speaking to Nachiketās about the structure of the Self "lodged in the heart of every creature," a perfect description of the physics of the unified field where infinity is seen at every point. He tells the boy, "The knowing Self is neither born nor does it die. It did not originate from anything, nor did anything originate from It. It is birthless, eternal, undecaying, and ancient. It is not injured even when the body is killed."

I called Wim every few weeks, as a friend, over his last months. He had restructured his engineers into teams to deal with some bad apples. "Every verse of the Veda describes the Totality, but in terms of the knower, the known and the connection between them, so I have given my teams a three-in-one structure. Totality at every point."

Wim's oncologist would call me with updates. She was Japanese and spoke Portuguese, but with her limited English and my Spanish, she managed to convey that he was physically slipping. Unlike her other terminal patients who appear to have the life drained from them, Wim's face appeared to her aglow with light. "He is accomplishing engineering miracles," she marveled, "with a brain full of metastases. He looks more alive than healthy men. It seems he's becoming timeless."

Living Immortality in Daily Life

Although our physical bodies are subject to the limitations of extreme longevity rather than true immortality, we can touch upon the field of immortality in at least four ways. First, we extend our influence far beyond the limits of our own bodies through the lives we touch when we teach and nourish a younger generation. Second, we leave an indelible mark when we influence our culture through inventions, art, compositions and other creations. Third, we pass on our DNA, which can literally become immortal. Fourth, we experience immortality every day when our settled awareness touches on the field of pure intelligence in our spiritual practices. Wim had been wildly successful at renewing his body and at bringing the structure of the unbounded into a metal and concrete buttress. In so orienting his attention, he seems to have unknowingly gained infinity on yet another level: living it in his daily life.

Wim delighted in finding *smaller than the smallest* in the same place with *greater than the greatest*; perhaps the reason for his business success was that he consciously integrated this principle into his brain functioning and his work, bringing infinity into the world of boundaries, whether it was designing a bridge or pacifying a team of temperamental engineers. This is living immortality in daily life, because even though we may appear to be just so much flesh, from the perspective of a quantum physicist, even our very physicality, the subatomic particles, and from there our atoms, molecules, tissues and organs, are all the expressions of an underlying, infinite, and immortal unified field.

At the end of his teaching, Death tells Nachikctās,

> "When all the knots of the heart are disentangled in this lifetime, a mortal becomes immortal. This much alone is the essence of my instruction."

We all have our knots, the twists and kinks in our brain's neurons from over- or underutilization of our senses, emotions and intellect; the excessive avidity of our neurons' receptors in the brain's pleasure-reward pathways for neurotransmitters caused by taking too much, or maybe too little, of a good thing; or the reef knots from the traumas of daily living. All these create boundaries in our brain's functioning: stresses, hang-ups, blockages, demons, call them what you like. Boundaries literally bind us and prevent us from living in the world of the unbounded, a cosmic playground of spirit that is the very nature of the world of our seemingly finite physiology.

I like to believe that Wim freed most of his knots. Through his spiritual practice, his intense pursuit of pure knowledge and the conscious application of his practice and knowledge to every aspect of daily life.

Like Wim's bridge, you also have a Vedic structure, and may indeed believe you were made in the image of God. Even if Death were to appear at your door to instruct you, you would never get a good idea of the marvel that awaits you on the other side until you finally arrive. This mystery is the most profound of all miracles, evoking the infamous graffiti, "Dying is the biggest kick of all. That's why they save it for last." In his yoga sutras Patañjali states, however, that you can get a good taste of infinity while still in this body.

You might be yet young but a sissy about growing old. Or you may be suffering in old age. In both cases, according to Vedic medicine, you still have a job to do: discovering the song of unboundedness in this lifetime and living immortality in daily life. The secrets of self-repair have been revealed by the ancient rishis (such as Jagu's ancient grandsire) specifically to give you the good health and time on earth that you need to experience your cosmic nature.

APPENDIX 1

THE THREE DOSHA PRINCIPLE
FOR A BALANCED PHYSIOLOGY

In the late 1970's several research colleagues and I were influenced by a visit from Belgian Nobel Prize winning physicist Ilye Prigogine. He had shown that non-equilibrium systems, such as a biological organism, create order out of chaos thanks to the influx of energy. He demonstrated the simplest and most elegant example of this, a thick, viscous fluid in a beaker over a source of low heat. As expected, after a while the fluid at the bottom rose to the top, where it cooled, and sank to the bottom. At first, it rose and sank in a haphazard way. With time, however, if the beaker and heat distribution were symmetrical, the rising and falling fluid would create convection cells with a smooth laminar flow. Eventually you could see a dozen perfectly polygonal columns surfacing at the top of the beaker where the rising fluid turned around and flowed back down. Symmetry and order had been created out of the chaos of the fluid.

The ingredients of this system are 1) the container 2) a source of energy to be dissipated, and 3) a flow of material. These are the requirements of any living system, because biological systems are essentially structures that create and maintain order amid chaos. Bacteria, amoebas, fungi, ferns, trees, insects and mammals all contain these three ingredients: (1) a physical structure or channel through which (2) flows a material due to (3) the dissipation of energy. In essence, we take in food; we move it via channels throughout the body where it is burnt to release its energy, which we then use to maintain order (keep our temperature constant, repair tissues, seek shelter, etc.). Health is a matter of keeping this dynamic in balance. The intelligence that guides it is the body's ancient song.

Physiological Operators

The ancient Vedic *rishis* (seers) also observed this biological phenomenon and recognized the same three elements: an element of movement or flow (*vāta*), the release of energy or metabolism (*pitta*) and the structure (*kapha*). They recognized that disease was a disequilibrium between these three elements and called them *doshas*. They are best characterized in English as *physiological operators*.

For example, vāta, being movement or transport in the body, is like the wind: light, cold and always moving or shifting. Vāta governs elimination, nervous system activity and locomotion. If imbalanced, vāta creates a drying, cold, brittle and irregular influence. Think of a tree at timberline, exposed to the wind and cold: it becomes dry, brittle, cracked and irregular in shape. Vāta dosha has a similar influence on our physiology, and vāta imbalances include osteoarthritis and osteoporosis (rough joints and brittle bones), insomnia and anxiety (excessive and irregular movement in the mind), constipation (irregularity and internal dryness) and aging, where we begin to look like that tree. There are many ways to aggravate (i.e. to increase out of proportion) vata in your constitution, but one of the best is to take on excessive activity, staying up late, and keeping irregular hours.

Pitta dosha, being metabolism or transformation of energy, is by nature hot, red, sharp and penetrating. When imbalanced, it expresses itself as inflammation or heat, so any disease ending in – *itis* (meaning inflammation) is generally a pitta disorder. Hot flashes, heartburn, rosacea and most other skin disorders are also attributed to aggravated pitta. Spicy or sour foods, overheating exercise, anger, and frustration are influences aggravating pitta.

Kapha dosha governs the fundamental quality of structure in the physiology, so its nature is solid, stable, heavy and inert. When aggravated, kapha manifests as obstruction, heaviness, or swelling. Sinus congestion, obesity, diabetes, and edema are examples of kapha disorders.

The Principle of Similars and Opposites

One important principle of Ayurveda called the Principle of Similars and Opposites states that the presence of a quality in your life or environment increases the effect of that quality in your physiology; opposite influences decrease that quality. Health can be maintained or restored by using this principle to structure balance in your diet, routines and environment. In other words: eat heat, get heartburn; eat fat, get fat. If a tissue is dry and brittle, it needs lubrication and nourishment. These may seem like simplistic principles to guide your health behaviors, but I am sometimes amazed to see how many ways most people choose to ignore this practical concept.

By nature, we are all born with certain predispositions that play a role in the diseases with which we may eventually be afflicted. Modern medicine has discovered the most obvious of these relationships. We know that heavy (kapha-type) people are predisposed to kapha disorders like heart disease, diabetes and edema. Sun-sensitive pitta people are prone to rosacea and other inflammatory skin diseases. Wiry, ectomorphic vata types are prone to brittle bones. Your mind-body type, called *prakriti* (nature or constitution in Sanskrit) has been the basis of many popular self-help books on Ayurveda. In this scenario, you determine your mind-body type and follow the corresponding dietary and lifestyle recommendations for that type.

The Problem with Body Types

There are several problems with this logic. Most importantly, this is not how Ayurveda works or how the best Ayurvedic physicians think. Most people have medical problems resulting from a lifetime of immoderation or neglect that may not be related to their body type. For example, the average American vāta-type person is statistically highly likely to have disorders related to our sedentary American lifestyle and rich diet, including risks of heart disease. Such a vāta person would be best prescribed a kapha-pacifying regimen including more exercise and a diet that reduces sweet, rich foods. A diet and exercise program based on her body type, however, would recommend liberal amounts of sweet, salty, oily foods and moderation in exercise, a prescription that would only make these chronic disorders worse.

When we take our car to the shop, we say, "Fix my brakes," and not, "Fix my car because it is a Chevy." Similarly, an Ayurvedic doctor focuses on your imbalances and their underlying causes when formulating your treatment plan, keeping your "make and model" in the back of her mind. In fact, even after the symptoms have completely disappeared and health is restored, your treatment should still be based on your previous imbalances and not on your body type. It is wiser to anticipate the likely recurrence of a previous disorder rather than the hypothetical predisposition to disease based on your body type.

APPENDIX 2

A PRACTICAL TEST OF YOUR DOSHA IMBALANCES

Here is a simple test to assess your dosha imbalances based on signs and symptoms of disorders, as opposed to your constitution (mind-body type). The results may help guide you to a more balancing diet, exercise, and lifestyle, including the types of music, aromas, leisure activities or even landscaping that may be therapeutic. These recommendations are listed in Appendix 3, which also describes the doshas in more detail. The recommendations in this book that address one or more of your significant, specific disorders should always take precedence over the results of this more general test. And the recommendations of your doctor should take precedence over this book.

Mark one point for a positive response in the appropriate box. In some cases, a positive response is weighted more heavily, even up to five points, because its presence, such as obesity or insomnia, overrides other imbalances. You can have points in several boxes on the same line or in no boxes. Add up the columns and write your scores:

A Self-Test for your Dosha Imbalance

	Vāta	Pitta	Kapha
Temperature regulation	Uncomfortably cold, or cold feet and hands	Uncomfortably hot, hot flashes, sweats	I often feel cold and clammy
Skin	Dry, flaky or scaly skin	rosacea, acne, easily sunburn, eczema, psoriasis (3 points)	Oily, waxy skin with large pores, edema
Mental imbalances	Anxiety, panic, distracted, forgetful (3 points)	Anger, frustration, irritability	Lethargy, melancholy
Disordered sleep	Sleep-onset insomnia or light, fitful sleep -- (3 points)	Sleep-maintenance insomnia: I awake and can't get back to sleep - (2 points)	Excessive sleep: I regularly need 9-10 hours per night
Joint problems	Cracking, rough aching, brittle, grinding	Inflamed, hot, red	Chronic effusion (fluid in the joints), loose
Upper digestion	Irregular	Heartburn, acidity, ulcers, reflux (3 points)	Sluggish: food leaves stomach slowly

With the results of this test, you can follow appropriate dietary and lifestyle guidelines to help correct the problems. Ayurveda is a satisfying science because the ancient texts describe the effect of nearly every environmental or dietary influence on our natural state of equilibrium, including the different kinds of drinking water, fruits and vegetables, hundreds of kinds of birds, fish, and animals. The texts describe what to avoid or favor to treat chronic disorders, making it easy and motivating for us to follow the proper program.

The Principle of Similars and Opposites (Samanya-vishesha siddhanta)

This principle states that in order to create a balancing influence in your mind and body, you need to adopt influences that have the opposite effect of the imbalance. To balance vāta, which is cold and dry, we naturally favor warm, rich, nourishing foods with sweet, sour and salty tastes. Pitta disorders need a cooling diet favoring sweet, bitter and astringent foods. Kapha disorders are the least fun to manage because they are helped by culinary restraint: light diets with less fat, sugar and salt, but plenty of spices with bitter, astringent and pungent tastes. Similarly, vāta imbalances are helped by calming, soothing influences in the environment such as classical music (vs. hard rock). Kapha imbalances require more stimulation, like eating spicy salsa, dancing the salsa and avoidance of siestas and television. Keeping a cool head – and body – by avoiding heating environmental influences, especially

	Vāta	Pitta	Kapha
I am underweight because I am:	I am too active and nervous to eat well (3 points)	My metabolism is too fast. I eat a lot and burn it off easily	——
I am overweight because:	I overeat due to stress and anxiety	I overeat due to an insatiable appetite (4 points)	I am sedentary and lethargic, despondent and lonely (5 points)
Constipation with:	Dry, small, hard stools	External hemorrhoids	Pasty consistency to stools.
Menopause	Insomnia, spacey, vaginal dryness	Hot flashes	Weight gain
Blood pressure	Elevated due to anxiety	Elevated due to anger	Elevated due to obesity and lack of exercise
Eyes	Dry	Red, inflamed	Excess mucus
Fatigue	Due to lack of sleep, anxiety, emaciation	Due to autoimmune or inflammatory diseases	Due to depression, obesity
Menstruation	Irregular or with scant, dark clots	Heavy flow lasting many days	Bloating, lethargy, fluid retention, fibroids
PMS	Anxious, edgy	Irritable, angry	Depressed
Heart	Arrhythmias	——	Coronary disease (5 points)
Headache	Tension	Migraine	Sinus
Other organs	Kidney stones, bladder and prostate problems	Hepatitis, gallstones (2 points each)	Asthma or bronchitis; sinusitis (2 points each)
My Totals			

during exercise and selecting soothing music and entertainment can help pitta imbalances.

This self-test assesses the presence of common disorders that can be helped by dietary and lifestyle changes to balance the three doshas. Proper Ayurvedic treatment of these and many other diseases involves more than superficial approaches to balancing the doshas. This includes strengthening the digestive fire, eliminating plaque or toxins, nourishing the tissues, and other interventions described in the specific chapters. Ayurvedic theory is intuitive and simple. As you see, in only a few minutes you have grasped a critical principle of this science.

Follow the guidelines in Appendix 3 for the dosha in which you scored the most points to improve your main imbalances.

APPENDIX 3

APPLYING THE THREE DOSHA
PRINCIPLE FOR SELF-REPAIR

This table has been conceived to give you a brief overview of the Ayurvedic three dosha principle, because this may be the only book on Vedic medicine to purposely avoid teaching about vāta, pitta and kapha. The understandings and recommendations described in the body of this book are the critical essence of Ayurvedic medicine, and usually neglected by books and courses that focus on Three Dosha Theory.

The Three Dosha Principle is presented as a table to allow for quick reference and not as a guide to be carefully followed. The recommendations for diet and lifestyle given in the chapters for specific chronic disorders always trump the recommendations given for a person's body type or nature. The Three Dosha Principle has been presented to complement these more important parts of your treatment plan. For example, if you read in Effortless Elimination, Chapter 19, that your constipation may be due to excessive dryness in the lower intestines (apāna vāta), you may find in this table additional information for eating according to a vāta diet.

	Vāta	Pitta	Kapha
Definition	Vāta is the physiological operator that governs movement and communication.	Pitta is the physiological operator that governs transformation and metabolism, the conversion of reactants into products thereby producing energy, heat and new tissues.	Kapha is the physiological operator that governs cohesion and structure.
Functions	Vāta is responsible for making everything move within the body and for making the body itself move, including circulation, elimination, peristalsis, respiration, speaking, natural urges, thinking, and locomotion. Vāta makes a person animated, enthusiastic, creative and witty.	Pitta is responsible for upper digestion, the biliary fire, metabolism of one tissue into another, the blood, the skin, vision, the intellect and the emotions, the luster of the skin, courage, hunger and thirst.	Kapha creates and lubricates the physical channels through which vāta makes the nutrients and wastes to flow and in which pitta oxidizes or transforms them. It regulates fluid balance, lubricates joints, holds the tissues and skeleton together, provides softness and suppleness and is the basis of immunity. In the mind, kapha creates generosity, persistence, understanding and forgiveness.
Composition	Vāta is composed of the primordial elements akāsha (space) and vāyu (ether, air).	Pitta is composed of the primordial elements tejas (fire) and, according to some texts, apas (liquidity).	Kapha is composed of prithivi (earth) and apas (liquidity).
Qualities	It is dry, light, subtle, moving, cold, quick, rough and hard. Vāta is increased in the body by any substance or influence having these same qualities. Except for being cold, it has qualities that are the opposite of kapha.	Pitta's nature is sharp, intense, acid, sour, hot, light, slightly liquid, and red or yellow. It is increased by any substance or influence having these same qualities.	Kapha is heavy, cold, smooth, unctuous, soft, stable, slow, slimy and sweet. It is increased by influences having these same qualities. Except for being cool, it is in every other way the opposite of vāta, so whatever pacifies vāta, such as rich, heavy and sweet foods, will increase kapha, a relationship that creates problems from using, for example, comfort foods to pacify vāta.
Locations	Vāta finds its main seat in the pelvis, the seat of elimination, but it is also in the nervous system, joints and all channels, such as vessels and intestines.	Pitta's principle seat in the body is the upper digestive tract, including the stomach, liver, spleen, gall bladder, pancreas and duodenum. Because of its relationship to fire and light, pitta finds a seat in the skin, eyes and blood.	Kapha's principle seats are in the stomach, chest, and head and it lubricates the joints.

	Vāta	Pitta	Kapha
Consti-tution (Prakriti)	People with significant vāta in their constitution are fun to be around because they are creative and lively. They tend to be on the svelte side, with slender digits, sinewy limbs, visible tendons and veins, and are always in motion, prone to taking on many projects. Traditionally they are held to have darker coloration, dark veins, blueness of the whites of the eyes.	People with significant pitta in their constitution have in general a good digestive fire and a sharp appetite. They may have a sharp appetite for projects and be entrepreneurial. Pitta individuals are creative, intense, possess good intellects and make good speakers, writers and teachers. They are courageous and warm hearted, even sentimental. People who are fair, freckled, blond or red-haired or have blue eyes tend to display more pitta in their constitutions. Pitta people sunburn easily and are prone to skin cancer.	Individuals with primarily kapha constitution are built in a solid, firm way. They will usually have ample flesh on large bones. Tendons and veins are hidden. They have large, well-formed, white teeth, large eyes (like a deer) and round faces, like a moon. They will move and function in a deliberate way, slow but steady. They will be faithful and dependable, possessed of sweet dispositions, and have good memories, being slow to experience anger and fear.
Symptoms and signs of increase	Insomnia, lack of energy, constipation with hard, dry stools, tremor, flighty thinking, garrulousness, weight loss, dry skin, fear, worry, nervousness, irregularity in habits, and accelerated aging	Excessive hunger and thirst, burning, craving cold drinks and foods as well as cold environments, fever, sleep-maintenance insomnia, yellow and red coloration of excretions, eyes and skin.	Since kapha is structure, increased kapha creates obstruction: excessive secretions, sinus congestion, phlegm in the chest with coughing, excessive heaviness, blockage of organs, dullness, lethargy.
Symptoms and signs of decrease	Depression, weakness, heaviness	Lack of appetite, feeling cold, sluggish digestion, pallor, lack of radiance to the skin.	Weakness and lack of strength with brittle, poorly formed tissues
Symptoms and signs of aggravated dosha	Vāta aggravation gives the appearance of something that has been left in a cold, dry wind: brittle, dry, emaciated, cracking, stiff and aged. This will express itself in the joints, skin, digestion, general vitality.	Signs of inflammation (heat, redness, swelling and pain), excessive sweating, heat and burning sensations, itching, discharge, anger.	Obesity, coldness, lethargy, impotence, excess secretions, excessive sweetness in the body (diabetes), dullness of mind.
Disorders caused by aggravated dosha	There are 80 disorders due to imbalance of vāta, including most problems of the central and peripheral nervous systems, digestive disorders, urinary and reproductive disorders, arthritis and many degenerative disorders associated with aging.	There are 40 disorders ascribed to pitta. When aggravated, pitta creates inflammation in the body, including most (non-infectious) diseases that end in −itis, meaning inflammation. These disorders include most skin diseases, especially those characterized by redness; gastritis and ulcers; autoimmune disorders; allergy, liver and gallbladder problems; and most blood disorders.	There are twenty disorders caused by aggravation of kapha. These include diabetes; edema; congestion of the head, neck, sinuses, lethargy; hypothyroidism; some tumors, masses or swellings. Obesity, while always a kapha issue, has its underlying roots in any of the three doshas (eating out of anxiety is a vata issue, excessively sharp appetite is a pitta issue).
Factors that aggravate the dosha	Any activity or influence involving movement will increase vāta. Such activities in excess will aggravate vāta: inappropriate work and exercise, overuse of the senses, traveling, fasting staying up late and keeping other irregular habits. Dry, cold, pungent, bitter and astringent foods. Cold and dry climates. Excessive worry, fear, trauma, stress and hardship.	Hot weather, poor digestion, spicy or pungent foods, salty and sour tastes, alcohol, anger.	Cold, damp weather. Cold, heavy, oily foods, dairy; heavy meals; sour, salty and sweet tastes. Sedentary lifestyles, sleeping during the day, lack of mental and physical activities; pampered lifestyle.
Factors that pacify the dosha	Activities or substances that create a lubricating, warming, calming influence.	Activities or substances that create a cooling, soothing influence.	Activities that create an influence of warmth, lightness and stimulation.

	Vāta	Pitta	Kapha
Food and spices to favor if the dosha is aggravated	Sweet, sour and salty foods. Rich, heavy and unctuous (lubricating) qualities. Any dairy, especially warm, whole milk; oil, ghee or butter; sweeter grains including wheat and rice; sweet, juicy and heavy fruits including citrus, banana, avocado; vegetables that do not create gas, ideally well cooked or stir fried in oil; seeds and nuts except peanuts; mung beans and red lentils that do not create gas; most meats, fowl and fish; any sweetener; sweet spices such as cardamon, cumin, cinnamon, salt.	Sweet, astringent and bitter foods with cooling qualities. Dairy: ghee, lassi, warm milk. Ghee and olive oil. Green leafy vegetables, squashes, zucchini, fennel, asparagus. Sweet, juicy fruits without excess acidity such as grapes, melons, apples, avocado, raisins and dates. Basil, coriander, anise, fennel, cardamom, tumeric, fresh cilantro.	Bitter, astringent and pungent foods. You can use almost any spice except excess salt. Use lighter oils, especially olive oil, but sparingly. Use bitter grains including barley, quinoa, millet, rye, and favor brown over white rice. Basil, thyme, coriander, oregano, cumin, turmeric, fresh ginger root and black pepper. Melons, berries, papaya, apples, persimmons, grapes. Use nearly any vegetable, especially dark, bitter ones including salads, greens, artichokes, green beans, etc.
Food and spices that aggravate the dosha	Bitter, astringent and pungent (hot) tastes; dry, cold and undercooked foods. Avoid chili peppers; vegetables and beans that create gas such as cruciferous vegetables.	Acidic, sour, pungent and salty foods. Hot chilies, green and red peppers, vinegar, pickled foods, sour or unripe fruits, tomatoes out of season, onions, garlic, cayenne.	Fat, fried and greasy foods. Heavy red meat and dairy foods including high fat cheese. Excessive quantities. Avocado, coconut, unripe or sour fruits. Use salt sparingly as it makes you retain water. Fewer heavy starches: potatoes, sweet potatoes, rich desserts.
First Subdosha	Prānavāta: Movement in the mind, intellect and senses as associated with the vital breath. Its location is in the head and chest.	Pāchakapitta: The digestive fire, synonymous with agni. It represents the combined action of the stomach, pancreas, duodenum, i.e. the secretion of digestive enzymes, acids and alkali, which literally cooks the food. Pacha = to cook.	Kledaka kapha: Located in the upper stomach, kledaka creates the gastric juices and provides the cohesion for the bolus of food. It functions like the oil in the pot of the digestive fire.
Second Subdosha	Udānavāta: Governs movement upward in the chest, including speaking, coughing, burping, sneezing, hiccoughing, spitting, etc.	Rañjaka pitta: Rañjaka could be called the biliary fire, located in the liver, spleen, gall bladder, pancreas. It converts rasa (plasma or chyle) into rakta (the cellular aspect of the blood), giving the blood its color, from which rañjaka derives its name, meaning *red* or *to color*.	Avalambaka kapha: Located in the chest, it provides the structure for the chest wall and back, and nourishes the heart.
Third Subdosha	Samānavāta: The wind that fans the flames of the digestive fire, samāna governs all movement in the upper digestive tract including peristalsis, flow of the food through the digestive tract, and its absorption.	Sādhaka pitta: Think of this as the emotional fire, located in the heart (hrdaya). Sādhaka is responsible for digesting all that we ingest in the form of perceptions, thoughts, intellectual activities, memories and sense of self (ahamkara). If it is working properly, the product of these faculties will be a sense of fulfillment and achievement, as well as clear decisions.	Bodhaka kapha: Located in the mouth, bodhaka is responsible for the perception of taste, which is the counterpart of apas (liquidity)
Fourth Subdosha	Apānavāta: Governs movement downwards through the pelvis including the flow of urine, stool, gas, menstrual fluid and semen as well as delivery of the newborn.	Alochaka pitta: Located in the eyes, alochaka transforms color and form (rūpa) into an image.	Tarpaka kapha: Located in the skull, brainstem and spinal column, tarpaka nourishes the nervous system including the flow of the cerebrospinal fluid
Fifth Subdosha	Vyānavāta: Governs functions of the autonomic nervous system including circulation and the flow of energy, as well as motility of the limbs.	Bhrajaka: Located in the skin, bhrajaka converts ingested and applied nutrients into strong, lubricated and lustrous skin.	Sleshaka kapha: Located in all the body's joints, sleshaka provides lubrication to joint surfaces.

APPENDIX 4

THE METABOLIC FIRES AND FORMATION OF TISSUES

Sama-doshah sam-āgnishcha
Sama-dhātu-mala-kriyah
Prasann-ātma-indriya-manāh
Swasthya-ity-abhidiyate

Balance of the doshas, and agnis (fires)
Balance of the dhātus (tissues), malas (wastes) and kriyas (organs of action)
Coordination of the cosmic Self with the senses and mind
This is the definition of health (swasthya)

> The definition of ideal health from Susruta Samhitā, the oldest textbook of surgery

Agni – The Digestive Fire

Agni, as it is used in Vedic medicine, is the gastric fire, that consumes or sacrifices the food to create energy and tissues. Agni is commonly called pāchaka pitta. Pāchaka can be translated *the cooking fire*, and is derived from the root PAK meaning to cook. It is said to reside in the stomach and small intestine, but also includes salivation and esophageal actions. Pitta by nature is sharp, and a proper digestive fire should be sharp. When the authors of antiquity refer to the gastric fire, they were referring to the physiological functions that literally cook the food or otherwise break it down to prepare it for absorption and subsequent oxidation. The concept of agni thus includes the secretion and action of hydrochloric acid, gut enzymes, bile acids and biliary alkali on the food bolus.

There are three disorders of this fire: too weak (mandāgni), associated with sluggish digestion; too sharp (tikshnāgni), associated with too much acidity, creating burning and dyspepsia; and irregular (vishamāgni), associated with both.

Dhātus and Dhātu-agnis –
The Tissues and Metabolic Fires

The human physiology is the expression of Veda, the reservoir of pure intelligence that governs creation, and nowhere is this concept displayed as clearly as in the sequential emergence of refined dhātus (tissues) from primordial plasma. Modern biology understands that the plasma provides nutrients for a cell to function, proliferate, and differentiate. The ancient Ayurvedic treatises describe the same processes. Plasma is the gross matrix for the other more refined tissues such as majjā (that which fills the bone, i.e. bone marrow, immune tissue and nervous tissue) and shukra (semen and ova), nourishing them and providing the milieu in which they can thrive. The immune system's recognition of hundreds of thousands of antigens that permits it to instantly mount an immune response, the complex executive functions of the nervous system, and the union of semen and ovum to form a new being are processes so refined they are true miracles. Ayurveda describes these phenomena as the emergence of life from pure intelligence.

The word dhātu comes from the root DHA meaning basis or foundation. Dhātus are created through the action of catalysts that convert one tissue to another. In this way, progressively refined tissues are created from their grosser precursors. The catalyst for this is another type of agni, a *dhātu-agni or metabolic fire.*

The Ayurvedic texts, like modern medical texts, state that proper functioning of agni, the digestive fire, breaks food down into its essence, ahārarasa, the chyle or liquid portion of the food which passes across the mucous membrane of the intestine. Ahārarasa is in turn transformed into rasa, the primordial plasma, by the first metabolic fire, the rasa-dhātu-agni. Think of rasa as the sap, similar to the colorless sap of a flower, that becomes all the various parts. The other dhātu-agnis sequentially catalyze rasa into all the other dhātus. The simplified schema goes like this:

Substrate	Catalyst	Product	English equivalent of product
food	agni (digestive fire)	rasa	plasma (sap)
rasa	rasa-dhātu-agni	rakta	Red and white blood cells
rakta	rakta-dhātu-agni	mamsa	Fleshy organs and muscle
mamsa	meda-dhātu-agni	meda	adipose tissue, fat
meda	asthi-dhātu-agni	asthi	bone and joints
asthi	majja-dhātu-agni	majjā	That which fills bone (marrow, nerves)
majja	shukra-dhātu-agni	shukra	semen, ovum, reproductive tissues
shukra	a wholesome lifestyle	ojas	essence of the dhātus

Ojas – The Essence of the Tissues

Ojas is the essence of the seven dhatus, the subtlest of material substances, and is created when shukra is made properly from the action of all the dhātu-agnis. It is created spontaneously from the other seven tissues as a result of proper diet, lifestyle, routines, staying rested, and spiritual practices. Ojas is responsible for physical and mental strength, radiance and beauty, immunity and well-being.

Srotamsi – Channels and Cavities

Any hollow cavity or organ in the body through which matter or intelligence flows is a srotas (pleural= srotamsi), according to the treatises. These include blood and lymphatic vessels, viscera, the heart, intestines, etc. Srotamsi are understood to be the flutes through which intelligence resonates, the physical expression of your body's ancient song. Ultimately, keeping the channels healthy and free of obstruction is the key to health according to Charaka. Different channels are held to be blocked by different kinds of āma (residues), a very modern concept.

Āma – Residues of Inefficient Digestion

Despite our best intentions, we fail to eat moderately of pure, nourishing fare. We eat too much, too heavily, too late at night, when we are still digesting a previous meal, or when we are anxious, upset or rushed. The result is a weak or irregular agni and inefficient digestion with the creation of an undigested byproduct, āma. The root [MA] means to ripen or cook, so āma means "uncooked products of digestion." Āma is the predictable result of failing to properly maintain agni.

Āma is what we call plaque, debris, or deposits in western terminology: substances that lodge in inappropriate locations to create pathology. We lay down plaque in coronary arteries, in nerve tissue (as in multiple sclerosis) or in the beta-amyloid tangles seen in Alzheimer's disease and in the heart muscle cells, or as the visible debris in the cytoplasm of aging cells.

The 13 Natural urges

Ayurveda describes 13 requirements of the body that should not be suppressed if good health is to be maintained. Suppression of these urges, the texts say, results in imbalance of the doshas or the agnis.

- passing urine

- passing stool

- seminal discharge or orgasm

- passing gas

- vomiting

- sneezing

- hiccoughing

- burping

- yawning

- hunger (and its corollary, the impulse to not eat if hunger is not present)

- thirst (and its corollary, the impulse to not drink if thirst is not present)

- shedding tears

- sleep (i.e. staying up doing activity at night when the need for sleep is present)

APPENDIX 5

RECIPES FOR IMPROVING DIGESTION

Pachakchūrna (Digestive spice powder)

- 1 part fennel seeds, dry roasted and ground to a powder
- 1/2 part ajwain seeds, dry roasted and ground to a powder
- 1/2 part licorice powder
- 1/4 part black salt
- 1/4 part cardamom powder
- 1 part cumin seeds, dry roasted and ground to a powder

Combine ingredients and keep them in a small spice bottle or jar. Take 1/2 to 1 teaspoon with the first bite of a meal to help digest that meal. It can also be taken after meals. All ingredients can be procured at an Indian grocery.

Kanji (Digestive rice broth or cracked wheat broth)

- Basmati rice or cracked wheat
- Water
- Salt, cumin powder

Kanji is the easiest of all possible foods to digest. It should be the first food to be taken after surgery, after or during a fast, or during abdominal problems such as bloating or irritable bowel syndrome. You can take it when no other foods are tolerated or when digestion is sluggish, such as during colds, childbirth, headaches or menstrual cramps. It is used following a laxative or enema, or during Ayurvedic purification programs (panchakarma). It is simple to cook:

Boil 1/4 cup of basmati rice (or cracked wheat) in 2 quarts of water, uncovered, for 20-30 minutes. It will boil down to about 1/2 or 2/3 of the original volume. Before the last five minutes, add salt and cumin powder to taste. If you prefer other spices, you may add a little grated ginger root or a hint of black pepper. Strain off the liquid and throw out the rice. Pour into a thermos and sip, warm or hot, throughout the day.

Dal (Cooked legume soup)

- Mung beans or red lentils (1/4 cup per person)
- Turmeric, cumin powder, mustard seeds, hing (asafoetida)
- 4 teaspoons ghee

Cooking time: 30 to 60 minutes (depending on type of dal used)

Dal is an excellent source of protein and is easy to digest. Dal should be a staple in the diet of anyone who restricts animal proteins. The best beans are:

- Yellow split mung, quick to cook, 20-30 min., easiest to digest

• whole green mung – longer to cook, about 45-60 min. Tastiest, retains some texture.

• small red lentils (masoor dal), quickest to cook, about 15-20 min. Becomes homogeneous and soupy

• brown lentils – require an hour to cook, tasty, retain texture, may create gas

Sort legumes to remove debris and stones. Rinse and drain, repeating the process until the water becomes almost clear. Legumes may be soaked overnight or even one hour before cooking to reduce the cooking time. Throw out the soaking water and use fresh water for cooking to reduce gas.

General rule of thumb: use 7 to 10 parts water to 1 part dal. Be sure to add enough water, especially if you have other things to do besides checking on your dal. You can always thicken the dal later by cooking without a lid if it is too thin. As the dal thickens, it may burn if there is not enough water. If you need to add water, the water should be boiling.

In a stainless steel pot with a lid, combine water and dal and bring to a boil. Use about 1/4 cup of dal for each person. Turn the heat down to low and simmer for the required time. When dal is well cooked, prepare the spices as follows: Heat 4 teaspoons ghee in a small skillet or saucepan over a moderate flame. Then add 1-2 teaspoons of black mustard seeds and 1-2 teaspoon cumin seeds and heat until the mustard seeds pop. Add 1/4 teaspoon hing, 1-2 teaspoons turmeric, and 1-2 teaspoons cumin powder to the ghee. Immediately stir the above spice mixture into the cooked dal and add salt and black pepper to taste. Optional for children: a teaspoon of raw sugar. Allow dal to set with the spices for 5 minutes.

Prior to serving, garnish with a few sprigs of fresh cilantro or parsley. During cold weather, add a teaspoon of fresh grated ginger to the cooking beans.

For variety, you may simmer it with one or a few of the following:
• chopped fresh tomato, chopped carrots or greens such as spinach or celery,
• 1-2 teaspoons of lemon juice,
• a few pinches of a spicier curry powder.

Khichadi

Khichadi (sometimes called kicheree) is simply rice cooked together with dal. It is the easiest solid food to digest and if digestion has been sluggish, khichadi should be the first food to be taken after kanji, which is nearly a clear liquid (see preface to kanji recipe).

Follow the instructions for making dal using split or whole mung beans, however, substitute rice for 1/3 to 1/2 of the dal. Basmati rice is the most digestible. Be sure to add even more water than for dal, as the rice absorbs a lot of water, and khichadi should not be too thick. Spice it more mildly than dal. See Chapter 21 for a quick Thermos Flask Lunch recipe to take khichadi to work or school.

Ghee

Ghee is the Hindi term for clarified butter – a staple of Ayurvedic cooking. It is considered the best quality oil for daily use, because it is simultaneously lubricating, light, and easy to digest. It can be used in the place of butter or cooking oil, but not on salads. Containing natural antioxidants, it has short chain fatty acids and its cholesterol fraction resists oxidation. It is therefore esteemed as one of the best foods for reversal of aging because it penetrates into tissues requiring lubrication, such as joints (See Chapter 29). Butter quickly scorches at high temperatures due to its milk solids, whereas ghee withstands high temperatures because it is the pure oil extracted from the butter. Ghee can be stored at room temperature or refrigerated. Ghee is available at delicatessens, natural food stores and Indian groceries, but is easily made at home.

Traditional (non-skimmed) Ghee

Place one or more pounds of unsalted butter in a deep stainless steel or Pyrex type glass pan on medium-low heat. Do not leave ghee unattended during this process and watch to make sure that the butter does not scorch while melting.

During the next 15-40 minutes, the water will boil away (approximately 20% of butter is water). Milk solids will appear on the surface of the liquid and on the bottom of the pan. The bottom of the pan must be frequently scraped with a metal spatula so it won't scorch. The solids will fall to the bottom of the pan; they add antioxidants and flavor. When the bubbling diminishes and the ghee becomes clear, the water will be almost gone. Turn heat to low. You should still see bubbles rising from the bottom when you take it off the burner. Remember that once the bubbles stop, there is no more water, and the temperature of the oil will rise quickly and scorch. The most common error in making ghee is allowing it to burn. Any residual water will continue to evaporate for ten minutes after you remove it from the heat, so don't take a chance – take it off too soon rather than too late. The butter oil will become clear and may smell nutty. Strain the sediment from the ghee while it is lukewarm by pouring it through a steel strainer into a clean glass jar for storage. You can leave ghee at room temperature or in the fridge. Be cautious making ghee as it can burn you as well as catch fire.

Lassi

Lassi is simply fresh yogurt blended with water. Yogurt is a curd and therefore hard to digest. Once yogurt is transformed into lassi, it becomes much lighter and aids digestion. Yogurt contains no lactose, which has been consumed by the bacteria. Thinning yogurt with water and blending it creates an emulsion that it is easily assimilated. It contains beneficial bacteria, and helps eliminate gas pains. It is traditionally taken after the main mid-day meal.

Digestive Lassi: Blend one part yogurt to three parts water, adding cumin powder, salt (and pepper) to taste. Optionally garnish with some finely chopped cilantro leaves.

Sweet Lassi: Blend one part yogurt to three parts water, adding cardamom, sugar, and rosewater to taste.

Ginger Tea
For weak digestion

- 1 quart water
- 1/2-2 teaspoons fresh ginger (less for sensitive stomachs). Or 1/2 teaspoon ginger powder.

Boil for 5 minutes. Strain hot into a thermos and sip throughout the day. Good for digesting āma, increasing the digestive fire and reducing congestion.

Ginger Stir-fry
(for sluggish digestion)

Grate 5 teaspoons fresh ginger root and fry it with a teaspoon of ghee. When brown, add some natural brown sugar, Succanat® or date sugar and fry a few seconds more until it caramelizes. Prepare and eat it first thing in the morning with a little hot water for up to eight days in a row. Wait one hour before taking any food or water.

Fennel Tea
(For digestion, nausea, bloating)

Put one teaspoon of fennel seeds into one to two cups of boiling water and boil for 5 minutes. Drink warm.

Cumin Tea
(For gas, bloating, sluggish digestion)

Put one teaspoon cumin seeds into one to two cups of boiling water and boil for 5 minutes. Drink warm. Excellent after supper to dispel gas and bloating.

Barley water
(For indigestion, fluid retention, tendency to gain weight)

Put one tablespoon of barley grains in one cup of water and soak overnight. In the morning, boil for 3-5 minutes. Drink one-half cup twice a day.

Coriander Seed Water
(for acidity, heartburn)

- 1 teaspoon coriander seed
- 1 cup water

Soak coriander seeds in water overnight. In the morning, strain and press the water out of the coriander seeds into the rest of the water and discard the seeds. Drink the remaining water.

APPENDIX 6

A THREE-STEP HOME PURIFICATION PROGRAM

The purpose of this program is to eliminate plaque and residues (āma) that are not otherwise cleared by the kidneys and liver. The Vedic texts recommend bathing the tissues with a lipid-based solvent to dissolve deposits. The solvent of choice is ghee, or clarified butter oil. The ancient Vedic texts describe ghee as having the quality of being extremely fine or subtle and therefore able to penetrate into tissues. Modern biochemistry has shown it to be composed of short-chain fatty acids.

This program is for generally healthy people. If you suffer from digestive, cardiac, pulmonary, kidney or other metabolic disorders, ask your physician before embarking on this program.

In order to be able to digest the significant amount of ghee required, however, you first need to strengthen your digestive fires. For that we will prime the digestion with fresh ginger root before taking the ghee. Finally, because ghee is said to carry the residues from the liver to the colon via the bile for elimination, you will eliminate the toxins with a gentle purgation. Be sure to calculate when you will be ready for the purgation, conveniently planning it for a weekend or a day off.

General Guidelines

- During this period, eat smaller quantities than usual (2/3 of usual amount). Favor lighter foods and semi-solids, e.g. soups, rice, lentils, dal and khichadi. See Appendix 5, Recipes.

- Drink 3-4 glasses of hot water per day on an empty stomach or between meals. During meals, sip hot water.

- Immediately following your laxative therapy, however, avoid eating or drinking until the effects of the laxative have worn off.

- Sip ginger tea for slow digestion, cumin tea for gas or bloating, or fennel tea for nausea.

- Eat if you are hungry; do not eat if you are not hungry. Do not intentionally fast.

- Avoid supplements and herbs during the home purification. Continue to take prescribed medications.

- Avoid consuming cold food (ice cream), cold drinks, meat, and heavy curdled dairy such as yogurt and cheese (pizza), these are heavy for both the digestive and metabolic fires (agnis). Your agnis will be working to digest the āma from the tissues.

- Avoid extra oils (butter, ghee, and fatty foods) except the days you are taking ghee.

- Avoid excessive physical exercise, which may deplete your energy during this period. If you have been exercising on a regular basis, then continue with a gentle program.

- Avoid exposure to the cold, taking particular care to cover the head and neck area. Your immune system and reserves may be depleted while you are eliminating toxins.

- Avoid alcohol, excessive caffeine and other stimulants.

- Stay rested. Go to bed early.

- Be regular with prānayāma, yoga and meditation.

Step One – Rekindling the Digestive Fire: Ginger Stir-fry

Follow the recipe and procedures for ginger stir-fry in Appendix 5 (Recipes), comfortably taking larger amounts – up to several teaspoons—of the tasty, spicy ginger every morning for 4 to 7 days. This will stimulate your digestive fire before step two.

Step Two – Oleation with Ghee (Snehana)

Every morning for four days, take increasing amounts of ghee on an empty stomach. Ghee can be purchased at health food stores or prepared at home from unsalted butter. See Appendix 5. If you are following this program specifically for improvement of mental functioning, use brahmi ghee. (See Resources). Ghee can make your digestion sluggish, so follow the dietary guidelines above. After oleation with ghee, you will feel light and supple. Research on individuals undergoing this program has shown that total cholesterol and the undesirable LDL cholesterol are actually reduced.[277] If overweight, you may lose weight.

Day 1: At 6-7 a.m. take 4 teaspoons
Day 2: At 6-7 a.m. take 8 teaspoons
Day 3: At 6-7 a.m. take 12 teaspoons
Day 4: At 6-7 a.m. take 16 teaspoons
Day 5: Massage and hot shower
Day 6: At 6-7 a.m. take castor oil as described below

Ghee should be measured (3 teaspoons = 1 tablespoon) and taken in a warm liquid form on an empty stomach on arising. Warming the ghee makes it more palatable and fluid. Sipping a glass of hot water 15 minutes after taking the ghee makes it easier to digest. If you have difficulty swallowing plain ghee, you can mix it with ½ cup of warm milk. If you feel nauseous, sip hot water with fresh lemon juice throughout the day. Treat yourself to a massage, even a self-massage, on Day 5, followed by a hot shower. The massage will encourage penetration of the ghee into the tissues.

Step Three: Laxative Therapy (Virechhana)

The purpose of laxative therapy is to hasten elimination of the impurities, which have been loosened by the oleation. Take the castor oil in the morning of Day 6 on an empty stomach. Before taking the castor oil, take a 15-20 minute hot tub bath or hot shower to increase the circulation and loosen the impurities in the body.

Most people do well with castor oil, which is held in Ayurveda to have beneficial effects aside from its laxative effect. If you have a sensitive colon, take only two teaspoons. If you are under thirty and have strong digestion, use five teaspoons for women and six teaspoons for men. You can swallow the castor oil by itself or follow the recipe in the box if you do not like its taste or smell. Two fresh oranges (or lemons) are needed for use in the recipe below. Read the complete recipe, arrange all the items conveniently, then proceed.

> **Painless Castor Oil Recipe:** Slice an orange (or lemon) into quarters. Prepare some boiled water. Place the prescribed amount of castor oil in an elegant teacup. Squeeze some juice from the orange (or lemon) into the cup. Add an ounce or two of hot water to make the thick, viscous oil thinner and stir it well. The smaller the volume, the easier it is to swallow. Listen to your body's song, bless your remedy and the Trajectory it will follow, hold the nostrils closed and drink the mixture quickly. Bite into the remaining orange (or lemon) for about 5 seconds. Tasteless castor oil can be purchased at most pharmacies.

If you cannot tolerate castor oil you can substitue two or three tablets of senna alkaloids (e.g. Senokot). You will notice a gurgling in the belly in 1-5 hours, followed by several liquid stools. Stay near home. Avoid eating or drinking until the purgation is completely stopped. You can sip small amounts of warm water during this time. When the purgation is finished, start sipping warm water or kanji (See Appendix 5, Recipes) to rehydrate. You may have little or no results. This is perfectly acceptable. The herbs are beneficial even without a strong laxative effect. In either case, continue to drink ample hot water (or ginger, cumin or fennel teas) for the next few days and follow the general guidelines above before returning to your usual diet. Your first meal after the purgation should be soup, dal or khichadi. Advance your diet cautiously, remembering that your digestive fire may remain slow for several days.

Enjoy your increased clarity of mind and lightness of body. You can repeat this program every four months if it was easy. If it was difficult, modify the quantities of ghee and castor oil accordingly.

APPENDIX 7

SEASONAL ROUTINES

There are six seasons (ritu) described in the ancient texts. Depending on where you live, you may find a season below corresponding to your environment's different climate changes throughout the year. Follow the guidelines in a relaxed way, because your diet and lifestyle also need to be determined by your constitution, your imbalances, your age, and your occupation.

Fall – cool and dry (Sharad Ritu)

The influence of a season on our health is not only a function of the weather. Fall (even more than spring) is the time of new beginnings in our social and economic world, and with this comes intense activity. Children go back to school, sports, and music lessons; companies launch new initiatives; TV networks launch new series; the cultural scene places its demands on us with late nights at the theater or other meetings. What a contrast to the easy-going, lazy days of summer. The heat of the summer has reached its peak and the days become shorter, darker and cooler (the opposite is the case in the southern hemisphere). We can anticipate cool, crisp days that will soon give rise to the peak of cold in winter.

- During this fall season, it is important to stick to a good daily routine and go to bed early.

- Avoid working, reading or watching TV late into the night. Get plenty of sunlight during this season to avoid mood changes that can come on as the days get shorter.

- This is a season for reducing weight and getting in shape, because you can now exercise abundantly without getting overheated.

- It is a good season to donate blood.

- Begin to take more hot beverages during the course of the day: hot ginger tea (see Recipes) can be sipped all day. In the evening sip cumin tea, made by boiling a teaspoon of cumin seeds in one cup of water for 5 minutes. At bedtime, try hot milk with a few threads of saffron.

- Most importantly, during this busy season, if you find yourself feeling overextended, just say "No!"

Early winter – (Hemantu ritu)

The cold season is beginning and the digestive fire, agni, is entering into the period where it needs to be most active, like your boiler automatically turning itself on for a cold winter morning. Agni can now digest heavier foods, which the body needs to stay warm.

- During the short days of winter, make an extra effort to expose yourself to sunlight. Your bones need vitamin D, synthesized by skin exposed to UV rays; even a half hour exposure of your face may be enough. In addition, your moods and even your libido are dependent on sunlight.

- Now, at last, you can indulge in heavier foods, enjoying an occasional dish au gratin or pizza. Use more oils in sauté, or dribble some ghee or butter onto your rice or toast.

- Enjoy hot, boiled milk, which Ayurveda regards as a rejuvenating tonic (always alone as a mid-morning or afternoon snack or at bedtime, never with sour, spicy or salty foods).

- Non-vegetarians can take heavier meat dishes during this season, especially as a soup or stew.

- Dress well, bundle up outdoors, wear a hat and scarf, i.e. remember what your mother told you.

- The ancient texts say this is the season for enjoying wine and sex more frequently.

Late Winter – (Shishira Ritu)

This is the coldest part of the winter, the season when the body gets dry, brittle and stiff. Even the air is dry from heating. Your joints may get brittle and crack. A self-administered oil massage with sesame or olive oil can be performed in the morning before a warm shower.

Follow the advice for early winter with even more vigilance.

In New England and Quebec there are traditions for dealing with the frigid dryness: pancakes with maple syrup and plenty of butter. Just don't overdo it: you may regret the extra fat you put on come spring.

Spring – (Vasantu Ritu)

Everything is coming alive. Buds, blossoms, trees pushing tiny leaves. The identifying factor for this season is the sun coming back. In some climates spring may be wet (see Varsha Ritu), for some it may be dry. In any case, the body's accumulated coldness and heaviness can lead to congestion, heaviness and lethargy.

- Favor a light diet. Avoid sweet, sour, salty and rich foods.

- Again, no siestas, as they increase heaviness and lethargy.

- Get outside and move, staying warm, however. This is a good time to enjoy the blossoming of nature.

- Use rough, bitter-tasting grains like rye, barley, millet, quinoa and buckwheat.

- Non-vegetarians should use leaner cuts of meat from animals that live in dry places such as fowl (except duck), rabbit, lamb or venison. Avoid heavy cuts of meat.

- In this season, oil massage is not as critical. Once a week, for example on your day off, may be enough unless your skin and joints are quite dry and brittle.

Summer – Hot and mostly dry (Greeshma Ritu)

This is the peak of accumulation of heat in the body. We just try to stay cool.

Follow a cooling diet, avoiding alcohol and hot, spicy foods. Take plenty of sweet, juicy fresh fruits.

- At last, you can indulge in a siesta after lunch. Cool drinks are fine. Try a dilute lassi made with mango, rose water or rose petal jam.

- Try soaking black tulsi (takmaria) seeds for 5 minutes in a little water and then adding them to any cool drink. They are delicious as well as cooling. (See Chapter 33 regarding their use for hot flashes)

- Ghee, milk, rice, wheat products and dal are all good for keeping cool.

- Exercise easily and in the cool of the day, and keep your bedroom cool and well-aired.

- Adorn your house with flowers and adorn yourself, if appropriate, with gems, especially pearls and a dab of sandalwood oil over your heart.

- Walking in the moonlight in the cool of the evening and swimming (or a cool shower if a pool or pond is not available) are useful if the heat is making you irritable.

Wet, rainy and humid spring or summer weather (Varsha Ritu)

- Humidity taxes the body and mind in this season and creates dullness.

- Practice moderation in all aspects of your life including diet and exercise.

- Siestas are not advised as they may create more heaviness in the body.

- Exercise in moderation.

- Foods should be warm and easily digestible.

- Honey is a good sweetener for wet weather. It is astringent and cuts mucus.

- People who enjoy alcohol can indulge a bit more.

- Hot baths and showers are important, preceded by warm sesame or olive oil massage. Inhale the steam deeply.

- Try to keep your living areas free of humidity.

- Stay dry.

APPENDIX 8

RESOURCES

I. Books on Ayurvedic Medicine

A Women's Best Medicine, Drs. Nancy Lonsdorf,
Veronica Butler & Melanie Brown

Perfect Health, Deepak Chopra, MD

Body, Mind and Sport, John Douillard, DC

Awakening Natures Healing Intelligence, Hari Sharma, Lotus Press,
Twin Lakes, WI 53181, www.lotuspress.com

Yoga of Herbs, David Frawley and Vasant Lad, Lotus Press,
Twin Lakes, WI 53181, www.lotuspress.com

Ayurveda, Science of Self-Healing, Vasant Lad, Lotus Press,
Twin Lakes, WI 53181, www.lotuspress.com

Fundamentals of Ayurvedic Medicine, Vaidya Bhagwan Dash
Charaka Samhiti

Ayurvedic Yoga Therapy, Mukunda Stiles, Lotus Press,
Twin Lakes, WI 53181, www.lotuspress.com

Ayurvedic Remedies for the Whole Family, Light Miller, Lotus Press,
Twin Lakes, WI 53181, www.lotuspress.com

Ayurvedic Healing: A Comprehensive Guide, David Frawley, Lotus Press,
Twin Lakes, WI 53181, www.lotuspress.com

Ayurvedic Beauty Care, Melanie Sachs, Lotus Press,
Twin Lakes, WI 53181, www.lotuspress.com

Ayurveda, Nature's Medicine, David Frawley and Subhash Ranade,
Twin Lakes, WI 53181, www.lotuspress.com

Ayurveda Secrets of Healing, Bri. Maya Tiwari,
Twin Lakes, WI 53181, www.lotuspress.com

Contemporary Ayurveda, Hari Sharma, M.D. and Chris Clark, M.D.
Heal Yourself, Heal Your World, Brian Rees, M.D.

Self Recovery: Treating Addictions, Using TM and Maharishi Ayur-Veda ed.
D. O'Connell & C. Alexander, Haworth Press

Science and Philosophy of Indian Medicine, Udupa, K.N. & Singh, R.H., Shree
Baidyanath, Lotus Press, Twin Lakes, WI 53181, www.lotuspress.com

II. Journal Devoted to Vedic Medicine

Light on Ayurveda Journal. Published by UMass Dartmouth
Center for Indic Studies. Subscribe online at www.loaj.com.

III. Ayurvedic Cookbooks

Ayurvedic Cookbook, Amadea Morningstar and Urmila Desai, Lotus Press,
Twin Lakes, WI 53181, www.lotuspress.com

Heavens Banquet, Miriam Hospodar

Ayurvedic Cooking for Westerners, Amadea Morningstar, Lotus Press ,
Twin Lakes, WI 53181, www.lotuspress.com

Sattwa Café, Meta Doherty, Lotus Press., Twin Lakes, WI 53181,
www.lotuspress.com

Cooking for Life, Linda Banchek

IV. Cassettes and CD's: Vedic recitation for healing and music therapy

Sāma Veda cassettes *

Rg Veda cassettes *

Gandharva Veda cassettes and C.D.s *

Available from **www.mapi.com, www.sanskrit.safire.com/Audio.html**
and other sources

IV. Books on Consciousness and Meditation in Self-Repair

The Bhagavad-Gita: A New Translation and Commentary, Maharishi Mahesh Yogi

Human Physiology: Expression of Veda and the Vedic Literature,
Tony Nader, MD, PhD.

The Physiology of Consciousness, Robert Keith Wallace, PhD

The Neurophysiology of Enlightenment, Robert Keith Wallace, PhD

V. Ayurvedic Herbs and Products

Because this book may be used in the absence of a trained Ayurvedic provider,
I have tried to recommend for each disorder one or two single herbs that can be
taken by anyone and without interactions with other medications, supplements
or conditions. This approach is called the *ekamula* (one plant root) school of
Ayurvedic herbal science. Avoiding proprietary formulas eliminates not only the
above potential problems, but also makes it possible to locate the necessary herbs
in any country. In alphabetical order:

Banyan Botanicals. Albuquerque, NM. 800-953-6424.
www.banyanbotanicals.com. Banyan's owners have made an effort to supply herbs
of the highest quality and freshness and attempt to find organic ingredients. They
have established their own organic farms both in the US and in Sri Lanka to
control all aspects of their product. They offer tablets and loose herb powders as
well as herbalized oils.

Bazaar of India, Berkeley, CA 800-261-SOMA.
www.bazaarofindia.com. Bazaar of India offers a wide variety of loose herbs,
groceries and encapsulating equipment.

Frontier Natural Products Co-op, Norway, IA, 800-669-3275. www.frontiercoop.com. Frontier carries a wide variety of loose spices and herbs that are seal packed. They sell capsules and encapsulation tools to allow you to make your own pure herbs.

Herbs of Ayurveda. One of the few suppliers of herbalized ghee, including brahmi ghee discussed in Chapter 24 on Brain Fitness. Herbs of Ayurveda is a small company that compounds their own herbalized oils and ghees, mostly for spas and practitioners. They keep supplies of bacopa brahmi ghee for shipping and compound special orders on request. www.herbsofayurveda.com.

Maharishi Ayurveda Products, Inc., Colorado Springs, CO. 800-255-8332. www.mapi.com. MAPI offers herbs of high quality that are extensively tested for purity. They specialize in formulas that take advantage of the synergistic value of the different ingredients. MAPI is also a good source for books, audio on Vedic recitation.

InterNatural is an online reseller of natural herbal and health products. They have a large selection of herbs and spices in various forms, including the Frontier Products. www.internatural.com

VI. Ayurvedic Schools and Programs

See the listings at the web sites of Light on Ayurveda Journal (www.loaj.com) and the National Ayurveda Medical Association (www.ayurveda-nama.org).

INDEX

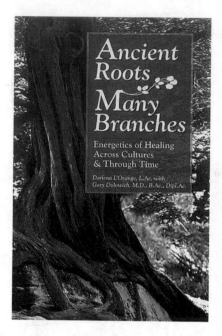